Citizen Participation: Canada

new press
Toronto
1971

Citizen
Participation:
Canada

A Book of Readings

Edited by James A. Draper

ISBN 0-88770-095-0 (paperback edition)
   0-88770-094-2 (hardcover edition)

Design/Peter Maher

new press
Editorial offices
84 Sussex Avenue
Toronto 179, Ontario

Order department
553 Richmond Street West
Toronto 133, Ontario

This book has been published with the help of a grant from the Social Science Research Council of Canada, using funds provided by the Canada Council.

Manufactured in Canada by
Web Offset Publications Ltd.

Acknowledgments

This book owes its existence in two ways to the contributors
of these readings. One stems from the thoughts and experiences that each contributor has chosen to share, and without
which there would be no book. The second relates to the support and encouragement that I have received from them.
While I am indebted to all of the contributors, I consulted, in
particular, Jim Lotz, Francis Bregha, Dorene Jacobs and
J. Roby Kidd.

In addition to those who contributed material, many persons made a contribution to the organizing and interpreting of
the book. These include many colleagues in adult education
and community development and persons who have participated in the O.I.S.E. course on community education and development. As well, I am deeply grateful for the help I received from members of my own department, particularly
Grace Benzon, Olivia Jacobs, Myrna Knechtel, and Richard
Williams.

The spirit of this book owes much to Maria, Diana, There-
sa and M.V.B., who have helped me to appreciate more fully
the communities of which I am a part, and those to which I
will likely never belong. Important too is the encouragement I
have received from these persons to focus on what I have and
less on what I thought I had lost.

Finally, this book is addressed to those who care about
their own self-growth as well as the growth and development
of others.

J.A.D.
June 1971

Contents

Section Six   Indian Participation

Section Seven   Application and Analysis

A Note to the Reader

This book of readings is intended to present ideas, provoke discussion, and indicate trends in matters relating to community development and citizen participation in Canada. The material is almost exclusively Canadian, although the concepts and principles expressed cross national boundaries. The book does not attempt to present a particular point of view. In fact, one of the strengths of the book is seen to be the variety of viewpoints presented within it. Neither does the book attempt to provide exhaustive coverage of its theme. Many more opinions and case studies could have been included. Many persons other than those contributing to the book were invited to submit articles, but for various reasons were unable to do so. One area that we would like to have seen covered more fully is the experiences of those working in the field; additional case studies and the sharing of field experiences would have been desirable.

The diverse backgrounds of the contributors of these readings, and the great variety of topics and issues covered by them, suggest that the book will be of interest to a wide range of persons and organizations, including individuals in voluntary social agencies; participants in training programs and courses dealing with community education, community organization, and community development; social-action groups; church groups; citizen organizations; various departments and levels of government; social-planning councils; professionals and field workers involved in community action, and others. Some will be selective in their use of the book, referring only to specific articles or sections. Others will use it as a general reference book, as a study guide, as a handbook, or even as a textbook for leadership training programs.

The reader will note that references to books and articles in the text follow the style of the American Psychological Association, naming author, year, and page number. Rather than include a selected bibliography at the end of each article, we have provided a comprehensive and cumulative bibliography at the back of the book. It should serve to guide the reader to sources that express additional points of view and enable him to pursue particular areas of interest. Footnote references, where they exist, appear at the end of the article.

The book is organized into sections. Each section includes an introductory paragraph, pointing out the elements or ideas that link the articles within it. Needless to say, a number of the articles could appropriately have been included in more than one section of the book.

It should be clear from the wide range of topics included in the book that we are not using any narrow and hence restricting view of such concepts as community development and citizen participation. And yet, all of the articles are linked by such ideas as the interaction of people, partnership, trust, self-responsibility, and participation. If the book is intended to inform and provoke, it most certainly is also intended to educate. It is hoped that the book will clarify the basic principles of citizen participation and aid in bringing about more understanding of these activities as processes of human development.

The views expressed in this book are those of the individual authors and do not necessarily represent the views of the editor of the readings.

JAMES A. DRAPER
June 1971

A Note about the Editor

James A. Draper has been involved in social development for many years. He has travelled extensively by foot and by hitch-hiking through Africa and Europe. He has been a seaman and has worked in logging and mining camps and at dozens of other jobs ranging from carpenter-millwright to labourer in a pulp mill to boys'-work secretary with the YMCA in Vancouver. In all these situations the common link was that of working and interacting with others. These informal aspects of the editor's learning have influenced him greatly and have nurtured an interest in the topic of citizen participation.

Professor Draper was born in Regina, Saskatchewan. He took his elementary schooling in Moose Jaw and his secondary schooling in Vancouver. He received his B.A. and Secondary School Teaching Certificate from the University of British Columbia, and his M.Sc. and Ph.D. from the University of Wisconsin, where he specialized in adult education, sociology and psychology, with additional concentration on anthropology and history.

Professor Draper taught public school in British Columbia before going to the University of Wisconsin. While studying there he also served as field officer for the Extension Division of the University of Wisconsin. From 1964 to 1966 he was advisor to the University of Rajasthan in India, as a staff member of the University of British Columbia. While in India he was also director of research and field studies. Immediately after returning from India, he was for eight months research director and special consultant to the Saskatoon Welfare Council.

He has taught community education and development courses at the University of Rajasthan, as well as at the University of the West Indies in Barbados. Presently he is an academic staff member of the University of Toronto's Department of Educational Theory (The Ontario Institute for Studies in Education). One of the postgraduate courses he teaches focuses on community education and development. Other particular research and teaching interests include international and comparative education.

Professor Draper is an advisor to a number of organizations and a member of many national and international bodies. In April 1970 he was commissioned by World Education, Inc., as a consultant on the evaluation of literacy and population education programs, at an Asian Conference held in New Delhi. He was chairman of the program committee that planned the Canadian National Community Development Workshops held in 1968 and in 1969 and is presently a member of the steering committee planning a third national conference. He has published many articles and books, particularly relating to adult education as well as community development in India and Canada.

Introduction

The basic principles of community development and social animation are not new. Many great philosophies and teachings
throughout history have elaborated on human interaction and
the ethical and moral relationships of man with man. What is
new today is our deeper understanding of these principles and
our greater attempt to implement them. This has meant a nar-
rowing of the distance between theory and practice, between
hypocrisy and truth.

Ignorance of what community development connotes often
has increased people's negative reactions and outright hostility
toward attempts to implement its principles. Nor have such
reactions come entirely from bureaucrats, politicians and traditionalists, for the same elements of distrust, fear and ignorance are also apparent in some of those who call for radical
change. If the basic ideas of community development were understood, then we would be much less surprised by its consequences.

Let us listen, and reflect, and understand, and learn. There
can be no doubt that changes of mind and in communities
will inevitably bring about organizational changes. Individuals
in social organizations have often been accused of having vested interests, frequently based on insecurities, that thwart
change. Such barriers must be examined critically. Some of
our present-day social organizations will not survive and new
ones will need to be created. Organizations adapt and change
because of the individuals within them, and organizations that
attempt to serve the people must understand the principles
upon which the people's ideology is based. If that ideology is
democracy then, by definition, participation of people must be
one of the basic principles.

The challenge is to be innovative and creative in seeking alternatives to the *status quo*. Let us remember too that the
change we are talking about is not that which comes about by
orders-in-council, but a change in attitude toward self, toward
others, and to the concept of people working together in artic-

ulating problems, identifying alternatives to the solution of those problems, making decisions, and co-operatively and responsibly activating and evaluating their decisions. That is the essence of community development and social animation. We are talking about the self-determination of people as a basic right.

The term 'citizen' as it is used here refers to the desire one has to belong to and be a part of something. Its meaning is not limited to statutory citizenship. Furthermore, citizen participation doesn't imply simply more people attending more meetings. It means the involvement of more people in dialogue. We have much to learn about how to achieve this. Communication is not a one-way process: to achieve dialogue, government must build into its own structure channels for the citizen to react and express opinions; the mass media and cable T.V. must think about two-way circuits; colleges, schools, and voluntary and other organizations that want to be community-oriented must learn more fully how to relate to their communities. How can human and material resources be utilized more fully in articulating common and vital goals? How can the great array of present-day technologies, and tomorrow's inventions, be used for educational purposes? Let us be as fearless and open as possible in accepting these challenges.

There is an Asian proverb that says:

> Go to the people
> Live among them
> Learn from them
> Love them
> Serve them
> Plan with them
> Start with what they know
> Build on what they have.

Do we understand what the proverb is saying? Do we believe that we can learn from others? Do we believe that we, as individuals, can learn and grow and continue to do so? Do we believe and practise the idea of *éducation permanente* or continuous learning?

There is little doubt that these basic ideals can be implemented and become reality, as long as one understands the concept of change itself. But let us also find a balance between reality and daring. It is assumed that power lies in the hands of those who make decisions. It is equally true, however, that power lies in the hands of those who define the alternatives upon which decisions are made. The solution to traffic congestion in our cities may not be just to build another expressway. The solution for a community impoverished and on welfare may not be to move everyone in that community to the city. But such decisions might in fact be made. We have been shown on numerous occasions that change in and for itself is not necessarily a good thing, nor is change for the largest number of persons necessarily a human principle. Moral and ethical values cannot be ignored by the decision-maker; the decisions of today must include a concern for tomorrow and beyond. Thus the people who are going to be affected by a decision must be involved in identifying and understanding alternatives, if we are ever to achieve 'that serenity to accept the things I cannot change, the courage to change the things I can, and the wisdom to know the difference'.

When we talk of citizen participation we are talking of certain principles and beliefs. We have attempted to encompass these in such terms as community development or social animation. Perhaps we need a new and refreshing term to encompass such principles. But let us clarify one more principle, which might best be done by distinguishing between community development and community improvement. The visible end result of both might be a community centre or better housing, but what distinguishes the terms is the process, or lack of it, that involves persons in making decisions. The process is an essential part of community development. To present an analogy, in travelling from point A to point B, where B is better housing, the value of the activity is not only arriving at B but the journey itself. In community development the journey is the learning, the skills and the confidence acquired by those participating in the process. Community development implies a very particular value system.

It should be clear that the basic principles about which we have been talking are applicable to a variety of settings, ranging from rural communities to congested urban areas to 'functional communities' that are based on the sharing of ideas and not entirely on geographical settings (although even the latter are linked by ideas). The philosophies encompassed by citizen participation are being adapted today, to varying degrees, in such institutions as universities, industry, government, schools, and voluntary organizations, to mention only a few. This phenomenon is exemplified by the frequent use of such terms as involvement, self-direction for learning, participation, co-operation, understanding, trust and communication. Environments are being created within which people can learn and grow. The educational component of these activities is essential and is, in large part, highly functional, practical and long-lasting; the results are the changing of attitudes and the improvement of social skills, including those relating to learning itself.

The action we take in this regard will relate to the view that we have of others. If we truly believe that man is capable of self-determination and all that that implies, then we will act one way; if we believe otherwise then we will act differently, and the consequences for society will differ accordingly. Good intentions and even strong convictions are not enough, for we know that these on their own have previously helped to destroy communities and the self-integrity of men.

It has already been stated that one of the reasons for the questionable respectability of community development is the lack of understanding about the principles upon which it is based. Another reason is our lack of knowledge of how people interact and become involved. It is necessary to take an interdisciplinary approach to improve our knowledge about community work. This calls for more research and documentation. We need to encourage more field workers to document and reflect upon and share their experiences. More rigorous attempts need to be made to establish baseline data prior to community action, so that we can evaluate more precisely its results and long-term effect. Apart from creating new knowledge, we need to utilize more fully the information we already have, derived from such disciplines as anthropology, applied psychology, communications, education, and social work. Following from this, we need to improve our skills in translating theory and knowledge into a form that will be usable by practitioners and field workers. The implications of these suggestions should be clear to any organization in terms of planning and budgeting for its community program. Some community programs have been unsuccessful because such planning and supporting services were unprovided. Community participation should be taken seriously as a research and planning problem.

It seems that we can hardly avoid making a decision about whether or not to become involved: whether or not we will make something happen, whether we will help something happen, or whether we will let something happen. Citizen participation is concerned with the development of communities and the self-growth of individuals within them. Such endeavours may culminate in greater economic independence, in increased social security, or in improved living conditions, but its worth especially lies in enhancing human dignity. These goals are inseparable from the challenges of maximizing the creative use of leisure time and the opportunities for learning, and of extending fundamental human rights to all.

JAMES A. DRAPER
June 1971

The Ideology of Participation

Citizen participation is based on certain ideals that have deep historical roots. The implementation of these ideals is not without problems and challenges. The concepts of representation, organizing for action, conflict, and power have taken on added meanings and call for rational reform. Legislative processes and organizational structures are challenged, as are some of the traditional ways of solving societal problems. The challenge is to be innovative in the democratic and planning process, so that desirable social change may be accomplished and the spirit of community participation strengthened.

This section begins with an article by Wilson Head that gives a brief overview of some of the historical roots of participation. These historical events are also elaborated on elsewhere in these readings. In the article by Head, various models for action are discussed, including those of Alinsky, militant models, and others. The way in which the data is analyzed and presented is in keeping with the strong action-research background of the author. Evaluation, he says, must be on two levels, accomplishment in social change and the ability to recapture the spirit of community development. His brief discussion on emerging trends and prospects is supplemented in greater detail by Francis Bregha (Chapter 5).

In Chapter 2, Michael Clague points out that citizen participation involves a process of decision making and that such a process frequently has a political connotation. Clague emphasizes that the structural forms of our legislative process shape immeasurably our patterns of participation. He points out the weaknesses of participation by ballot and concludes his article by making some suggestions for reform.

E.R. McEwen expresses his concern about organizations perpetuating themselves and the work they do; too often the result is to keep the poor people poor. He says that schemes that do not emphasize the development of people do little to eliminate poverty. It is fundamental to the democratic process that government reflect the desires of people; the role of the planner is also important in reflecting the desires of people, and McEwen mentions the traditionalist, humanist and pragmatist approach to planning. In suggesting ways in which participatory democracy in Canada can be developed, he leads us naturally to the last article in this section, written by Steven Langdon. Langdon's deep involvement in the student-power movement has given him particular insights into the politics of participation. He expresses the view that in the last decade students have

become one of the leading exponents of the politics of participation, giving a fresh impetus to the concepts of equality and
decentralized popular control. His student case-study gives us
an example of the positive aspects of confrontation and
conflict.

The Ideology and Practice of Citizen Participation

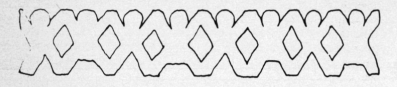

Wilson A. Head

Historical Background

Many differing views of the nature of citizens' participation or involvement are held by various observers of the current situation in Canada and the United States. The concept of citizens' participation is a very important part of the liberal-democratic theory of politics. It is well ingrained in the North American scene. In fact the term 'citizens' participation and involvement' seems almost superfluous in a democratic society. It could be argued that democracy is by nature 'participatory', and that the citizen is a source of all political power. Political theorists have long recognized, however, the fact that society is composed of a multiplicity of different interest-groups. In fact James Madison, writing in *The Federalist Papers* in 1787, recommended a republican form of government as a means of maintaining popular control of democratic structures in the United States. Madison was aware of the fact that powerful interest-groups would develop and would tend to dominate governmental institutions unless held in check. Madison and others anticipated John Galbraith's concept of 'countervailing power'. Modern citizens' participation and involvement, therefore, may be viewed as a form of countervailing power, possessing, at least to some extent, the possibility of checking the influence of other powerful groups exerting pressure upon government on behalf of their own interest.

This process is not new in North America. Canadians as well

as Americans are, as de Tocqueville observed more than a century ago, a nation of 'joiners'. The country is characterized by innumerable citizens joining themselves together as interest-groups for the purpose of achieving common objectives. The extent of these developments in Canada is illustrated by a recent study published by the Department of National Health and Welfare, Ottawa, December 1969. During the course of this short, four-month study, a total of 215 low-income groups were identified in Canada, most of which had been organized during the preceding two years. The study was concerned only with groups in which at least one half of the members were classified as 'poor'. It is now known that a considerable number of other groups could have been identified and interviewed had time been available.

Historically, the most widespread aspect of citizens' participation has been the use of the ballot-box. In theory, the citizen participates in a democratic government through the exercise of the franchise, and governments get their authority from 'the consent of the governed'. In practice, some groups make far more use of the ballot-box than other groups. The reasons for this are many, but among the most important is the fact that many groups have a tradition and practice of constant participation in meetings and other group activities. There is ample evidence, from the studies of social scientists among others, that members of the middle classes are more prone to organize to protect their interests than members of the lower socio-economic groups.

Much of what has been called 'citizens' participation' in the past has been a phenomenon of these middle-class groups. Canada has its Rotarians, its Kiwanians, and other service clubs, its Chambers of Commerce, its women's organizations, its Boy Scouts, its professional associations, its ratepayers, and other similar groups. These and other middle-class bodies have undoubtedly contributed a great deal to the social, economic, and cultural objectives of Canadian society. In addition, many interested groups have frequently played an overtly political role in the community. They have succeeded, on occasion, in influencing the acts of governments at the local, provincial, and federal levels. This activity by volunteer groups has generally been considered a valuable part of the development of Canadian society as a whole.

In recent years, however, there has been both a qualitative and quantitative change in the nature and extent of citizens' participation and involvement in neighbourhood and community affairs. This development in Canada, as in much of the Western World generally, has been rapid and dramatic. Citizens' groups represent, in part, an aspect of a world-wide movement by the poor and other disadvantaged people to take action to change their immediate situation. The movement is closely related to the civil rights movement in the United States, the world-wide revolt by increasing numbers of youth, the drive by women to achieve full equality, the effort of Canadian Indians to secure rights guaranteed by treaties over the past two hundred years, and other similar movements. The new citizens' participation movement includes the activities of tenants demanding decent homes for their families and children at reasonable rates, and of welfare recipients who are organizing against welfare bureaucracies which have often been oppressive in their treatment of welfare recipients. But perhaps the largest single activating element in the increasing scope of citizen participation has been the activity of high-rise developers engaged in urban-renewal activities in the larger cities of Canada. Often urban-renewal activities have been at the expense of poor people who lived in neighbourhoods slated for redevelopment. Urban renewal has all too often meant the displacement of the poor. Their neighbourhoods and homes have been destroyed in order to build new high-rise developments for the benefit of the middle class who could afford to pay the increased rents.

The continuing incidence of degrading poverty in the midst of a generally affluent society, the depersonalizing effects of rapid urbanization and technological change, and other massive social and economic problems have led to a pervading sense of powerlessness and despair, particularly, but not exclusively, among the low-income people. The 'hip' generation provides evidence of considerable alienation even among many youths from more affluent sectors of the Canadian society. While different groups experience economic, psychological, and social deprivation in different ways, the evidence suggests that the poor suffer the results of alienation much more acutely than other sectors of the population. It is within this context that citizens' participation has become not merely a desirable factor but a virtual necessity. It is no longer a question of whether or not participation is a good thing: this is now accepted. For example, the importance of citizen participation was recognized in the Congressional stipulation that the recent 'War on Poverty' in the United States would be conducted with the 'maximum feasible participation of the poor'. In a recent address at the first Ontario Provincial-Municipal Conference held in Toronto in April 1970, the Provincial Secretary and Minister of Citizenship of Ontario stated:

> In many ways the present interest which people are express-
> ing in formation of local neighbourhood groups may indeed
> be considered a natural outgrowth of the very complexity of
> our modern society and institutions.

The Minister of the Department of National Health and Welfare (Ottawa), in a paper presented at the Canadian Conference
on Social Welfare held in Toronto, June 1970, made the following comments:

> A democratic system, to succeed, must be much more than a
> general vote one day out of every three or four years. It must
> be a vital, on-going contact and exchange between govern-
> ments and their constitutents . all of them, not just the
> rich and the powerful. This is the crucial role of citizens'
> groups – to organize and mobilize their people into a politi-
> cal force, so that their views can be heard in their own right,
> not filtered through a massive super-structure of agencies
> and committees and officials.

Although these sentiments were expressed by high government
officials, a considerable body of evidence suggests that much of
the public, and particularly the poor, have little faith in participation in formal democratic structures.

At the electoral level, some evidence supports earlier findings
that citizens from low-income areas participate to a lesser extent in elections than do those from more affluent areas. The
recent *Don District Study*, published by the Social Planning
Council of Metropolitan Toronto (March 1970), found that
only 21.6 per cent of the eligible voters in the District voted for
aldermen in the 1966 municipal elections. The range was from
a low of 14.6 per cent in one census tract to a high of 29.0 per
cent in a tract including a public-housing project. The more
affluent district immediately north of the Don District recorded
a 41.0 participation by eligible voters in the same election. The
same study also found a low degree of non-electoral or social-
group participation:

> With the exception of participation in labour unions, few of

the low income respondents indicated more than minimal participation in the various groups and organizations which existed in the neighbourhood.

These findings suggest that direct participation of the individual citizen in the process of government and public affairs has long ceased to exist in any meaningful way. The current movement towards increasing citizens' participation appears to revive once more, in varying degrees, the involvement of citizens in the governmental process. This process must be recognized as a political activity. Political science has strangely paid little attention to this process in the past; it is time that its practitioners take this new movement into account.

The Rationale of Citizens' Participation

The ideology of participation appears to be focussed upon the following assumptions: that the ordinary citizen possesses the right to 'participate in the decisions which affect his life'. This concept was given modern expression in the *Port Huron Statement*, a document expressing the objectives of the Students for a Democratic Society in the United States in 1964. This and similar declarations have become a part of the ideological basis of much of the new, low-income citizens'-participation activity in both the United States and Canada. As indicated earlier, the concept, 'maximum feasible participation of the poor', was written into the 1964 act creating the 'War on Poverty' in the United States.

This ideology is supported by much of the democratic and liberal ethos of Western societies: an ethos based largely upon faith in participatory democracy as an ideological assumption of great importance. Participatory democracy has been viewed as a reflection of the responsibility of the individual for his economic and political station in life. Emphasis upon hard work, freedom of enterprise, thrift, and prudence reflects this dominant value in Western societies.

A second assumption relates to the often-expressed attitude of some leaders of disadvantaged groups that the poor have 'had enough' and are ready for revolt against the 'system' if their demands are not met. Confrontation tactics are seen as the only way in which disadvantaged groups can demand their share of the fruits of an affluent society. The new slogan, 'power to the people' derives directly from the Black Panther movement in the United States. Some groups have used confrontation tactics with considerable effectiveness, particularly in certain situations in which this tactic is appropriate for the achievement of short-term goals.

There is some evidence, however, that even in many low-income communities in which citizens' groups operate, the majority of citizens do not support militant action for achieving objectives. The Don District Study, for example, found that the large majority of respondents gave little support to militant tactics. Most of the respondents in this study felt almost totally powerless in influencing the behaviour of government at either the local, provincial, or federal level. With the exception of the small number of residents who indicated membership but little active participation in labour unions, the extent of participation in community life was minimal.

Ravitz (Loring, Sweetser & Ernst, 1957) found in Detroit that while there were differences between the degree of participation between whites and Negroes in neighbourhood associations involved in urban renewal, the majority of all residents were uninterested in participating in any type of program of neighbourhood improvement.

A third assumption frequently stated by leaders of citizens'-participation groups, whether in middle- or low-income areas, is that they 'represent' the citizens of the area. Undoubtedly, such groups represent the interests of some of the residents of the area; the question is to what degree do they represent the interests of the total area. This is, of course, a rhetorical question in that it is almost impossible for any one group to represent the diverse interests of all residents of any area. Neither membership figures nor levels of participation in groups reflect more than token interest by the majority of residents in most groups. This is not to suggest that a small membership necessarily reflects insignificance and lack of influence. Many well-led groups with few supporters have accomplished impressive results, particularly in terms of their ability to 'veto' action of which they disapproved.

The problem of representation, however, raises a number of basic questions relating to the nature of democratic government. A recent study, *Neighborhood Participation in Local Government*, conducted by the Toronto Bureau of Municipal Research (1970) called attention to the importance of clarifying this problem. The following questions are posed: (a) Can elected government officials delegate decision-making (political) power to voluntary groups? (b) How does this delegation relate to their official duty to represent their constituents, since by law the elected officials are the duly elected decision-makers in a democratic society? (c) Can a neighbourhood expect that a self-selected, voluntary interest-group will actually represent the interest of the entire neighbourhood rather than merely the interest of its members?

This study points out the extreme complexity of defining the 'public interest' to the satisfaction of all groups in a given community. In addition, most neighbourhoods are composed of not one but a number of interest-groups, each competing with others to influence public opinion and to achieve goals important to themselves. A further problem is that the achievement of goals considered important to one group may be perceived as detrimental to the interests of other groups. For example, the success of home-owners in securing low-interest loans for rehabilitation of properties generally results in raising rents to tenants. Tenants may not view this achievement as in their best interests.

A fourth assumption made by many low-income citizens'-participation groups is that their activities are 'non-political' and above the negotiations and compromises of partisan politics. This assumption ignores the central fact of community life that any attempt to alter the economic, social, or political structure of society is, in its broad sense, inherently political. The Don District Study was unequivocal in stating that 'citizens participation has created its own political terms of reference. Instead of placing major reliance on the municipal electoral process ... participation focussed upon citizens activity between elections. As a result elected politicians and political aspirants are finding it desirable to court neighborhood groups in order to remain in or obtain public office. There has been little doubt that citizens participation has begun to change the entire concept of the political process in redevelopment.'

This is not to suggest that politicians welcome the development of citizens' groups. The evidence suggests that most politicians prefer the old concept of the citizen restricting himself to merely voting in periodic elections. But some politicians are beginning to perceive that citizens' groups can be a source of strength, and are actively consulting and listening to local groups interested in community improvement and change.

The final implicit assumption relates to the fact that many of the programs designed to help the poor involve, at least to some extent, the concept that the poor are responsible for their own poverty. The problems of poverty, slums, etc., are defined in terms of helping the poor learn 'responsible behaviour', a type of behaviour patterned upon middle-class standards and values. The result is the establishment of retraining programs designed to equip the poor for low-level jobs, 'head-start' programs designed to deal with the handicaps of the 'culturally deprived' children of poverty areas, or programs designed to teach parents middle-class child-care methods. The question is rarely asked whether programs based upon these values are appropriate in terms of helping poor people escape from poverty. There is very little evidence that these programs actually help the poor to escape from poverty, although a few of the most capable and socially mobile poor do manage to escape their plight.

Many community-action programs begin with the assumption that the problems of poverty are basically problems of social and economic inequalities and that a massive redistribution of power is the necessary goal. This stance, however, raises a number of basic questions. One of the central questions, involving the issue of citizens' participation, is whether it is possible for a local citizens' group to achieve change in the status of its members through an attack upon the social, economic, and political structures of contemporary society. If the massive problems of modern industrial society persist, in spite of increasing affluence, rising levels of education, better health care, and other effects of modern technology and knowledge, how can the local citizens' groups be expected to achieve meaningful structural change?

There is little evidence, either in the United States or in Canada, that the poor alone can plan, operationalize, and conduct major programs directed at major structural change in modern societies. It is difficult to understand why anyone could have expected that the poor alone could accomplish a task that no other group has been able to handle. Although there are no answers to these questions at the moment, the emergence of citizens'-participation groups are based upon the assumption that citizens' groups, whether low or middle income, can, through organized action, release major sources of energy and ability which have been largely untapped in the past. Although there is no evidence that they have been able to effect major structural changes in society, the activities of most low-income groups are beginning to result in some significant change and improvement in the services available to the poor. The concerns of citizens'-participation groups represent and reflect the fact that, to a significant extent, community agencies and organizations, presumably organized for the purpose of meeting the needs of local citizens, have largely failed in achieving that goal.

Some Experiences in Community Participation

The rapid increase in the number and focus of citizens'-participation groups, particularly in low-income communities, has introduced an entirely new situation in Canadian life. While the organization of groups for the protection of their interests has been commonplace among middle- and upper-income groups, most of these groups have been organized during the last two or three years. Low-income citizens'-participation groups, according to the survey financed by the Department of National Health and Welfare (Carota), are concerned primarily with what may be termed the 'bread-and-butter' issues affecting the daily lives of people living in poverty. They organize to fight against the abuses of the welfare system, the practices of some slum landlords who charge exorbitant rents for inferior accommodations, the arbitrary and frequently inhuman treatment received from private agencies and government bureaucracies, and as a means of regaining some degree of self-respect and control over the community institutions whose decisions vitally affect their lives.

Within this context, citizens'-participation groups tend to focus their concerns and activities upon community agencies and institutions that do not meet their needs, as perceived by their members and leaders. Welfare-rights groups, tenant-rights groups in both public and private housing, groups organized to obtain increased day-care facilities for children, groups organized to promote the rights of racial and ethnic groups, and groups organized to improve the education of their children are predominant among the new citizens'-participation groups in Canada. In spite of the attempt by the American Office of Economic Opportunity (Metropolitan Applied Research Center, 1968) to define community action in terms of *action* and *power* goals, a study in that country discovered that in actual operation, the traditional social services, not the action approach, dominated the programs. In other words, the community groups wanted and insisted upon social services, opportunities for retraining, and educational programs. Of 51 anti-poverty projects studied, a total of 116 programs were basically educational, including head-start programs, and an additional 103 were traditional social-services programs. Only five programs were actually focussed upon organization of the poor for action directed towards basic social change. Although leaders of many of the groups apparently wish to lead members of citizens' groups into theoretical or ideological positions as a basis for revolutionary action, there is little evidence that these attempts have succeeded to any significant extent. The focus is generally upon institutional change rather than broadly conceived ideological change, i.e. an overthrow of the 'system'. Respondents in the Don District Study indicated a preference for 'sending deputations: or for writing briefs in attempts to influence the behavior of government officials. None of the organizations interviewed indicated that they preferred resorting to militant action such as holding demonstrations, confrontations, marches, etc.'

This is not to suggest that militant actions will not be taken, if all other attempts fail to achieve desired results. The unresponsiveness of many private and public organizations to the needs of residents of low-income neighbourhoods may, and occasionally does, lead to the use of militant action simply because other methods fail to achieve results. Demonstrating in front of City Hall is not limited to low-income groups; ratepayers' associations, farmers' organizations, and other middle-class organizations have been known to engage in militant action when their interests are directly threatened.

The reluctance of low-income groups to become engaged in militant action or direct confrontation with the community power structure may be based upon an accurate if intuitive assessment of their own limited power to influence change by this strategy. Second, most citizens'-participation groups do not possess the information and knowledge required to meet 'the Establishment' on its own terms and risk humiliating defeat in a frontal encounter. Third, the problem of adequate leadership is an ever-recurring problem in low-income groups. Many leaders are upwardly mobile, and are ready to move into middle-class positions when their groups succeed in improving their condition of life, thus effectively depriving their groups of leadership at crucial periods in their development.

The conflict model of citizens' participation, although quite attractive to many groups, also has its limitations. The successes of Saul Alinsky, the great American exponent of radical conflict strategies, are frequently cited as examples of what the poor can achieve through the use of confrontation. Alinsky is a tremendously impressive middle-class community organizer of great experience, who has achieved a considerable reputation for helping communities accomplish objectives. Alinsky has also had his share of failures in this endeavour.

The utilization of conflict models does not guarantee that citizens will succeed in defeating the impersonal and frequently dehumanizing bureaucracies which frustrate them in their attempts to deal constructively with their environment. Direct confrontation tactics can be evaded or aborted by the power structure; the energics of citizens may be dissipated by resilience, indulgence, intransigence, delaying tactics, and other skilful manoeuvres. Or in the final analysis, the power structure may, as it has often done in the past, resort to the application of superior force, including the use of police power. Resistance may occur at the neighbourhood, municipal, or other levels of government.

A major criticism of many citizens' groups is that the frequent practice of confrontation and conflict, employed by some groups, particularly in the United States but less frequently in Canada, results in increasing alienation, bitterness, and distrust among the various groups within the community. When fear, distrust, and hostility reign, it becomes difficult to focus upon the real issues and problems of the people. These criticisms appear to have a considerable validity, at least as they relate to some groups. There have been occasions in Canada when the leaders of the more militant groups have succeeded in dividing the community into hostile and warring camps, each attempting to eliminate its opponent and become accepted as the only voice of citizens in the community. Moderate leaders may become immobilized and unable to function, thus ending the possibility of effective joint community action.

These criticisms of the possible effect of confrontation tactics, however, are not to suggest that they are always inappropriate in all situations. The limited evidence available suggests that neither the use of confrontation nor consensus or other models is necessarily decisive in achieving the objectives of citizens' participation. A major problem in the decision to employ various strategies in achieving community change is the general lack of an adequate analysis of the nature of power and its effective utilization. While space does not permit an adequate and systematic analysis of power relations in modern societies, an examination of citizens' participation in community action programs suggests that certain characteristics of power must be much better understood than they have been to date.

In the absence of this type of analysis and understanding, certain citizens' groups tend to substitute militant rhetoric for effective action. The facts are that, except for the ability to veto action by government and other bodies, most community action programs have failed to produce the basic changes in community conditions originally sought. This failure is stern testimony of the ineffectiveness of rhetoric unless accompanied by clearly defined goals and strategies appropriate to those goals. A definition of this kind must recognize (a) the reality of power in the particular situation and how it can be dealt with; (b) the ability to organize and utilize the power inherent in citizens themselves for effecting change; (c) a realistic assessment of the power of the resistance blocking change; and (d) an analysis of the possibilities of achieving goals in view of the significance of this examination.

The importance of leadership in developing effective citizens'-participation programs has been repeatedly demonstrated in Canada as in the United States. In the past the development of leadership in citizens' groups has been a precarious process, largely because of the lack of an adequate body of knowledge relating to community action. Although there have been instances where capable leadership has emerged from the membership of citizens' groups, this is often a precarious asset. It is difficult for groups to maintain adequate indigenous leadership over an extended period of time. Thus professional leadership is often necessary for considerable periods of time if the groups are to function successfully. In fact the availability of professional leadership was the indispensable component in the growth and development of every neighbourhood association observed in one American study of the Metropolitan Boston area in 1958. Local neighbourhood leaders simply did not possess the skills necessary to handle the organizational activities required by the projects conducted by the citizens' groups. The constant change in leadership and the need for constant recruitment of new leaders demanded much time in order that the association could be kept alive and functioning (Schaller, 1966).

Trends in Financing

Unfortunately there are few examples of local citizens' groups raising adequate operating funds without resorting to appeals to outside groups. While groups may find the idea of securing funds and employing professional organizers attractive, the financing of staff presents its own special problems. Citizens' groups have frequently found that granting-bodies, whether private or public, demand certain conditions as a requirement for making funds available to the organization. These conditions may or may not inhibit the freedom of the association in taking action it may deem essential in carrying out its objectives. On the other hand, many citizens' groups have sought and have succeeded in obtaining funds for operating purposes.

Saul Alinsky's Industrial Areas Foundation, perhaps the most militant of the American programs combatting poverty and supporting radical social change, is financed by middle-class churches and big foundations. The initial stages of the American 'War on Poverty' were conceived and supported by middle-class organizations including the Rockefeller, Ford, and other huge foundations. In Canada, the federal government has financed the Toronto Community Improvement Association (C.I.A.), an association of tenants in Regent Park, a public-housing project. Other local groups are seeking funding from local and federal government sources. The community organizers employed by the Trefann Court Residents Association, perhaps the most publicized community-participation group in Canada at this time, were partially financed by the United Church of Canada.

Emerging Trends and Prospects

Although the present development of citizens'-participation groups in Canada is still too recent for making valid judgments as to their proper role in initiating and pressing for effective social change, some general observations may be in order. First, it is apparent that local citizens'-participation groups cannot alone solve the massive social problems of modern society. The pressing problems of unemployment, the drug problem, poor schools, inadequate housing, poor social services, pollution, war, and the apparent alienation of an increasing number of citizens, both adults and the young, reflect a pervading sense that our society is failing to meet the needs of all of its citizens. Citizens' groups obviously cannot solve these problems, but there is some evidence that they may begin the task of relating the individual to his society through community action. Through community action, he is beginning to break through the impersonal bureaucracy of big business, big government, big educational systems, big health bureaucracies, and the other structures that dominate his life at every level.

Several trends are now emerging in this connection. One of the most pressing problems in low-income neighbourhoods in Canadian, as in American, society is the remoteness of control of the agencies and institutions presumably serving the needs of the population. Boards of directors of community agencies tend to be composed largely, if not exclusively, of middle class people from outside the area. Community-participation groups are mounting an attack upon this situation, and are achieving some results. The control of these agencies and institutions has been the prerogative of middle-class people for a long time, however, and it will require sustained effort to make more than token changes.

For example, local citizens' groups could be delegated the power to involve themselves fully in the control of their own neighbourhoods. These groups could encourage the entire community to become involved in the decision-making process, a first step in helping the people feel a sense of belonging and participation in community life. Control of the educational institutions, hospitals, the police force, social agencies, and other agencies serving the local neighbourhood is an essential step in ending the state of alienation and hopelessness so prevalent in many communities today.

The decentralization of the decision-making process through encouraging citizens' participation should help government to become more responsive and to reflect more adequately local needs and aspirations. The question of representativeness is important here. Some method must be developed to insure that community groups actually represent the various interests in the community, or that in the event they only represent one group, this fact be well understood and taken into account. The present practice of some government agencies of holding public hearings, particularly with respect to zoning by-law changes, etc., provides a model for an expansion of this concept. Citizens' groups could hold public hearings on government proposals, inviting comment and criticisms from all sectors of the population. These groups could also conduct public hearings on the quality and quantity of government services in local neighbourhoods. Some welfare-rights groups in the United States are presently involved in this type of action.

Citizens must be helped to move beyond exclusive concern with immediate problems to an awareness of the interdependence of problems at all levels. This responsibility, however, demands that citizens' groups be willing to assume responsibility for decisions made. When citizens are given the right to participate in decision-making, then they must be ready to assume responsibilities for action taken to implement plans. They cannot sit back and permit public officials to fend off attacks by other segments of the community, who may not agree with decisions made by local groups.

One of the most important findings of the Don District Study was the fact that citizens increasingly do not trust professional planners and other 'experts'. The planner or other government official will normally work to achieve the goals of urban renewal or other programs as conceived by public political bodies or by his own knowledge of the situation. The citizen is more likely to be primarily concerned with protecting his own family, his own property, or the interests of the local neighbourhood, rather than those of the general community. The interests of the professional planner and those of the citizens' group may coincide, but quite often they do not. It is important that the citizens' groups be involved from the initial stages in the planning process. This will require some redefinition in the role of the professional planner in the total planning process. There is evidence that some planners understand this requirement and are beginning to consult citizens' groups on a regular basis.

There is little question that these practices will, as they have in the past, be inefficient, require the resolution of differences between various neighbourhood interests, tax the patience of 'experts', and cost the taxpayers more money. Many groups will need expert help; this is already happening in Toronto where the City Planning Board has loaned a professional planner to a citizens' group to work with them in formulating plans that may differ sharply with the plans of the city itself. Citizens' participation is not an end in itself. In the final analysis it must be evaluated on two levels. First, citizens' participation is concerned with social change and must be evaluated in terms of its accomplishments in this area. Second, citizens' participation must be evaluated in terms of its ability to recapture the spirit of participatory democracy or community involvement. It must enable the citizen to involve himself meaningfully in his society, making his voice and aspirations heard and understood in community decision-making. Much has been achieved in both areas; the future of human society may require that the entire community become involved in this process.

WILSON A. HEAD was born in Atlanta, Georgia, U.S.A. He attended Tuskegee Institute, Alabama, where he received the B.S. degree in Education with a major in social science. Following a short teaching career, he entered the Atlanta University and graduated with a Master of Social Work degree, with a major in group work and community organization. He completed post-master work at the University of Chicago in social welfare, group dynamics, counselling, and adult education. He was awarded a Ph.D. degree in Education (Adult) in 1958 by Ohio State University in Columbus, Ohio.

He has a wide variety of work experiences, including relief work with the United Nations in Poland and community organizing in community centres in Philadelphia, Indianapolis and Chicago. For six years he directed the group-services program at the State of Ohio Juvenile Diagnostic Center in Columbus, Ohio.

In 1959, Dr. Head came to Canada as Executive Director of the Windsor Group Therapy Project in Windsor, Ontario. Two years later, he became Director of Social Planning for the Windsor United Community Services. In 1965 he became Director of Planning and Research for the Metropolitan Toronto Social Planning Council, later becoming Associate Executive Director for Research and Development. Following four years of part-time teaching, he joined the staff of Atkinson College, York University, on a full-time basis in September 1970. At Atkinson College he is responsible for developing a social-welfare-education program for part-time students.

Citizen Participation in the Legislative Process

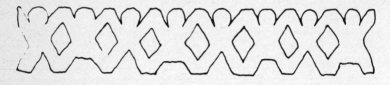

Michael Clague

Any delusions about the security of democratic participation in Canada should have been dispelled by the events of autumn 1970 in Quebec and the implementation of the War Measures Act. Wherever one might stand on the issues involved, no one with a commitment to civil liberties can be complacent about the results of those turbulent days. Basic rights of association and privacy were abrogated by the federal government, supported by the government of Quebec and the civic administration of Montreal, as were normal safeguards in procedures for detention. A passing aberration? We will only know with the passage of time.

Against this background, any consideration of citizen participation in the legislative process must be concerned with questions of fundamental change in structure and process as well as reform. A crude instrument of legislation was invoked to deal with a complex situation. Perhaps one result was the apprehension of those who tragically claim to seek social improvement through the necessity of violence: a futile and profoundly destructive view. But perhaps another result was the further alienation of the disaffected in society, compounded by the October civic election in Montreal and the pressures and charges brought to bear on the Front d'action politique (FRAP) by some municipal and federal politicians (Katadotis, 1970). Young people, the militant poor, and some labour members are disenchanted with 'the system.' The legislative process is at the core. Is reconciliation possible?

It seems to me that the old dictum, 'We are so much at one that we can safely afford to differ,' is still fundamental to a democratic, collaborative society. It is incorrect to assume that such a society would be blandly homogeneous. It is naive to assume that the pluralism possible in society is infinitely elastic. Virtually by definition decision-making in a democracy is a tough, messy business, characterized at best by compromise arrived at through pragmatic idealism – unless, of course, one believes in man's ultimate perfectibility!

The test of any legislative process is the extent to which the boundaries for citizen consent and dissent can be in continuous evolution, sensitive to new forms of participation to meet the issues of the day. Only on this basis can there be some assurance of the timeliness and creativity of legislative decisions.

Matters of Substance and of Process in Political Decision-Making

The listing of our societal ills is by now an all-too-familiar litany. The size and pervasiveness of all forms of organization and bureaucracy, the pace of change, and the complexity of the issues are overloading our capacity to understand and our procedures for sound decision-making. At a gut level there is simply the question of the sheer stamina required to sustain the working-through of decision-making procedures that produce results that are democratic and technically competent.

The dilemma of participation increasingly faces all classes in society, though it is the poor who experience most forcefully the inadequacies of current participatory means in seeking redress of inequities in our social structures and in our distribution of resources. Sydney Verba (1967) suggests that there are four causes contributing to this situation:

1. The economy is expanding and changing rapidly in ways that benefit some and not others.
2. There are great mobility opportunities for some in the social structure.
3. There are emerging values that reject traditional means of social control.
4. The expansion of government intervention in the economic and social life of the nation increases the stakes of participation (p. 55).

That the stakes are high is revealed in the substantive magnitude of contemporary issues. Matters of pollution, of resource scarcity, and technological response allow for only slim margins for error, if any at all. There is a sense of finality about the decisions before us, which, once taken, seem irrevocable. The character of a city can be sealed through the development of a freeway network; the fate of a river system can be determined by hydro-electric dams. We desperately need uncomplicated information and the means to predict with some accuracy the consequences of any given course of action:

> In the conduct of human affairs, our actions inevitably have second-order consequences. These consequences are, in many instances, more important than our original action (Bauer, 1966, p. 2).

Given this climate of complication it is inevitable that there be pressures for technologically correct substantive decisions at the expense of democratic processes. Yet it is not simply an issue of 'the people versus technology'. Pollution is a case in point. The tone of the debate sometimes suggests legislation by fiat against further technological defacing of the environment without sufficient concern for the welfare of those affected by such action. Inevitably, those whose livelihood is affected are in opposition to the environmentalists. Somehow technology needs to be rerouted in a manner that ensures basic securities as well as protection of the environment. Sensitivity as to what constitutes basic securities is really only possible through democratic means.

Significantly, there is also a growing concern today for the processes of decision-making. Indeed for some the values and norms expressed in how a decision is arrived at are more important than the decision itself. There is the implicit assumption that if people are effectively involved, then the decision will be correct. This existential mood is reflected particularly among the young and the counter-culture and within the human-potential movement. Though too frequently isolationist and over-simplified, it is a philosophical stance badly needed in a technocratic age. The pressures for benevolent, totalitarian decision-making will undoubtedly grow, nourished through our frustrations in trying to manage technological life.

The strength of the dual concern for both competence in technological management and a democratic process in decision-making is that we are forced to ferret out and develop new options that are hopefully more harmonious in solution to both people and the environment. The options available for creative compromise are increased. In the freeway debate, for example, the options cannot simply be a number of expressway-route alternatives. Rather they must include non-freeway proposals which deal with the effective movement of people, goods, and services. Questions then to be asked should include considerations of factors least disruptive to urban life, and indeed those options that can enhance it for the foreseeable future.

Similar magnitudes of compromise should be operative in proposals for further large hydro projects. The arguments of those suggesting the damming of the Fraser River, for example, are based on the apparently insatiable need for electricity and the alleged fact that hydro power is less a pollutant than nuclear energy. Yet surely the discussion should be broadened to question how wisely we use our present electrical resources. In a culture of conspicuous consumption, in which electrical energy is at the forefront, there must be some power uses that are less than essential. We should examine what we might give up as well as what might be needed for future power uses. This is where tough compromise is called for.

Decisions are proposed and made on a grand scale affecting whole communities and whole societies, yet the individual human scale needs somehow to be protected and enhanced. There is the greater good and there is the particular good. Again, compromise can be too narrowly defined and rationalized through the 'greater good of all the people' arguments. Nowhere is this more evident in Canada than in regional economic planning. The infusion of development funds and the introduction of new industrial, agricultural, or fishing patterns are intended to raise over-all living standards and contribute to the wealth of the designated area. In order to gain the support of local people, funds are also spent on social-development programs that can enable residents to become involved in the planning process. Such involvement ranges from simple participation in information meetings, organized by the planners, to responsibility for developing various stages of the regional plan.

Citizen involvement in area-development plans has not to date been a resounding success, however. The difficulty centres on the greater good v. particular good dilemma. Stephen Guisinger, in an unpublished paper, has suggested that the goals of large-scale, macro-economic planning and those of community and social development are not fully compatible, and conflict between the two emphases can therefore be expected (Guisinger, 1969, p. 56).' People in target areas for economic development frequently prefer planning and resources that strengthen their existing life-styles to changing employment and residence to suit the requirements of the new industries.

Too often, it seems, there is an implicit assumption that the larger public purposes which foster an area-development plan are in fact accurate reflections of the public good. In his report on the subject, McCrorie (1969) states that ' . . . if the larger society itself is not questioned then planning is incomplete and a key factor in involvement is ignored' (p. 97). Perhaps the values local residents stubbornly protect are worth nourishing for the greater good too. One can only assume that effective compromise in planning produces an economy more resilient and ensures maintenance of the best in local values and participation. Citizen involvement is limited in the spectacular economics of large-scale development while the potential for vast, bureaucratic decision-making is unlimited.

Scope of the Legislative Process

In the final analysis the quest for technically competent and democratically rooted decisions must centre on our legislative process. It is the formal means by which people in society determine and sanction their collective actions, affecting the breadth and depth of individual, group, and community life. The structural forms of our legislative process shape immeasurably our patterns of participation. The crunch comes in terms of the adequacy of current legislative structures and procedures to suit the needs of the times. Mrs. Doris Power's statement on behalf of the Just Society (1970) to the Special Senate Committee on Poverty – 'we will not legitimize this type of social bullshit' (p. 18) – reflects with precision the gap between the legislature and many poor people in Canada.

Increasingly, the poor are not alone in their powerlessness. A city politician has about as much trouble and possibility of success in dealing with a federal Manpower Department or a provincial welfare department as does the man on the street. Identifying who has pertinent information and who is responsible for decisions in the vastness of bureaucracy is a never-

ending search. It underlines the gap between the world of Ottawa and the legislative process – one reality – and the myriad of
interests and needs of the country-at-large – another reality, or
almost so it sometimes seems.

In a recent issue of *Maclean's* George Woodcock has calculated that a Canadian eligible to vote federally since 1921
would ' . . . have been allowed to exercise his political competence federally on exactly fifteen days . . . fifteen being the number of elections held during the past fifty years' (Woodcock,
1971, p. 14). Participation by the ballot-box alone is indeed one
of the serious weaknesses in current legislative procedures for
the general populace. The federal Task Force on Government
Information summed up the problem well:

> Since governments are inevitably increasing their effect on
> the day-to-day lives of citizens, it follows that the citizens
> should be able to increase their say in what governments do
> . . . participatory democracy suggests the citizens' continuous
> and broadly based involvement in the process of government
> (Task Force . . . 1969, p. 17).

Participation avenues need to be designed to give the citizen
direct, on-going access to the formal decision-making processes
of government when the citizen's interests are involved. For
citizens – and not the candidates – elections are essentially a
passive affair, more in the nature of a broad referendum of
approval or removal.

Another serious weakness lies in the growing misalignment
of our three formal legislative levels in Canada, among themselves and increasingly to the populace as a whole. The importance of urban affairs still receives only grudging recognition
from the provincial and federal levels. And within the large
metropolitan centres there is considerable distance between
City Hall and the needs at the district and neighbourhood levels. Some argue that the latter represent a needed fourth level
of government to get action on issues and ensure local participation.

A third weakness in effective citizen participation in the legislative process is the information problem. Whatever the final
hoped-for results of Information Canada might be, citizen,
legislator, and bureaucrat are unable at present to maintain a
communications flow that informs, educates, and instructs all
parties involved. The mysteries of technology need simplifica-

tion, the bureaucratic ramifications of political decisions need clarification, and the nuances and idiosyncracies, the beliefs, and emotions of the moods of a variety of publics need expression to responsive, legislative ears.

Finally, it is important to identify, understand, and manage in a more democratic manner the vast grey area of quasi-legislative decision-making that occurs within the bureaucracy. The scale of social and economic planning today (especially the latter) requires a broad, formal legislative sanction that permits an overly generous bureaucratic discretion in the development and implementation of the specific details of policy. Political accountability gets lost in the process. Similarly the growing number of review boards and quasi-judicial tribunals within the bureaucracy represent in a very explicit manner substantive decision-making that fleshes out and refines the intent of formal legislative decisions. Welfare-appeal boards and workmen's-compensation-appeal boards are two such examples. Another illustration is the zoning-appeal-review board in town-planning procedures. Here, particularly, it is important to ensure that citizens in areas proposed for zoning review have the political clout and legislative means for negotiating with the developers, real-estate interests, and city planners.

The existence of the weaknesses identified here means that the scope of the legislative process is simply not broad enough to accommodate the political responsibilities and involvement requirements of citizens today. Restricted in the range of participative options available within the current legislative structures, people are increasingly seeking alternative ways of affecting directly political decisions:

> ... the right to speak, to picket, to demonstrate are the chief instruments through which poor people can effectively influence legislative policy (Canadian Civil Liberties Assoc., 1970, p. 20).

Mass meetings to protest a proposed road development through an expensive residential area of Vancouver, and the coalescing of numerous citizens' groups to fight a high-density, 'Four Seasons' development in the same city, suggest that other income groups are having to resort to extra-legislative procedures as well, if their views are to be heard.

Towards an Open System: Some Suggestions for Reform

Clearly it is imperative to increase the range of participatory
options available to the citizen in the legislative process. The
answer does not lie in some yet-to-be-discovered participatory
form that is inherently correct for all time. Rather it lies in the
responsiveness of organizations, in the availability of resources,
in free access to information, and in a political planning process that is accountable to the citizenry. Thus, the act of involvement is governed by democratic norms, while its structure
is essentially determined by the nature of any given issue and
the particular interests involved. The implications of this approach to participation are explored more fully below.

Organization and Participation

Our traditional forms of organization are characterized by rigid, mechanistic systems with elaborate vertical hierarchies.
Their boundary systems are 'fixed', i.e., their engagement with
social systems beyond their own is relatively static, reflecting a
time of less-rapid change than is the case now.

The concept of participation that is used here, however, is
characterized by open, temporary arrangements of resources –
both human and material – designed to fulfil functions for a
given period in time and then be subject to rearrangement.
Such an organization is less vertically complex and more open
to collaborative relationships among its members. It is also
more open and sensitive to influence from other systems and
events, reflected in the continuous development of its boundaries. The 'open organization' is one that appears more suited to
an age of constant change.

There is still very much a need for the kind of participatory
base line that is characteristic of representative government,
but it badly needs supplementing with the flexible use of organization resources described above.

The Importance of Information

The function of information in the relationship between citizen
and government is to ensure two-way communication about

existing and proposed policies and practices, to assess what are, and to test what should be, the programs of government. Information practices should therefore be based on the concept of out-reach; informing those directly affected by government actions in a manner that is sensitive to their particular needs. Policies, rules, regulation and operating procedures of legislation should be readily available. Every program should explain the rationale for the practices it employs.

There is also need of a single source of help to guide citizens through the labyrinth of bureaucratic practices. In this regard, the citizen advisory bureau concept, recommended by the Information Task Force, has a special role at the city-wide and neighbourhood levels (Task Force . . . , 1969, p. 294).

The question of government privacy of information needs re-examination. Certainly there can be no rationale for keeping from the individual personal information on himself in government records, except in those exceptional instances where national security is threatened. A welfare recipient should be able to review all files a department has on him; so too for an individual receiving Manpower counselling or unemployment insurance.

Information is a source of control. It is also a source of understanding, learning, and participation. Government information policies must be designed to do the latter, not the former. More advanced forms of communication are required, utilizing the media and developments in computer technology. One successful example, it is reported, occurred on an American campus during the Vietnam Moratorium last year. Virtually all faculties had geared into a variety of protest forms, based on their educational orientation. Fine arts churned out posters, political science provided the political analyses, law the legal arguments against the war, and so on. To keep track of the burgeoning activities, up-to-date information was fed regularly into a computer. The inquiring student wanting to know what was going on simply checked with a computer terminal.

The significance of this illustration is the fact that information was quickly and easily available to all on campus. There was no need for the large network of co-ordinating committees that would customarily be operating in such a situation. Gone too was the inevitable small group who knew more of what was occurring than anyone else.

Government should move towards organizing its informa-

tion services in a similar manner. Then it would be less suscep-
tible to the charge of shaping information to suit its own ends,
for citizens would have full access to the same resources.

The Distribution of Resources

Unless one is prepared to devise and propose means for more
equitable distribution of income and financial resources in
Canada, all other proposals for increased citizen participation
are bound to founder. Mal-distribution of wealth and unequal
access to the country's resources mean that some will have
more influence, power, and means to effective participation
than others.

Major redistributive measures, such as the guaranteed income and tax reform, are fundamental. Less elaborate changes
can be introduced as well. A ceiling could be set on campaign
expenses in elections, or perhaps a public fund set up out of
which all properly nominated candidates draw equal amounts
of dollars. As well there could be increased use of public funds
to support the activities of citizens' groups, particularly those
among the poor. Chambers of Commerce receive indirect government subsidy to act as political lobbyists through tax-de-
ductions. Why cannot the organizations of the poor receive, as
Alan Borovoy (Canadian Civil Liberties Assoc., 1970, p. 37)
has suggested, a similar benefit?

Money given by government to citizens' groups should be
viewed as aiding citizen development and social change. The *ad
hoc*, informal, and spontaneous characteristics of many citizens' groups are a source for fertile ideas and for experimentation that may not be possible within the most enlightened formal structures of bureaucracy. Grants to a tenants' association,
to a welfare-rights group, or to a pollution-control group
should be very liberal in their support of unique and imaginative proposals, even when these run contradictory to established policies. It is a conscious way to keep government on its
toes.

Federally, much credit should be given to the Secretary of
State and the Department of National Health and Welfare
for the assistance provided to citizen groups with a minimum
of qualifications. Recent political uncomfortableness (within
Parliament and at the local level) over the actions of some
groups receiving these funds is a sign that they probably are

being used to good effect. It is important now, however, to acknowledge formally the validity of such grants as a legitimate part of the political process.

The Planning Process for Decision-Making

Planning in government remains fragmented and parcelled by jurisdictions that do not or cannot consider the interdependency of contemporary issues. There are economic plans, urban renewal plans, and transportation plans. There is no over-all planning process that links these with social needs. Thus, there is little effective political accountability for the results of planning, particularly in the social sphere. Consequently, the citizen has no significant opportunity to participate in a coherent social-economic planning process at the community, regional, or national levels. Participation in this sense is more than affirmation of broad legislative proposals. It includes direct participation in the shaping of the proposals by all interested parties, with formal legitimization occurring in the legislature. It includes the intensive dissemination of information and its acquisition from the public in a form that reveals the consequences and implications of given policy alternatives. And it forces greater commitment and accountability from the formal politicians and bureaucrats in the implementation of decisions.

The Future of the Legislature

What is necessary is that citizen participation in legislative decision-making occur through a dynamic movement of individuals and interest groups into and out of the government sphere, the engagement being determined by whatever needs and interests are current at any given time. This applies as much to a House of Commons as to a city council or provincial government. The intent, as Professor Gordon has described it, would be to supplement Parliament with '. . . theoretically, non-party forms of representation to speak for special occupations and interests' (Task Force . . . , 1969, p. 10).

Inevitably such a development would lead, as the Information Task Force Report observed, to ' . . . alterations in some traditional parliamentary forms' (p. 17). The role of 'The Official Opposition', for example, might be altered. To too great an extent the scope of the opposition-parties' concerns is narrower than that of the latent opposition within the province or country as a whole. The posturing of being in official opposition seems greater than the disputes or alternatives that are under consideration. To speculate for a moment: if indeed technology was able to facilitate a means for effective mass decision-making (the global village idea) in continuous process, would there be a need for an official opposition? Would those in government be more visible and therefore more responsible in their political actions and, consequently, subject to more immediate censure, removal, or approbation? Perhaps, but for the here and now there are a number of changes in current legislative practices that would be an improvement.

Involvement in the Formal Legislative Process

Citizen input is required in both reviewing existing legislation and in developing new proposals for enactment. The customary methods for obtaining a sense of public opinion and suggestions at the federal-provincial levels have been the debate following publication of a White Paper, fact-finding committees of the Senate and the House, Royal Commissions, and, of course, the government platform at election time.

These consultative devices need to be strengthened. One way is through the inclusion of concerned citizens as advisory members of legislative committees. For example tenants, landlords, and private home-owners might serve as advisers to a committee of the legislature reviewing housing policies. A trend along this line is noticeable in some municipal governments. In Calgary, for example, members of a welfare organization have participated in a sub-committee of the City Social Service Committee. The thorny problem of freeways in Vancouver has resulted in a special Committee of City Hall, 'The Transportation Liaison Group', which includes both elected officials and citizens from the areas potentially in the path of the highway. As well, Vancouver has set up a planning advisory committee for a large community-services complex in the east end, which is composed of six citizens and four public officials. This committee will be responsible for supervising and recommending for approval all aspects of the centre's planning to City Council and the participating boards (Parks and Schools).

Another approach for improving involvement would be

more developmental in style; it would place prime responsibility upon the target publics involved in potential legislation – rather than the legislature – to develop proposals for government action. For example in situations where regional development is being considered, the use of the community self-study technique might be appropriate. Algonquin College in Ottawa has done some pioneering work in using community self-analysis to have broadly representative groups of citizens identify all possible areas of need and local opportunity, and then move to the difficult process of open bargaining and consensus-building to arrive at a set of community-wide priorities. Used on an area-development basis, this technique allows for more accurate expressions of local desires than do any of the current imposed formats. In effect, the results of such an exercise constitute a local mandate for government action. An equally important result is the greater degree of community interest and participation that is generated. Less ambitious, but still quite valuable, variants on this approach include Thunder Bay's 'Town Talk' program, the 'Encounter' experiment in Halifax, and 'Action 70' in Ottawa.

The concept of councils advisory to government, to the legislature, or to the general public is well established in Canada. The most prestigious perhaps is the Economic Council of Canada. Others have included the Canadian Council on Rural Development, the Science Council of Canada, a Manpower advisory council, and the National Council on Welfare. The councils' function is normally one of persuasion and education. For those that are advisory to a single department of government, their effectiveness in influencing policy is critically dependent upon the interest of the minister of the day.

Advisory-council dependency could perhaps be lessened in two ways. Those bodies that receive budget and staff services from the department they ostensibly counsel could benefit from independent funding directly from the legislature. As well, departments and ministers could be required to consult the council in the formulation of legislation for the House. The National Council on Welfare should be able to be a critic, an advocate, and an endorser of department and government action – or inaction – in the social-welfare field. (Indications so far are very much in this direction for this new body.) Finally, the council-appointment process needs opening up. Patronage is rife. The criteria for selection should be well known and the means democratic (open to all applicants whose qualifications suit the responsibilities of the council). Civic politics are notorious for distributing the appointment spoils, yet it is at the municipal level where interested citizens could contribute most directly and easily to community life through the advisory-council process, regardless of formal political affiliation.

Involvement in the Administrative Process

Administration in government is the vehicle for carrying out legislative policies. As noted earlier, the complexity of legislative policies today means that a kind of quasi-legislative function is developing within the administrative sphere, as the intent of government programs is fleshed out and refined. There is a need therefore to include citizens in both advisory and decision-making capacities in the administrative process. They can give life and reality to administration, limiting the dehumanizing pressures of bureaucracy.

Welfare-appeal boards, required in each province participating in the Canada Assistance Plan, would be considerably more credible if they were separated from the immediate control of welfare departments. They should obviously include in their membership, perhaps even as a majority, citizens who have been or are receiving social assistance. Manitoba is the only province to date that has included welfare recipients on the board.

Administrators need advice as well on the efficacy of their operations, the degree to which they are achieving the objectives expressed in legislation. An advisory group, like the National Council on Welfare, might review the various federal funding programs for citizens' groups and make suggestions for any changes required. Or at the community level a local Manpower office could benefit from a citizens' committee that helps formulate Manpower priorities to meet local needs.

The watch-dog function is evident in all of these examples. It might be argued that the institution of the Ombudsman office in government would more effectively perform this role. However, citizen participation in the administrative, quasi-legislative responsibilities of the government bureaucracy complements well the responsibilities of an Ombudsman. The latter responds once administrative wrongs are brought to his attention. The former is engaged in the process of administrative action to ensure that the chances of administrative error or malpractice are minimized. Together they ensure strong protection and perhaps even enhancement of individual and group liberties.

Credibility: Fundamental to the Legislative Process

Technical and democratic competence in the management of contemporary issues is the optimum goal for legislative reform. To the extent that the means exist for a broad range of participatory activities in the legislative process, there is a basis for legislative action that fits in tone and substance the needs of the day. Legislation that is less clumsy and more refined to suit the problem should be the result. It is essential that people know they have an effective option to help create, shape, and determine legislative policy. Indeed, knowledge of and confidence in the existence of the option is as important to political morale as the number of times it is utilized.

MICHAEL CLAGUE participated in a recreation-and-leadership-development program on the Musqueam Indian Reserve while studying political science at the University of British Columbia. He later became Adult Program Secretary with the Toronto Central Y.M.C.A. Branch. The establishment of an adult-education program at the Ontario Institute for Studies in Education provided an opportunity to formalize his working experience to date and to pursue studies in areas of special interest, such as community development. From OISE, Mr. Clague joined the Citizenship Branch, Department of the Secretary of State, as a National Liaison Officer. This position afforded him extensive contacts with the voluntary-agency community in Canada, and he had an opportunity to observe at first hand the growing institutionalization of relationships between government and the voluntary sector by means of public-funding schemes. In February 1969, he was lent to the Special Senate Committee on Poverty. Committee responsibilities included arrangements for the public-hearing program across the country and research and writing on the subjects of participation, the law and the poor, and the social-service system. Since November 1970, Mr. Clague has been a community worker in the Grandivew-Woodland area of East Vancouver for the Neighbourhood Services Association. He is also active in the Canadian Association for Adult Education.

The Politics of Participation: A Student Case

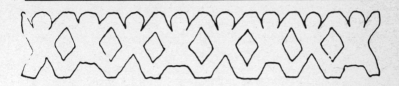

Steven Langdon

The student role in Canada hasn't always been very helpful to the historic thrust for democratization and equality in our community. When William Lyon Mackenzie's populist rebels came marching down Yonge Street in 1837, one of the armed contingents that fought them was made up of Toronto students. When Mitchell Hepburn decided industrial unionism was subversive in the Ontario of a century later, a significant number of his anti-U.A.W. 'Hepburn's Hussars' were University of Toronto students.

So there's nothing inevitably progressive about the student population in this country.

In the last decade, however, students have become one of the leading exponents of the politics of participation; their protests and their experiments, indeed, have become contributing factors in the spread throughout the community of the ideals of democratization that this book is about. Students didn't develop the concepts of equality and decentralized popular control, on which the participation thrust is built; but they did give fresh impetus to those ideals in the sixties. Accordingly, the example of student power had a significance well beyond the student constituency from which it was articulated.

That's one reason for examining the student-power movement in a volume of this sort, largely concerned with the politics of participation on the level of less specialized communities. More important, there are some useful conclusions that can be drawn from the student experience; any efforts towards community participation will benefit from those lessons. That is the primary focus of this paper.

The first point of analysis is the process by which student power became articulated and defined on Canadian campuses, the way in which the movement for student power developed; from this we may establish some general framework for the growth of movements for community democratization. Secondly, we consider the strategy that the student power thrust has used; again, the purpose is to draw some general conclusions about strategies for radical change in Canada.

The Process of Student Participation

The student-power movement grew from the interaction of two factors: a social process that established the roots for student protest; and an institutional initiative by which the student leadership on campuses accepted and propagated a commitment to participation. The progress of the movement was marked by two further developments: the progressively tougher definition of what participation really meant; and the increasingly more obvious decentralization and broadening of the student-power movement. This section of the paper examines each of these points in turn. [1]

It was undoubtedly the new emphasis on technological and managerial skills for modernized industry that provoked the widespread expansion of university education in the sixties in Canada. The needs of our much more sophisticated economy dictated a much better educated labour force. As a social process, however, this massive expansion of post-secondary schooling had a dramatic impact all its own. Its size alone was spectacular; in Ontario, for example, university enrolment grew from 25,659 in 1959-60 to 73,805 just eight years later (Minister of University Affairs, 1967, p. 27). And its size established two realities.

On one hand, the process put together in their own institutional context a great many young people; a much larger percentage of the youth population than ever before was isolated in educational institutions. Students were, in an important sense, set apart as a particular social grouping within society; and their numbers were, for the first time, large enough to give some social significance to their reactions to the role they were given to play. The growth of a distinctive youth culture is in some degree a reflection of this social isolation. And in the same way, the grouping together of so many students, sharing similar frustrations and hopes, established the basis for a student-power movement. The power implicit in the new numbers of students could respond to the problems that grew in the institutions in which students worked.

Similarly, the expansion of universities provoked major dilemmas inside those institutions. The old *élitist* college style let professors and students come to know each other well; it let them develop informal influence over each other. But the new mass 'multiversity' lost this personal character; huge lectures, impersonal contact, institutionalized authority became the pattern; the university learning experience became depressingly conventional and standardized (Presidential Advisory Committee, 1967; Adelman & Lee, 1968). At the same time, studies indicate that contemporary students come to university with expectations as high as ever of an exciting and creative education (Stern, 1966); the reality, however, could no longer meet these hopes. This factor, the educational failure of the mass university, became the most important basis for the student-power thrust in Canada; the drive for student participation and for educational reform was one and the same.

These social developments established the roots for a student-power movement in Canada. But the movement itself did not arise spontaneously. It was consciously provoked by a small minority of students, most of whom were involved, in Canada, in organized student-government institutions. This conscious minority recognized many of the dilemmas of the mass university by the mid sixties; and from that point it began to develop programs to win student participation.

At the University of Toronto, for example, the Students' Administrative Council (SAC), then an *élite* student government far removed from most students, began to raise questions about student participation in the mid sixties. At the national level, the Canadian Union of Students (CUS), an even more isolated group of student leaders, did likewise. (In the case of CUS and to a degree–through CUS–in all local student governments in English-speaking Canada, the increasingly militant syndicalism of the Quebec student movement was an important external influence.)

From the questioning, the first conscious efforts devel-

oped to win significant participation for students in the governing of their educational institutions.

These first efforts began the process of defining effective participation. The original point of reference was the proposals of
the 1966 Duff-Berdahl Commission on University Government: advisory consultative committees for students in departments; possibly one or two student representatives in the Senate; the election of a non-student Rector to speak for students
on the Board of Governors. These suggestions were quickly
rejected by students, who argued that mere voice in university
decisions was not enough; participation demanded a voting
role, even if a limited one.

The student thrust passed into the 'representation' stage,
where the introduction of elected students onto existing decision-making bodies became the object. At first there was considerable administrative resistance to the idea – until a few examples of representation were tried. The result of these experiments was two-fold: a good many students found that the
experience of working as a small minority within existing decision bodies was frustrating, and ineffective so far as achieving
the changes they sought[2]; similarly, administration and faculty
found that such limited student participation was relatively
easy to accept. Consequently, students developed a more rigorous definition of effective participation; and administration-
faculty moderates successfully established limited levels of student representation in a great many Canadian universities.

From the experiments with representation, students developed a new concept: parity. The councils, committees, and
boards of the university, it was argued, should include equal
numbers of student representatives and of faculty representatives. From this equality would come a better student chance to
win reform and a more valid level of student influence in their
own education.

The Commission on University Government (cug) at the
University of Toronto provides the best support for this position – partly because the structure of the Commission itself involved parity. More than that, however, the Commission endorsed parity in its exhaustive final report (1969), concluding
that 'the strongest arguments for parity between faculty and students are based both on the student commitment to and interest
in the learning process, as well as on very important political and
psychological realities: unless students feel secure in their influ-

ence and are, indeed, given considerable influence, participation becomes merely token.'

Again, though, the parity model includes some drawbacks, and a number of students began to suggest even more far-reaching structural changes. The basic goal was to establish a sense and reality of participation in decision-making for all students, to have them all develop the feelings of psychological equality that CUG suggested were essential to non-token participation. The problem with parity, it was argued, was that only a small number of students actually took part in the making of decisions, and the great bulk of students remained as far as ever from a sense of control over their educational institutions.

From this emphasis on broad democratization, the student-power movement, particularly at Simon Fraser University and the University of Toronto, began to define effective participation in terms of 'parallel structures'.[3] That model, as the SAC brief to CUG defined it, 'maintain(s) the committee system by making joint committees the major innovative bodies and the forums for detailed discussion and compromise between faculty and students. Committee decisions must, however, be approved by dual open meetings, one of all faculty, one of all students, within a given jurisdiction' (Students' Administrative Council, 1969, p. 15). Each element of a department, in short, is given a veto; from this comes a real equality and influence that makes participation effective for all students and faculty.[4]

While the meaning of 'participation' was being worked out in the process of seeking it, other developments took place in the student community. The *élite* student-council leadership succeeded in its efforts at making democratization an issue – because, as we saw, the roots for such a thrust were present. But the first target of student demands for effective participation became those *élite* student governments themselves; the radical agitation for change in which student councils were involved provoked reaction from students, reaction meant to control those governments in a democratic way. At the University of Toronto, for example, several colleges and professional schools held referendums on whether they should withdraw from the SAC; and while the council won those referendums, they marked the beginning of much more open, participatory student-unionism on campus. Mass open meetings, referendums, much wider SAC communication became the new pattern.

The Canadian Union of Students was far less able to adjust and reform its *élite* structure; and consequently the radical cus agitation for democratization claimed the national union itself as a first victim.[5]

Two other developments became obvious as well. First, the impetus for the student-power movement spread beyond the student-union leadership. Informal radical thrusts grew up on many campuses (the Toronto Student Movement at U. of T., for example); and the movement for change became widely decentralized, to departmental course unions, for instance, or to local college and professional-school student associations.

Secondly, the basic commitment to student power became widely shared throughout the whole student community; the belief in participation became internalized. Thus, at U. of T. for example, in student elections for cug, all four candidates pledged to student power were elected.[6] In 1969-70, surveys in the political-economy department found most students committed to parity – though rather vaguely.[7] And last fall an overwhelming majority of a high turn-out, in Arts and Science at U. of T., supported student parity in a referendum.

The general framework within which student power grew, then, is clear. The basic ingredients for the movement's relative success were: (a) the shared experience and condition of its potential base; (b) the existence of at least one critical problem on which discontent was focussed – educational failures, in this case; and (c) the activity of a small but significant student leadership in articulating the student-power alternative. The process of defining effective participation, and of working to get it, brought a radicalization in the student-power thrust; more and more fundamental reforms came to be seen as necessary. And as the potential base of the movement developed a commitment to participation, the original *élite* leadership was replaced by a decentralized, much more informal drive for change in many different parts of the university. Student power began as a vague ideal in a student *élite*; it developed into a broad-based movement throughout the student community.

The Student-Power Strategy

There are some useful conclusions that can be drawn from the growth process of the student-power movement: the necessary ingredients for a successful community power thrust are suggested; and the pattern by which a movement matures is implied. Similarly, the strategy that the student-power drive developed points to some valuable insights for the effort toward community participation in Canada.

The early student attempt to establish participation in the university relied on reasoned argument and negotiation. And it failed, not so much because the arguments were poor, but because those in authority refused to take the student demand very seriously. Moreover, those students negotiating were cut off from their potential base of support, because the locus of discussion was closed meetings with university administrators and faculty.

Two strategic conclusions were drawn by the student leadership involved at that stage. The first was that openness had to be a prior condition of any negotiations with university authorities. Otherwise it would be impossible to maintain the confidence of supporters. As the SAC put it at U. of T., 'all discussion would be open unless a decision were made to close discussion of a particular topic. All members of the university have a right to know the decisions made by those governing them and the reasons for those decisions' (Students' Administrative Council, 1969, p. 18). Significantly, the CUG also endorsed this position in its report.

The second strategic conclusion was that students would have to show how seriously committed they were to major reforms before they would get them. The student leadership recognized that participation was inevitably a question of power, because in so far as it gave students important influence, it reduced the influence of other elements in the university; the faculty perceived this reality with special clarity in the case of departmental decision-making. The student strategy, then, had to recognize this conflict for power; it had to develop some way of mobilizing the only strength that students had in the conflict – the power implicit in their large numbers.

The result was a politics of confrontation. By using confrontation tactics, students were able to persuade authorities that they were, in sizeable proportions, serious about major reforms in the university – that they were serious about winning effective participation.

Ever since the student dissent of the sixties developed momentum, there has been a great deal of nonsense written about

confrontation politics. The confrontation style has been con-
demned as a threat to 'law and order'; it has been rejected as
the introduction of uncivilized violence and force into our essentially humane and peaceful community. Such criticisms have
missed the point.

Confrontation politics is a perfectly natural style of protest
by which men and women, affected by particular institutions,
attempt to gain power in decision-making by organizing together and demonstrating collective strength to those in charge
of institutions. Conflict arises, of course, because those who
now make decisions are being challenged. But from the
perspective of democratizing the community, the conflict is useful. For one thing, confrontations themselves begin the wider
distribution of power within society; more people are pro-
pelled into politics and, by their motion, shift authority even
as they demand participation for themselves. Moreover, confrontations have a long history of bringing about egalitarian
social reform – just as direct action brought the ballot to
women in the early years of the century, gave workers improved status in their factories, and won civil rights for American blacks.

The use of confrontation politics, however, raises some serious issues. There is a spectrum of confrontation methods
across which we must make distinctions. Confrontations can
be legal, illegal but non-violent, or violent (defining violent
confrontations, as the Campbell Committee on Discipline did
at U. of T. as those 'that endanger the safety of persons or
destroy valuable property of the University or its members'
[Presidential Committee, 1969, p. 72]).

Students at various universities in Canada have used all three
types of confrontation. Legal demonstrations and boycotts
have been used everywhere. Violence, though, has been used
very rarely; and where it has been used, as in the destruction of
computers at Sir George Williams, the result has been devastat-
ing for the student-power movement. Partly for these tactical
reasons, students have rejected political violence; but even
more important, the student movement, by and large, has rejected violence for moral and ethical reasons. Students have felt
that those who suffer most from a climate of social violence are
the poor and the powerless, rather than those in authority.

A violent strategy seems likely to be self-defeating, to hurt those already victimized, and to destroy the eventual possibility of a humane, participatory community in which radical social reforms will have been instituted.

Then there is the more difficult category: that of illegal but non-violent protest. Here again there is a long and honourable tradition, that of civil disobedience; from Thoreau to Gandhi to Cesar Chavez, it has brought non-violent change. This is a strategic approach which the student-power movement has, perhaps hesitantly, accepted. Thus non-violent sit-ins, occupations, threatened occupations, and so forth have marked the fight for participation at many Canadian universities. Usually such serious moves have convinced authorities that students were deeply committed to change; and significant reforms have followed.[8] Such illegal confrontations in Canada have almost always been marked by complete non-violence in the sense the Campbell Committee defines it.

At the same time, though, confrontations can escalate, initiate violence, and destroy the basis of support for a movement's thrust for participation. That has meant that careful planning and self-restraint have been a necessary part of the strategy of most successful student confrontations. Militant action has had to mean disciplined action. Those prepared to confront authority in the drive for participation have had to recognize a deep responsibility to keep protest non-violent.

The strategy of the student-power movement, then, suggests several points: (a) the need to move beyond leadership negotiation, both to win supporters and to achieve participation; (b) the importance of openness in keeping the confidence of supporters; (c) the significance of confrontation politics in developing a movement for participation and in reaching the democratization goals sought; (d) the critical need to reject a strategy of violence; (e) the responsibility, in a confrontation strategy, to underline a non-violent style.

The student-power thrust has been relatively successful when its strategy has been broad-based and militant enough to convince most students to support it and most authorities to respect it. At the same time, that strategy has emphasized non-violence so as not to destroy the ultimate goals it sought, so as not to lose the large-scale sympathy of the student community, and so as not to bring powerful state repression down upon it.

Conclusion

This is a very brief review of a complex social movement, which has grown everywhere in the industrial world; even within Canada, attention has been centred on relatively few campuses in the article. Moreover, my analysis has concentrated on the growth process and strategy of student-power movements, where they have been reasonably successful. And the focus of concern throughout has been the aspects of student power that relate to the participation ideal. The student-power movement involves wider aims, beyond the democratization of educational institutions:[9] these have been ignored.

All that is to emphasize that this paper presents no definitive conclusions about the history and purpose of the student-power movment. Instead, it has attempted to point out some significant factors in the growth process of the movement and some useful insights into its strategic approach to provoking social change. These may be of some value to community-based groups attempting to win for themselves the power to affect the society that shapes them.

That may be where the student-power thrust is most important in any analysis of community participation. The example of student efforts may help many, whose material conditions and oppression are much worse, to organize effectively to force large-scale change.

Certainly the student effort over the last five years has shown that well-organized action can bring significant reform. At the University of Toronto, for example, the movement for student power has brought considerable change – not enough, of course, but still considerable. The pattern of education is now much less inflexible, with experimental courses offered for credit in a number of fields; final examinations are given far less emphasis than used to be the case; course content within departments is much more varied and innovative than it was in the early sixties. The attitudes of faculty towards students are much less reserved and authoritarian than formerly. Student institutions, such as residences, are self-run. And everywhere students have at least a limited role in decision-making. The university is much less secretive than it was five years ago, too. Confrontations, it is clear, have shaken people's minds, forced them to think again about their institution, and brought essential changes.

Much remains for the student-power movement to do – particularly at the level of many departments; for it is at the departmental level that much of the real power rests in shaping the style and content of education, and senior faculty continues to hold that power securely and defensively. That level, in fact, is the focus of the most bitter conflict in the university today, as students maintain their effort to gain full participation in all aspects of educational decision-making that affect them.

Nonetheless, the student-power movement has demonstrated that militant organization can win widespread reforms. The relative success of students in doing this is, possibly, the most important point other community power movements can grasp. The politics of participation, and a strategy of non-violent confrontation, can provoke serious improvements in the lives of those now powerless and exploited in the Canadian political economy.

FOOTNOTES

1. The conclusions and analysis in this section, as in the whole paper, reflect my own personal involvement in the student-power movement, particularly at the University of Toronto, but also, through the Canadian Union of Students, on a national level. It need hardly be pointed out that the perspective from such participant observation is less than definitive.

2. At the University of Toronto, for example, fourteen students were given places on the thousand member Arts and Science Council in 1968; within four months the students were convinced, in the process of discussing educational reforms, of the relative uselessness of their role. For an indication of how widely this pattern was followed in Canada, see the survey in *University Affairs*, 10:6 (July 1969), 9-21; for a well-argued statement of non-student support for a limited, but voting, student role in government, see the Ontario Government's *Report on the Ontario College of Art* (Toronto: Department of University Affairs, Sept. 1968).

3. Student Power Research Sub-committee, *Report*. Vancouver: Political Science, Sociology, and Anthropology Department, Simon Fraser University, June 1968.

4. Significantly, the parallel structures system would go a considerable distance towards preserving for faculty a sense of control in the sensitive areas of hiring, tenure, and promotion decisions; faculty would have a veto on all student suggestions.

5. There were, of course, other factors involved as well; see my

on the union's demise: 'cus', *Canadian Dimension*, Feb.-Mar., 1970, 6-8.

6. The complex voting-system used meant that a huge majority of those voting was required for such a result.

7. Political economy course critique, University of Toronto, 1969-70, p. 70.

8. The occupation of the political-science department at McGill, for example, led to significant student participation in departmental decision-making – including the controversial areas of hiring, promotion, and tenure. Similar important changes took place at Windsor after an occupation there. The pattern is repeated in less dramatic terms at many other campuses.

9. These aims include reforms in particular matters of student concern – financial-aid legislation, for example – and radical democratization of the society at large. Canadian independence from the web of U.S. economic and political ties has been a major priority as well. These are all student-power aims in the sense that the movement for student participation has also worked for such goals. For an even wider perspective on student power, in the United Kingdom, see Alexander Cockburn and Robin Blackburn (eds.), *Student Power* (London, 1969).

STEVEN LANGDON is presently studying at the Institute of Canadian Studies at Carleton University. He is also working as Ottawa columnist for *Maclean's* Magazine.

He was an honours graduate in political economy from the University of Toronto, and while there was very actively involved in the student-power movement: as full-time President of the Students' Administive Council, 1968-9; as a member of the Trinity College f Stewards; and in the Political Economy Course Union. He a member of the 1969 Presidential Advisory Committee on ary Procedures. In 1969, he visited Africa as a representative adian Union of Students.

don worked as an editorial writer for the Toronto *Star* in 1969, and continually from April 1970 to mid February e months as the Ottawa-based editorial writer for the tributed regularly to *Canadian Writer* and to *Cana*- has contributed to the first issue of a forthcoming *dies for the Secondary School*, and has published ann's book *The Underside of Toronto*. Mr. the provincial executive of the Ontario New

Citizenship Development and the Disadvantaged

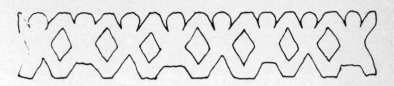

E. R. McEwen

There has been a nation-wide upsurge of concern at the failure of governments and voluntary agencies in Canada to meet the basic needs of its citizens. The concern is focussed on such facts as: the increasing pockets of poverty; the widening gap between the poor and the rich; increased industrial output and rising unemployment; the preparation of youth by schools and universities, for work that does not exist; the pollution of the air; and the degeneration of lakes and streams into open sewage systems.

This concern has expressed itself in the past few years in a rash of agencies committed to bringing about the needed changes in Canadian life: the Company of Young Canadians; the National Film Board through its Challenge for Change programs; anti-pollution councils, tenant associations, community-development agencies, and many more. Probably the most notable development in this respect has been the growth of organizations of the Indians, Métis, and Eskimos, dedicated to improving their position in the Canadian scene.

It would appear that the over-all aim of the current movement for change is to insure that all Canadians of all ages and economic brackets are knowledgeable of the democratic process and motivated to use it; to guarantee that all levels of government, industries, and public and private institutions are indeed true reflections of the desires and aspirations of the people and accountable to them. Despite all the expressed concern, however, the old order of things still grinds on.

It should be recognized that the present order of Canadian life is influenced, and to a large degree controlled, by international financial forces. The economic life of Canada is not something that our government can readily control. Too often expediency or 'tokenism' is the basis of government action, not by desire, but by necessity, due to forces at work both internally and externally.

It would be foolhardy to expect civil servants and the staffs of welfare institutions to be realistically dedicated to the irradication of poverty, since its existence provides them with a livelihood. When a person has invested years of toil doing good works for disadvantaged people, he becomes dependent on the perpetuation of the system for his own survival.

Traditionally, governments have offered programs for disadvantaged people cafeteria-style. The menu is prepared behind closed doors and then put on display to be taken or left without question or complaint. There is a constant building up of 'incentive packages' by experts, for the good of people deemed to be in need of them. In the present order of things, the creation of the package is not solely for the disadvantaged people, but often to serve the career ambitions of those who conceive it.

The Canadian Social Conscience

There is a marked lack of social conscience in Canadian history except on the part of some left-wing parties and splinter movements. Professor John Porter in his book *The Vertical Mosaic* notes that the great vision leading up to Confederation and since was and still is that of a nation stretching from sea to sea, spanned by railroads, with a vigorous flow of commerce east and west. The accent has been and still is on the material things.

The United States, because of its eighteenth-century origin has had, throughout its history, the philosophical concept of liberty, equality, fraternity. Before and during the War of Independence and during the building of the constitution, these concepts were articulated as basic ingredients for building a new nation. It can be argued that these are American myths. But such myths have an important function: they provide a basis for planning and action which, it can be argued, is in keeping with the traditional goals of the country. They provide the basis for the 'new deals', and human-rights movements.

Throughout American history, there has been an interplay between two basic concepts: the Jeffersonian, which has confidence in the capabilities of the common man to govern; and the Hamiltonian, which believes that only an *élite*, the leaders of industry and finance, can govern. Hamilton's approach was that businessmen should insure a vigorous economy and the common people should be encouraged to accept their leadership.

Canada came into being a century after the United States, not in the Age of Enlightenment, but in the age of British imperialism, the very peak of British industrial power. The philosophy that conceived it was pragmatic – the preservation of British interests in North America against a reunited, rapidly industrializing giant that shared the continent with it. The Anglo-Saxon element, with its ties with the motherland, found no need to enter into serious dialogue with its French-Canadian fellow-citizens about the social and cultural goals of the new nation.

The United Empire Loyalists, who played a large part in our early history and traditions, had, to a great extent, rejected the egalitarianism of the American Revolution and came to Canada where the colonial tradition still obtained. Many of them, like latter-day exploiters of Canadian resources, were induced to come by generous land-grants. Canada, under British rule, was a safe place in which to invest. Others had simply made the mistake of putting their money on the wrong horse. They had expected a British victory and had anticipated preferential treatment when the rebels were crushed.

The presence of this powerful political element in Canada was negative rather than positive in terms of the development of a social conscience.

The image of Canada that has been portrayed at home and abroad in the manner of colonial countries is of a land of vast material resources where prosperity is within the reach of everyone and, conversely, poverty, illness, etc., are the result of flaws in character. Welfare is provided for the destitute but it must never be sufficient to rehabilitate the recipient, as this would remove the punishment of those who have chosen to be poor in the midst of endless opportunity. This is the social attitude that has been perpetuated for generations in our schools, our churches, our politics.

Unfortunately, there is little progress taking place in the elimination of poverty as new schemes and packages are being ground out and offered up cafeteria-style. While there are federal and provincial programs for disadvantaged regions, their application is such that those who have something get assistance in proportion to what they have. There is little or nothing for the illiterate Métis squatter.[1] Token upgrading and retraining programs are offered hither and yon as the budgets permit, but these in far too many instances fail to result in employment. It appears that our government needs to accept a few basic assumptions around which policy programs and priorities can be established. These assumptions, in the interest of social justice, should be as follows:

1. Every citizen is entitled to a reasonable level of income. This would mean that the government would have to pay far more attention to the planning and controlling of the economy.

2. Every family is entitled to a reasonable standard of housing – poor housing generates illness, curtails education attainment, etc.

3. Every citizen is entitled to a good level of education in keeping with his interest and potential.

4. Every citizen is entitled to health services.[2] The accent needs to be on the building and maintaining of positive health rather than on curing and rehabilitation. In recent years, the government has made notable progress in the introduction of comprehensive health-insurance programs. It should be noted that this progressive move was vigorously opposed by the national and provincial medical associations and the private insurance companies.

In the democratic system, governments can accept only assumptions that are recommended by the population in general. Our traditional values and our history offer few precedents for the changes that are necessary in insuring social justice in Canada. New means must be created that will give the Canadian people, young, old, new, poor, and rich, knowledge and experience in using the democratic process to insure that our governments, at all levels, and public and private institutions, are reflections of the desires and aspirations of the people, and, equally important, are accountable to the people they serve. There are many people, young and old, ready and willing to work to this end.

Characteristics of Planners

Planners of programs for the development of human resources appear to fall into three categories.

1. The Traditionalists

This group believes that the complete realization of the potential of a community (whether local, provincial, or national) is the object of planning. Their immediate goal is to meet material needs – food, clothing, and shelter. A well-developed citizen is one who produces and/or acquires more than he can use. A good home, two cars, a summer cottage are distinct marks of success.

The adherents to this approach believe in sound education, a reasonable standard of housing, good health, and motherhood, since all these contribute to productivity, growth, and expansion. Rugged individualism is an unquestioned virtue. There is an assumption that there are unlimited material resources and opportunities available (a hangover from pioneer days). Poverty arises mainly from lack of initiative. The poor and disadvantaged groups are viewed as stagnant ponds or puddles isolated from the mainstream of Canadian life. The task of developers is to dig channels linking these ponds to the mainstream. The pollution of the stream, where it ends, etc., are not seriously questioned.

2. The Humanists

Adherents of this group believe that human growth and development is the main concern of any planning. Each person is viewed as a 'bundle of powers and possibilities'. The goal of society should be to help individuals realize their potential as human beings.

Humanist planners strongly maintain that the various structures and administrative systems must be such that they can respond to the expressed desires and aspirations of individuals and communities. They believe that program creation should begin in local communities, where the consumers of the service provided have a share in its planning; further, that organization at the municipal, provincial, and federal levels should arise out of complete knowledge of local conditions and needs.

Both in making plans and in carrying them out, communication is absolutely essential. Information concerning needs at the local level must go in a steady and systematic way to the policy-makers and providers of resources for development. The planners and providers in turn must communicate in the same way with the beneficiaries of their programs. This two-way flow of information, with its accompanying dialogue, is participatory democracy.

The adherents of the Humanist school of planning would reverse the main thrust of 'Information Canada'. Instead of streamlining the flow of information from Ottawa out, they would establish mechanisms to encourage individuals and community groups to examine their situations, articulate their concerns and aspirations, and channel what comes out of their 'local hearings' to the appropriate agencies at the three levels of government or to local chambers of commerce, voluntary agencies, etc.

This kind of activity – with built-in counterbalances to insure equitable consideration of the concerns and aspirations that will emerge – in due course results in the development of policies, programs, and priorities closer to the wishes of the people for whom the programs are designed.

The humanists tend to be idealistic in their concepts and action. Their critics point out their lack of realism and general failure to understand the dynamics of the existing social, economic, and political systems and the difficulty in effecting change.

3. The Pragmatists

Adherents of this school of planning are less extreme than the traditionalists and the humanists. They tend to sympathize with the humanists, but believe that more progress can be made by pursuing a middle course between them and the traditionalists. They recognize the necessity to act realistically in satisfying material needs, a central concern of the traditionalist. They believe that social change can be attained through a disciplined process that combines the best of the traditional and humanistic approaches.

Adherents of this view recognize the need to challenge vigorously prevailing attitudes, social goals, and existing administrative procedures in order to usher in the new day, but are prepared to exercise patience. They talk 'grass-roots' philosophy, but tend to favour pilot undertakings hither and yon with the hope of piercing the armour of the *status quo* at critical points. The hope is that the people and the governments will gradually get the message, and the needed basic changes will come about.

I would opt for the humanist approach. Human growth and fulfilment must be the goal if improvement of our society is to take place. The goals and values of the traditionalist need to be challenged. Pragmatism has a function in the early stages of development, but the tendency of 'tokenism', which characterizes the pragmatic approach, should be watched.

The political-science faculties of Canadian universities have given little attention to ways in which the democratic system can be developed so that it functions for the benefit of all the people. They do little more than describe political life as it is. Leadership is needed among political scientists to find ways and means whereby Canadians in general can be helped to understand why things are as they are and the power of the ballot-box in the democratic system to change them if they so wish.

Today's electronic mechanisms make it possible for citizens to communicate with each other, sharing views and experiences in order that they can make meaningful decisions affecting their communities, local, provincial, national, and international.

Political leaders, the framers of policies and programs, have the means of ascertaining in very short order the views of citizens on any or all basic problems that concern them, if they choose to use the existing communications system.

Having the communications facilities is no guarantee they will be used for the common good. In the present private-enterprise system, the mass media, with the partial exception of the C.B.C., is an extension of manufacturing. It is the selling-arm of the goods and services the private-enterprise economy produces. Cable systems, the most effective means of mass communications in cities, are entirely privately owned.

Unless there is government intervention to insure that the communications system is used to enable nation-wide dialogue on the problems that confront all Canadians, it will be used to perpetuate the *status quo*.

The C.B.C., as a publicly owned national broadcasting system, should have a clearly defined role in participatory democracy. It should place its facilities at the disposal of those groups at all levels working in community development. Sustained, in-depth dialogue leading to consensus and political action would not only win awareness but would also meet the corporation's problem of Canadian content.

In conclusion, I would like to suggest a few guidelines which I believe would aid the development of participatory democracy in Canada.

1. Since the present government of Canada has as one of its election promises the encouragement of participatory democracy and a just Canadian society, it should give one of its departments a clear mandate to provide leadership in promoting citizen participation across Canada. The Ministry (Without Portfolio) for Citizenship was a positive move in this direction. However, the terms of reference or mandate of this embryo department are rather vague, and it is grossly under-financed. This Minister Without Portfolio responsible for Citizenship should be given the clear challenge of giving leadership in the creation of the necessary mechanism to guarantee that the policies, programs, and priorities of the government are in keeping with the aspirations of Canadians in general. The challenge would be that of giving disadvantaged groups a voice and a fair share in decision-making and action. A significant beginning has been made by the Minister responsible for Citizenship, through funding of the native associations and other minority groups, Information Canada, etc. Such programs as the N.F.B.'s Challenge for Change, the Company of Young Canadians, and Opportunities for Youth, under the aegis of the Secretary of State, are making a significant impact. In my view, the program would be enhanced if a number of additional steps were taken.

(a) The Minister responsible for Citizenship should be given a clearer mandate to co-ordinate the resources devoted to social change of the Secretary of State (Challenge for Change, the C.Y.C., special programs of the C.B.C., the Canada Council, etc.). These programs need to be given a clearer focus.

(b) Information Canada centres should be converted into listening-posts to find out more about the concerns and desires of the people at the community level – the data received to be fed systematically to government departments at all levels, as well as to agencies of the private sector. All information centres should be similarly re-oriented.[3] The accountability of the providers of services to the consumers should be a key consideration.

(c) Citizens' groups should be provided with funds to enable the holding of 'community hearings' on all matters of public concern such as housing, employment, education, human rights, etc. These hearings would be mechanisms for dialogue at the grass-roots level.

(d) Research and technical services should be provided to support the proposed community hearings.

(e) Necessary information should be provided for the people for whom government programs are designed to assess the adequacy and relevancy of the programs by the governments at the three levels and by agencies of the voluntary sector.

The over-all aim of the program would be to create machinery to insure that bureaucrats and political leaders are accountable to the people.

2. All voluntary agencies should be encouraged to reconsider their role in Canadian society. For example is there a need today for such organizations as the Imperial Order of the Daughters of the Empire, the Y.M.C.A. and the Y.W.C.A? It is not suggested that these organizations be curtailed in a free society. They should nevertheless be prepared to rewrite their constitutions to bring their activities in line with the needs of the times. The Empire no longer exists for the I.O.D.E., the Y's are no longer associations of Christian youth. Voluntary agencies should be prepared to make changes as well as agencies of the governments.

3. The new Department of Communications must be given a clear mandate to insure that the necessary electronic and other equipment is available to permit community, provincial and national dialogue on matters of public interest.

4. The terms of reference of the C.B.C. must be revised so that its main function is that of facilitating the current movement for participatory democracy.

Canadians need to deal effectively with the traditional myths that have set the pattern of our thoughts in the past, and to work quickly for changes needed in finding answers to our present problems. Failing this, there is a danger of Canada's disappearing from the scene as a nation, with or without bloodshed.

FOOTNOTES

1. Under the ARDA/DREE programs, farmers with small holdings are entitled to assistance in obtaining larger areas of land to insure the viability of their operation. There is no provision for the squatter who is without property to begin with. His only outlet would be upgrading and retraining to enable him to enter the wage economy, but with the chaotic state of the economy there is no assurance of employment.

2. The medical practitioners have applied the free-enterprise philosophy in their field. Disease and health breakdown have contributed to their material gain, and insurance companies have capitalized on the fears and anxieties that people have of illness and loss of income.

3. The information-centres movement appears to be based on the assumption that lack of information is the major problem. It is suggested that a lack of relevancy of programs to needs is a far greater problem.

E. R. MCEWEN was born on a farm near Dauphin, Manitoba, receiving his elementary education in a one-room country school. He took normal-school training and taught at Brandon, Manitoba, in the early thirties; he received his Bachelor of Arts degree in 1937 from the University of Manitoba and a degree in theology from United College in 1940.

In the early years of World War II he served as the Y.M.C.A. Senior Supervisor for their services to the R.C.A.F. in the United Kingdom. He was later commissioned in the Education Branch of the R.C.A.F. and served in the Middle East, at Cairo, and in England. He retired from the R.C.A.F. with the rank of squadron leader.

On returning to Canada, Mr. McEwen was appointed Assistant Director of the Canadian Youth Commission. Later he joined the staff of the Canadian Welfare Council as head of their Division on Youth Services and Recreation.

In 1963 he was appointed Executive Director of the Indian-Eskimo Association of Canada. He retired from this position in February 1970. Mr. McEwen is currently serving with the federal government in a consulting capacity as a special program adviser on Indian-Eskimo participation. He is also currently President of Jadar Ltd., a newly organized toy- and souvenir-manufacturing industry.

Mr. McEwen served as Secretary of the Canadian Committee for the World Assembly of Youth from 1949 to 1951. He was a Canadian delegate to the World Congress on the Irradication of Illiteracy held at Tehran, Iran, in 1965. He also served as a consultant to the World

Council of Churches at the meeting on racism in London, England, in 1969. He has written a number of articles and pamphlets in the field of community organization and community development.

Section Two

Change and Intervention

In Canada the phenomenon of social change has some unique characteristics. These greatly affect the ways in which individuals and communities interact, the institutions that we construct, and the manner in which community energies are channeled and organized. However, social change and intervention are not without their problems of implementation and practice, not the least of which is the ethics of intervention itself. There are risks involved and answers to critical questions need to be found. Understanding some of the societal and organizational trends will help us meet the challenges as constructively as possible. It is important to be constructively critical of events, so that what is learned from these experiences can be maximized. The multiplicity of our communities and their problems call for interdisciplinary action and understanding.

In his detailed discussion of the problems and strategies of community development in Canada, Francis Bregha deals with the characteristics of Canadian social change. He points out that there is a need for community development to define clearly its area for action and the issues it will tackle. We need to harness community energy and distinguish between community development and service-oriented strategies. Like McEwen in Chapter 4, Bregha points out the need for a new type of planning.

In defining community development, we also say something about how its purposes will be achieved. In sharing his perceptions of some of the trends in social participation in Canada, the late William Baker comments upon the direction toward non-institutional and rehabilitative measures in meeting some of the challenges of today's society. He speaks of the interdisciplinary nature of community development and the increased importance of social-science research, including an emphasis on an interdisciplinary and comparative analysis of community political systems. Such analyses are discussed later in the articles by Norman and Fay McLeod (Chapter 14) and Donald Willmott (Chapter 18).

Bert Deveaux's wide range of field experiences has given him particular feelings about the factors that inhibit community development and citizen participation. He comments on the Manitoba program, the Company of Young Canadians, and the ARDA programs. Other points of view on these programs are expressed elsewhere in this book by Lagassé (Chapter 16), Compton (Chapter 27), and Hendry (Chapter 30). Supporting services are essential to the community worker, a viewpoint also expressed by Whale (Chapter 13). Deveaux emphasizes that to become free is to become responsible. To become responsible is to question, to have ability to take action, to make decisions, to be effective, and above all to have power.

The essential need for communication between the community worker and his sponsoring organization is dealt with in greater detail in Hedley Dimock's article. The failure of attempts at social intervention is often due to the lack of understanding of the underlying philosophy. In talking about the helping relationship, Dimock raises a number of ethical questions. Like other writers in this section and elsewhere in the book, Dimock points out that there are organizational problems in sponsoring community-development programs. Organizations that wish to become involved in social intervention may themselves have to change.

Community Development in Canada: Problems and Strategies

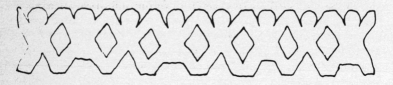

Francis J. Bregha

The upsurge of interest in citizen participation and community involvement in Canada no longer needs to be documented. It is all around us, visible at party conventions, meetings of interest groups, student demonstrations, tangible in the often bitter struggle of the poor or of other disadvantaged minorities. It crystallizes around new problems and issues, such as pollution or drugs, constantly rejuvenating people's thrust for increased self-determination. It is perhaps not surprising that in such a situation an almost inevitable confusion arises about the real meaning both of participation and of involvement. For some, these terms acquire a connotation of 'mass mobilization', leading, they hope, into one or another form of revolutionary utopia; for others, these words are tantamount to 'interest articulation', headed towards the emergence of new and strong pressure groups promoting concerns hitherto ignored; for still others, participation and involvement essentially mean the broadening of existing *élites* so that power and decision-making would be shared in a more equitable way. For this reason, the author of this contribution refuses to discuss generalities that unavoidably dilute the meaning of both terms; rather he will focus on one sharply delineated area: the use of community development in a Welfare State.

> I cannot believe that, when the people have become sovereign, they will choose to leave their Welfare State as that rather shallow, bureaucratic, strongly centralized, institu-

tional machinery, manipulated by crafty organizational entrepreneurs and vested interests, which it is doomed to become if it is not vitalized by citizens' participation to an even
higher degree.

Gunnar Myrdal's profession of faith fixes quite forcefully the
boundaries within which community development in Canada
should be discussed, at this late hour of our industrial society's
drift into the complexities of post-industrialism. The sovereignty of the Canadian people, never fully realized, seems now
even more difficult to achieve, and the future of the Canadian
Welfare State appears even more problematical than in Myrdal's description.

That community development has as yet made no significant
contribution to the tackling of these issues is generally admitted. In fact, many voices are asking whether community development can help at all in solving the more important problems
of Canadian society. This scepticism is both understandable
and justified. After some initial enthusiasm, when fast trans-
plants from the underdeveloped world seemed to take root in
programs *for* the Indians and *for* the rural poor, the inner
logic of the Canadian scene, cultural and political, reasserted
itself. In spite of the pioneering work done under the Agricultural Rehabilitation and Development Act (ARDA) and of several enterprising private groups, such as those in Montreal
and in Halifax, the difficulty of evolving a Canadian model
for community development became obvious. For the impa-
tient young at the universities and in the Company of Young
Canadians, community development acquired the look of a
pretentious methodology for mouthing trivialities about unimportant social problems; for the bureaucrats in governments
and agencies, the endless intellectual discussions of community
development were substituted for action.

One of the more evident reasons for this rapid transition
from unfounded optimism to an equally unfounded pessimism
is the fact that community development in Canada still has to
define its area for action, as well as the issues it should tackle.
Unless community development comes to grips with the problems of our society and its developmental needs, its function
will, of necessity, be taken over by another philosophy and
another approach. Though the basic tenets of community development may seem universal, there is no assurance that our

society in Canada could not develop on lines quite different from those in other countries. The search for its proper field of application in Canada will, therefore, constitute the major focus of this analysis.

In order to proceed to a global perspective, we must briefly identify the major trends in and salient characteristics of contemporary social change in Canada. We will do so through a summing up of the main propositions formulated in recent writings by Gross, Trist, Vickers, Emery, and Chevalier.

Firstly, an irreversible change-process proceeding at an accelerating rate increases social, economic, and political inequalities within and between countries. This constitutes the principal characteristic of a drift from industrial to post-industrial society. In the latter, the energies of most people will no longer be required for the production of goods and services, as modern technology will make them abundant. This is even now leading to the paradox that a growing proportion of the population is subsisting on minimal incomes, often below the poverty line – basically on unearned income provided by welfare – at a time when sufficient productive potential is available to supply the needs of everyone. The problem of equitable distribution of income and assets is therefore beginning to take priority over the problem of production.

Secondly, the transition from industrialism to post-industrialism will be accompanied by increasing social turbulence, created by the complexity and size of the total environment as well as by the impact of communications. While the interdependence of the parts will be more readily recognized, the unpredictability of connections between them will also increase, thus widening the area of uncertainty for individuals and organizations. Society will hence face a growing number of meta-problems, for whose solution a comprehensive attack alone will become the accepted strategy. We already have two such meta-problems in Canada: pollution and the whole area of French-English readjustment under a new constitution. It is probable that other meta-problems are appearing on the scene, though they may not yet be perceived as such by most of us: for instance, the increasing difficulty of creating employment opportunities while fighting inflation.

Thirdly, whereas evidence for the above-described change is already available, what has not yet occurred is a corresponding transformation in our cultural values, organizational philosophies, and ecological strategies. Growing alienation and social disintegration are the inevitable results.

Finally, under these conditions, welfare and development are becoming increasingly interrelated, one impossible without the other.

The validity of this sketch, though argued about in its details, has been generally accepted. Those trends that are perhaps more visible, such as the fast urbanization of Canada, the inability to eradicate poverty in our midst, and the explosion in the 'learning force' which is now more numerous than the 'working force', complement rather than contradict the analysis. Detailed studies of changes taking place between the late 30's and the mid-60's, particularly those done by Trist and Emery, substantiate the over-all picture by singling out factors in the lives of the individual, the family, and the whole society. Within this framework, the transformations they have noticed in ecological strategies are of first importance to our attempt at identifying community development's proper field of application in Canada. According to their categorization, these are the most remarkable changes that have occurred in the last thirty years: strategies moving from 'responsive to crisis' to 'anticipative of crisis', from 'specific measures' to 'comprehensive measures', from 'requiring consent' to 'requiring participation', from 'damping conflict' to 'confronting conflict', from 'detailed central control' to 'generalized central control', from 'small local government units' to 'enlarged local government units', from 'standardized administration' to 'innovative administration', and from 'separate services' to 'co-ordinated services'.

If we accept this broad analysis of contemporary social change in Canada, it becomes immediately obvious that community development here cannot simply be concerned with development-as-increase in resources or productivity (as it primarily is in the emerging nations) but also and foremost with two closely linked problem areas: the allocation of assets within our society (which our War on Poverty has somewhat beclouded), and the allocation of power. Development-as-reallocation will nevertheless remain another empty formula, unless the nature of its process and the possible role of community development within it be clearly perceived.

When C. Wright Mills was describing the seeming collapse of our historic agencies of change, he pointed out: 'One of the most important of the structural transformations involved is the decline of the voluntary association as a genuine instrument of the public.' And in another place he stated: 'The middle levels are often a drifting set of stalemated forces: the middle does not link the bottom with the top. The bottom of this society is politically fragmented, and even as a passive act, increasingly powerless: at the bottom there is emerging a mass society.'

The reasons for this are, of course, inherent in the transition to post-industrialism. Among all the democratic freedoms defined at the beginning of industrialism and used as its political motor, the one of association is possibly most open to the pull of tradition, which is bent on institutionalizing accepted patterns of collective action with the risk of becoming blind to new needs and to new strategies. In fact, the traditional exercise of this freedom has created in our society institutional icebergs that presently are among the greatest obstacles to the harmonious flow of development-oriented transformation. While throughout history social groupings have been among the most important vehicles of change, we seem to be in the peculiar situation of seeing their role downgraded by the technological aspects of our society, or misused by those who intend to control both power and assets regardless of how obsolete or inappropriate their title to them may be.

Simultaneously, our society appears to be undergoing a divisive process of a new character: some groups in it maintain a degree of ability for self-triggered transformation, others are merely changeable. The former category includes the upper and higher-middle classes and various tribes of young activists, while the latter involves a growing number of more or less clearly defined 'problem groups' – the poor, the Indians and the Eskimos, the unemployed, the rural migrants, the aged, the physically or mentally handicapped, etc. The lower-middle class seems to be rapidly drawn into this second category as its inability to secure proper housing, higher education, and better-paying jobs is forcing it out of the so-called mainstream of Canadian life. Thus, while the number of masters of their own fate (relatively speaking) is shrinking, the number of dependents of all sorts is vastly increasing. For the latter, social change based on self-help or mutual aid becomes more and more unrealistic as their powerlessness calls for environmentally triggered transformation, depending, among other things, on the attitude of the people in the first category.

This process is accompanied by the paradoxical phenomenon analysed by Gunnar Myrdal in his *Beyond the Welfare State*: the very success of the Welfare State decreases stimulants to participation in decision-making. In short, dependency becomes more and more total as traditional measures for combatting it are applied by the State. Cloward and Piven arrived at the same conclusion in their 'The Professional Bureaucracies: Benefit Systems as Influence Systems': ' . . . welfare programs debilitate and demoralize; the attitudes and ways of life into which clients are forced inhibit their effective participation in even ordinary social roles and surely inhibit political activism.'

Nor should it be assumed that the different policies of the Welfare State are the only ones that create, enhance, and, finally, institutionalize dependency. The educational system, by attempting to cater to the increasingly sophisticated and complex demands of the job market, introduces another, perhaps more subtle, form of it. So, in fact, does all publicity, advertising and public relations, be it on behalf of industry or governments. These things all contribute to what, in reality, amounts to a case of addiction to artificial consumption, unrelated to real needs of freely chosen priorities. While many of these forms of dependency may appear to be willingly accepted by the public, they promote powerlessness and alienation in the long run.

It has now been widely recognized that the liberation of man – from whatever type of dependence – springs not from an act of his free will alone, but also from a joint act of a community encouraging him. The question then is how to harness community energy in such a way that it may be mobilized and released for man's liberation. In a society that, however unwillingly, promotes the apartheid policy of segregating the 'haves' from the 'have nots' and the powerful from the powerless, this is of crucial concern for community-development strategy.

Among the first steps needed for the implementation of development-as-reallocation of assets and power is the consistent application of community development to the area of social utilities. The latter have been defined by Alfred J. Kahn as ' . . . a social invention, a resource or a facility designed to meet a generally experienced need in social living.' Most prominent examples are the basic educational, health, housing, and welfare services, cultural and recreational opportunities, therapy, and rehabilitation. While the idea of making these services substantial rights instead of charity or privilege is gaining ground, there is as yet no efficient mechanism for making the right to social utilities an enforceable one. Even more importantly, the provisions for effective planning of social utilities, or for bargaining over their quantity and quality, are clearly inadequate. Community development offers a formula for bringing the consumers of social utilities into both the planning and the bargaining processes.

As for the first, the planning process, H. Waisglass pointed the way: 'Planning councils must have a people base in contrast to the money base of the community chests. Planning councils will have to establish a power base. Community development and neighbourhood organizations seem to be the most promising foundation on which to build a viable and purposeful social planning system.' Because so much of social planning is, in growing proportion, performed by different levels of government, the latter should, by the same token, admit representatives of the consumers of social utilities into their own planning bodies. This principle is making some progress in the field of urban renewal; it should, however, be extended over the whole scale of government-provided social utilities.

Nor is the recent willingness of our governments to set up new appeal procedures and to publicize the availability of them enough. At issue is the joint planning administration of services. The fear of certain governments, particularly the municipal ones, that a new 'parallel structure of government' would emerge is understandable, as the present monopoly they possess in decision-making about quantity and quality of certain services is, in fact, threatened. The whole point, however, is that this monopoly should be broken. Once the desirability of citizens' involvement is accepted, effective channels have to be created for it: channels that are legal and institutional and go far beyond the present game of 'participation by invitation only'.

In regard to the bargaining processes, a separation of the action and service functions into discreet citizen organizations would be necessary. Professor Grosser, in his review of community-organization programs in the United States, concludes: 'The experience of the projects illustrates that dispensers of public agency services are congenitally and organizationally unable to distinguish between the protest and service function when practiced by the same organization.' Hence, while citizens would sit on the boards of public and private service agencies as representatives of the consumers, they would also establish independent action groups that would permit more effective bargaining from the outside. This double-pronged strategy would, on the local level, be rooted in the same functionally differentiated community-development process.

While consumer participation in the planning for and decision-making about social utilities is of obvious importance to the attack on dependency, it would be far from sufficient for really eradicating it. The liberation of man requires also his conviction that he can influence as much the conditions that put him in need as the ill effects of these conditions. Society can have the best unemployment schemes and yet remain unable to create jobs for everyone; the best housing policies, yet leave the original structural reason for them untouched; the best hospitals for physical or mental illness, yet no capacity to control the conditions that lead to disease. In short, services and utilities, however excellent, are not enough if men can do nothing about the situation that created the need for them.

This is what distinguishes community-development strategies from more service-oriented strategies. The provision for and the delivery of services is only one and perhaps the least important aspect of community development. Its main thrust and principal *raison d'être* as a method of intervention is to transform the causes and conditions shaping the quality of life in a society so that as few people as possible would depend on any kind of service.

Such an approach would, quite evidently, require a new type of planning: one that would be less crisis-oriented, less grounded in more or less artificially defined sectors or problem areas, but much more directed towards prevention and towards comprehensive programs, than is the present planning. Such planning would also represent an on-going process, with high levels of citizen participation, which would facilitate the fast feedback needed for constant readjustment and up-dating of policies and plans of action. The implications for the education of planners, for the strengthening of planning bodies on all levels, and for an expedient processing of specific plans by the political decision-makers would, of course, need detailed spelling-out so that the basic community-development process would be enhanced by them.

It is in this perspective that the reasons for identifying development-as-reallocation of assets and power as the emerging field for community development in Canada become more apparent. There has been a tendency here to encourage community-development approaches only to situations where development-as-increase had local priority (among Indians, in rural sections, in underprivileged regions) or where service-orientation prevailed as the traditional pattern for coping with social change (among the urban poor). Yet this corrects only slightly the inequalities in our society – most frequently it simply perpetuates them. The evolution that occurred in the ecological strategies, mentioned earlier, forces us to reconsider these initial concepts and to update them so that the real nerve-centres of change can be touched.

In addition to identifying these nerve-centres of change, there is the concomitant problem of how change is to be channelled. Traditionally, governments and private groups in Canada have developed skills for 'reacting to change'; now, it is necessary to plan and to guide change. From the passive reaction towards change that has resulted in a vast patchwork of programs and legislation, we need to move towards an active reaction and master the skill of shaping change according to plans that will tackle causes and effects alike preventively.

This necessity leads us inevitably into the political and social-action arena. Here are the nerve-centres that govern the essential part of social change in Canada. As the complexity of problems-to-be-solved increases, Canadian governments tend to enlarge the scope and the depth of their intervention on all three levels: municipal, provincial, and federal. This happens because of the progressive weakening of voluntary associations and because of the latter's inability to cope with large-scale problems. Gradually, Canadian governments, sometimes forced by public opinion, sometimes of their own will, gravitate towards the establishment of an effective monopoly on developmental activities in Canada. Given the nature of the governing process, local communities or groups are frequently left more 'underdeveloped' in terms of their ability to reach their own decisions after the government's intervention than before it. This is so because the State most often prefers to implement its policies by increased control over individuals and groups, by propagandizing and manipulation of ideological symbols, and by influencing mass behaviour rather than by enhancing the people's own ability through local leadership and community cohesion. Instead of maximizing the conditions favourable to the emergence of strong voluntary associations on the local level, governments tend to impose bureaucratic controls for dealing with citizens on a one-by-one basis within a docile and voiceless mass society. To believe that this process can be 'sweetened' by the governments' apparent willingness to encourage popular participation through advisory bodies, task forces, and all sorts of commissions, avoids the crucial issue: real participation occurs not when it is centrally decreed, but only when citizens recognize it as meaningful and effective on their own terms.

Moreover, participation on governments' terms, that is, as defined and regulated by them for their own objectives, is unlikely to eradicate the basic inequalities in our society simply because the groups invited to 'participate' – the Indians, the poor, etc. – resist integration into the mainstream as long as this integration aims at preserving the same power mechanisms that segregated these groups in subordinate positions in the first place.

For this reason, strong and consistent social-action thrust, correcting the excesses of bureaucracies, limiting the power of politicians, and softening the rigidity of administrative systems, is the most dynamic basis for community-development programs in Canada. Precisely because governments can so easily destroy effective and meaningful involvement of the people by defining the terms of participation solely in the light of their own objectives, it is essential that autonomous centres of power be created within, around, and sometimes against the institutionalized clusters of political and developmental processes. Only in this way can the latter be modified, humanized, and brought closer to popular needs and hopes. The naive belief that popular will spontaneously 'percolates' upwards to the upper levels of government is dying fast as the increased complexities and accelerating rate of change illustrate more and more frequently the need for sharp reactions by organized citizen-groups on a vast variety of issues affecting their lives. There is little doubt that this need will be greater as post-industrialism takes hold on Canada. There is little doubt, too, that the philosophy of democratic government will have to undergo a thorough scrutiny, with the mechanisms of 'representative democracy' (political parties, nomination and election procedures) having to strive for both greater representativity and greater responsiveness.

Many of our values assume community-wide participation,

political democracy for example, but the changing social reality requires their constant activation and reinterpretation. Economic or administrative considerations of expediency keep imposing new controlling layers on our society, which then has to rediscover its freedom. In this continuing interplay, community development encourages new types of co-operative associations, suggested by new goals or new pressures, becoming thus an on-going process through which citizens strive to revitalize their basic human rights.

After this excursion into the political and social-action arena, it should now be possible to circumscribe that vast and changing area in which community development – both as a philosophy requiring participation and as a technique enhancing development – can best contribute to the guidance of social change in Canada. Geographically, the country will become even more predominantly urban instead of rural as it was in its first years. Moving from the development-as-increase focus of its infancy, it will increasingly tackle the issues of power and assets, thus reflecting the fact that in a post-industrial society problems of just distribution have priority over problems of production. In so doing, community development will come very close to political processes, in fact meshing with them often so thoroughly that its contribution will appear mainly political. Its programs, related to government-citizen interaction, will be oriented towards making the people's involvement effective and meaningful; for this reason, the form taken will most often be the one of active. occasionally aggressive, social action. Through keeping governments on their toes, community development will tend to promote a pluralist approach to planned development; by revitalizing democracy and by humanizing public administration, it will help in redefining the role of a modern state in the post-industrial era. From its present preoccupation with special groups, it will gradually shift its emphasis to problems defined geographically, cities and regions becoming its main units of analysis. The concern for groups defined in a different way will, however, not disappear; wherever disparities or inequalities threaten the goal of over-all development, special projects and programs will intervene to correct the situation. As social utilities, including a guaranteed annual income, become universal, community development will gradually dissociate itself from the service function, though maintaining a bargaining position over the quantity and quality of services, and will address itself to those causes that created social dysfunction in the first place. As it does so, it will increasingly become part of a total situational-planning approach, by and large preventive and comprehensive. In the measure that it succeeds, the drift in Canada towards post-industrialism will give way to planned social change.

FRANCIS BREGHA, professor at the School of Social Work, University of Toronto, was born in Prague, Czechoslovakia, where he studied law and economics immediately after World War II. He completed his studies in economics at Laval University, Quebec, after his arrival in Canada in 1949.

He has been economic adviser to the Prime Minister of the Province of Quebec, lecturer at Laval University, and a frequent participant in C.B.C. public-affairs programs.

After four years in England, France, and Germany, where he was editor of a European economic journal, he went to South America as regional director for an international program in economic development. There he 'discovered' community development and started to apply this approach to developmental problems of the Pacific Coast countries.

Since his return to Canada in 1967, he has been teaching at the University of Toronto and acting as a consultant in community development to the federal government, as well as several provincial and municipal governments. In addition he has continued his interest in Latin America, where he now spends several months a year on missions for international development organizations, including the Canadian International Development Agency. He is Chairman of the Canadian Committee of the International Council on Social Welfare, Canadian representative in several international associations, and an active participant in local community-development in Toronto.

Community Development in Changing Rural Society [1]

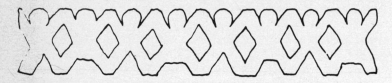

William B. Baker

Belief in the efficacy of community action as a response to life conditions has been a distinguishing characteristic of North American society. This is particularly true of rural areas with their more pervasive experience with government extension and economic services. In today's multiple communities, rural-urban dichotomies are still real in detail but blurred in the larger affairs of modernization. Social differentiation and integration have further transformed the community context of the genetic belief. Certainly, the historical vehicles of the belief require redefinition. Community development is one redefining response of the enlargement of social-contact space and the elaboration of communication systems.

Community development is not a new concept. Its historical antecedents extend back to the beginnings of rural life on this continent. Sanders (1958), Bruyn (1963), Warren (1963), and others have traced both rural and urban land lineages. Community development is achieving scientific and clinical relevance in contemporary society as a more sophisticated ideological object and as an instrument for administered social change. It reflects an enormous increase in the number of decisions which impinge upon individuals and families under conditions of rapid social change. As Janowitz (1961) has defined it in *Community Political Systems*, the community must be understood as a social reality, a political context, and an ideological symbol, if contemporary political behaviour is to be analysed. A summary statement on community development will therefore reflect the tension between a full grasp and interpretation of historical fact and the identification of the emergent abstract and general relationships.

Definitions of community development reflect the fluid and pregnant nature of current trends. No attempt is made in this paper to review and compromise its varied connotations. It is sufficient to observe that, when deep-rooted beliefs become incorporated in explicit processes of administered change, some codification is necessary. In one sense, latent aspects of the relatively closed system of the pioneer community must be rediscovered and made manifest. Community-development ideology thus represents a more or less explicit and consistent set of ideas about how its purposes are to be achieved. Four commonly accepted ideas will clarify the concept as it will be used in this paper. Written in the form of value judgments, these are: (a) members of a community should share in decision-making about matters affecting community affairs; (b) individuals and local groups should be presented with current environmental realities; (c) new complexes of community norms should be facilitated by a general diminution of bureaucratic and centrally determined prerogatives; (d) special emphasis should be placed on the reintegrative effects of creating relatively tight-knit, intercommunicative, and personal role-sets.

These ideological components provide the frame of reference for episodic but sequential community social action focussed on 'felt needs' or designated problem situations. A common unifying assumption is that such action is primarily a learning process, and the specific tasks are of secondary significance. Theoretically, as a community experiences sequential social action, a learning gradient is established that facilitates community identity, renewed confidence, and rising skill levels in resolving ever more complex social and economic issues.

When one moves from the ideological framework for community development and attempts to assess its relevance to the larger structural context of North American society, the evidence of ambiguity is impressive. It is difficult to avoid the impression that its more outspoken proponents assume the community to be an independent entity requiring only marginal reference to outside resources of expertise and finance. While this may be an exaggeration, it underlines the dangers of an unrealistic emphasis on processes isolated from prevailing imbalances, trends, and needs of exogenous institutions. These now provide the major community inputs. Unless community development can be related to the changing character of these inputs, only marginal responses can be anticipated in terms of reintegration. The above-mentioned assumption also neglects a prevailing trend that downgrades space and location as major social and economic variables. Unless it is assumed that community development will achieve a spread effect through the generation of a social movement, it must operate as an integral part of the warp and woof of the existing social fabric. Only tentative and highly speculative statements can be made about how this might be accomplished.

The expanding role of government, as reflected in the welfare state of the Western democracies, is a major contributor to vertical differentiation and integration. This, combined with a strong humanistic view, has provided a powerful instrument for turning the course of culture in the direction of man's vital needs. Selznick's *T.V.A. and the Grass Roots* (1949) provides a highly relevant, contemporary commentary on the organizational implications. In many respects Selznick provides a model for predicting consequences with a direct bearing on future conceptions of community development.

In its initial stages, welfare statism pursued objectives designed to ameliorate the more obvious symptoms of social and economic imbalance. This was done primarily through categorical and institutional extensions: schools, hospitals, old-folks' homes, subsidized housing, marketing and credit agencies, and so on. While this remains the dominant policy, due in part to continued population growth and mobility, it is clearly not working for a growing incidence of disadvantaged groups in a modernizing society. More attention is now directed towards non-institutional and rehabilitative measures. In part, this also represents a shift from moralist to causal interpretations of deviant behaviour. The trend is illustrated by criticism of the euphemistic 'golden-years old-folks' home'. In some quarters, this has become a caricatural 'pre-cemetery cold-storage vault' symbolizing isolation of the elderly from the normal relationships of the community. Recent social innovations receiving serious attention are foster homes, day-care centres, meals-on-wheels, and so on. Thus the institution is moving towards the community as a result of more imaginative diagnostic practice.

A shift in public policy from quantitative to qualitative approaches to disequilibrium touches on a widening range of community-based situations: long-term physical and mental illness, premature retirements, chronic low income, school dropouts, functional illiteracy, prejudice, housing renewal, delinquency, and so on. Improved diagnostic and prognostic insights and techniques are tending to view the community as a therapeutic milieu in both the treatment and prevention of these disabilities.

A clinical orientation to the community milieu is also facilitated by the increased professional component in the civil service. This is becoming dominant both at the top policy level and in those 'helping professions' mediating between community and government administrative systems. Wide discrepancies exist between the specialized technical skills of the helping professions and the knowledge and skills required as community 'change agents'. Only a small proportion has been exposed to any systematic training in the behavioural sciences, but this does not detract from the fact of much imaginative and experimental non-institutional programming. Clinical questions about community phenomena are certain to become more sophisticated and penetrating.

It cannot be assumed that these orientations have emerged as the result of conscious planning. As Selznick (1949), Myrdal (1960), and others have implied, the response is tangential to the rationally ordered functions and goals of formal bureaucracies. No doubt theoretical developments and research in such crucial areas as the diffusion process have pointed out fundamental differences between the formal structure of bureaucracies and the diffuse structure of community social systems. A more cogent reason may be that administered change requires some correlation of dynamic factors impinging on what might be called the target sectors of the community system: adapted (modern), adapting (transitional), and unadaptive (traditional-anomic). Disadvantaged target groups are frequently located in the unadaptive or retarded-adapting sectors. Resolution of their difficulties often requires mobilization of the total community environment (industrial development). Two major public programs illustrate this: the Agricultural Rehabilitation and Development Administration (ARDA) in Canada and the Rural Areas Development Administration (RADA) in the United States.

An even more appropriate demonstration of tangency is found in the new professional-administrative and professional-non-professional role-sets that even partial community mobilization requires. The influential agricultural extension systems in North America started out with an orientation towards improvements in physical production by working through individual farmers. Later, this devolved into broader programs of farm and home management working through group processes. Still later, the devolution was towards broad public-policy discussions. Today, rural development is becoming the major instrumentality for progress through the co-operative – extension systems. In general, the time-order of community-sector involvement associated with these trends has been: adaptive (progressive farmers),⟶adapting (transitional farmers,⟶unadaptive (chronic low-income farmers),⟶total sector involvement (community systems).

An interesting contrast is presented by the experience of organized social welfare. Here, the early emphasis was on individual case work. Later, this devolved into group work and family counselling. Still later, the emphasis shifted to a concern with broad social policy and, today, it is focussing on community development. Thus, the time-order of sector involvement has been as follows: unadaptive (indigents),⟶adapting (upwardly mobile),⟶adapted (family breakdown),⟶total sector (community system). Other helping professions may be located along this continuum. Of course, this has not been a linear devolvement, but the outlines appear to have general validity. One result is that the helping professions are sitting on each other's lap. The consequent social system and professional role linkages may be the critical factor in the formulation of public policies supporting total community development as a politically legitimate function. As a result, agricultural-extension systems, long the primary legitimate agency of rural-administered change, are passing through profound problems of institutional adaptation.

These trends are under way when the definition of what constitutes a viable community system remains inadequate. Multiple community boundaries are incomplete, transitory, and unrelated to local government jurisdictions. The underlying process requires much more systematic study. Individual 'market' decisions of farmers (larger land-holdings, shifting trade-centre patronage, etc.) continue to have aggregate effects largely unanticipated at the point of original decision. Thus dispersion and social disorganization persist. The latter requires collective and externally administered decisions to adapt. The centripetal tendencies of metropolitan communities (central city to suburban satellites) can be contrasted with the centrifugal tendencies (satellites to central farmer cities) in rural areas. Modern service technologies in production, consumption, and distribution appear to find a new point of equilibrium well above the capacity of thousands of smaller rural trade centres. When caught up in the often pathological throes of survival, these centres detract from the potential realization of larger community systems adapted to current development requirements.

We need to know more about the consequences of presenting environmental realities to citizens through community-development processes. Vidich and Bensman (1958) and others have documented 'the social psychological consequences of rural surrender' resulting from autonomously induced change. It is assumed that reality presentation will enhance the processes of group representation and the formulation of community consensus. Community-development approaches have demonstrated that it is not difficult to create short-run 'emotional hothouses', but there is no good evidence of sustained learning gradients. The displacement of integrating or maintenance orientations (a primary concern in community development) by task orientations will likely accentuate as external agencies promote programs in the name of community development. Administered change will test the fragility of spontaneous involvement of citizens, and surrogate reward patterns will likely evolve. But the goal-displacement tendencies of external change agents may create dysfunctional reward patterns through such devices as precommitted grants-in-aid, payment for part-time leadership, delegation without adequate role retraining, and intrusion on private living through an unwitting emphasis on continuous programming. Leadership tends to pyramid in all communities and places inordinate demands on a dedicated minority.

Community voluntary organizations are usually involved through community councils, development associations, or some equivalent horizontal co-optative mechanism. Improved operational definitions are needed on how these mechanisms are related to community power-structures, shifts in leadership complexes, the allocation of responsibility between council and constituent units, and the management of community consensus. Community-wide decision-making is complicated by vertical differentiation of voluntary associations and the continuing intrusion of exotic organizations in the absence of any common control over access. Experimental activity with publicly unrecognized disadvantaged categories (handicapped children) has been a traditional function of voluntary groups. Substitute activities are needed as formal agencies assume this function in the form of sophisticated and expensive research. The dilemma of community chests and welfare councils has been well documented in this respect. Where governments have sought to relate voluntary associations to bureaucratic structures, as in The Netherlands, these associations tend to become formal, professionally dominated, and inflexible to the point of retarding rather than facilitating growth. This does not imply that retardation is always an inappropriate reaction to rapid change.

Local government is usually involved through national, provincial (state), and municipal covenants as the local official intermediary in channelling financial and technical assistance from higher levels of government. In general, local government units have been slow to respond to approaches requiring anything more than passive citizen participation. (Rossi and Dentler document this in *The Politics of Urban Renewal, 1961*.) This is even more characteristic of small urban and rural municipal units. The prevalence of the 'low-tax ideology' studied by Vidich is partly explained by shrinking and unstable sources of local tax revenues. Confused jurisdictions have resulted from the proliferation of local administrative districts. Frequent use is made of the co-optative mechanism through formally appointed committees unrelated to the community political system. With the exception of such Canadian provinces as Alberta and Saskatchewan, there has been a long history of failure in local-government reorganization. One can safely generalize that local government, whether traditional or reorganized, cannot be considered an appropriate substitute for the more diffuse processes of citizen involvement in community development, but it is an indispensable ally.

Some of the most difficult aspects of community development emerge in attempts to articulate the vertical and horizontal components. As one moves up the network of control, communication, and decision-making, there are nodes of concentrated activity: community, district, state, region, nation. In Canada and the United States there are no known programs equivalent to the fully integrated type of community development found in some of the centrally planned countries. On this continent, the adaptive and/or the project-type approaches are most common. These approaches require little change in prevailing administrative arrangements; they permit a geographical flexibility appropriate to widely dispersed problem areas, and they encourage diversity and experimentation in field operations.

A final word is necessary on the expanding role of the social sciences. Governments are recognizing that development of any kind without a firm research foundation is likely to become self-defeating. Both ARDA and RADA make fairly generous provision for research funds. There are many unresolved questions as to how such funds should be allocated and administered. Questions of economic viability have high priority in any development program. Economists thus occupy a favoured position, but they are now more vocal about the need for study by other social disciplines. Community development requires emphasis on interdisciplinary and comparative analysis of community political systems. Very few such studies have been attempted. An immediate need could be met by a synthesis of the partial analysis already done by the various disciplines.

It was Kolb (1959) who observed that the fundamental community is a composite of many expanding and contracting feature communities possessing the characteristic pulsating instability of all real life. Most citizens still meet and try to cope with life situations in the fundamental community. Community development represents a convergence of historical tendencies that assumes this basic fact. This paper has reviewed some of the trends in North American society which may facilitate, inhibit, or invalidate the purposes and the ideology of community development. The tentative conclusion is that the growing edges of society – whether rural or urban – may rediscover the functional significance of the fundamental community and that its development may become an integral part of broad programs of social and economic development. Unless studied in this perspective, community development may be little more than a series of platitudes to delude the unwary.

FOOTNOTE

1. Paper prepared for joint program of the American Sociological Association and the Rural Sociological Society (Montreal: August 1964).

WILLIAM BAKER was born in Verigin, Saskatchewan, in 1919. In 1944 he received his B.S.A. with distinction from the University of Saskatchewan. He did postgraduate studies in rural sociology at the University of Minnesota (1945-6), the University of Kentucky (1948-9), and the University of Michigan (1951-2). In 1964, North Dakota State University conferred upon him a Doctor of Laws (*honoris causa*).

Some of the positions held by Dr. Baker include the following: Director, School of Agriculture, University of Saskatchewan, 1946-56; Chairman, Saskatchewan Royal Commission on Agriculture and Rural Life, 1952-6; Consultant on Adult Education to the University of New England, New South Wales, Australia; study-team member of community-development programs in India under Carnegie Foundation invitation, 1956; member of the North American team, Conference on Adult Education in the African Universities, University of Ghana, 1963; Canadian delegate, International Conference on Plan Implementation, Caracas, Venezuela, 1966; and member, Panel of Experts on Organization and Administration of Agricultural Development, Food and Agricultural Organization, United Nations, Rome, 1967.

One of the last documents written by Dr. Baker was a *Progress Report on a Three-Part Research Program* on the relation of welfare and development in Canada's post-industrial society, dated October 1968. He was directing this important project from the University of Toronto, where he had been appointed Cassidy Research Visiting Professor on July 1, 1968. He was attached to the School of Social Work at the time of his sudden death in November 1968.

The Enemies within Community Development

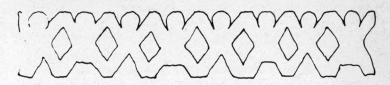

Bert Deveaux, with Kaye Deveaux

Objectivity is the way one comes to terms and makes peace with a world one does not like but will not oppose; commonly, these 'objective' men, even if politically homeless, are middle class and operate within the boundaries of the social status quo. In some part they tolerate it because they fear conflict and want peace and security, and know they would be allowed considerably less of both if they did not tolerate it.

Alvin W. Gouldner

My own personal experience in the field of community development has led me to two positive conclusions. First, community development is simply a method; it is not a program or an end in itself. As a method it seeks to encourage, pursue, and execute the democratic process. Second, because this method examines and questions the roots of events, often challenging the 'square' roots of society, it is essentially a radical method that is not popular for long with governments.

To have democracy as an aim, however, implies that such a state does not already exist, and to admit this is to admit a contradiction personally and universally. Fully realizing this contradiction for the first time, the individual may do one of two things: he may hide, vacillate, conduct 'studies' to determine poverty levels, and so on, until he finally loses sight of the contradiction; or he may take up the cause of the oppressed, admit the contradiction, and commit himself to action. There is no room in this business for arm-chair radicals.

The Chess Game (as Played by the Radical v. the Government)

Personal risks are high for the radical organizer, regardless of where he or she finds himself or herself. The individual may be a high-school student working for more participation in school affairs, a woman reacting to female oppression and job discrimination, a community developer on a remote Indian reserve, a tenant worker in Toronto, or anyone, anywhere, who sees injustice and follows the imperative for action. In Canada some of these individuals have chosen to be employed by government 'community-development programs'. I would like to begin by examining some of these.

The earliest one in Canada was in Manitoba and began in response to the study entitled 'The People of Indian Ancestry in Manitoba', conducted by Jean Lagassé between 1956 and 1959. The community-development program was launched in 1960 and achieved a number of successes before racing to its decline by mid 1968. To date, it has been the longest-lasting program in Canada, and this is owing to three reasons:

1. Because most of the people it served were Indians, the Province was not directly involved; and because Ottawa is geographically removed from Manitoba, the buck could always be passed to the Indian Affairs Branch and the federal government;
2. The program was under the imaginative direction of Freeman Compton, a man of strong conviction regarding the grass-roots approach plus the talent for keeping the administrative wolves at bay; and
3. The sincerity of Deputy Minister K. O. MacKenzie, who did an excellent job rationalizing the program to government.

But by 1968, as the program began to involve the Métis, who were a provincial responsibility, and as the philosophy of community development began to spread and become a source of embarrassment to more departments, the government began to check the progress of community development and the chess game began in earnest.

Their first strong move was to eliminate the autonomy of the community-development branch in the Department of Welfare, making every community-development worker responsible to regional directors of welfare instead of their community-development director. (The king is castled and the pawns lose ground.)

These regional directors, needless to say, did not necessarily hold to community-development theory, but still had authority to hire and fire community-development workers.

To legitimize this action of removing power from the director and putting it into the hands of regional welfare directors, the government gave the reason that community development was a good method and its technique should be put to use in government. (Repressive tolerance and the old co-optation deal.) Then the purge began.

The director and his community-development consultants were pushed into a small group known as 'The Consulting Group' with no authority to hire or fire, or even to visit community-development workers without clearing first with the regional welfare director. The field-workers, consequently, lacked any consistent support from anyone well-grounded in community-development techniques.

Ironically enough, the majority of the community-development workers and consultants, realizing they had been co-opted, did nothing, and unlike true radicals fell in step to the tune the government piped. It was the first time the community-development program had been so challenged, and if ever an opportunity had arisen to test their ideals – this was it! They failed to meet the challenge and became 'objective men'. Thus did the government of Manitoba separate the Machiavellis from the Mavericks.

The new 'Consulting Group', still in its infancy, died a more honourable, but still as final, death. Originally, Compton bought the structural reorganization because he had been assured of real involvement with other branches in the Department. Naturally, this promise was not fulfilled, for to put democratic principles such as the sharing of information into government would inevitably lessen the power of the Minister and his deputies.

Compton's difficulty was that he really believed in those democratic principles such as the sharing of information into ernment had planned its strategy well. In August 1970, and without any prior knowledge, Compton received a letter indicating that his Consulting Group was disbanded and that he was to be transferred to the unrelated field of 'Publications'. The government could declare 'checkmate'.

In the true Machiavellian fashion, then, the Manitoba government rescinded its community-development mandate. Similar programs in Ontario and Alberta suffered the same final outcome: Alberta's program lasted four years while Ontario's effort, for political reasons, again, was cut after just two years. While I can understand the political realities of our so-called 'just society', I have yet to overcome those gut reactions I get whenever I witness community developers turning into 'objective men' at their first confrontation with government. In short, the quest for a democratic state is okay so long as one's job is not at stake. And this is the stuff of which most community developers in Canada are made.

The Company of Young Canadians

Probably the best-known example of community development operating within government was the C.Y.C. experiment. At any rate, it certainly became the most notorious. Volumes of truths, half-truths, and outright lies have been written about it. My own personal reflection after two years' involvement is that, if it came in like a lion, at least it went out like a lion. But it stands tall in Canadian community-development history because of its real radicals. Probably because of its youth participation, it rocked more boats, hit greater heights and depths, risked more encounters with the Establishment, dared more things, and roused more anger, animosity, and law-suits on the Canadian scene than any other program before or since. For five years it survived four Directors, daily newspaper attacks, a parliamentary inquiry, Council meetings that resembled a Mad Hatter's tea party, and a great turn-over of vocal and misguided volunteers before the government figured out its checkmate. In 1969, the radical Director was replaced by an uncommunicative school teacher, the vacillating first Council by young Machiavellis, and the Mavericks fell by the wayside frustrated and out-manoeuvred by a government-appointed Comptroller. If it served any real purpose, it certainly was a testing ground for those who believed in democracy. Inexperienced volunteers were introduced to the way it really is: the poverty scene, bureaucratic pass-the-buck techniques, landlord oppression, middle-class repulsion over the volunteers' non-conformist appearance, the deaf ears of government, and finally the reality of just in whose hands the power of the people lies.

I joined the C.Y.C. in February of 1968 to head a community-development project in the industrial part of Cape Breton. Because Alan Clarke was Executive Director at the time, my terms of reference as Project Director in Cape Breton were quite clear.

Initially, I was to assess the climate for C.Y.C. entry into the area; we did not want to dump uninvited volunteers there. This required very close and frequent consultation with miners, fishermen, tenants, citizen groups, and local councils. After five months, and in response to requests by communities, the decision was made to start a project. My responsibilities then became centred mainly on the selection and training of volunteer workers.

Because the volunteers responded directly to those problems considered important to the miners, fishermen, and tenants, our project soon developed a strong community base. The volunteers were not typical government experts giving solutions but, instead, were working democratically with these people on problems already selected by the community.

Our undoing was that we expected the same democratic relationship between ourselves and the Executive Director of the C.Y.C. in Ottawa that we practised with the Cape Bretoners. While Alan Clarke and Stewart Goodings were Executive Directors, the necessity for volunteer participation in C.Y.C. affairs was both permitted and encouraged. With the arrival of Claude Vidal, all hell broke loose – for here was a man who did not like to be questioned; here was a man who insisted on being 'in charge'. The volunteers on the Cape Breton Project, on the other hand, were equally insistent that they have a voice in Company affairs and refused to be silenced by Vidal and his deputies. The struggle was on and Ottawa was chosen as the battleground.

In November of 1969 when the C.Y.C.'s permanent governing Council met – the Council that has since been rendered powerless by the federal government – it voted to freeze the Cape Breton project, pending an official 'evaluation' by a federally appointed Council member, Dr. Michael Kirby of Halifax.

Kirby was a business-administration professor at Dalhousie University and a prominent Nova Scotia Liberal, but he was neither radical nor a community-development expert. Nevertheless, he wrote a glowing report of the project's 'substantial community base' and 'favourable reaction' from local people.

He mentioned the local Cape Bretoners working as volunteers and pointed out 'Many of the community leaders I talked to believe that the reason the C.Y.C. is likely to achieve success with its Cape Breton project is because the volunteers themselves are very concerned with the communities in which they live.' He urged that the project be 'unfrozen' and expanded.

Instead of accepting this recommendation, which the Council had asked Kirby to do, Claude Vidal decided to ignore it and play the chess game alone. I had challenged his methods of dealing with volunteers many times. He understood nothing of grass-roots work with the poor and denied the basic premise of community development – that a program evolves from the people themselves and that you do not design a program first and manipulate the people to accept it later. Vidal had the power, decided to wield it with a vengeance. In so doing he counted on the internal confusion of the new Permanent Council.

Just before Christmas, two Cape Breton volunteers of 'trainee' status were informed by mail that since they hadn't applied for full volunteer status (which they hadn't done because the project was supposedly frozen), their contracts were expiring and they would be dismissed. A third volunteer who *had* applied for volunteer status was informed that, since he had done so while the project was still frozen, he would be dismissed too. You have to hand it to Claude Vidal – I have never witnessed such a corruption of the rules of the game and seen the player get away with it so easily. By this action he disqualified himself even to play the government game. The government, however, having realized the implications of the C.Y.C. as an instrument for real social change, was determined now to checkmate the program.

We protested the manoeuvre, but we were ignored. At the same time, the government was busy setting up a bureaucracy, so that in March they announced that the C.Y.C. would be governed by an *appointed* council of nine members (instead of the Council with a majority of volunteer-elected members that had been provided for in the C.Y.C. Act). The Council and its chairman would be government-picked, and if it did not meet with government expectations, the government could disband it. The battle had lasted through five years of moves and countermoves, but in March of 1970, the government could sit back and smugly declare to its opponents: 'Checkmate.'

The Cape Breton project disbanded itself in January, two months before the government decree.

Canada's War on Poverty – a More Common Example

So far, we've looked at programs that were aimed directly at initiating democratic action. A more familiar kind of government program is the ARDA (Agricultural Rehabilitation and Development Administration) type that seeks to offer 'holistic' or package-deal solutions to economically depressed areas. Since 1963, several of these ARDA programs have been set up. If you look at ARDA operations in the Manitoba Interlake Region, Newfoundland, Prince Edward Island, Quebec, or Nova Scotia, you will find they all have a common approach: a common 'research' approach. This common 'research' approach was designed by government to yield those problems that government itself could relate to. It was not designed to help local communities articulate their own personal or local problems.

ARDA and Paper Proposals for Participation

The ARDA Act of 1961 made no provision for any participation; the idea of participation is one that developed over a period of time.

The first mention of it was in the ARDA General Agreement (1962-5) signed with all the provinces. This Agreement mentioned 'local' advisory committees as part of the structure needed to implement the programs. When FRED (Fund for Rural Economic Development) was sanctioned in July of 1966, furthermore, it was *stipulated* that 'participation by the residents of the area in carrying out the program be *provided for* in a comprehensive plan'. This legislation led to the signing of the first agreement between Canada and New Brunswick to implement a comprehensive plan for the development of the area designated as north-east New Brunswick. Section 6 of this Agreement is quite clear:

> Canada shall not participate in, nor contribute to, the program hereunder unless there exists the effective involvement

and participation of residents and local people of the area through the establishment of local advisory committees as provided for by the Act.

Now that local participation was official policy, it had to be defined, and the United Nations' definition of community development was used:

The term 'community development' refers to the process by which the efforts of the people themselves are united with those of governmental authorities to improve the economic, social and cultural conditions of communities. . . .

Corruption of the Mandate by the Bureaucrats

Realizing that Section 6 of the General Agreement was an accomplished fact, the senior ARDA Planner for North-eastern New Brunswick at the time (1966) said:

The local population might be effectively involved to participate in such a way which will *smooth the operation, speed up the implementation*, and improve the effectiveness of the program rather than *hamper or delay the whole operation.* (Italics added.)

The program implementers who arrived on the scene were technicians. They had come to design a plan and then to implement it. This strategy might be acceptable, if the plan did not affect the local population so deeply, but in the case of north-eastern New Brunswick, the ARDA bureaucrats came up with a relocation program.

Thinking that the involvement of people might somehow facilitate things, the provincial ARDA officials wrote a report, at the time, enumerating the benefits of local involvement. Among the many points listed were the following (italics added):

1. Much of the success of the Northeast development program depends on an effective mobility program in which people *will move voluntarily as compared to forced mobility following land expropriation.* Local people *must be involved in developing situations and attitudes that will facilitate this*

program. [Again, we're back to the old story of making the people fit the plan. One cannot help but get the feeling, also, that this 'plan' is seen by the professional implementers as being the 'answer' to most things.]

2. It is important that the whole population of the area *accepts and participates* in the rural development program. [Why is it not equally important for the rural-development program to fit the needs of the people?]

3. Many experienced and highly trained people are involved with local committees and can contribute their training to the overall development program. For example, local physicians, engineers, educators, lawyers, clergy, etc. . . , can contribute much through local committees toward supplementing or complementing *the work of the recognized professional program implementers.*

4. Irresponsible protests and action by dissatisfied persons and groups will be minimal if there are effective local committees which have ready access to the program implementers.

The ARDA approach, then, was to implement a plan which – to ARDA's way of thinking – would be good for the people.

Local Reaction to ARDA Plans

The initial reaction of the local people to the ARDA sales pitch was one of naive hopefulness. Communities in northern New Brunswick had long been neglected by government, and the people now misconstrued the ARDA effort to read that government authorities were finally taking notice.

In Madawaska County, the first step of the ARDA technicians was to have the communities conduct studies. Somehow, it was felt that these would keep people involved and co-operative. But even to the unsophisticated farmer who was prepared to give government a chance, it soon became clear that the survey forms were predesigned to yield those problems already foreseen by the government technocrats and not those local ones felt deeply by the community people. And yet the studies were completed; enough, in fact, to paper the Great Wall of China. After presenting these completed studies to the ARDA implementers, the people sat back and waited for results. They had little choice but to sit back and wait, because the ARDA implementers had not encouraged the people to be responsible for decision-making, for planning or proposing, or for being the body that in point of fact would be the *final pusher*. Instead, the ARDA implementers, both federal and provincial, had directly created this role for themselves – a role they could not possibly fulfil by virtue of their being federal and provincial employees and, hence, politically powerless.

When I arrived in Madawaska County last fall, the local people began a review of the ARDA effort. They tried to determine why six years of conducting studies had not produced results. Their conclusion was simple: instead of organizing, they had spent six years conducting studies. As a result of this simple conclusion, the Regional Development Council has changed its objectives; they have just recently endorsed a community-development mandate and have workers out in small communities totally involved in grass-roots activity.

Communities two hundred miles away in north-eastern New Brunswick were less fortunate, for the ARDA implementers in that area were preoccupied with the notion of a relocation program that just had to be pushed through. At the beginning of the ARDA program, they had organized a Regional Development Council in the area (comprised mostly of Establishment people from the larger French communities) to take care of Section 6 of their General Agreement. This government-financed Council was to support the ARDA projects until 1968, at which time it occurred to a few non-Establishment people that they too had a right to sit on the Council. At the same time, it was decided by someone to encourage the people of the area to participate in the setting of priorities. The Council *animateurs* then entered communities and began their grass-roots activity – the effects of which were almost immediate. Being seriously consulted for the first time, the people were anxious to voice their disapproval not only of the ARDA programs, but of members of the French Establishment who appeared to be the only real recipients of this federal-provincial anti-poverty program. The confrontation between these two groups was inevitable. Members of the Establishment – who were also strong supporters of Louis Robichaud, then Liberal Premier of New Brunswick – were not about to give up their positions easily.

By spring of 1970, however, results of the grass-roots activity were quite evident. Delegates at the annual meeting of the Regional Development Council turned out to be angry representatives from local communities, and ten directors of the Council were quickly dismissed.

No longer dominated by the Establishment, the Council now became the official voice of the people. Again, the Machiavellis and Mavericks were quick to separate. With a provincial election due in the fall, the Liberal organizers and members of the Establishment (also Liberal) were quick to see the new 'people council' as the enemy, and the smear campaign was on.

In July of 1970, Robichaud announced he was withholding government funds from the Council, pending an investigation into its affairs. The three-man ministerial committee appointed by the Premier soon reported their findings: the Council was to keep in closer contact with the traditional organizations. Later, Robichaud advised the Council that the organization would soon be replaced by a new organization representing traditional leadership.

Robichaud lost his election in the fall, and the new Progressive Conservative government is still trying to define new policy covering organizations like that of the north-east. At present, the Council is receiving its funds on a month-to-month basis.

The ARDA implementers are still in the area, but will have little to do with this new organization, which now truly represents the people.

Tackling the Problem of Poverty

We cannot accept any optimistic conception of existence, any happy ending whatsoever. But if we believe that optimism is silly, we also know that pessimism about the action of man among his fellows is cowardly.

Camus

The first problem to be tackled is a political one: political in the classical sense that the people are the body politic and any problems the people have as a whole are political problems. Consequently, solutions really become political solutions. It is a question of being concerned, of simply looking up and taking an interest. To do that is to be political.

In the process of being political, of course, one discovers the absence of freedom. Yet at the same time, one sees, in a Platonic sense, the potential for freedom. Herein lies our dilemma — for freedom is a fact and therefore the object of an imperative: to become free is to become responsible. To become responsible is to question, to have the ability to take action, to make decisions, to be effective. In short, it is to have power – for power is simply the ability to act.

But the poor by their very situation do not have this 'ability to act' and in order to obtain it they will need to fight for it – for no one is going to give it to them. No one ever has.

How does one really begin to organize the poor? Nicholas von Hoffman, one of the chief organizers for the Industrial Areas Foundation in Chicago, gave this reply with studied casualness: 'I found myself at the corner of Sixty-Third and Kimbark and I looked around.' Simplistic perhaps, but very real. The rehabilitation of the alcoholic, the salvation of the emotionally disturbed, and the self-respect of the poor all require the same ingredient – empathy for their condition.

Community development can only be successful if those involved adhere to its methods and principles. The following paraphrase of Biddle & Biddle's *Community Development Process* will indicate how it may be achieved.

First, community development is a *process*, and thus is something other than a formula or recipe that – if precisely applied – will render exact results. In fact, an outline of process presents a method for seeking, a method by which citizens may evolve their own formulas which serve them best. The process simultaneously involves learning by individuals (including the worker), and changes in their interrelationships. It is a process of education that requires a conscious act of participation and action on the parts of all involved.

And finally, a note of warning. If we fail to heed the demands of the poor in Canada now, we must face the consequences later. The conflicts, problems, and disorders we are presently faced with from Indians, Negroes, and white people alike, will not, and cannot, become less urgent by themselves. Their problems will not disappear. Community development has a major contribution to make to society. I cannot appeal too strongly: let the enemies of community development reconsider their position, before it is too late.

BERT DEVEAUX'S earliest work experience, after leaving St. Francis Xavier University in 1960, was with the Children's Aid Society in Amherst, Nova Scotia. From there he moved to New Brunswick to work as a Classification Officer at Dorchester Penitentiary for a year and a half. In 1961 he and his wife, Kaye, accepted teaching positions in northern Ontario and spent two years with the Indians of Sandy Lake.

Mr. Deveaux's interest in Indian problems led to a position with Community Development Services in Manitoba in 1964. On the Oak River Reserve, twenty-seven miles from Brandon, he worked with the Sioux people to form the Community Development Council, which developed self-help techniques. Four years later, in February 1968, he joined the Company of Young Canadians as Project Director in Cape Breton, Nova Scotia. In May 1970 he was asked to implement a community-development mandate at the University Settlement of Montreal. His next position was in New Brunswick, where he was invited to do community development at the grass-roots level.

Mr. Deveaux is presently working with the Provincial Department of Agriculture and is attached to CRANO, a regional development council working with economically depressed communities in the north-western part of the province.

Social Intervention: Philosophy and Failure

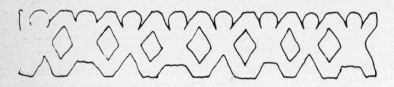

Hedley G. Dimock

Over the years I have been involved in helping relationships in a wide variety of situations, some of which have focussed on social or geographical communities. I have had a great deal of difficulty in working out my personal stance or philosophy in a helping relationship – why am I helping, towards whose goals are we working, and who gets to decide what in the relationship? This is additionally complicated in community situations, as there is usually an outside organization, who likely have their own goals for what I am to accomplish, sponsoring my intervention in the community. In looking at strategies for community change we find some who answer the ethics questions by saying they are just doing a job for their organization – the question of who does what and why is then the organization's responsibility. Others describe themselves as catalysts, or neutral entities, who just bring existing elements together in such a way that things happen (and thus the question of ethics does not come up). Some helpers have the community set their own goals for development, and their job is just to help them accomplish these ends (this places the responsibility to decide what's best on the community). And then there are some, including the radicals, who say they have the answers and know what is best for the community, and the militants add that the end justifies the means (hence, any change may be better than no change, or the goal is change, not people). This question of who gets to do what in a community, and why, is a major problem for me in social interventions.

The other problem I want to look at is the breakdown in communication between community workers and their sponsoring organizations, which results in the project's being discontinued. There are, in Canada, a surplus of competent workers anxious to make socially significant interventions in a community, and an increasing number of organizations who see their future linked with their involvement in community action. However, organizations that sponsor community-development work are often not able to integrate the new thrust, they lose communication with their workers, and then discontinue this program that now seems to be working against their best interests.

The Community Helping Relationship

In any helping relationship it is essential for me to know who is involved and why, and who gets to decide what is going to happen. The medical model, where a sick person seeks the help of a trained expert and pays for that help, does not hold up when I look at community interventions. Members of the community in which the intervention takes place rarely ask for help and usually do not pay for it (and may not even be grateful that help is offered). The doctor typically attempts to restore the health of the client, and both parties agree on the goal – mend a broken leg, lose weight, cure an illness, or remove a tumor. In a community situation the goals are probably not clear, and it is quite possible that 'clients' and 'helpers' do not agree on them. And, there is usually an outside organization that is footing the bill. It is also clear that in the medical model, the doctor knows what is best for the client – the client's role is doing what the doctor suggests. Obviously this goes against all the goals of community development – full participation of clients in goal-setting, utilization of the resources of the community, and the development of self-reliance in the community.

My own early experiences in helping relationships were in high schools and hospitals. The medical model of the helper knowing what should be done and doing it for, or to, other people was accepted without question. But as I worked with the patients in a children's hospital, I found that the last thing needed was another person to direct and control the situation. I sought other models of helping relationships and found the

Rogerian Model (Axline, 1947; Rogers, 1951). Here, the helper is a neutral catalyst who helps the client see where he is and what he wants to do more clearly. Freeing his capacity to see his goals then puts into gear his natural drive for more maturity and effectiveness. This worked well for some time, and then I found a number of things happening. Probably most important, I began to lose touch with my own values and feelings in this neutral, facilitating role. I was not clear why I was helping and what I hoped to get out of the relationship. I also found that people had no guidelines or models against which to test their own positions. I was a mirror simply helping them see their own needs, interests, and feelings more clearly. This eliminated any challenge, any learning through confrontation or examination of other ways of doing things, and left change up to the innate drive for maturity. While I found this a safe position, as there was little of me that anyone could attack, I found my own learnings limited, as my own behaviour could not be tested and could not receive feedback.

In a way, there was a strong temptation to go back to the medical 'I know what's best' model, but I had too much respect for the integrity of the individual and his right to make decisions concerning how he wanted to live his life. Through my research I had found that the opportunity for clients to participate in the decisions that affected them was a most important factor in the learning that took place. And workers who were able to facilitate this participative orientation to decision-making were most likely to be rated as highly competent by their supervisors (Dimock, 1970). But I had found, too, that I wanted my needs and interests to be part of any situation in which I worked.

Now I see a collaborative model as the one that is most worth while for me. I like to enter into negotiations with a community or group and have their interests and mine identified. If they do not have any interests or goals they can state immediately, then the first part of our collaboration is getting to know each other and experimenting to see if we have some interests in common. Once goals and priorities emerge, it becomes important to test the commitment of all parties to these goals. If they do not include enough of my interests or open up new opportunities for my learning, then I, like anyone else, am free to withdraw. The association continues as long as the collaboration has real meaning to those involved.

Examples from the Field

Let us now look at some examples of these stances, and examine their more logical components. I have described my personal orientation, as I am convinced that personal needs rather than philosophical assumptions determine behaviour (my biases are therefore now clear).

A great deal of overseas work has started from the assumption that we know what would help the people – health, agriculture, birth control, education, and communications – and we'll do it with them, or for them, demonstrating North American know-how. Some of the community-development work of ARDA, the Agricultural Rehabilitation and Development Administration, of the Department of Forestry, has started out with the predetermined goal of eliminating the small, marginal farmer. The Department of Fisheries has been busy for several years in moving isolated fishing-communities in Newfoundland into more viable – larger and more accessible – units. Some community-development work of private community-serving organizations has worked in the same predetermined way, with branches of the organization being set up in the newly 'developed' community.

An exception within the private sector was the pioneering social intervention of the National Council of Y.M.C.A.s in Lanark County, just outside of Ottawa. In this project the Y refrained from transporting its traditional program into the community and setting up a Y, complete with building, there. Rather, it unleashed a worker with a strong back-up team of resource people and attempted to relate to the problems and interests in this rather depressed community. The project continued for three years, with a considerable amount of citizen participation in decision-making, community action, and leadership-training programs. Today, three years after the program was discontinued, there is still activity in the community that is related to the social intervention (Jackson, 1971).

Ten years ago I spent some time with a resident of a Maine paper-mill town, who was a key person in the company's community-development plan. The company felt they would like to involve more citizens in the operation of the town and reduce the mistrust and apathy in relations between the mill and the town. A major community-development program was initiated, involving outside consultants with company financing (Klein,

1965). In the process the citizens developed some of their own goals, but the question of who got to decide what remained a concern as long as the company was financing the program. A few years later I talked to the president of a company that was just setting up a town with the largest paper mill in Quebec about citizen participation in organizing and operating the town. He did not feel there was any viable alternative to his company's taking the responsibility, as they had a virtual monopoly on the talents and resources in the town.

After close to a century of paternalistic control and 'we know what is best for your development', the Indian Affairs Branch became interested in participatory action using self-help and launched a major program of social interventions in Indian communities. Soon, there were two conflicting systems at work, as the community workers helped the Indians to identify and communicate their version of their needs to an authoritarian system that knew what was best for them. Following a series of confrontations, Indian Affairs reduced the community development program to a meaningless level.

The Company of Young Canadians (C.Y.C.), established in 1966, was the most independent of all government-sponsored, social-intervention programs. Free from the usual bureaucratic control, company workers used their social-animation approach in a broad range of situations. Working sometimes with the people on problems they had identified, and, at other times, setting the goals themselves and aggressively organizing the people to support them, they achieved results that varied a great deal (and depended partly on who was reporting the results).[1]

A need for clarity concerning goals and for specificity of programs remained a concern for the federal government, and presented a continuing problem for the Company, as community development is a type of helping relationship and not a task- or production-oriented program. Last year I encountered a similar problem when our Centre at Sir George Williams University applied to the Canadian International Development Agency to support our proposed work in Jamaica. Following the collaborative model I developed above, we had established a number of contacts in that developing country and clearly described our interests in such collaboration. CIDA replied that they only supported projects that had predetermined, specific, activity-type goals. This seemed to me to continue the 'we'll do something for them' approach.

In summary, we have a number of philosophies of social intervention, which range on a continuum from the authoritarian and paternalistic 'we know what is best for us to do for them', through a mid-point collaborative strategy where both parties put out their positions and seek overlapping areas of common agreement, to an end where they decide and we just help them do it. Thus, the interveners may have total say in what happens, an equal say in what happens, or no say. It is perhaps ironic that many of the intervention orientations of the radicals who are determined to change the authoritarian and dehumanizing Establishment involve only a few people, who autocratically decide what is best for everyone else. Then they attempt to manipulate the results in the same dehumanizing way that the Establishment does in order to achieve these ends. We can quickly test ourselves on this continuum by answering the following questions: Should farmers be free to remain on unprofitable land? Should Indians be allowed to continue educating their children to a hunting and trapping life-style (when all signs are that this industry is rapidly failing)? Can the poverty-stricken choose to remain in sub-standard housing when a new housing-project is available? And, can the Newfoundlander stay in his remote outpost without health, communication, or educational services? As you see, it's a question of who gets to decide what happens to whom. That is the question that gets to the nitty-gritty of social-intervention philosophy.

Organizational Problems in Sponsoring Community-Development Programs

As early as 1966, Dick McDonald observed that a major problem in community-development projects was that the organizations sponsoring them were not able to continue to relate to them for any period of time (Dimock & McDonald, 1967). It seemed that the more successful the social intervention (judged by community interest and participation), the more conflicts and pressures organizations encountered in the community-development process. The literature then, as now, contained very few descriptions of Canadian community-development programs that had succeeded in helping communities take responsibility for their own destiny and become more reliant on their own resources. Programs that continued were paternalistic, and the communities became more apathetic and dependent. And programs that produced participative citizen-action were later immobilized by their sponsoring organizations. Thus, while I have questioned the ethics of social interventions where a few people are moulding decisions about what a lot of other people should do, it is also clear that *participative programs fail as they are not able to maintain support from their sponsoring organizations*.

A typical example seems to go as follows. A government or community-serving organization finds it has lost communication with a large element of its community and sees a growing apathy among other elements. In an effort to break through its traditional structure, the organization gives some priority to a program where workers will establish communication with the community and attempt to activate interest and participation in areas related to the organization's goals. As the social intervention takes hold the community reports back to the organization describing areas where they would like the organization to modify its policies and procedures. This stands to reason, for if there were not differences in interests and procedures, the organization would not have lost contact with this part of their community in the first place. It looks as though this was the organization's purpose in initiating the community-development program, and all seems well. But the organization may have been naively hopeful that the new communication and interest would support its traditional ways of working and that it would not have to make any changes in policy and procedures.

However, the communication back from the new elements in the community continues to seek its own set of needs and one way or another the organization is unable to support this continued pressure for change. The most obvious examples come from situations where the social intervention produces an aggressive or militant pressure on the organization to change, such as Indians seeking radical reforms in Indian Affairs practices when it appears that the community-development program is supporting, if not initiating, the pressure. With some C.Y.C. projects, it appeared that the federal government was spending about ten thousand dollars to keep each of its workers in the field and that the workers were 'creating' a series of situations to put pressure for change on provincial governments. Part of the strategy was to seek wider support by extensive coverage through the news media, and this made the pressure more unbearable for the organization.

In less obvious examples the organization has harmonious relations with its community-development participants, but the pressure for change still remains. The Y.M.C.A. project in Lanark County, and other out-reach programs typical of community-serving organizations, may be phased out through a lack of funds. Most community-agency programs bring in some money through program fees or other forms of support. Social interventions are not programs, and participants are rarely able or disposed to support them. The lack of a specific production orientation in a social intervention makes it hard to receive outside support from foundations or government. The cost of the community-development program soon begins to affect the budget of the sponsoring organization, especially if the program grows and requires more resources. Stopping the community-development thrust may be excused as due to a shortage of funds, but that is only a superficial reason. How an organization spends its money reflects its priorities. What it is really saying is that the community work is not of great enough interest to us compared to the other things we are doing to warrant our support. The 'other things' are usually the traditional programs. What we have seen is an application of the principle that 'change in one part of an organization requires changes in other parts of the organization if it is to continue'. Thus, a change in program focus (community development) requires a change in budgeting and priority setting around how available funds will be spent.

This inability of the organization to respond to change and to integrate the innovative challenges of the social intervention requires the demise of the social intervention to protect the organization. The implication is obvious – any organization initiating a social intervention needs to give as much time and money to integrating the project and dealing with its own organizational change as to the project itself.

Social interventions and community development have not had a significant impact on the major institutions of Canadian life. As attention shifts from launching new programs and training the leaders working in them, to solidifying a participative orientation to community work and dealing with the change these programs necessitate, more tangible results should be forthcoming.

FOOTNOTE

1. The work of the Company made it clear that it was not just 'established organizations' that thought they knew what was best for other people and that had a minority of outsiders making decisions for the majority of residents. Some of the Company workers moving into communities across Canada made the same kind of outsider minority decision for the many local residents. The decisions and method of expression were different, but the form of 'we know what is best for you' was the same.

HEDLEY G. DIMOCK has been working in the helping professions since he started as a camp counsellor during his summers at college. He was resident master of a school for handicapped youth, headed a department of group guidance in a children's hospital, worked on educational programs with nursing and para-medical staff, co-ordinated training for a metropolitan Y.M.C.A., and taught university courses on a part-time basis. During the past decade he has been at Sir George Williams University, Montreal, as Professor and Chairman of the Department of Applied Social Science, and Director of the University's Centre for Human Relations and Community Studies.

Following the completion of his Doctor of Education degree in Group Psychology from Columbia University in 1955, he has been a consultant to many community-serving organizations. Most of his work is with helping professions, where he specializes in human-relations problems in training and organizational development.

His major research interest is identifying personality factors associated with effective group and team leadership, and assessing the success of different types of leadership-training programs. Another application of this research is identifying leadership profiles of successful street-workers in community-oriented programs. The measurement tool developed during ten years of research has been published as the Dimock Leadership Inventory. Other publications include three books, the 'Leadership and Group Development' monograph series, and many articles.

Community Development and Learning: Concepts and Implications

An essential prerequisite to the implementation of community development is an understanding of its philosophy. Important too is an understanding of the supporting services and organizational structures necessary to relate to communities successfully. The individual and the community not only must be understood specifically, but also in the broad context within which they function. In discussing the philosophy of community development, planning, implementation, and evaluation are to be seen as part of a continuous process, and are dependent upon a clear statement of objectives. One of the primary objectives of community development is the process of learning skills and attitudes, as well as the acquisition of knowledge.

Jim Lotz begins this section by discussing aspects of community development in Canada to determine whether it exists, either as a coherent body of theory or as an operational validity. His discussions are conducted in a historical, domestic, and international context.

J. Roby Kidd points out that terms such as "involvement" and "participation" have always been an integral component of democracy and that the significance of these notions for adult education has long been understood. He points out that there is a close link between learning and participation, and reinforces the fact that learning and change are essential components of community development. Furthermore, learning is linked to action. Kidd's discussion touches upon other basic principles of community development; he refers to the obstacles to change, the ethic of community involvement, and some attributes of the change maker, a subject discussed further in a later article by Whale. In keeping with points made by Lotz, Kidd agrees that community development is not yet an art, and it is far from being a science, but a strategy of community development is emerging.

Out of his vast experience in the French-Canadian context, Michel Blondin elaborates further on the philosophies and practices of *animation sociale*. A positive note is followed throughout his article when he assesses the effect that *animation sociale* has had on poverty and the contributions it can make to the urban phenomenon. Brief mention is made of the role of the *animateur* and the place of citizens' committees.

R. Alexander Sim continues to probe, in depth, questions relating to the ethics of intervention and helping relationships. (The latter is also the major focus of Dimock's article in Section II.) Is community development innocent of creating or perpetuating injustices? What has community development in Canada accomplished? Who is accountable for the practice and implications of social intervention? In discussing three types of innocence, he points out that innocence is a quality that must be placed in a moral context.

Taking off from the previous discussions on philosophical, ethical, and organizational and supporting structures, W.B. Whale zeroes in on the community worker, the key to community development. Since the community worker is usually employed by an agency, Whale asks how the worker can serve three masters: the community in which he works, the organizations by which he is employed, and himself. The worker must understand himself and the philosophies and methodologies to which he is committed. The role of the worker is to apply his knowledge and understanding of process to the community, his agency, and other agencies.

Does Community Development Exist?

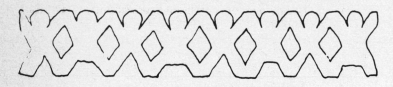

Jim Lotz

In the movie *Jumbo*, Jimmy Durante is endeavouring to smuggle an elephant out of a circus. He is stopped by a guard who asks him, 'Where are you going with that elephant?' Durante looks surprised and innocent, moves his body in front of the animal, and asks, 'What elephant?'

His reaction is reminiscent of someone who has been accused of doing community development.

The term 'community development' occasions a highly ambivalent reaction among those in the field of development these days. To unskilled newcomers, the concepts of community development seem to be the answer to all problems and to provide a simple, common-sense way of resolving complex human difficulties.[1] If the local people can only be persuaded to help themselves, buckle down, stop squabbling, and co-operate cheerfully, that bridge will be built, that new crop planted, that road repaired. And, of course, it will all be done in a co-ordinated manner. A recent case study in community development – one incident among many – should indicate that this sort of simple-minded approach to development will no longer work (Griffiths, 1970). Experienced professionals in the field of development – especially the specialists – will tend to laugh bitterly at the mention of 'community development', and dismiss its techniques as those of simple-minded amateurs as full of naive goodwill as they are empty of substantive knowledge. In the fall of 1970, the Anglican Church withdrew staff from Venezuela where a $300,000 community-development project came apart, and there are plenty of other examples of agencies and individuals launching community-development projects with wild enthusiasm and then slowly seeing them wrecked on the rocks of reality.

Community development does not seem to have achieved those prerequisites of a scientific discipline: a coherent body of theory and a close relationship to reality. There is a pervasive feeling in the writings on community development that community development is not academically respectable (because it lacks a body of substantive theory) and also that community development does not work as a technology (because so many disasters in development have been identified as community-development projects). On the other hand, when a vogue for community development appears in a country, as is the case with Canada at the present time, the representatives of established disciplines appropriate the field of community development and claim it for their own. Social workers say that community development is just a new word for community organization. Adult educators state that they have long been involved in doing community development. Like the man who discovered he had been using grammar all his life, the mention of community development makes specialists examine what they are doing and see how it relates to community development. This is a useful function for the term 'community development', in that it forces people in development roles to pause, and to be specific about their own operations. The problem of defining and recognizing community development from its theory and practice may be less one of discovering something new, than of rediscovering something that has always been happening in human relations.

It is the purpose of this article to look at some aspects of community development in Canada, and to determine whether community development – either as a coherent body of theory, or as an operational reality – exists in this country. This may seem strange, but the aim is to take nothing for granted. In a recently published handbook (Canadian Council for International Co-operation, 1971) on non-governmental Canadian agencies involved in overseas development, 374 community-development efforts are listed in countries abroad by a wide variety of agencies. No less than fifteen community-development projects by as many Canadian agencies are being carried on in Nigeria. The Presbyterians, the Lutherans, the Evangelical Church, the Mennonites – as well as the Boy Scouts of Canada and the Sudan Interior Mission – are named as being involved in community development in that country. One might expect a wide range of diversity in their approaches, not to mention in their philosophies. A number of provincial government departments have community-development branches, and the Department of Indian Affairs and Northern Development accepted the community-development approach about five years ago as a way of solving the problems of the indigenous peoples in Canada. No evaluation (or should it be autopsy?) exists of the Indian Affairs Branch's program, but my own knowledge of it seems to indicate that it was not considered a success. On October 22, 1970, the Minister of Indian Affairs and Northern Development announced the signing of an agreement that gave the Federation of Saskatchewan Indians the authority to manage community-development services in the province. A similar agreement was signed with the Union of Nova Scotia Indians in September 1970, and with the Manitoba Indian Brotherhood in October 1969. One thing that Indians in Canada have learned is that they usually get what the white man does not want – the 'old-clothes syndrome'. It is interesting to see community development being moved out of the hands of the federal government and put into the hands of Indians at this time.

Basic to a scientific approach to any problem is scepticism. Transferring community-development services to Indians, in the light of experiences with the technique elsewhere in the world, does not suddenly validate this approach to solving problems in socio-economic development. A concept is not made real because the government and Indians sign a paper. Community development may simply be a form of ritual magic, a form of pseudo-academic astrology that has no relationship to reality. The mumbling of words like 'self-help', 'co-ordination', 'felt needs' are used to avoid evil, and to give comfort to people who want to solve human problems but don't know how. One thing has become painfully obvious in Canada in recent years: if people are interfering in the lives of other people, and they don't know what they are doing, they usually identify their efforts as 'community development'.

Traditionally, the twin bases of community-development approach have been self-help and the concept of co-ordination. In the period after World War II there was a rush to 'help' the 'underdeveloped nations'. At that time, it must be admitted, our knowledge of these areas was somewhat vague. If every English schoolboy had been drilled to learn the main exports of Peru, very few people understood the reality and complexity of life in that country. Rote learning about another country, coupled with some ethnocentrism, seasoned with a dash of fantasy based on the works of such writers as Rider Haggard, accompanied by a large amount of goodwill and a belief in the perfectibility of man, are not ideal qualifications for tackling the serious problems of other cultures. In Canada there is an abysmal ignorance about the reality of life in other cultures. On a Canadian talk-show in September 1970, the interviewer remarked to an East Indian girl who was with a singing and dancing group, and who had mentioned that the troupe was going to Trinidad, that 'they have their own music down there – steel bands'. He was obviously ignorant of the fact that large numbers of East Indians live on the islands.

What some might ascribe to ignorance, others might see as racialism. All the concern about human rights and civil liberties in the world will mean nothing if there is no awareness of the concepts on which other cultures are based. Advertisements for rum in middle-class magazines such as *Saturday Night* show a well-dressed white couple at a table in the West Indies, surrounded by black, uniformed waiters. A cartoon commercial for a children's cereal on Canadian TV in 1970 showed a sea captain being captured by cannibals and prepared for the pot. Oddly enough, a British TV commercial in the same year showed the same thing in live form. In each case the cannibals were bought off by the advertised product. These commercials reveal a great deal about Western society, or about the atavistic fears of white men.

The 'gee whiz, aren't the natives cute, let's pitch in and help them better themselves' stage of development is long past in places like Britain, the United States, France, and other Western countries. Development specialists still go out from these countries, but they have skills needed elsewhere, and are usually invited by the recipient country. If they perform satisfactorily in their technical jobs, and can relate as human beings to the people with whom they are working, they usually finish their tour. If they cannot operate in human and technical terms (and the former is the most important consideration), then they may well be 'invited out', or 'de-selected' – the bureaucratic euphemism for being fired. In the annual report of the Canadian International Development Agency for 1969, white Canadians are usually shown, in photographs from developing areas, as supervising people. This sort of propaganda subtly reinforces the idea that only whites are suited to teach. In the CUSO Bulletin a nurse aho went out to teach in India expressed astonishment that Indian students had difficulty grasping abstract concepts (CUSO Bulletin, 1970, pp. 6-7).

In one class that I gave in community development, a group from CUSO 'took over' one evening. The men discussed at length why anyone should help people in developing areas. A former woman volunteer, after forty minutes of aimless academic discussion, pointed out that this was not the problem, and that people from Canada would simply be invited into countries to do specific jobs. Identifying the wrong problem has caused a great deal of grief in development.

France has sent men out to Canada to teach, and to help reorganize *L'Evangeline*, the Acadian newspaper; those involved accept these assignments in lieu of military service. Meanwhile, Canada sends graduates to Francophone countries in Africa. To my knowledge, the French 'Co-opérants' in Canada do not claim to be helping Canadians to help themselves, nor do they see themselves as co-ordinating the activities in their areas. They are more likely to be polarizing people.

By bringing the two basic concepts of community development – self-help and co-ordination – home to Canada, it is possible to understand why the community-development movement has aroused such hostility in the developing nations when done by outsiders, and such confusion when carried out by nationals. The concepts of community development may be seen as a deliberate attempt to interfere in the lives of others. The very words 'help' and 'aid' have become suspect in development; while many agencies and individuals have claimed that they are helping others, they are obviously also doing very well themselves.

The basic problem of community development is not in the developing nations, or among the poor. It lies in the individualistic views of the Western liberal tradition. Traditional societies were based on mutual aid, and reciprocity of relationships. Kropotkin pointed out in *Mutual Aid* (Kropotkin, 1955) that co-operation, not competition, could be the key to social survival. In Ottawa's Lower Town, self-help projects were launched in an area undergoing urban renewal. Research showed that the citizens there had been practising mutual aid for years (Shulman, 1967). Just as in the developing nations too many people were in too much of a hurry to pull the peasants out of their misery, so in Ottawa's Lower Town there was no attempt initially to work with and through existing citizens' groups and leaders, and to build on the past history of the area and use it as a resource. The decision was made to 'renew' the area, so that life could be made 'better' for the citizens there.

In a recent book on the Company of Young Canadians (Hamilton, 1970), the difficulties in dealing with community development in Canada are revealed. The C.Y.C. espoused the use of community development as their method of changing society, but nowhere in the book is there a definition of community development, or an account of its origins and practice, either in Canada or the developing nations. With the C.Y.C., the process was seen as fighting 'the system', 'the Establishment', 'society'. In common with other early community-development efforts, the technique with the C.Y.C. began as a mystique – 'Community development is the key to social change'; then it became an ideology –'Learn community development techniques, and we shall conquer. In community development, you are fighting the system'; finally it became a dogma – 'People who are fighting the system are the only people who are doing community development. Anyone else is not doing community development.' The C.Y.C. fell apart through lack of a proper relationship between headquarters and field staff, through inadequate selection and preparation of volunteers, and through financial mismanagement. The Company was not 'co-ordinated'.

A whole mythology in community development revolves around the concept of co-ordination. Any peasant now knows that when the white man talks about co-ordination, he means control. Development to date has attracted a certain type of person. Indeed it should be possible to describe the culture of the developer. Among the characteristics of this culture (or perhaps 'personality type' might be a better description) would be a strong belief in progress, a penchant for rationalism, a middle-class origin, an individualistic, liberal bias, an ability to deal with abstract concepts, a university degree in economics, administration, or a similar 'hard-headed' discipline, and a mechanistic, reductionist approach to all problems, combined with a specialized understanding of one aspect of reality. The middle class, in the nineteenth century, became masters of the machine, and commanded the abundance thereof. They saw themselves as being in total control. But more and more it seems the world is out of control. Such diverse phenomena as sky-jacking and the threat of pollution seem to convince the middle class that the world is on the brink of chaos. In the Canadian North, for example, the government in 1969-70 alternated between enthusiasm about the oil-rich Arctic and concern about pollution of the cold environment.

We are passing through a phase that marks the end of empires. Most Western schoolchildren are taught that the Roman Empire was a 'good thing', a glorious period in the history of man. Only later does realization come that maybe the whole concept of empire is a shabby trick in which 'savages' are dazzled with the symbols of power, or overcome by force of arms. Opposite the Forum in Rome is the Mamertine Prison. Here the 'freedom fighters' of an earlier time, including Vercingetorix and Jugurtha, were executed or left to starve to death after the Roman triumphs. It is a cold and clammy place, and shows the other side of those straight Roman roads and orderly Roman minds and the white cities with their amphitheatres and baths baking in the sun of the Mediterranean.

The Romans were great co-ordinators. They also had that restless urge to bring civilization to (and exact tribute from) barbarians. But the urge to push outwards and the internal tensions in Rome proved too much, time and time again. There was not enough energy to hold the frontiers and to keep the centre under control. The 'fall' of the Roman Empire has been discussed over the past two centuries. There was no sudden 'fall', but rather a replacement of certain concepts by others (Chambers, 1966). The same sort of change in concepts is going on today as the nineteenth-century empires crumble, and their dominance fades.

In the developing nations, the problems of co-ordination have been complicated by rivalry among specialists trained in the West. The way in which the advocates of one approach have tried to impress *their* ideas on the local people, and the way in which other specialists quarrelled with them and confused the local people, is a phenomenon that is all too familiar in the community-development field. In the Canadian North, the problem changes every time a new specialist arrives. The aggressive, assertive, single-minded Westerner with his vested interest in his own speciality or profession, oblivious to any other approach, is a familiar figure in the literature of development. These people are 'muscle men', and their habits and mores are rooted deep in the Western tradition. It is this muscle-bound, Western approach to problems that has caused difficulty in the past. Westerners throw out signals all the time. Accustomed to manipulating machines and tools, they unwittingly use terms and techniques that suggest they are manipulating people. Now we are moving from the extension of muscle to the extension of mind. The process of development becomes cerebral; concepts, ideas, assumptions, methods must be examined before they are used.

There are reasons for the muscular approach to development, which lie in the last two hundred years of history in the West, as the machine became the central fact of civilization. Inanimate nature was made to work for the good of man, for 'progress', for a better life. Energy was harnessed and made to produce material goods. Progress as an increase in the *quantity* of goods and services now has been replaced by the concept of *quality* of goods and of the environment. The Gross National Product as a measure of national prosperity is being challenged in the United States (Bird, 1970). At a time when many people in the developing nations are reaching a threshold in their awareness that life can be improved, that they can get better housing, purer water, greater opportunities through urbanization and mechanization, messages pour out of the Western world that resources are being depleted, the environment ruined, and life made miserable for people by the machine and the city. There is a swing back to a Rousseau-like romanticism, and the Western world goes back to the eighteenth century and to the delights of unspoiled nature in man and landscape.

In community development, the wheel has come full circle. What Westerners say or do may mean nothing in real-life terms among the 'poor', 'the underprivileged', or the 'underdeveloped'. But it tells a great deal about the assumptions of people in the developed nations, and it is from these assumptions that development begins. Always, in community development, the idea arises that the problems being dealt with are those of 'other people'. This, again, is a middle-class bias – the belief in an 'objective', controllable world. In Canada over the past five years, there has been a tremendous ferment about the problems of the poor, yet very few people seem to realize that to call people poor in an acquisitive, capitalist society is to call them failures in the terms of that society. Great stress is being placed on 'citizen participation'. In Ottawa during the 1960s, a citizens' group organized to get the National Arts Centre built. Their initial estimate of the cost was about $8 million. The Centre was eventually built with public funds totalling $46 million. A citizens' group among low-income residents in Toronto, which sought $16,000 from the city in October 1970, was refused the money, and accused by elected officials of being Communist.

A series of reports from Newfoundland (Iverson; Matthews, 1968) assesses the impact of resettlement on the outports. What emerges from these reports is the sense of integrity in the life of the outports, and a complete lack of understanding by the provincial government of what life in these parts of the province is really like. The outporters maintain a tradition of self-help, coming together to do things (such as moving house) that are beyond the capacity of individuals. Then they return to their individual lives and to patterns of informal interaction. Social scientists 'study' remote areas, but only management specialists can question the operations of the government departments, and measure their 'productivity'. Studying the values and assumptions of the bureaucracy, or prying into the politics of the capital, would, of course, be considered a subversive pursuit (Smith; Fischer, 1970).

Governments have always been happier to have social scientists romping around in the field, and in remote villages, than examining the structure of decision-making and the distribution of money and power in the large cities. Usually Canadian social scientists quote Weber ('the routinization of its own existence') or Merton ('displacement of goals') on the problems of bureaucracy, but they never provide any data on the empirical reality of modern-day power structures. While working in a government research agency between 1962 and 1966, I found I was always able to get funds for studies of Indians and Eskimos. But suggestions for studying the department's activities met a blank wall. Research workers would be deterred by being asked to sign a form that guaranteed that any information they gathered would be kept confidential. And only in 1970 was the first report published by the research unit on whites in the North, and *their* problems (Parsons, 1970).

In 1970, someone finally turned things upside down, and published a study of the power *élite* of Toronto (Kelner, 1970). At a session on community development at the Canadian Sociology and Anthropology meetings in Winnipeg in 1970, I suggested that there should be more studies of the affluent in Canadian society, and especially in the Maritimes. If we assume the 'poor' have failed, it would be useful to have some models of what constitutes success in this country. This suggestion was greeted by a bellow of rage from a sociologist who had studied Africville, the Black area of Halifax. He claimed that 'we all know the system is rotten', despite the fact that his research had been funded by government, and that he himself had been appointed the youngest head ever of the department of sociology at the largest and best-endowed university in the Maritimes.

Coser (1965) has dealt in detail with the dilemmas of the liberal, intellectual approach to social problems, the ambivalent role of the intellectual, and the conflict between idealism and reality. In the United States there appears to be a complete disenchantment with the ability of intellectuals to aid in the solution of real-life problems. The idealism of the 'new frontier' era was followed by the pursuit of impossible dreams, and then by a growing concern for reality and the need to devise approaches to solve concrete problems. In 1969 a new Community Development Society was formed in the United States, and the material from this society has a familiar ring about it.[2] Americans going abroad to do community development found that they lacked an understanding of empirical realities other than those of an advanced Western country. They were also forced to face their own 'internal' reality. At the same time, there was increasing evidence of poverty and misery at home. The liberal dream of the rational man held that as civilization progressed and man was liberated from the chains of superstition, a new era would dawn in which harmony would prevail. Only eliminate the irrational part of man's nature, and the age of Reason and Human Harmony would arrive. Stanley Loomis' description of the Jacobins in power (Loomis, 1964), and of the careers of Marat, Danton, and Robespierre shows, in terrifying detail, the results of such thinking. Eradicating the evil in society was too difficult. The pursuit of abstract goals led to the persecution of individuals. It was easier to kill an evil-doer than to create a perfect society.

It's a long way from the French Revolution to contemporary Canada. But the roots of many of Canada's problems lie in attitudes of mind that developed two hundred years ago, and that, because of cultural lag in Canada, still persist in the thinking of decision-makers. Changes in society come about when attitudes of mind alter under the impact of new realities and concepts. They do not occur through hysterical reactions to modernization and mechanization, through the isolated actions of radicals, or because people collect together in conferences to deplore pollution, urban sprawl, poverty, etc.

Because of the slowness of change and the increasing evidence of preventable human misery, it is tempting in Canada to see community development as a technique for taking on 'the Establishment'. Hopefully, however, the era of simplistic approaches to serious social and economic problems has passed with the first phases of such social-action agencies as the C.Y.C. The romantic notion of community development sees the developer as Lawrence of Arabia, raising the tribes against the corrupt government. An early attempt in the western provinces in the mid sixties was led by a man who publicly espoused the belief that community development involved 'fighting the Establishment'. If this person saw community development as a form of revolution, he forgot one of the main rules of revolution – don't tell anyone you are starting one. Early attempts at community development in the federal Indian Affairs Branch seemed to be based on the same premises of fighting the system from within. Such programs as the National Film Board's *Challenge for Change* seemed to have been initiated in the belief that films and film-making would radicalize the poor. There was much talk of the 'objective' eye of the camera, which ignored the considerable amount of research on film-making that stresses that the camera – like any other tool – is not an objective extension of man, but can be used for a wide variety of purposes, both positive and negative. These early, amateur attempts at community development in Canada were not noted for much intellectual content, or for any regard for the efforts of others, either those of the past or going on at the time. They ignored the second rule of revolution – if you are going to topple the system, don't try to do it with the system's money and while working for the system. All these attempts ignored the fact that 'the enemy' was not an abstract force like 'the Establishment' or a wicked individual like the local politician or businessman, but our own ignorance of the limits of reality.

The liberal concept of objectivity is under attack. The work in theoretical physics that was done in the 1920s and 1930s is only now filtering into our consciousness. This work has shown that there is no such thing as an 'objective' world; there are only degrees of subjectivity, based on relationship to reality through measuring instruments. The idea that the use of Fabian tactics will bring about social change is a prevailing myth in Canada. Put objective information and 'facts' into the hands of decision-makers, and you will be able to bring about change, goes the theme.[3] No one questions whether the decision-makers are able to understand the information, or whether they have enough awareness to match the right piece of information with the right problem. Or whether they understand the politics of the use of information and knowledge. Decision-makers are swamped with written and oral information, and have to make political choices related to their position in the social and economic structure. Two young volunteers from the C.Y.C. went into a settlement in Alberta, after briefing themselves thoroughly with all the information on the area that they could get their hands on. But they did not seem to understand how to use this information, what their role was, and what their relationships were to the separate white and Métis communities. Eventually they were forced to move out, after polarizing the community.

In the twentieth century we have become familiar with the concept of the electromagnetic spectrum. The concept of a spectrum destroys the notion of polarities (black/white, good/bad, rich/poor) that is embedded in Western thought. Where this concept of polarities originated is in dispute, but Hauser (1962) believes that it came about when men began to settle in villages. They began to gain some control over the environment, and to see themselves as separate from it. With the growth of cities came polarization into classes, into the 'we' and the 'they'. The concept is a key one in human society, and through the years has found expression in Zoroastrianism, Greek drama (with its masks of tragedy and comedy) and the Manichean heresy.

In development, we are involved in a change in concepts, and not simply in a change of tools. The developing nations will not become just like the West. The evidence indicates that they adapt to urbanization and industrialization in a variety of ways. The West is showing its incapacity to deal with its own internal tensions, and every 'primitive' society had some way of doing this. The Eskimos murdered people who were threats to the group. In Canada, there was concern in 1970 over the question of Arctic sovereignty, and this led to the rationalization of a number of schemes by the Department of National Defence for 'defending' the area – the use of obsolete aircraft, the establishment of an icebreaker fleet, the construction of nuclear submarines. Yet a group of young unemployed people in Vancouver were evicted only with great difficulty from an armoury that had been used as a summer youth hostel. The enemy is considered to be 'out there'. Concentration on an external threat avoids examination of one's own frame of reference.

In castigating entrepreneurs and their excesses, liberal critics fail to understand that these men took considerable risks. And it is becoming obvious that development is a difficult and risky business. Various pressure groups have demanded that Canada devote 1 per cent of its Gross National Product to overseas development. And yet, in 1968-9, Canada was unable to expend its foreign-aid allocations. In Hansard, Mr. Macdonald noted that, in 1968-9, $7,682,314.75 allocated for aid to Latin America was not spent. He also noted unspent allocations for Colombo Plan areas ($22,374,810.52), 'various countries' ($2,458,020.01), French-speaking African states ($9,368,732.55), Commonwealth Caribbean Assistance Plan countries ($13,006,839.72), and Commonwealth African countries ($10,341,270.22).

Waterston points out that the most difficult problem in development is to determine good possibilities for investment of money, time, and effort (Waterston, 1965). In development overseas, what can Canadians do abroad that the Americans have not tried to do with money, and the local people cannot do themselves? The Canadian International Development Agency has boomed in recent years, and is now a large, Ottawa-based organization. The creation of large organizations with all the 'experts' located in one place has been shown to inhibit the processes of development, rather than aid them. Again, the goodwill of people in such organizations as CIDA is not in doubt. But between 1922 and 1967 only five Ph.D.s in anthropology were awarded in Canadian universities; only two anthropologists and two sociologists in Canada claim to have a specialized knowledge of Latin America (Connor; Curtis, 1970). How can any country be serious about development (which necessitates an understanding of cultural factors), when it has not encouraged its citizens to study and appreciate other ways of life, and has not trained the manpower needed to fill the roles that are opening in development? In addition, of course, there is a federal ruling that only Canadian citizens or immigrants who have been in the country for over five years can be employed by government – unless the government cannot find a suitably qualified Canadian. In an era of nationalism, it is unlikely that non-Canadians will be hired for employment in development, which, after all, reflects national values and goals. And so in Canada we face a double bind. There are few well-trained people in the field of development, and entry into government development agencies is restricted for non-Canadians. Since development involves money and power, it is very difficult to determine whether money spent in the name of development is not being used merely for political slush-funding. Development makes demands on people to perform, and to do so they must understand the theoretical and empirical bases of modernization.

What seems to have happened in Canada in the past is that community development has been used as a gimmick, and as an escape. Calling a project 'community development' allows people time to determine what the problem is, and then to tackle it realistically. Or it can be used as a vague portemanteau word to cover up the confusion in the developer's mind. In a report on the Fogo Islands, a sociologist studying religion was called in to study resettlement (Dewitt, 1969). He concluded that the people were suffering from anomie, and recommended that the government station a community-development worker on the island.

It is becoming obvious that using community development as an escape route is no longer a paying game in Canada. For one thing we know far too much about what has happened in the name of community development abroad to assume that a community developer is part of the solution to any problem, and not part of the problem. Secondly, we have a great deal of theoretical and empirical information on development that indicates that it is not a simple problem of getting the natives to do what someone else thinks is good for them. Thirdly, we are beginning to understand the shape of Canadian society. The country is half way between an advanced technological, market-oriented society, and a subsistence economy. This dualistic economy is marked in places like Newfoundland and the Yukon (Brox, 1969). The federal method of tackling economic problems has been the traditional one of endeavouring to lure large companies into a 'lagging' area to open up primary producing plants or new industries. In Canada this strategy is obviously failing. For one thing, at a time of increasing nationalism, the voters are unable to equate subsidizing American companies with an increasing national desire to have control of the country's industry and resources. The Churchill Forest Industries development in The Pas, Manitoba, has shown up the inadequacies of public subsidy for primary resource development by groups who have only an exploitive interest in an area. The fate of such projects as the Glace Bay heavy water plant, which, despite expenditures of over $100 million, had not got into production by late 1970, should also give pause to anyone who sees only 'economic' solutions in developing areas.

Community development in the rest of the world has been tied in with national development, and with the creation of a certain *ethos*. The community-development process is an expression of the national goals and the emerging *ethos* of a nation. The movement towards self-help and co-ordination is a reaction to the imposed colonial standards, and to the fragmented approach to life that characterizes Western society. Basically, community development does not accept the primacy of the Western way. Development is always political, and this implies conflict over the distribution of money and power. The serious problems in development revolve around attempts to maintain an evolutionary approach to change (which implies growth and feedback) as opposed to a revolutionary approach. In Canada there is still a lingering belief that equates the practice of politics by local people with the operation of original sin. But local groups are learning politics. The aggressive statement by Andrew Nicholas about the weaknesses of the old way of handling Indian problems is identified as 'conservative militancy' (Nicholas, 1970). It ties in with the ideas of Bennett on conservative innovators among people in the Canadian west (Bennett, 1970). Innovation and conservation are not seen as opposed poles; they can be synthesized through the actions of individuals with status, as Bennett's study shows.

In development, the whole of man is involved – not merely

the political aspects. Social innovators have to be effective at the psychological, social, economic, and political levels. This demands a high standard of performance, and an understanding of the limits and possibilities of reality. It is the complete opposite of the fuzzy, vague approach that characterized such bodies as the C.Y.C. And yet, initially, community developers have to be vague as they determine the limits of the possible.

The thrust of development may be political, but the impact is always personal, social, and economic. The sort of simplistic nonsense that has passed for community development in Canada, and elsewhere in the world, seems to be on the way out. Canadians still retain an innocence about the complexity of their own country. If innocence can be combined with scientific scepticism (which has much in common with the disbelief many low-income people have about any attempts by governments and other formal bodies to help anyone but themselves), and if this can be tempered with humanism and informed by knowledge of social-science theory and practice, we may yet develop strategies and tactics in Canada that could be useful in developed industrial countries and in developing rural areas. The greatest shortage in development in Canada at the present time is of trained, skilled, and experienced people to handle social and economic problems at the theory-practice interface. In a country of 4,000,000 square miles, with a population of 21,000,000, the problems of human development, both personal and national, are becoming apparent very quickly. The Special Senate Committee on Poverty has shown the extent of poverty in Canada, and its attendant misery. Unfortunately, the approach to poverty in Canada to date has been problem-oriented rather than solution-oriented. The 'solution' to the problem of poverty is seen in simplistic terms, and the chairman of the Senate Committee has repeatedly gone on record as favouring a guaranteed annual income as the way to eradicate poverty in Canada. The chairman also got very tense in the Yukon Territory when someone criticized one of Canada's sacred symbols – the R.C.M.P. Yet the visit of the Committee to Prince Edward Island sparked the establishment of a citizens' group. In November 1970, an investigation of irregularities in the distribution of welfare on the Island resulted in the dismissal of two R.C.M.P. officers.

Each nation has its own approach to community development. In Canada, what is emerging as the main strategy of community development is the transfer of money and power from those who have it to those who do not, in a sane and humane way. The guaranteed annual income scheme is a safe way to do this, through the traditional mechanism of transfer payments from the federal government to the citizens of Canada. This approach tends to create 'hammocks' – it provides a stable income for those who are considered to be incapable of competing in the economic system. But a 'springboard' approach is also needed if the guaranteed annual income is not to repeat the stigma of the Speenhamland system, and reduce everyone to dependence on one standard of performance, and one standard dole. A springboard approach would stimulate people to develop tactics whereby they could obtain access to money and power, and opportunities in the larger society. This will depend on a flow of information. For example, the Minister responsible for Citizenship stated that $35,000,000 would be available for voluntary groups in Canada, for citizen participation.[4] Who will get this money – the traditional citizens' groups who do voluntary service, manned by professionals skilled in politics and raising money, or the newly emergent, grass-roots organizations? In 1969-70, the federal government made available $200,000,000 for experimental housing. Who got these funds – and how did they secure them? Is the federal government really encouraging innovation and experimentation in social and mechanical technology, or is it merely sluicing money into the economy in an attempt to keep people quiet? Or are these experimental projects merely ways of paying off political debts? Experimental projects in Canada usually end up in trouble from both the accounting and the accountability end, as witness that great experiment in social change, the Company of Young Canadians.

If any of these attempts are based on a nineteenth-century sentimental-charity approach to socio-economic problems, instead of on rationality and justice, then it is unlikely that governments will be able to sustain the pressures on them to adapt to changing demands. One peril in Canada is cultural lag, but an offsetting factor is the realism and humanity of Canadians in general. Canada is being rushed rapidly into the post-industrial society, where knowledge and information are the keys to growth and development. Because of the late start the country got in community development, the nation has an excellent chance of training people to handle the stresses of change in both a scientific and humanistic manner. People can be quickly trained to understand the dimensions of a problem, and to deal with it. What is needed is not reliance on community development as a simplistic technique, but an understanding of the complexity of 'internal' and 'external' worlds. The concept of self-help must be complemented with the idea of enabling other individuals and groups to develop their potential. The concept of co-ordination must not be used to enforce ant-like conformity. In Canada a life-style can emerge in which individuals can come together to form groups to undertake projects and programs that benefit everyone in the groups, and others with whom they come in contact. What seems to be emerging in Canada is a new sort of society that can avoid the extremes of selfish individualism and of conformity. Such an approach could link personal, individual development with the development of a national community. Canada, as a 'middle power', could feed out the results of the Canadian experience in socio-economic development to all nations caught between the stable past and the uncertain future. This will demand honesty and openness, the use of science and a concern for humanity, that seems, on reflection, very Canadian.

FOOTNOTES

1. I have discussed community development elsewhere: 'Is Community Development Necessary?', *Anthropologica*, N.S. IX (2), 1967; 'Community Development and Urban Research', *The Lower Town Project*, Canadian Research Centre for Anthropology, Ottawa, 1969; 'Whither Community Development in Canada', *Community Development Journal* 4 (2), 1969; 'The Community Developer: Outsider in the Middle', *International Review of Community Development*, N.S. 21-2, 1969; 'Training in Community Development', *Journal of the Community Development Society*, 1 (1), 1970. These papers, together with additional material, will be compiled into a book for submission for publication under the title *The Process is the Product*.

2. See *The Journal of the Community Development Society*, published by the Society.

3. See, for example, *Canadian Urban and Regional Research: To Do It and To Use It*, Canadian Council on Urban and Regional Research, July 1970.

4. "Stinging personal attacks chill meeting on Social Change", *The Globe and Mail*, October 31, 1970.

JIM LOTZ is a staff member of the Coady International Institute, Antigonish, Nova Scotia. Until September 1971 he was Associate Director, Canadian Research Centre for Anthropology, and Research Professor in Community Development, at Saint Paul University, Ottawa. He graduated with a B.A. in geography from Manchester University in 1952, and spent a year as a trader in West Africa before coming to Canada in 1954. He served with several Arctic expeditions, and joined the (then) Department of Northern Affairs and National Resources in 1960, working first as a Community Planning Officer, then as a Northern Research Officer. In 1966 he joined the Canadian Research Centre for Anthropology as Research Director. He is the author of numerous articles and papers on the North and community development, and of the book *Northern Realities: The Future of Northern Development in Canada* (1970).

Adult Education, the Community, and the Animateur

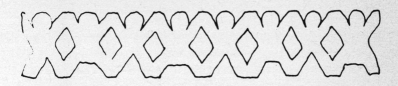

J. Roby Kidd

You should never wear your best trousers when you go out to fight for freedom and truth.

Ibsen

I believe in getting into hot water. It keeps you clean.

Chesterton

Introduction: Learning and Participation

During the 1960s many people, of all ages, began to use words such as 'engagement' or 'involvement', and talk about concepts under some label such as 'participative democracy'. Some were self-styled activists and social revolutionaries, some were politicians, and some were simply concerned citizens. It almost seemed as if these words had just been coined and these notions had just been discovered. Of course such concepts have always been an integral component of democracy. And the significance of these notions for adult education was understood long ago. Involvement, participation: this is no new idea for adult education; it has been an accepted and fundamental principle for at least four decades. In adult education the community has been the setting, not the individual classroom, nor the institution. Adult educationists may have failed often in expressing the notion in practice, but they neither ignored nor misunderstood the values. And many adult educationists have felt constrained to act in their private roles as citizens as well as in their professional roles as social-change agents.

To be a participant in community life and action was the boast of every Athenian' citizen. It was his privilege, and his honour compelled him to exercise it. Participation enlarged him, made him more of a man, added to his dignity. The man who refused this opportunity missed what was precious in his life. This view is reminiscent of the retort of King Henry V of England, spoken to a laggard earl who arrived after a hard-fought battle had been won: 'Hang thyself, bold Crillon. We were at Arques, and you were not there.'

Can participation in community politics, or housing, or planning, or rent control, or rat control, be likened to the activities of the Athenian citizens? They can and they are. Not all community action is glorious or even exciting. Some of it is frustrating, wearying, corrosive.

On the larger side of it, neither the community nor the state will flourish if citizen action is weak and irregular. There are mounds of evidence from all over the world to support this contention. The reverse is also true. No city has recovered from the onset of urban blight until a group of citizens has called a halt and said: 'We care about our community. We are concerned about its future and we will stand and work and fight for its honour.' This is the lesson of Athens, and Coventry, and Oslo. Money and talent are needed, of course, but first there have always been citizens who cared.

Of course the cynics deride these notions: 'You can't beat city hall,' they say. 'If you can't beat them, join them.' 'Things aren't so bad for us, so why worry.' 'The people who are living in bad housing would soon make a pig-sty out of good housing if you gave it to them.' They also say, 'What the community really needs are smart operators, not do-gooders.'

The cynics can supply considerable supporting data and they make it sound convincing. Their claims must be examined and their charges refuted. Part of the task of the involved citizen is to evaluate community progress, honestly and rigorously, and subject the claims of the cynics and reformers alike to honest scrutiny.

But our primary concern, in this paper, is not with social action but with learning. Is learning closely and directly related to participation?

I have believed for many years that no one learns anything

well without involvement. I am convinced that when someone has learned something well he ought to express that learning in action. From personal experience I know that learning of depth and power occurs when one takes part in significant action and reflects, studies, analyses, observes one's own behaviour and that of others engaged in action. I even see temporary withdrawal from action to seek quiet and reflection, which is the contribution of Asian scholars in particular, as part of a total process of engagement, not of disengagement.

It is a cardinal principle that citizens of a community ought to have the opportunity, and perhaps the obligation, to give something back to that community, through responsible community involvement. I know that such service will enlarge them as persons and is one cure for the alienation, boredom, and corrosive loneliness which is the sad lot of so many.

I assert these principles; I shall not try to offer proof. But these are not simple matters. And when I hear some of the clichés about community action, about change, about citizen involvement, frankly I shudder. It is an achievement when statesmen, as well as humble men, speak approvingly about the principle of participative democracy. But they and we may tumble into folly unless we know how to express such principles in appropriate action.

Since these principles are ours in adult education (although we don't own them), we have a special obligation to contribute to clarification and rationality, as well as enthusiasm and motivation.

For example, we need to be clear about the primary goals. Is the involvement to lead to some kind of improved community as well as enlarged human beings? Or is involvement itself the goal? Much current talk suggests that participation is itself a desirable end, a kind of therapy. If that is literally true, then all we need to do is organize more bingos, more horse races, more 'love-ins', more protest marches, and strikes. In all of these, the amount of involvement is considerable. But it is conceivable that, at the conclusion of such engagements, no single practice and not one person in the community will have altered in any significant way. Involvement, engagement, participation, these are not goals; they are all means.

By the way, the same question may be asked about change, or progress. It is popular now to speak of change, all change, as being both inevitable and desirable. Not so. Some changes are to be resisted like the plague. More crude and evil things have been wrought in the sacred name of progress than any man can count.

The Issues

In my opinion, we are wasting valuable time and breath in talking endlessly about and debating some worn or false issues. The question to be asked is not really, 'Will we do something?' but 'How will we do something?' or when, or where. Let me illustrate with five kinds of issues on which we will need to straighten out our thinking:

1. Not, *should we participate?* but, *how will we participate?*
2. Not, *is our commitment to change?* but, *to what kinds of change?*
3. Not, *are we motivated for change?* but, *what is the kind and quality of motivation?* I am assuming that most of us have some commitment to the improvement of our communities. I also think it likely that our motives are somewhat mixed and that personal needs and wishes are intertwined with social goals. A mixture of motives can be a source of strength, but it can also confuse or corrupt. How much of our drive is an effort to buy off our own consciences? Or to obtain a better job or more pay, or to demonstrate our intellectual or moral superiority, or to achieve fame, or simply to practise the kinds of skills that we are good at?

Recently a boy playing in the baseball Little Leagues was asked about a game, and he replied, 'It was a great game until the third inning when we never got to bat because some of the fathers got into a fight.' Some parents and coaches take part in the sports activities of their children because of their own emotional needs and vanities. Any social reformer, young or old, may engage because he is determined to prove something, perhaps prove something to himself. In community development we may need to be gentle and understanding about the motives of others, yet clear-headed and critical about our own motives.

4. Not, *will we work with community forces?* but, *how will we co-operate?* I am assuming that if we plan to work in a community we will understand that this means co-operating with many or most of the elements in a community. Not everyone has been prepared to do this. Some reformers in the past have

stubbornly refused to work with other citizens, with 'bad people', people in another church, or a different social-economic class, or age group, or with someone like a bartender, or a newspaperman, or a politician, or a representative of the 'Establishment', because in this association they might become contaminated. There are cases in the present where reformers have refused to work with churches, or social agencies, or the Y.M.C.A., or unions, or corporations, or governments, presumably because they might become corrupted. But such behaviour is the denial of community. Of course we may be betrayed or corrupted, by our own hungers or angers or ambitions, or by others'. But, if we are too fearful about our own integrity to work with others in the community, perhaps we should take up some vocation such as lighthouse-keeper. Anyone who is apprehensive that his clothing may be stained by the dirt of compromise, or by the colour of another's ideas, ought really to stay at home.

5. Not, *will we use special tactics such as confrontation?* but, *what tactics are best suited to our goal?* There are fads in tactics as there are in dress, or living-styles, or educational techniques. Not so long ago some people attempted to pursue all learning objectives in the same 'tried-and-true' method, the lecture. Even if the goal were to learn to give a speech, or to counsel, or to administer a program, they tried to learn through being lectured about speaking or counselling or administering. I remember one year when every single conference, no matter what the purpose or under what auspices, had 'buzz groups' all over the place. It became so prevalent that one minister asked: 'Can you imagine Moses or Jesus having a 'brainstorming' session to pound out the Ten Commandments or to decide what miracle should be performed?'

For a year or two the labour unions employed exclusively the sit-down strike as a tactic. Now various kinds of confrontation tactics are in vogue for individual change and growth and also to achieve social change. For some of these purposes, protests and confrontation tactics seem to have been effective, and we may have much to learn from people who use them well. However, some of those with little experience or imagination, or those who are proud of their skill with such tactics, tend to employ them on all occasions, whether suitable or not. Tolstoy wrote of the man who 'never chooses an opinion, he just wears whatever happens to be in style'.

There is a wide range of methods and tactics suited to different conditions and objects. By using some tactics one can win a battle but lose a war. It's easy sometimes to gain a particular goal but in so doing forfeit the confidence and trust of one's associates or make implacable foes of one's opponents. Our present knowledge of the tactics of social change may be almost as primitive as the 'bloodletting' stage of medical science. But we should employ all that we know, not practise accommodation, or confrontation, just because we like it, or are good at it, or because it is in style, or we have neglected to consider any alternatives.

Responses That May Be Expected from Others

Recently a Canadian sociologist listed six forms of response to our present opportunities and predicaments:

1. Some are not involved – they are *opting out*. Much attention has been given to some young people who have chosen not to participate. But many others opt out: for example, those men and women who choose to live with and for alcohol rather than live with and for a community. It is a melancholy fact that more than 100,000 men and women have chosen to opt out in this way in Ontario.

2. Some are *copping out*. These are the people who snatch an unfair advantage from the situation, the criminals who steal, and their smarter brothers who perform sharp practices to enrich themselves at the expense of others, yet manage to do so without breaking the law or at least without getting caught. No one knows their number, but the total, whatever it is, is much too high.

3. Some are on a free *escalator ride*. They 'go along', take free advantage of all the opportunities in the economy and society, the good luck that every Canadian possesses to live in such a privileged society, the results of the planning and hard labours of others, and never deign to give anything back. Alas, these too seem to be legion.

4. Some, a few, want to bring about swift, radical change, and hope to do it by confrontation, protest, and abrasive 'wearing-away' tactics. These people are much in the news these days. They feel themselves a part of society or the community but are angry at its injustices and imperfections and are determined to

transform it. They engage, but only on their own terms, and often tend to be derisive of others.

5. Some, likewise a few, are alienated from society but from time to time do engage in responsible ways to improve the community. They choose certain causes and turn their backs on others. There are similarities between the last two categories, but their values and goals may be quite different.

6. Another minority are *system smashers*. Some of them seem to have no defined goals, but enjoy, and seem to obtain some personal gratification from, destruction. Others do have goals, which they believe will only be accomplished by first effectively destroying the community. Some are romantics; they assume that good always blooms if an evil is destroyed, failing to read history and note that the outcome may be a greater evil.

People who seem to be the antithesis of the 'system smashers' contribute to the same effect. These are purists who will do nothing, and counsel that nothing be done, until the motives of all of us and our behaviour to each other and our schools and communities are decontaminated. They often talk against any form of international development. This kind of self-righteousness also ends in nihilism.

Is there a seventh category? Are there significant numbers of people who will deeply engage, who have thoughts about, perhaps have agonized about their goals, who will pay the price of learning effective methods, and who have developed a morality and an ethic about change? I believe that there is this seventh corps, and it is they with whom we should ally ourselves.

Just as it seems possible to identify seven distinct classes of people in relation to their involvement or participation, it is also possible to show the position of people on a continuum that runs from one extreme position, where education is valued but involvement is negated, to the opposite extreme position where action-involvement is valued but education-learning is negated.

1. There are still those in education who would like to live in a comfortable tower of ivory or plastic, where they would study, contemplate, save their own souls, become men of wisdom and refinement, but take no part in the uncomfortable, dirty world about them. The famous sociologist Park was not one of them, but he is often quoted as speaking for them. One day a young student, at Park's suggestion, had gone out to see the slums of Chicago. Frightened and angered by what he found, he re-

turned to the university and demanded: 'Professor Park, Professor Park, what are you going to do about the slums?' The Professor puffed on his pipe and replied calmly: 'Not one damned thing, except study them.' Many who take seriously this extreme position of 'detachment' do not even bother to study phenomena where real people live and die; their research is more remote and refined. Some educationists have attempted to study the community at a safe distance, through statistics and models, uncontaminated by blood and sweat. In recent years, their number may have declined, and it will be interesting to see how many will survive present happenings inside university halls.

2. There are many educational programs from which, it is planned or it is hoped, community action will follow. Such programs are designed as educational experiences that are intended to lead on to action. One familiar example of this was 'National Farm Radio Forum'; another is the study groups in co-operative housing projects, which typically are conducted for a full twelve-month period in advance of building any houses.

3. A third approach is the insertion of an educational component into a larger plan. For example, efforts are now being made to introduce education and citizenship participation into the Metropolitan Toronto Waterfront Plan. It is now understood in social-economic projects in developing countries that no scheme of irrigation, or improved agriculture, or new industry, will have much impact unless, along with the new technology, there is an effective educational-training program.

4. A fourth approach is community action that is not designed for, but it is hoped may lead to, education as a by-product. In the forties most of the block-development projects in American cities featured efforts to destroy rats, or to build small play-areas for children, but the hope was that with the achievement of a small success, people would thereupon study together how to deal with other community problems.

5. There are cases of community action where education is neither intended nor rejected; it is simply not considered relevant. Most of the activities of private land-developers fall into this category.

6. Examples can also be found of community or individual actions that are anti-educational, planned and carried out by people who claim that the community is so evil that it should

be destroyed and that any outcome will be an improvement.

In presenting these approaches on a continuum I have tried to do so without ascribing blame or value. Nevertheless, you will hardly be surprised at my own emphasis upon the need for a combination of education and action. Education without action can be sterile and, in the deepest sense, irresponsible. But so can action without education. I sympathize with those who find progress agonizingly slow and want to act quickly. But whose need are they responding to: their own frustrations, or the people whom they claim to be serving? Action without education can be destructive and tyrannical.

What Can We Learn from Earlier Experience?

Assuming that we can learn from the experience of others, there is much for us to study about community action and involvement. Some examples come from abroad, particularly from Scandinavian countries, or post-revolutionary societies, such as those in Russia, China, and Cuba. The involvement of men and women in their factory and community life in Russia or on the communal farms of China offers a fascinating study and is not without meaning for us. But if you are sceptical of anything beyond your own continent, there is still much to consider at home.

Most of us have forgotten the variety and extent of community organization and action during the depression and war years. During two brief decades, settlement houses where middle-class social workers had moved in to offer help to the poor were changing into community centres based on substantial citizen participation; urban block-plans were being devised to give crowded, yet isolated, alienated people some face-to-face association with which to identify; the notion of the community educationist or *animateur* was being developed; vast recreation programs were being operated by community people without a single professional in view; hundreds of thousands of people began to learn participation in unions; politics in Alberta and Saskatchewan were based on active local units; and there were scores of neighbourhood self-help movements of which the Saul Alinsky program in Chicago was the best publicized.

These are activities and movements rich in suggestion and

also in warning. They can and, in my view, should be studied for concepts and for insights. In these case studies we can learn about power, and how it must be used if change is to come, and also how it can and 'did corrupt. We can see how the cynical can destroy all they touch, and how the foolish, ignorant optimists, heedless of risks, can fail themselves and drag down others by their failure.

These stories can encourage us about the power of people, when aroused and educated, to do something about their environment and their lives. But we can also find examples repeatedly where notions based on false or over-simplified assumptions soon peter out. Most people can be helped to eliminate some obvious blight such as rats. But the assumption that people who banded together to destroy rats could easily organize to eradicate poverty or eliminate boredom has been tried and found inadequate scores and scores of times. Yet this is precisely the kind of romantic notion held by many today who prate about community involvement. Some social ills are not easily overcome; they may need months and years of patient, united effort. They are not dissolved by magic, or enthusiasm, or the power of positive thinking, or the involvement for a few weeks in summer by young students.

These decades and these events have never been fully analysed or chronicled. But much information is available. And those who go about repeating the same elementary blunders and insist on reinventing the wheel every decade deserve neither our patience nor our sympathy.

Is There an Ethic about Community Involvement? Yes!

Those who decide that communities must be changed or that you or I must be changed have a serious ethical problem to face. For myself, I have found it a useful test of a person's sincerity to ask him if he has ever considered his ethical responsibility for change.

When I was growing up it was still quite common to be stopped by a stranger and asked 'Are you saved?' And then to be exhorted to give up my sins and accept one form of religious expression or another. Now we have even larger numbers of self-appointed evangelists who insist on our reading their tiresome polemics, or attending their boring plays, or buying their magic products, or endorsing their slogans, or living in their planned, stultifying communities, or baring our souls in groups for their cleansing. The new salvationists are no less arrogant, no less self-righteous, no less contemptuous of my right and power and responsibility for self-development than the old. This is equally true of many who are determined to improve our communities. They remind me a little of that old comedian, Fred Allen, playing Santa Claus to a little girl who refused his gift of a doll, shrieking at her, 'You take this doll, see! You like this doll, see!'

We could tell each other many stories of community action that failed through the lack of an ethic.

On the whole I am an admirer of Saul Alinsky and have been since I first visited his work more than twenty years ago. But I deeply distrust some of his methods, at least those he practised in the earlier years. The famous 'back-of-the-yards' movement in Chicago in the early forties was an excellent example of how people can be encouraged and trained to solve some of their economic and social problems. But that campaign, lacking any deep ethical foundation, has had one truly dreadful consequence. The 'poor white' immigrant families back-of-the-yards were encouraged to develop goals and adopt touch tactics limited to their own individual and group advantage. Subsequently many of them have been the most bitter determined opponents of other people, like the blacks, having any rights or obtaining he means to decent living to the area. Not only have they denied human dignity and opportunity to others, they themselves have coarsened and sickened for lack of broad human objectives.

Action without thought may not be nearly so dangerous as action without morality.

Is There a Strategy for Community Development?

I think there is. It is not yet an art, it is far from being a science, but a strategy is emerging. First comes the recognition that adult education is not walled in by the classroom or the institution; it occurs all over the community, and not always among groups. There is also a recognition that the adult educationists have, and should collaborate with, many allies – teachers, librarians, recreation specialists, broadcasters, unions and management, civic government, and ethnic and other groups.

The agent of the strategy has often been described, using a mindless and misleading analogy, as a *community catalyst*. This suggests that the agent is not a man at all but some kind of impersonal force, and that in the process of community action he is unchanged and unchanging, bearing no ethical responsibility for what happens. If we continue to use words that are so misleading, it is little wonder that we behave badly.

A much more appropriate term has come from the French – *animateur*, or *animateur sociale*, or if you must, *social animator*. There is no final or precise agreement about the role of the *animateur*, but some of the elements in his work can be perceived:

1. He stimulates people to think about, and develop the will to take part in, their own personal development and community improvement.
2. He supplies information about methods and helps develop skills of community education and community action.
3. He assists people to discover and develop qualities of leadership in themselves and in each other.
4. He helps people assess and develop standards of value and judgment about their own growth and about community change.

The *animateur* is concerned about change and realizes that any change may be blocked by those who benefit most from the *status quo*, by prevailing value systems, by what is loosely called the power structure of a community, and even by some community institutions. He tries to understand and work with community forces as well as individuals. His emphasis is on attitude change, the development of trust and self-confidence.

He does not undertake his role as a mercenary or as an adventurer seeking escape or amusement or power. The *animateur* possesses social skills, but they are not for parlour games. And his involvement is not an exercise in personal therapy. Notice how close all of these elements are to the role of any good teacher.

Where does one learn to be an *animateur*? The writing on the subject is increasing both in volume and in depth. Much of it is coming from our colleagues in French Africa and French Canada, men such as Michel Blondin. You will remember that one famous fictional character suddenly realized that he had been writing prose all his life. Alan Thomas once said that he had suddenly realized that he was an existentialist. Perhaps most of us have perceived or will perceive that we are all *animateurs*. Unless, of course, you operate like Clarence Darrow, who once said: 'I'm a friend of the working man and I'd rather be his friend than be one.'

What Are the Main Obstacles to Change?

1. Assuming that we are clear about the changes we wish to achieve (and this is a large step that is often lacking), who are the people who can be expected to oppose the change? Are they people whose jobs are threatened or who may perceive that they are threatened directly by the change? If so, resistance will be stubborn. Are they people whose values may be displaced by the change? Does their present ideology stand against your proposal? Or is the opposition simply a kind of apathy, of people leaning against change not so much from conviction, but because the present they know seems more comfortable? The tactics that you will employ with these three general classes of oppositionists will, of course, be very different. Many campaigns seem to fail because no account has been taken of what motivates the opposition and therefore how it may be remotivated.

2. There may be formidable blocks or barriers to change in the kinds of administrative arrangements or legal sanctions that prevail. For example, it is now obvious to most individuals who have thought about the problem, that fixed retirement plans at sixty or sixty-five are extremely unsatisfactory for many people, and result in a waste of priceless talent and experience. Much greater flexibility concerning retirement should prevail. Unfortunately, the fixed plans have become enshrined in legal ordinances, in hiring practices of many groups, in union contracts, in pension plans of all kinds. Accordingly any move towards greater flexibility lags far behind the development of understanding of what would be reasonable.

3. There may need to be changes in the law. This is often the case with proposals for community improvement and housing, sometimes in proposals for amending training requirements for jobs.

4. The change may cost considerable sums of money. You will need to make a realistic assessment of the financial resources

and the financial outlay involved. For example, if everyone were to give up cigarette-smoking because of danger to health, what would this mean for tobacco growers, or cigarette manufacturers, or advertisers, etc.? If reformers do not face such questions squarely, they can always expect resistance from those who are obliged to face them.

5. The whole social situation requiring change may be exceedingly complex and the very complexity may constitute the chief barrier. Where do you start? For example, if you wish to do something about alcoholics in your community, do you begin with a drying-out clinic in the hospital? Or educating the doctors and nurses about alcoholism? Or in counselling with the family, or counselling with the employer, or with the courts, or with A.A., or with all of these? Because no single change will, by itself, contribute very much to the solution of this complex social problem.

Ignoring the people increases the risk of loss of alternatives. Often they know most, have the clearest ideas of what can and should be done about a problem.

6. When, where, and how do you involve the people who are disadvantaged, or who may be helped or hindered by the change, in the process of study and decision-making? When Father Jimmy Tompkins was assisting the miners of Cape Breton to build their own homes, he engaged them in a study of housing and community life for an entire year. Does it take twelve months to learn how to buy lumber or drive nails? Of course not. But it takes time to reach agreement about goals, to learn about each other, to learn to trust each other, to attain confidence about our ability to push forward. Many programs of change ignore the people who must choose to change, and the initiators are upset because the people seem apathetic, or stupid, or stubborn. People who are ignored tend to act like a man who received a book mailed to him to improve his mind. He sent it back to the publisher with the note: 'I didn't order this book. If I did, you didn't send it. If you sent it, I didn't get it. If I got it, I paid for it. If I didn't, I won't.'

Who Are Our Allies?

1. What kinds of people now support our proposal or would be led by their needs or values to support it if they understood

what is involved? Can these allies be reached and their support obtained? Is it a case where little or nothing can be done unless some group members will themselves take some action? For many years it has been clear that no permanent solution to the problems of the Canadian Indian are possible until he becomes confident enough to stand up for his own rights. What organizations and what kind of leadership may be needed? Is some training of key personnel required?

2. What changes that have been occurring in law enforcement or in people's expectations or in the new resources that are now available favour your proposal? Has the 'time' for it arrived? Does the emotional climate support the change?

Designing the Plan

Now that we have listed some of the factors of resistance and the factors favouring change, it may be possible to begin to put together the plan.

I am sure that most of us will understand that 'who plans?' is a crucial question. As I noted above, the engagement of many people in making the plan may be the most important step in the whole process. This is not easy, and we need not fall into traps of naiveté or sentimentality. Obtaining the necessary widespread involvement and consensus in various stages of the planning is no substitute for hard strategic thinking by those in a position to think. A conglomerate of people is no more likely to draft an intricate design for social change than a conference can design a functional, beautiful building, or a committee can write a poem.

You will need to obtain general agreement about goals and policies, but you will also need small groups (sometimes, perhaps, a group of one) of people technically qualified for specific tasks such as:

1. Estimating the inputs in the plan both in dollars and human energy.
2. Studying the probable changes needed in the law or in administrative arrangements.
3. Examining the kinds of leadership that may be needed and proposing forms of leadership training.
4. Estimating realistic time-budgets for the preparation of the plan, obtaining commitment, taking action, and the various follow-up stages.

Any specific plans thus proposed should be based on the needs and interests agreed upon by the larger groups of participants, and be discussed, amended, and adopted by them. Success will depend on commitment, of course, but also on how rational and realistic the plan, including the time dimension, is.

Testing the Plan

It is excellent practice, of course, to test out all factors and action steps, at least in your mind. Later it may be possible to test simulated models of community action by computer.

You may wish to scrutinize in some depth some cases from the past. One example, which I myself have drawn on often for illustrative purposes, occurred during and after World War II. In the days after Pearl Harbour, when Japanese naval craft sailed close to the shores of British Columbia, some fearful or bigoted people became excited about the loyalty of Japanese Canadians living in B.C. Accordingly, thousands of Canadian citizens were rounded up, dispossessed of their homes and businesses and relocated, first in camps in the interior of B.C., and then in many parts of Canada. The story of this shameful episode and the eventual success of those who banded together to end the outrage is fascinating and full of incidents and practices useful as a case for study. Some of the steps then taken were to organize different kinds of groups for pressure and action, obtain commitment to continue the struggle until all the major aims were achieved, obtain involvement of the victims (the Japanese Canadians), engage in many forms of publicity and propaganda, lobby in Parliament, win changes in the law, collect funds for the costs of court cases, and so forth. No single step, by itself, accomplished much, but the total campaign did.

One can obtain excellent guides for assessing plans and strategies by examining actual cases. Of course, every new plan of social change must be, as they say, 'tailor-made', based on specific needs, particular people, and unique events.

Excess Baggage

Christopher Morley once said, 'The enemies of change are always the very nicest people.' Nice people, who are comfortable, are not found too often in the vanguard working for change. Yet, in addition to having problems with conservatives and reactionaries, the *animateur* also has problems with people who claim they are change-oriented. He may even have problems with himself, or with some of the rest of us. Note some of our attributes:

1. *Naiveté.* Some change-makers seem to feel that good intentions are enough. They do not seem to realize that some efforts not only fail, but backfire, and that failure in the early stages of a project may make it twice, or many times, as difficult to succeed next time. By their well-intentioned clumsiness, they create difficulties for everyone else. Of course, no one will accomplish very much if he waits until conditions are perfect; they rarely are. Most efforts to change involve a calculated risk, and some degree of failure will be experienced by anyone who tries often. But the risks ought to be calculated, not be the result of ignorance or sloth or stupidity. Moreover, many who have failed to estimate the risks often seem unprepared to cope with failure; they give up easily, or quit too soon, or turn and flee.

Communist strategists consider that those who fail have not just failed, but have made blunders in planning. If the error damages future operations, the unsuccessful are considered immoral as well as failures. We need not accept Communist strategy or values, but we may be able to learn from anyone the value of preparation and realistic assessment. For example, it will be instructive to assess the record of such innovations as the Company of Young Canadians or Rochdale College in Toronto. These projects were excellent in terms of their goals, but ran into serious difficulties. What has been the impact of these efforts on subsequent efforts?

Of course, you may argue that if we always knew the difficulties we might rarely begin a project. Someone has said, 'There are two kinds of people, those who want to get things done, and those who want to be right.' And the great successes, it is alleged, are often won by those who are oblivious of the dangers they court. In World War I the Canadian Army stormed and took Vimy Ridge after the English, Australians, and French had all failed. It was said that the reason for the Canadian triumph was that no one had told the Canadian troops that the ridge could not be taken. There may be something in the general argument that confidence is a key to change. Yet, if risks must be run, it seems certain that they will most often be surmounted by those who know the chances and consequences, not those who may seem to be shielded by their ignorance.

2 *Self-righteousness.* The badge of many reformers is a 'holier-than-thou' stance. Self-righteousness is their favourite apparel. H. L. Mencken used to mock the church as 'a place where gentlemen who had never been to heaven brag about it to persons who will never go there'. Yet today self-righteousness seems much more prevalent outside the church than inside. Nothing becomes us so ill, and nothing so irritates others, as moral condescension. It makes us smug and contemptuous of our friends. It makes us refuse to work with people we despise or denigrate. It dulls our perception of the problem, or the need for allies. It interferes with, or breaks communication with, others. It causes us to expect gratitude and to be hurt when thanks are not accorded. This is a kind of self-indulgence that afflicts us all through life, in middle age, but also in youth.

Realism in Tactics

We need not denigrate sound principles as a basis for sound action. And we can expect, and ought not to be upset, to be labelled idealists or 'do-gooders'. But we ought to be as practical and as realistic as is possible in the choice of tactics. It's not much good using an elephant gun when the enemy is a black fly or mosquito. We ought not to choose tactics that are unsuitable for the circumstances. Because of the falling birth-rate in France, certain measures were adopted to encourage conception of children. The same incentives were also applied directly to French colonial territories like Martinique and Guadeloupe where no encouragement is needed to increase the birth-rate. Thirty years ago in the United States, measures were adopted to improve life on the Indian reservations, and well-meaning people tried to make these same reforms operative in Alaska where there were no ghettos or reservations for anyone. By this attempt to be consistent and generous, a seriously retrograde step was nearly taken. At the end of World War II, some well-meaning Canadians kept saying that the Japanese had every right to go back to British Columbia and were determined to make them go back even though it was not in the best interests of all of them.

No Time Sense

A Texas millionaire once asked the President of Harvard University what it would cost to build a Harvard in Texas. The President replied, 'A hundred million dollars.' When the Texan took out his cheque book, the President added, 'And it will take a hundred years.' We don't have a century for change. But some kinds of change may take a generation, or at least a decade. Those who yell, 'We want it now,' have to be considered, but most of them don't know anything about the conditions for effective change, and many of them are not really interested. Those of us who believe in change have to learn what can be accomplished quickly and what cannot, and develop appropriate style and stamina. We are obliged to train for the hundred-yard dash and the six-mile run and the marathon, and understand the tactics for each, and value each.

Conversely, we need not expect security or continuity of present practices. We should heed the words of a college football coach who was given a lifetime contract. 'I guess it's all right,' he said. 'But I remember another coach with a lifetime contract. He had a bad year and the University President called him in, pronounced him dead, and fired him!'

All Action – No Plan

Some of us seem happy only when there is overt action, as long as we are moving, no matter in what direction. We are like the hockey player who, when the puck was shot into the crowd and was lost, shouted impatiently, 'To hell with the puck, let's get on with the game!' We forget that, in military parlance, one has not only to capture a position but to hold it, and to maintain good communications. Napoleon drove everything before him as far as Moscow and then lost his whole army. Likewise, single social goals can be won while the position and the entire campaign can be lost. In social action, arrangements must be made for developing commitment, for servicing the project when the advance has been won, for leadership training, for continuing renewal of the participants.

What we need not at all is the person who has no time sense or time plan, who gives up easily or refuses to work unless his special tactics are followed.

What We Do Need

There is much we can do without. But there is much that we need.

1. *Training in* animation sociale *or community development*. The time is past when the lucky adventurer or the well-meaning first-time operator can be put in charge of social-action projects. We no longer expect much success from raw recruits working on other problems. Please note that age is not a requirement. Many of the most successful *animateurs* have been young – but they have usually had both training and field experience, or have been prepared to obtain it. Why would we assume that in a process as complicated as community action there would be effective substitutes for experience and trained intelligence? Canada needs several programs of training for *animation sociale*. Some are required at the highest professional level, for those who will be responsible for large-scale and major campaigns, for teaching, and for research. Some should be at the level of the skilled practitioner, perhaps to be carried out in a community college along with appropriate field-work. Some should be provided for the hundreds of adult-education workers, social workers, and community workers who are already engaged in some form of *animation* but wish to improve their understanding and skill.

2. *Commitment.* I keep using the word 'commitment'. I do so because unless we achieve commitment, and deserve it, not much social change will result. First of all, it rarely develops in a mass meeting, or a large conference. It rarely or never develops from programs using the mass-media, although commitment can be strengthened and reinforced by utilizing the educational technologies. The usual source of commitment is in some intimate face-to-face group, a family, or with congenial staff associates, or workmates, or some close friends. People tend to commit themselves deeply under circumstances like those in which they will dare to make a dramatic break with their past or make a marked shift in attitude. If we are serious about social change, we must multiply the number of experiences in which commitment may occur. Trust is a necessary condition and you can't buy trust, you have to earn it.

3. *Timing.* For many important kinds of social change we must have a time plan that goes far beyond a single year and may last five, or ten. We must attract people who will work together

until success has been achieved, and obtain financial resources that can be renewed or will not run out long before the job is finished.

4. *Resources and Institutions.* I have suggested earlier that we need programs of training, given either in institutions already established, or in new institutions that we must create. We need also to find ways of involving people and of obtaining some form of co-operation for the entire duration of a social campaign. Financial resources on a scale many times greater than at present will be needed for research, training, evaluation, and the publishing of experience.

Conclusion

Recently a Catholic priest was telling me about a young man from northern Ontario who came to Toronto for work. While here he 'slipped from grace' and committed a certain kind of indiscretion which he duly reported at confession and received a fairly heavy penance. Later the young man lived for a while in Montreal and, alas, fell into the same error and once more confessed. This time he received a much lighter penance. Surprised at this he told the priest about what had happened in Toronto and asked him to explain. 'Oh,' said the priest smiling indulgently, 'what know they of sin in Toronto?'

Well, in Toronto and Ontario we know of many kinds of social sin and failure. We have reason to quote Thoreau: 'City life! Millions of people being lonely together.' Or Rousseau: 'As soon as any man says of the affairs of the community, what does it matter to me? the community may be given up for lost.'

In this paper I have reviewed some of the forms of response to both the illnesses and advances in the community. Both perils and mistakes, and the opportunities for engagement and involvement, have been mentioned. I have described what is the essential task of the *animateur*, admitted that we have no well-developed methods of training him, yet noted that all of us must play the role and that we must deserve, and learn to work with, colleagues, in the community.

Canada has begun to borrow from Scandinavia and New Zealand the idea and the office of the ombudsman, the man who is charged with protecting the citizen from being crushed by the state or by giant power-blocks. Every province may need

one, but even more important than a guardian and champion
of the private citizen is the existence of many persons who will
encourage and sustain people to build and renew communities
where all human beings can live in dignity and fulfilment.
That's what adult education is all about.

J. ROBY KIDD has worked on road gangs and taken part in many social-
and political-action projects. While he now holds a university profes-
sorship, most of his 'teaching' has been in trade-union, farm, ethnic,
and community groups, as well as in the West Indies and India.

From 1951 to 1961 when he was Director of the Canadian Association for Adult Education, that national agency was in the forefront in
helping the 'public' understand social issues; it was here that such
organizations as the Indian-Eskimo Association were initiated.

Dr. Kidd has been awarded several university degrees, and has giv-
en courses or lecture series at ten universities in almost as many countries. But his experience in community involvement came as a citizen.

He has studied community organization and group work professionally, but his observations are those of a practitioner who reflects,
not of a scientist who has followed rigorous procedures.

His writings include ten books, as well as pamphlets and study
reports. One of his books, *How Adults Learn*, has been translated and
published in four languages. His first book was a manual on day-
camping for city-bound children who had little that was constructive
to do during the summer months. He is editor of *Convergence*, the
international journal of adult education.

From 1966 to 1971 he was Chairman of the Department of Adult
Education at the Ontario Institute for Studies in Education. He is
presently professor of adult education at OISE.

Animation Sociale[1]

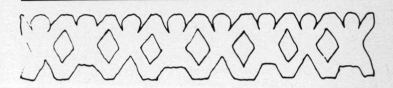

Michel Blondin

Methodology of Animation Sociale

Animation sociale concentrates its efforts on a group of persons who want to bring about changes in their environment. This group is composed of persons who are representative of the environment in that they are essentially similar, in their manner of life, in their values, and their mental outlook to the people of their area as a whole. It is not the job of the group to provide services, although one of its tasks is to see that the different bodies responsible, whether private or public, develop services that will adequately meet the needs of the community. But its essential task is to initiate the majority of the people of the district in participation.

This group, which most often is formed of inexperienced persons, goes through three phases.

Phase A:

First, communication must be established among all the persons in this group, providing for exchanges of views so that the broad outlines of the *common situation can be defined*. This is the starting-point for defining goals that will command universal support.

Phase B:

It is by basing our efforts on this common awareness that the *goals of the group* are set. The members will then support these goals and act to change the society in which they live. Each member of the group must rise above ideological differences and the usual interpersonal conflicts. In addition, there must be a desire to define these goals in relation to the needs and the values of the community to which they belong, where members of the group will act as a leaven.

Phase C:

Success in carrying out the common goals demands concerted action and the overcoming of the usual obstacles, which are: inadequation between the end and the means, desire for self-sufficiency, and reluctance to translate intentions into action.

The goals defined by the group are not achieved unless efforts are co-ordinated, tasks and responsibilities shared, and actions verified and controlled.

Animation sociale is, therefore, a technique of social intervention in a given society by a group that undertakes this task. Obviously, the process of *animation* gives rise to a process of self-education, the essence of which is a heightening of the capacity for self-determination.

This desire for self-determination through the introduction of a rational approach to action requires a willingness on the part of the government to plan, that is, to exercise control and introduce rationality into the socio-economic changes that are taking place, plus the desire to involve as many people as possible in the planning.

One of the fondest ambitions of *animation sociale* is to achieve self-determination in a group of people, so that it becomes autonomous, that is, freed from its besetting automatisms and determinisms. Autonomy means that ability to make decisions and choices freely and to take the consequences.

This brings us back to our goals, for there is no possibility of choice without access to decision, without machinery for participation.

Role of the Animateur

The instrument by which *animation sociale* is carried out is the *animateur social*. A few remarks about his various roles are in order here.

The animateur *as an agent of rationalization*

The *animateur* enables the group to reach a decision that is as
coherent and autonomous as possible. To do this, he subjects
the group to a discipline of thought and action based on strict
rationality and a desire for independence from the usual pressures, of whatever kind they may be.

The course of action followed by the group under the leadership of the *animateur* is as follows:

1. Analysis of the situation – description of all angles of a situation, including constraints, and understanding of its precise
   meaning;
2. Search for solutions – formulation of different alternatives
   for solutions, analysis and criticism of these approaches, and
   choice of one of them;
3. Carrying out of the action by identifying the tasks, their
   proper sequence, and the deadlines for each, deciding on a
   division of labour, and checking on performance of the
   tasks;
4. Supervision over the performance and over the proposed
   action taken;
5. Assessment of the results and thinking about the work as a
   whole from the angle of results achieved.

This first role of the *animateur* also includes training the
group in the basic techniques to be used by the committee:
agenda, minutes, sub-committees, duties of president and secretary, and so forth.

This work pattern, which the group assimilates gradually,
becomes the channel through which the autonomy of the group
and of the individuals who comprise it is built and developed.
Thus, the group's energy ceases to be destructive or unused
and becomes constructive and creative instead. The group is
then able to achieve real participation.

The animateur *as an agent of socialization*

The group owes its existence to the cohesion that is formed
among all the individuals who belong to it.

First it is necessary to foster the expression of a thinking that
is common to the group and shared by all members of the
group. The interaction that takes place among the members of
the group, and the exchanges of views by which it is achieved,
gradually lead the group to the formulation of a common out-

look based on a common perception of the situation and of the goals of the common action.

As cohesion is not solely a rational phenomenon, the *animateur* must make it easier for persons with differing sensitivities and emotional make-ups to get along together. Interaction among the individuals in a group is, of necessity, an emotive interaction. There is as great a need in any group for emotive cohesion as for rational cohesion.

Recent experiments have led to the discovery that a genuine action of social transformation can only become a reality when there is an intense group spirit. The group then becomes the test-bed for group participation and the emotional pattern for the other organs of group participation that must be set up.

It should, however, be clearly understood that such a group, far from being inward-looking, is open towards the neighbourhood and welcomes any other person who has the desire to join in the same task.

The animateur *as a channel of information*

The group cannot draw from within itself all the knowledge it needs. It must acquire a working knowledge of the techniques that it will have to use regularly to secure further information.

The *animateur* will first help the group to identify its information requirements in relation to its goals, and thus really develop its awareness.

He will then guide it to the sources of information (documents, experts, services) so that it can acquire the information it needs by itself.

He will then make sure that the group assimilates the information and derives the necessary benefit from it.

The animateur *an an instigator of participation*

Finally, the *animateur* must firmly believe in the objective he is seeking to achieve in his work, namely participation, and must identify all of the possible implications of it as he goes about his daily work. However obvious this may seem, it must be reiterated that the task of the *animateur* calls for great sincerity and consistency, demands it is impossible for many *animateurs* to meet. The *animateur* must at all times be consistent in his behaviour towards individuals and groups. He must be a firm believer in participation and must use every means, great or small, to further this end. If through small and apparently insignificant acts, the *animateur* betrays these attitudes, which means that he takes responsibilities for the group, it can be expected that genuine participation will not be engendered.

This is all the more imperative as the *animateur*, as a person, is usually strongly motivated towards a change in society that would accord to the underprivileged the place they have never occupied, for lack of means and resources. He is thus torn between the profound demands of his profession and his own motivation to act.

The Citizens' Committee

In its present form, the most visible element of social animation is the citizens' committee, a group of about twenty average persons from the district who are organized for action. The citizens' committee has several characteristics:

1. It is a group of militants who think about what they are, what their problems are, and what factors enter into those problems. This leads to a realization of their position in society. On the basis of this stock-taking, goals are set that will tend to encourage participation, the ultimate goal of their action. This requires that henceforth the attitudes and values that characterize this participation must be clarified and practised within their group, an instrument that they can forge in their own way.

2. This group of militants first sets itself the task of awakening the population of its district, i.e. of rousing it from its apathy and passivity, so that people will ask questions about the present situation, the source of awareness and of action. The citizens' committee refuses to become the spokesman of a population that is not changing. For the citizens' committee, the awakening of the neighbourhood population becomes the priority objective of its action.

3. It is hard for this awakening to take place without starting small actions which are the expression of the awareness of the militants, the means of achieving needs already felt by this population, the starting-point for a progressive awakening, for the desire to be active and effective, for assuming one's responsibilities and shaping one's future. Action based

on needs is the best way both to avoid embarking on meaningless ventures and to foster new attitudes of participation, taking care to verify whether what one perceives is really what other persons in the district feel. This probably explains why the problems related to children (schools, parks, etc.) and those related to housing are chosen first.

4. It is only after this that such activities as exerting pressure on the authorities, expressing the thinking of certain workers for public opinion, can have a meaning and an impact that are not in contradiction with the objectives pursued.

These four characteristics are not present, of course, to the same degree in all committees, but most of them tend in this direction, only deviating from it from time to time.

Why Has Animation Sociale Developed in Quebec?

So little is known about group phenomena that any answer to such a question is risky. Nevertheless, the matter is worth considering, because it may throw some light on the significance of *animation sociale*. It is all the more important to ask this question because there is very little *animation sociale* outside Quebec.

During the past five or six years, Quebec has been going through a period of soul-searching and self-examination, in a desire to develop its potentialities and gain control of its destiny. Thus Quebec is willing to face up collectively to the changes of every kind that are radically transforming it.

The present ferment in Quebec encourages pioneering and trailblazing in many areas of life. New ways are greeted with comparative tolerance, more especially as Quebec has now become a pluralistic society in terms of race, religion, and ideology. Everything is being challenged, re-examined and reassessed.

The Quebec government, for its part, has even set up machinery for consultation through bodies such as the Superior Councils on Education, the Family, and Labour. Whatever their shortcomings, these Councils and their extensions have nevertheless marked a first step towards the establishment of machinery for participation. It is even probable that consultation machinery may be set up at the regional level in a year or two by the Quebec Planning Board to prepare the way for public participation in major decisions by the population of the various regions.

The Commission on Welfare and Health (Castonguay Commission) launched an operation called *Comité d'Expression Populaire*, an opinion-gathering body. In this way the commissioners were able to sensitize themselves to the outlook and modes of living of twelve groups of low-income workers and social-welfare recipients, brought together for the occasion by the *animateurs*. The commissioners thus became aware of a radical questioning of everything by the very people who were most directly affected by these programs and who were usually the last to be consulted.

It is this climate of questioning, and the desire of the people to take their future into their own hands, that constitutes a favourable climate for activities like *animation sociale*.

Animation sociale in a rural environment originated with a government project, le Bureau d'Aménagement de l'Est du Québec, known in English as the Eastern Quebec Planning Bureau, whose funds came partly from the Agricultural Rehabilitation and Development Administration (ARDA) and partly from the Quebec government. A characteristic feature of the B.A.E.Q. was its desire to take the whole population into partnership with the experts in their planning operations, not only at the operative stage, but, more particularly, during the exploratory phase and in the setting of goals. These are essential phases with which the fate of these people is closely bound up.

Animation sociale can, therefore, develop in Quebec because a large part of the population and some technocrats and politicians are anxious to set up machinery for consultation and information, and because these people feel vaguely that participation in its fullest sense is necessary to a society in the process of being built.

About the same time, le Conseil des Oeuvres de Montréal made its first attempts at *animation sociale* in Montreal. It was no longer a question of a context of planning or of regional development, but of an attempt to find an answer to the disorganization that prevails among the working-class in the large urban centres.

During 1966 the Economic Advisory Council of Quebec, which is to become l'Office du Plan du Québec, a planning-board, set up a working party on *animation sociale* with the task of clarifying the vocabulary, exploring various related areas such as machinery for consultation and information, and making recommendations to the Quebec government.

What Is the Impact of Animation Sociale on the War on Poverty?

It is generally agreed now that the real significance of modern-day poverty is not only that a person is deprived of food, clothing, and decent housing, but, above all, that he is deprived of his fundamental right to be a citizen who is on a par with any other citizen. The poor man has no part in defining collective goals for our society. The poor man is the one who, in spite of appearances, is forgotten when it comes to making decisions. The poor man does not count in our society, and our society prefers it that way. The poor man is, and feels like, a second-class citizen, not so much because of his lower level of material comfort as because of his being left out of the decision-making process and the scant importance attached to his values and his view of the world. To put it briefly, in spite of all the transfer payments made to him, the poor man counts for very little in our society. One has only to observe who is the target of advertising.

Poverty is a victim of its invisibility. An evil that is so unapparent loses its impact on public opinion. *Animation sociale*, far from sweeping poverty under the rug, makes its presence conspicuous and more embarrassing, which is the first serious step towards its solution.

Animation sociale accords a large place to participation by the 'little people' of our society – the poor and the working-class people – because it seeks to give them back a real place in our society, to give them a share of power like any other social class.

Animation sociale thus becomes a basic weapon in the war on poverty, by placing in the hands of the poor some instruments for securing their advancement as a community.

What the *animateur social* knows, and what many others suspect, is that once these people, who comprise 30 to 40 per cent of the population of our towns and cities,[2] become participants, at that very moment all our institutions and all our structures – social, economic, and political – will have to be re-examined. To work from below, to build with those who are the cast-offs, means to rebuild, to re-invent our society, no longer to serve the interests of the well-off, but to serve the needs of the whole population, beginning with the less fortunate. And we are convinced that the choices that then would be made by the underprivileged would meet the aspirations of other social classes, because the things that are troubling our society are felt by more than one class, as they have so little to do with material comfort.

What Contribution Does Animation Sociale Make in the Face of the Urban Phenomenon? [3]

Our work in the underprivileged districts of Montreal brings us into daily contact with the major weaknesses of city life as it is found in Montreal. And Montreal is only one of many examples.

The city as we know it today is the product of unplanned actions and of decisions taken without reference to other decisions and with no overriding goals in view. This absence of coherent decision leads to social segregation (water-tight distribution of social classes by geographical areas); to an uneven distribution of community amenities (the less the residents have green area of their own, the less park space is provided for them; the oldest and worst-equipped schools are found in the run-down districts); to arbitrary action (working-class families are evicted more readily than middle-class families; and police behaviour differs from one district to another).

We live in urban concentrations, but the urban institutions (city council, municipal administration, taxation system, etc.) are decidedly ill-suited to our needs. We live in a new environment, and we rely on a system of values that is better suited to the needs of the beginning of this century than to 1968. This is how I see our desire for home ownership, for living in bungalows an hour's drive from work, for driving private automobiles in the downtown area. Although the malaise is felt by many, it is felt mainly by those who cannot afford the means to 'get away from it all' by living in the suburbs, taking long drives, and owning second homes in the country.

To deal with the present problems of urban living such as housing, genuine solutions are needed. These solutions will have to deal with the varied aspects of the problem. Accordingly, the philosophy on which the old solutions were based will be completely called into question. The new solutions will have to be based on other philosophies, including participation.

In a more general way, the necessity for control of urban

development will soon be admitted. Chaotic development such as we now have will be increasingly resented, and identified as one of the key situations that must be swiftly and radically changed because its effects are so disastrous.

The shortcomings of urban development will be increasingly felt, and the need will arise for new solutions to be devised. These solutions will have to meet other than purely economic and financial requirements. Urban development will have to provide an adequate answer to the various needs of all the urban population, regardless of social status, and at the same time provide for machinery making possible both citizen participation and the creation of flourishing community life.

Urban development will probably be the first level at which the general problems will be identified by the citizens' committees. It is likely that the problem of urban development will be felt and perceived at the same time by various specialists and various organizations. Combination of these efforts will make it possible to initiate projects for radical change.

In a more general way, various structures and institutions will be examined with reference to the criterion of participation and of a real community life. A review of these institutions will become an absolute necessity.

This questioning of the *status quo* will begin with challenge and defiance of arbitrary decisions, such as are made every day. In more and more communities, each decision will be examined in the light of two criteria: the needs of those people with whom we work, and the way in which the decisions are reached.

From this will emerge the need for rational forms of action that will give rise to planning activities, the only ones over which the population as a whole can exercise control. This planning will have to be on a participating basis or it will not take place.

Participation will be the essential characteristic that will make possible the re-invention of the urban institutions and structures. Only then will we live in a city whose institutions and structures are the result of the considered action of the whole population.

What Lessons Emerge from Results Already Obtained?[4]

The results obtained appear to the *animateurs sociaux* and to some other observers to centre around three themes: (1) fewer arbitrary decisions; (2) improvement of the district; and (3) development of leadership.

The first to react to the creation of the citizens' committees were the public-school and municipal authorities. They reacted to the birth of this movement with fear and tried to avoid head-on clashes by acceding to demands quickly. For this reason, we see that the public authorities are making fewer arbitrary decisions, for fear that they may be required by the citizens' committees to justify them. These same authorities, especially in the area of urban renewal, are endeavouring to improve information services and establish machinery for communication with certain citizens' committees.

Generally speaking, major improvements have been made in these districts as a result of pressure by committees such as the Education committee, working on such projects as construction of new schools, provision of pre-school classes, certain curriculum changes, and development of detection services; the Urban Renewal committee concerned about better rehousing services, improvement of information services, and reassessment of public housing, in terms of both rates and management; and the Facilities committee, which has been working on such projects as creation of parks and playgrounds, improvement of safety measures, more school-crossing guards, traffic lights, better road signs, and better maintenance of streets and parks.

But the most important results stem from the creation of local leadership, which is trying gradually to spread its influence through the district and transform it. These new leaders have begun to gain self-confidence and discover their strength, to experience the birth of a hope that gives them the strength to undertake great tasks. These same leaders are gradually developing their social consciousness and are becoming capable of understanding and interpreting many events whose ramifications extend far beyond their own district.

This brief description of some of the results obtained shows that improvements in amenities for these districts are easy to obtain, but the transformation of the inhabitants is a much slower and more difficult job. But some pioneering has been done and there is no telling what the effects of this will be.

What the response will be to the expectations of *animation sociale*, only the future will tell.

FOOTNOTES

1. This paper was originally prepared as background material to explain *animation sociale* for a tour of ten major Canadian cities by Michel Blondin late in 1968 at the request of Community Funds and Councils of Canada, an affiliate of the Canadian Council on Social Development (formerly the Canadian Welfare Council).

2. According to the Report of the Economic Council of Canada, 1968.

3. I have dealt with these questions at greater length elsewhere: Michel Blondin, 'Vie Urbaine et Animation Sociale', *Recherches Sociographiques*, Department of Sociology, Laval University, July 1968.

4. I have attempted a more detailed subjective analysis elsewhere: Michel Blondin, 'Quels changements apporte l'animation sociale?', *L'Animation*, Cahiers de l'institut canadien de l'education des adultes, Montreal, September 1967.

MICHEL BLONDIN is presently working in Latin America as a consultant in one of the few centres of research and experimentation in adult education on that continent: INDICEP (Instituto de Investigación Cultural para Educación Popular), linked with Radioemisoras Bolivia (Oruro, Bolivia).

In 1963 he was the first social animator to work in an urban setting in Canada. From the work of the team of social animators at the Social Development Council of Metropolitan Montreal (Conseil des Oeuvres de Montréal) which Michel Blondin directed, stemmed the citizens' committees and similar peoples' groups that exercised a considerable influence on a large number of similar experiments across Quebec and in Canada.

Michel Blondin has written a number of articles on social animation, a number of which have appeared in *Recherches Sociographiques, Convergence, Les Cahiers de l'Institut Canadien d'Education des Adultes, Bien-Etre Social Canadien*, etc. He has delivered many lectures on the same topic and in 1968 made a speaking tour that took him to the major cities of Canada.

In February 1970 he left his post with the Social Development Council of Montreal and spent some time studying at CIDOC (Centro Intercultural de Documentación, Cuernavaca, Mexico), before beginning his work in Bolivia.

The Innocence of Community Development

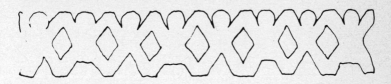

R. Alexander Sim

I

In the quarter-century since World War II ended, technological change, social revolution, and political upheaval have dominated the world scene. In this period, many types and varieties of actors and agents have been at work to hasten change or retard it; to promote disorder or maintain order. In the clash and chaos of the times, community development has been active in one form or another almost everywhere, in the ill-understood process of helping others to help themselves.[1] In spite of protestations, community development has been in most times and places on the side of the *status quo*, employed by the régime, domestic or foreign, that wielded the most power, willing to serve what seemed the best of all humanitarian means for unquestioned, often unknown, ends. By avoiding conflict, in most cases, and in almost all cases violence, it has been out of tune with the temper of the time, out of touch with its realities. Yet it has acted as an accessory to repressive forces, been all too willingly used as their plausible and well-seeming agent. Thus unwittingly, community development, by avoidance of basic issues, has helped to promote the ultimate chaos that follows delay and postponement of facing up to fundamental problems, and has contributed to the deluge that comes when redress is too niggardly, when justice arrives too late. If history notices what community development has done in this past quarter-century at all, its judgment will be harsh. Posterity will say it was innocent because it was too naive to understand the consequences of what it had done, or it was guilty because it did understand, but feared the consequences of acting boldly, lacked the necessary nerve to fly into the eye of the storm.

Since community development is involved in shaping events, we must look back and try to understand. The record of community development must be examined, its innocence weighed, not to judge the living or the dead, but to fit us to face the hard days ahead.

Our theme is innocence. Three types are applicable to the record of community development. In each case the intentions and accomplishments of those who undertake to help others, which is the presumed aim of community development, will be examined. Innocence must always be considered against a framework of legal assumptions and moral values. The assumptions about what should or should not change shift through time, but the action discussed here has to do with change itself! Values are a deposit of experience in time past, but action is in the present, a projection into the future. The action in which community development participates usually has to do with things, but the consequences are experienced by human beings. The things are objects, 'its', third-person items, but the human beings are 'thous', to use Buber's categories. The rhetoric of community development has been impeccable, its understanding of the complexity of what it purports to do, shallow.

There is the innocence of the child, of the archetypal child in the Garden of Eden who has not as yet eaten of the fruit from the Tree of Knowledge. There was, at one time, an era of real naivety, where one class or group believed it had the right and the wisdom to help others. If they acted with humility and a true sense of charity, one could be persuaded of their innocence, even though the consequence of their action is now seen as disastrous.

Then there is the innocence of that which is established by a jury of peers. Its counterpart is guilt as established by admissible evidence.

However, innocence is a quality that must be placed in a moral context. It cannot be considered alone; one must be innocent of something. Goodness cannot be imagined without the presence of evil, nor darkness without light.

Finally there is the innocence of the saint who, like Dostoevsky's Idiot, is so devoid of self-enhancing calculations as to be considered mad. This quality of innocence is child-like, but it has the component of knowledge that the child lacks. The ordinary man may do what is wrong because he lacks the courage or the creativity to do what he should. The saint knows what is right, and acts on this knowledge regardless of the law or popular morality. His innocence stems from his apparent disregard of the consequences. He may not earn his sainthood in his own lifetime, when he may be judged mad, ignored, or put to death. Late-ripening social wisdom judges him right. By then the shell of his thought has become a popular orthodoxy used as a whip on new 'truths'.

It is easy to postulate innocence because it is impossible to foresee the consequences of action. The inventor of the internal combusion engine is innocent (by this argument) of the death toll on highways, and the effects of the snowmobile on wild life. The extension of this argument has interesting consequences. The nineteenth-century missionary on the plains of North America is blameless for the spread of syphilis and alcoholism among Indians. The engineer who plans superhighways is blameless for the destruction of urban neighbourhoods. The economist helping to modernize agriculture in India has no responsibility for the resulting population explosion, the challenge to the authority of the cillage elders, or the known effects of herbicides on the ecology. As for the agronomist, someone might say: before Rachael Carson he was innocent, after Rachael Carson he was responsible for the consequences of his efforts, however small or ineffective, to modernize agriculture in that great country. But supposing he is working there today, but was too busy helping India to read to even hear of Rachael Carson. Or his professors refuted the ecological argument to his satisfaction. Or he believed it better to relieve hunger today by recommending the use of herbicides, even at the risk of injuring the descendants of those spared to procreate by his intervention. Or he was asked by his superiors not to question the policies of his own country which had sent him to India (danger pay included), or the policies of the Indian government, which presumably asked for his services.

Soon we are lost in a jungle of relevancies and irrelevancies; ultimately, if Eichmann and Calley were guilty, each individual must answer for his own behaviour no matter what collective guilt is shared by his professional colleagues, his countrymen, or the whole wide world.

II

Community development has been a movement and a technique. Yet it has been a movement in a limited time/space scale. In no sense can it be considered a social movement with spontaneous support of the masses. It has worked almost exclusively with Western democracies, and in their pay, directly or indirectly.

There has been no correspondence with China or Russia, so we cannot examine their methods of bringing about change at home and abroad. It has had no philosophical link with the powerful transnational movement, which is skeptical of all state enterprises, communist and capitalist. It was unprepared for the present attitude of revulsion towards the technological revolution represented by the various counter-cultural movements. It has opposed what it believed to be irrational values and tradition-founded structures. Thus it has explicitly supported actions that implicitly accepted urbanization and industrialization of regions that might otherwise have escaped the blight that is now evident in 'developed' regions.

As a movement it has been dedicated to orderly change, usually to the improvement of the living standards of the poor and disadvantaged. As a technique it has used what were believed to be humanistic methods of helping people to perceive their own needs and to discover the means of satisfying them. But the needs have been regularly the unstated assumptions of the national bureaucracies and larger corporations. Its emphasis has been on things (latrines and tractors), on relocation, on retraining, on getting people to accept objectives determined elsewhere yet put to them as a benefit, or a gain. In fact the changes have often destroyed community structures, disturbed familial and kinship bonds, and caused incalculable psychological damage to individuals.

The numerous definitions of community development all seem to stress the technique of community development, usually recognizing a linkage between locality and the state. The commonly accepted U.N. definition states boldly it is a 'process by which efforts of the people themselves are united with those of the government'. Others have been less explicit: Biddle sees it as a social methodology 'to encourage people to help themselves, utilizing the co-operation of many professional people and agencies' resources to urge people (even apathetic ones) to learn how to discover their own initiatives'. He goes on to say that agencies should learn 'to restrain themselves until their aid will strengthen peoples' responsibility to contribute to their own problem solving' (McEwen, 1968, pp 7-9).

What is implicit in Biddle, and in other definitions I have studied, is some kind of intervention from the outside, because community development never refers simply and wholly to the actions people take and always have taken at the local level. Even Biddle's rebuke to agencies 'to restrain themselves from helping' implies their impatience to get on with the job and suggests if they will only wait, the local people, even the apathetic ones, will take some initiative and ask for help.

The riddle in community development up to now has been not the timing of intervention, but the ethics of it. Today, unlike yesterday, we have rightly learned to suspect any means of 'getting' people to do something for their own good as the good is defined by someone else, whether it is offered by a church, a state, or a big cartel selling pesticides, or a public authority building a dam or pushing through a superhighway. A benign community-development worker employed by any of these does not make the means cleaner, regardless of his own personal caring. It has regularly been the practice for men and women to accept employment as community-development workers from agencies that did in fact have predetermined goals for communities and whole regions. They were thus placed in the ethically untenable position of helping people discover goals already on the drawing-boards of a distant bureaucracy. That these workers often helped to ameliorate the impact of the changes that were coming, that they often acted as advocates of the unfortunate victims of social and economic progress, does not soften our judgment of their innocence. Having eaten from the Tree of Knowledge, they must now toil in the vineyards east of Eden.

Community development, however defined, has been a change agent. Now that change is in question, so are its agents and their sponsors. The changes that have been proposed and effected have not proven their worth. Landscapes have been sullied and people have been destroyed. Decades after the concept of progress has lost its philosophical coherence and its moral force, technical assistance abroad and regional development at home are mounted and activated on the limited and outmoded indices of economic productivity.

Community development was a legitimate heir of philanthropy, adult education, and applied anthropology. It descended from settlement-house activity, latter-day colonial administration, and missionary work. Each in its own way identifies (if missionary work is taken as a prototype) two sorts of men, clean and unclean, we and they, the elect and the damned, the developed and undeveloped.

In the blander idiom of the day, we now speak of the advantaged and the disadvantaged. Whereas the clean and unclean dichotomy often served as synonymous for skin colour, the current one, of advantage or disadvantage, refers to differences of caloric intake, G.N.P., and extent of industrialization. It is peculiar inversion to find that the self-styled clean elect are now the dirty polluters, currently damned.

The missionaries, the settlement-workers, the colonial administrators are now being weighed in the balance of historic perspective. They seem now to have lent to, and to have provided, cover for forces that were unworthy of the ideals they expressed, that were incapable of achieving the ends they set – for others.

The thrust of the settlement house and its successors in the welfare state accepted poverty as an unfortunate given, and the poor as the objects to be changed, not the conditions that created their conditions. By the same token, those who have attempted to reform colonial administrations (whether in the great empires, or here in our own north, our urban slums and our Indian reserves) were applying cosmetics where surgery was needed. Their well-intentioned liberality simply distorted the prognosis, and delayed the inevitable changes. There is little evidence that community development has been allowed to attack, or wished to work at, fundamental problems.

The progenitors of community development are many and of diverse origin, but it is more a child of the industrial revolution than of the French upheaval of 1792, more akin to Yankee clockmakers than to Jefferson and Lincoln. As Europe emerged from feudalism, as cities grew, as the abuses of the factory system became evident, as knowledge of the brutalities of colonialism spread, there was a responding surge of humanitarian sentiment that had reform and gradual change as its theme. A steady stream of movements followed: the abolition of slavery, child-labour laws, prison reform, universal suffrage, and trade-unionism.[2]

There was a widely held assumption that as man, the superior creature, had evolved, so would the good life 'as freedom slowly broadens down from precedent to precedent'. Some battles were lost by the Luddites and Chartists, but their leaders were misguided. The imaginative proposals of the Rochdale pioneers provided space for idealistic experimentation without challenge to the major industries, without urging state intervention. The alternatives offered by Marx and Engels were accorded the limited freedoms of Hyde Park or the brutalities of Mussolini's castor oil, or Hitler's storm troopers. The prevailing mood of optimism was justified at the level of values by the mythology of rationalism. Science and technology would work together for good: if not for the good of all, for the good of the greatest number. Enlightening conservatism counted on polite turbulence to help the system correct its own mistakes and abuses.

If there is anything we have learned in the days of Black power, Red power, student power, and tenant power, it must be the hard facts of the hard times ahead for well-intentioned, or not-so-well-intentioned, workers and soldiers who want to help or save others. The distance may be shorter than it seems from Berkeley to Watts, from sunny California to Vietnam, from Gaspesia, Caughnawaga, and Prince Edward Island to every city's inner city: from persuasion to pacification.

In time it was only yesterday that North Americans discovered poverty and pollution, but ideologically it was an eon ago. With that charming innocence that Mark Twain and Walt Whitman saw in us so clearly we continue to send herbicides to India, turbines to Africa, humanistic psychology to the Netherlands, and square dancing to the West Indies. But is any thoughtful person serious about exporting technology and ideology any more? I doubt if the exporters are serious now; by no means can we say they are innocent. I suppose we keep on because we do not know how to stop. Yet we are exporting ideas and things that have failed here.

But as we face a crisis of values, it is doubtful if minor revisions in the theory and practice of changing others is enough. The problem organized religion has already faced awaits the helping and healing professions, which have accepted too unquestioningly superficial theories of pathology and deviance originating with the supposedly value-free behavioural scientists.

Organized systems of explanation function to organize our consciousness of self and our belief as to what is and what may come to be (Cassirer, 1944, Chap. I). These explanations are inevitably grounded on assumptions on the nature of human existence. These assumptions are selectively chosen, yet they become the foundation of a world-view. In a complex society such as ours, groups operate side by side, in the same city, drink the same water, and watch the same commercials on television. But they listen to different music, speak different dialects, worship different gods. When one appears in a court presided over by the other group, and basic assumptions about justice and rectitude lose their utility, a political trial results. The judge becomes another protagonist, for he and the accused respond to systems of explanation of such differing magnitudes that commonplace objects like flag, pig, hair, fence, fountain, alarm clock have totally different meanings. Community development thus comes to bridge between two, and many more, cosmologies, though they all may be served by the same sewage, water, and ambulance systems.

Thus, the progenitors of community development are less than useful, for they were a gentle breed who chose to work behind, in Tawney's phrase, 'the decorous drapery of political democracy': missionaries, settlement-house personnel, workers'-education tutors, applied anthropologists struggling to prevent or slow down the destruction of native cultures, missionaries who added improvements in agriculture and small industry to evangelism, and, in later days, human-relations trainers who hope to change society by changing those at the top first,[3] or, if not that, to concentrate on changing attitudes without attacking inequities imbedded in structures that in fact generate and regenerate attitudes that must be altered before inequity is removed.

III

Community development has been one of the mute handmaidens of more than one level of government in Canada. Its demonstrated incapacity to translate the expressed wishes of people into hard political currency can be explained in part at least by the innocence of community development. Where political turbulence has resulted from community-development work, the funds have been withdrawn or the worker dismissed.

I wish now to show that the failures of community development are attributable less to innocence than to the timidity of political and bureaucratic leaders who have used a technique of local consultation to buy time, and in the gamblers' parlance 'to cool the mark'. I wish to argue that this reflex avoidance of conflict is short-sighted and is the most certain of all strategies to guarantee the destruction of the institutions that this timidity is supposed to protect. For community-development methods cannot be used to improve society without creating disequilibrium. Conflict provides the energy that generates change, in the sectors of society where the greatest inequities exist. Change without conflict is no doubt the dream of every politician and public servant, but this is not the way society operates.

A community-development movement is needed that is as free as possible of the self-protecting tactics of political persons and powerful bureaucracies. It appears, therefore, that those who wield power, and oppose, with subtle cunning, proposals to redress inequities, are actively promoting revolution, whereas many of the groups that are regarded as enemies of law and order may be doing more than anyone to preserve a stable society.

A sophisticated view of the function of conflict in a changing society is required to understand the forces now at work in society. An interesting paradox was stated by Georges Simmel, which applies to this situation. He said 'The most effective prerequisite for preventing struggle, the exact knowledge of the comparative strength of the two parties, is very often obtainable only by actual fighting out the differences.' He puts it this way:

> How men quarrel in terms of certain of their customary allegiances, but are restrained from violence through other conflicting allegiances which are also enjoined on them by custom. The result is that conflicts in one set of relationships lead to re-establishment of social cohesion (Gluckman, 1965, p.2).

A recognition of the use of conflict in bringing about change is particularly important in developing government policies in relation to the poor, and other groups not adequately represented in the power structure in Canada.

The federal government is likely to continue to make financially costly gestures to disadvantaged groups. As each gesture is made, the political consequences can be assessed. The consequences could appear to range from harmless local busy-work to a direct assault on the state: thus a spectrum of consequences are envisaged, ranging from soft and benign to hard and malignant.

Making such assessments is not easy, for what appears to

have soft consequences can result in hard ones, and vice versa. There is also a difference in time and personal perspective. What appears soft today is found to be hard tomorrow. What appears hard this year may be experienced as soft next year, and so on.

Let us examine the paradoxical consequences of community action at the two extreme ends of the continuum.

In stating a policy for support of a more militant community development, it will be necessary to state it in the form of a paradox. The more benign the action taken by disadvantaged groups, the less political turbulence will result in the short run, the less change will occur in the long run. The more benign the action taken, the less likely major institutions will correct inequities and abuses, the more likely these institutions will suffer retribution in the long run. On the other hand, the more hard and malignant the action taken by groups stimulated by community development, the more quickly other jurisdictions and the public, reacting to stimulation from the mass media, will begin to bring about a termination of support to such groups. As a consequence, essential corrective actions will not be taken and major institutions will ultimately suffer the most.

Let us illustrate the two extremes. A benign action is one that keeps people busy at the local level dealing with minor adjustments to the system, but effectively cutting them off from involvement in major issues (Sternlieb, 1970). These actions cannot be discounted, for they have many positive effects; they do correct local abuses and at a level where people can perceive changes in the system and the benefits thereof. For example, a tenants' group can persuade or force a landlord to repair the laundromat system in a housing project. There are some positive effects from such an action, besides the advantage of having a place to do laundry: a confrontation with a landlord on a minor issue such as this may develop leadership that is later ready to move on to more critical issues. It corrects an abuse, and there are immediate satisfactions, physical and psychological. The negative effects are that a series of such actions makes no fundamental change in the status of the poor. Paradoxically, if the landlord refuses to fix the laundromat, the confrontation escalates, and the chances of fundamental changes to major institutions are increased.

Hard, malignant action is directed at the basic assumptions upon which the system operates. They may succeed in correcting major abuses. If they do, the ultimate extinction of major institutions may be delayed or averted, even though they may be severely modified. However, hard action is more likely to bring about a political backlash. The resulting political reaction forces the termination of support for community development, and, more tragically, it may result in the loss of some social gains. The hard, malignant line does not always have beneficial results. Polarities often result without changing anything, without even mobilizing the people. In such cases, the action proposed is often too abstract and too theoretical, because the leadership is out of touch with items like laundromats. The relevance of such action, when urged on the people, is often misunderstood, and so the support that might be forthcoming from the people themselves is not proferred.

It is quite possible that hard-line actions will recruit a measure of local support, but this simply creates another serious risk. Good local leadership can be drained out of the locals so quickly that the power base of the persons moving up the scale of influence is lost and they are cut off from their followers.

It is obvious from a politically operational point of view that the two extremes must be avoided, since they will both have the same result. In the centre, the same paradox is at work and the same dichotomy is present, but, if extremes are eschewed, the effects may become operationally practical.

At the soft end, action must be relevant enough to create some change. At the hard end, the resulting turbulence must be sufficiently contained that the public and other jurisdictions will not bring about their untimely termination, yet must carry sufficient power to effect needed change. In summary, the paradox is as follows: if change does occur, it creates short-run turbulence, but avoids long-run disequilibrium; if these disruptive adjustments are avoided in the present, the delay simply increases the survival risk to the institutions that are seeking protection from immediate change and modification.

There is an additional paradox. Some problems are so intertwined with others that they must run their course before the economic and cultural realities reveal themselves. The political leaders must ride the storm until a certain critical point is reached. In some cases it is reached too late. If it is reached too soon, the characteristics of the problem are not fully evident, the way it affects other elements now in balance are not known, the effects of remedial action are hard to assess. The problem might go away without a prescribed remedy, whereas the remedy, if applied too soon, may create other problems. Moreover, a remedy applied too soon is a form of paternalism that stifles the growth of leadership and viable problem-solving mechanisms. The most important function of a strong organization among the normally unrepresented is this: to bring abuses and inequities into public view and to make adjustments before it is too late – too late for those suffering from the inequity, too late for the institution involved to benefit from self-correcting measures.

We must find a middle ground that combines a base in locality with action that has sufficient force and scale to be significant. Personal and local relevance must be combined with theoretical coherence. Unfortunately, the two seldom come together.

We look for a practical involvement in the abuses that people feel and for which they need redress, and a theoretical framework for a social movement with leadership of broad, sufficiently intellectual vigour and sophistication. Thus the pressure on major institutions will be such that the changes of fundamental significance will result.

This is not to suggest that society ought to be a smoothly working machine, and it could be so if only management of the major institutions was more humanistic, less intent upon career enhancement and the survival of the organization.

A model of the ecology of change can help to illustrate how community development might help free us from the fear of innovation. Vichers has given this notion a characteristically imaginative airing:

> Like the life forms of the physical world, the dreams of men spread and colonize their inner world, dash, excite, modify and destroy each other, or preserve their stability by making strange accommodation to their rivals (Vichers, 1968, p.32).

Ideas and values can move, compete, and destroy with a fluidity that is seldom reflected in the writings of students of the sociologists of knowledge.[4]

Growth in nature is not a static condition, since there is a continuous struggle between species for space, sunlight, and nutrients. Into this delicately balanced arrangement, new species are constantly moving, creating imbalance and scarcities. The result of this invasion is conflict, and eventual accommodation when a new precarious balance is established. In nature conservationists quite properly deplore the rapidity with which new technologies are allowed to diffuse their influence on nature. In politics, repression is like a deadly herbicide that 'defoliates' the most delicate of all properties, the flowering of the human spirit.

In a healthy ecology, there is constant change; some species suffer, others thrive, yet the total scene is thriving and vital. Our communities must not die but live, for they are the habitat of human beings. A healthy societal ecology, in which ideas and institutions fight freely for survival, will keep our communities and our societies alive. This survival depends on the unrepresented having a voice, sharing power.

In nature a wide diversity of species compete for space in the environment. There is also, in nature, a fantastic profligacy in the production of seed in relation to the number of surviving organisms. Every acorn does not become an oak tree, every semen seed does not become a man. Yet in the realm of ideas, the natural creativity of man is systematically stifled, by the social order, the family, and socializing systems. This is signally true of the modern state which, as it becomes more powerfully centralized, seems with its timorous leaders to fear, more and more, the free exploration of alternatives. Thus individuals become sterile and communities become parochial, when they could be the breeding-ground of artists and innovators. The ultimate absurdity of the state decreeing 'Let nothing grow in Canada but maple trees' is obvious. Yet in social and political life we approach this folly.

IV

The loss of innocence is not the inevitable product of experience except for those capable of learning from it. Those who cannot learn are then neither innocent before law nor in the judgment of history. Our task then is to see if instruction is to be gained from the successes and mistakes of community development over the last two or three decades. We could look beyond the immediate past to the various forms of private and state intervention that have gone under the name of philanthropy, therapy, economic development, wars of intervention, or simply helping others. We could also look at the immediate present to read what we can from counter-cultural movements, liberation parties, unpopular music, and unpublished poetry. We could study and, better still, live among those who have chosen to do something themselves, and say something for themselves without a social animator sent by an outside institution with its own inevitable, partially hidden agenda. We could imagine action without encouragement from others, without outside money, sometimes without permission, sometimes in spite of the law.

It appears that something is emerging that the wise and sophisticated do not understand. It is something only the innocent could intuitively grasp or take seriously. It is not a new ball game that is shaping up, not a new shape of ball, not a ball park, not a new shuffle, choosing sides again to mix the losers with the winners. Playing ball is passé, or so it seems.

The ecological disasters now upon us were predicted decades ago by unconventional experts and by wise old farmers and fishermen who were then considered obstacles to the diffusion of new ideas. What is evident now is that the rational scientific approach to problem-solving in a linear sequence of analysis does not only effect change, it creates new problems. At the level of values we are groping now for new definitions of the concept of the problem, and at the same time we grope for new pieties, as witness new theories depicting Christ as a political agitator, or as a troubadour or jester. It should not be difficult to accept totally new ways of helping others, ways so unfamiliar there is no language in use capable of describing such a process. What is being looked for is a concept of help that is actually an exchange where initiator and helped are conceptually indistinguishable.

There may be open space ahead for innocents and 'idiots' to work. If there is, the need for and relevance of the professionally trained and qualified to 'heal' and 'help' others will diminish. Laing tells of a research psychologist who pronounced a woman mentally ill because she did not respond to needles he thrust into her flesh. Today Laing can ask 'Which one was mad?' and his question resonates in everyone who has ever tried to help a community or heal an ill person. Right now no proposition is too weird. Suggest that the meek shall inherit what is left of the earth, and a lot of innocents of all ages will say 'yes'. Now there is a notion that a new type of community development could take seriously.

FOOTNOTES

1. In this paper, community development will be personalized as

though it were accountable. By this means I hope to put into some kind of form my own thinking and reading, and, more pertinently, my experience. In 1938, I was engaged by McGill University to set up an adult-education program in the Eastern Townships of Quebec. During the war years, I was able to observe the dysfunctional co-operation that existed between the farmers of that region and the various governmental agencies with a mandate to increase food production through the use of wartime incentives and restrictions. It was instructive to commute between two realities: that of the bureaucrat with the over-all picture reflected in charts, graphs, and misleading reports from the field, and that of the local community and the individual farmer's bank balance. Yet, by means that were grossly inefficient by any standard the bureaucrat could imagine, production went up, morale was high, the war, we were told, was won. It was humanly degrading to the farmer, if sharing in decision-making is a criterion of full citizenship.

In recent years as a consultant to federal and private agencies, I have occupied this middle ground in various roles, and have observed others trying to do the same, many of them (like Bill Baker) my friends. The views expressed in this paper are not just a reflection of these experiences, they are even more a part of a search for a means of personal and collective survival in what is left of the twentieth century.

2. Richard M. Titmus *Essays on the Welfare State* (London, Unwin University Books, 1958). If Titmus is read carefully, it will be seen how well the early attacks on the system mounted by the Fabians fitted the thesis that reform did not disturb but actually supported the way things are. His excellent essay on the irresponsible society is a stern lecture to the insurance industry that their investment policies should take more account of widows and orphans and do more 'to relieve squalor'. See Chapter Two.

3. For a bland acceptance of the assumption that Africa needs T-groups, see Donald Nylen, *Handbook of staff development and human relations training: Material developed for use in Africa* (Washington, D.C., National Educational Association, 1967). For contrast, read such studies as Ladislas Segy, *African sculpture* (New York: Dover Press), and Melville Herskovits, *The human factor in changing Africa* (Hilda Knopf, 1958).

4. It is surprising this notion has not been used more often, for instance by Robert E. Park, the urban sociologist, since he made such brilliant application of the ecological model to change in the city. A student of Park reports that Park saw meteorology as a possible model for change.

R. ALEXANDER SIM was born in Gap View, Saskatchewan. He was a frequent school drop-out sometime before it was in vogue to be one; none the less he has been around schools and colleges all his life in a respectably uneasy liaison. When not in or near academe, he has worked for and advised governments and voluntary organizations.

He worked for the Canadian government in the Citizenship Branch for a number of years, where one of his responsibilities was the administration of a grants program. Most of his life he has worked in projects and on studies financed by grants from foundations and governmental agencies. He has recently made reports to the Secretary of State and the Central Mortgage and Housing Corporation on questions of citizen participation and funding citizen organizations.

He has been involved in a number of social innovations. In 1935 he was first-chairman of the group that organized student co-operative residences at the University of Toronto, from which Rochdale College can trace legitimate descent. In adult education, he was first Director of Extension Services at Macdonald College in Montreal. He used radio as a means to bring community groups together, first in Canada's famous 'National Farm Radio Forum', then in the Arctic with Delcap programs. In 1943 he started a bicultural training centre eventually run jointly by McGill and Laval universities.

As a teenager he became interested in folk schools, and is still looking for ways (and means) of combining residential education with a farm setting. He wants to see a place created where people can grow through physical work, meditation, and free exchange of ideas and fantasies, thereby helping an individual find his true creative self and his responsible political personality.

One of his publications was *Crestwood Heights*, which he co-authored. His poetry, which blossoms infrequently, is the side of his creativity that has lost out to work in the social field and to work on his farm at North Gower, Ontario. He is also a consulting sociologist and lecturer in community medicine, University of Ottawa.

Critical Questions for the Agency-Based Community Worker

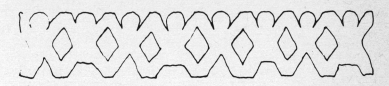

W. B. Whale

Most community development in Canada happens because a government department, a voluntary association, or an educational institution has established objectives and designated resources to meet some kind of development need. More often than not the agency with development objectives employs a field-staff to work towards achievement of those objectives. Field-staff members thus employed are, of course, accountable to the agency that pays their salary. But the agency requires its field-staff to meet a community need. That, in one way of looking at it, makes the field-staff accountable to the community. Each member of a community-development field-staff, therefore, faces the same dilemma as anyone who attempts to serve two masters. Whose aims and objectives does he work towards? Those of his agency? Those of the community his agency has a desire to serve? Those he has for himself? Depending upon his philosophy of what community development is all about, the community worker could logically work towards any *one* of the three. This article will consider the possibilities of working towards *all* three. It outlines a series of critical questions the community worker faces as he attempts to effectively meet the demands of his role and at the same time maintain some element of his own individuality.

The Difference Philosophy Makes

Any community-development program probably gets its start

with the identification of a need. That need probably has to do with some problem of inequality in the style of life within a segment of the population. Examples might be substandard housing, under-employment, unemployment, lack of recreational opportunity, below-average levels of education, and so on. The problem is identified in general terms as one that exists over a wide area of the province or country. Resources are made available and policies set for using the resources. The result is a program – a housing program, an educational upgrading program, a recreation program. The terms of reference for the program are general so they will apply over the whole area where the need is identified. The program is handed to the community-development personnel to interpret and implement within the local situation.

There are several differing philosophies regarding how a community-development program should be implemented. Using a housing program as an example, one way would be for the field-worker to make local municipal government aware of the terms under which assistance for building of houses may be obtained. The local government proceeds to condemn and possibly expropriate substandard housing and to provide alternative accommodation for its occupants within the terms of the program.

A second approach to implementing the housing program could be for the field-worker to make the terms of the program as generally known as possible. He would engage in a process by which the opportunity for improved housing could be considered by the community along with opportunities for other kinds of development. The objective of the process is to have the community decide whether or not housing should receive top priority from among all the opportunities open to it.

A third approach might be for the community worker to provide the local government and others with details of the housing program. Then, he might involve the local people who are living in substandard housing, attempting to have them decide what kind of housing would meet their needs most effectively.

Where the community worker is not involved with the community, other than to advise the local authorities of the terms of a program, there is no doubt that he is accountable only to the agency providing the program. His success as a professional in the field will probably be judged by his agency on his ability to have the program utilized to the full extent of the resources provided. To have the program utilized will indicate to the agency that it was correct in its judgment that the program was needed. To have all the resources that were provided used up will indicate to the agency that its estimates of the extent of the need were accurate.

Where the community worker is involved with the community to the extent of having community members make choices about the kind of housing they want, he is still accountable largely to his agency for the implementation of the program. But he is also accountable to the community for the kind of housing they get. The worker's success is now judged by his agency in the same terms described above. His success is also judged by the community. Whether or not the kind of housing the community indicated they need actually materializes will determine whether the community worker is a success in the eyes of community members.

Where the community worker engages the community in a process to decide whether or not housing is to receive priority attention, entirely different criteria are brought into play, both by the agency and by the community. From the agency's point of view the worker is still accountable to it. The agency will likely judge the success of the worker, however, on whether or not there is an involving process and on whether or not the community comes to a decision on its own about housing, even if the housing program is rejected.

The community too may hold the worker accountable to it. Because the worker caused a process to take place, the community may expect the worker to accept responsibility for the outcome of the process. Even though the community rejects housing as a first priority and even though community members may be aware that the worker's agency has resources only for housing, there may still be an expectation that the worker can also provide the resources for whatever the community considered to be first priority. If the worker cannot fulfil the expectations, frustrations result in accusations by the community that the worker didn't do his job, that the agency is an inflexible bureaucracy, and so on.

The approach the agency and the worker take to implement community programs has a considerable influence on both the accountability of the worker for his actions and on the criteria by which his success will be judged. The critical questions for the community worker are:

1. What does my agency believe to be the best way for its program to be implemented?
2. What is my particular role in implementing the program?
3. Do I have the ability and the attitude that will let me do a competent job within the agency's terms of reference?
4. What does the community expect of my agency and of me?
5. How does the community's expectation compare with what my agency can actually provide?
6. Do I have the ability to assist the community to establish realistic expectations of my agency?

Fragmentation of Resources, A Bane of Community Workers

The resources available through any development agency are limited, not only in extent but also in kind. For example, the resources needed for development in agriculture are available in one group of agencies. The resources needed for development in areas of housing, or recreation, or educational upgrading, or skill-training are likely to be available in separate agencies.

Needs identified within a community seldom conform exactly to what can be resolved using the resources of a single agency. For example, the resources required to reclaim agricultural land into viable economic units may be available through agricultural agencies. The resources to help people adjust to new social and economic circumstances, which may be the result of the agricultural development program, may be available through other agencies. The result is that either inter-agency co-operation and co-ordination is required, or only a portion of the development task can be achieved.

There are examples of successful inter-agency co-operation in development in practically all provinces of Canada. But, by and large, it would appear that agencies prefer to operate independently of one another. This preference is understandable when one considers how difficult it is to justify the existence of an independent agency, when a large portion of its budget and staff resources are used to work towards the objectives of another agency.

The community worker tends to fall victim to the fragmentation of resources, and the matter of accountability comes into question again. If he attempts to achieve even limited participation by citizens, the limitations of resources become evident. The objectives of participation are to achieve an understanding among citizens of the proposals placed before them. It is also to have citizens take some part in decision-making on the proposals. In order to achieve understanding, all the elements of the situation within which proposals are to be implemented need to be examined. That examination is useful to allow the citizens to understand what portion of the situation can be looked after, using the resources offered. It also points out other resources needed to take care of the entire situation.

The community worker is faced with two alternatives. If he feels strong accountability to the community, he will likely take the time to involve other agencies to work out a co-ordinated program to cope with the entire situation. He thereby places the community's interests ahead of any desire his agency may have to maintain independent programs. If he feels strong accountability to his agency, he may decide not to go beyond making the resources of his own agency available. Of course, the alternative he chooses may be determined by whether or not the agency's policies provide for co-operation with other agencies.

The critical questions for the community worker are:

1. Does my agency's policy permit me to seek a co-ordination of efforts so that a total situation within a community may be resolved rather than just that part for which my agency has resources?
2. What are the agencies that have resources that are likely to be of benefit to a community along with those my agency can provide?
3. Do I have the ability to give leadership to a co-ordinated effort and still let the other agencies maintain the sense of autonomy they will require to meet their needs?

The Tyranny of Time

Time invariably comes into the picture. Community-development programs are operated within the fiscal policy of the development agency. That means financial and personnel resources are allocated and accounted for annually. In some cases, resources are allocated over longer periods. Few agencies, however, have become adept at accurately predicting the amount of time required for a particular development project. Particularly in agencies that answer to the public, administrators become anxious if resources are not used according to estimates. Pressure is therefore applied to have money and time spent on the projects planned. If it seems improbable that this can happen, then pressure is applied to divert the money and the energy of people to other uses.

The time factor often gets in the way of meaningful citizen participation. Time allocated to get a development project under way and showing results often does not take into account time to have people involved. The more intensive the involvement, the greater the time investment. People who are expected to take some responsibility for development decisions in their community have a right to expect enough time to understand the consequences of their decisions.

From the community point of view, the nature of the time problem will be determined by citizens' perception of the role of the development agency. If the citizens expect the agency to do the developing for them, then any attempt at citizen involvement may be viewed as a waste of time and a hedging of responsibility. If the citizens expect and want to be involved with the agency in decisions about development, they are likely to want to take as much time as seems necessary to make wise decisions.

Again, the community worker is faced with a dilemma. There are three factors of time. There is the amount of time the agency has estimated to be required to conduct the project. There is the amount of time the community judges is needed to do the job. There is the amount of time the professional community worker considers to be necessary to engage in the processes by which most effective development can take place. There are likely to be pressures on the community worker from all three sources.

The critical questions for the community worker are:

1. To which of the pressures of time do I yield?
2. If there are serious gaps in the thinking about time between my agency, the community, and myself, do I have the ability to help bring about understanding so the program can proceed?

The Central Question of Accountability

The general question underlying all of those posed thus far, and perhaps the most critical of all questions for the community worker is: To whom am I accountable?

It is easy for the agency to say the worker is accountable to it. After all, the agency provides the resources for the worker's employment. It is just as easy for the worker to agree. But to do that, two facts may be overlooked. The first fact is that the development program is intended to serve the community. It is the citizens of the community who must accept the consequences of the program. The second fact is that the community worker is himself an individual who thinks, has feelings, has an integrity of his own.

The question of accountability must be clearly answered in order that a single set of criteria may be established by which the program's effectiveness may be judged.

Judgment suggests evaluation. Evaluation is a term that has long been the centre of controversy among community workers and others involved in the field of community development. At one extreme, evaluation is looked upon as destructive to creativity or to the emergence of self-determination. At the other extreme, evaluation to a sophisticated set of predetermined criteria is built in as an essential part of every community-development project. Both viewpoints may be valid up to a point. Both may be completely wrong, if adhered to without flexibility. The fact does remain that judgments are made about the effectiveness of community work. Decisions regarding the expenditures of thousands of dollars intended for the benefit of deserving people are based on those judgments. The welfare of deserving people may, therefore, be at stake. Professional careers of community workers and their administrators may rise or fall based on those judgments. With consequences such as these, there can be little doubt that one cannot afford to take lightly the process by which the judgments are made. Whether or not it is called evaluation is relatively unimportant as long as the process is a deliberate and sound one.

There Are At Least Three Centres of Judgment

When considering a process of evaluation, the points of view of all of those directly involved are of consequence. That means there will be a minimum of three points of view where agency-based community work is concerned. The community will certainly be making judgments about what is going on; the agency will be making judgments; the community worker will be making judgments. It is when each of the three is making its judgments and using unrelated criteria that damaging difficulties are likely to arise.

Often, the community worker may not be considered to be making judgments separately from the agency with which he is employed. That reduces the number of centres of judgments to two, and thus simplifies the matter. That also reduces the community worker to a cog in the agency machinery; he has no individuality.

To gain the satisfactions that everyone seeks in his employment, the community worker needs to make his independent judgments. In fact his judgments are probably the most critical of all, to himself, to the community, and to the agency he serves. There are at least three additional questions that are critical to his survival and growth as a community worker. The answers to these will help in answering at least some of those raised earlier.

1. What do I believe to be the fundamentals of development for any community?
2. What are my own capacities to conduct processes or programs based on those fundamentals?
3. What are the kinds of policies that indicate whether or not any particular agency is conducting its program based on the same fundamentals I accept?

Knowledge of Self is Key to Community Worker's Own Satisfactions

Armed with answers to such questions, a community worker can know himself well enough to make decisions that are crucial to his effectiveness in development work. The community worker's satisfactions from his employment depend upon whether he knows himself well enough to make his own judgments about his effectiveness. His satisfactions will also be determined by whether he knows himself well enough to judge which agencies can permit him to achieve to a level close to his potential. He has a definite advantage if he can judge his own effectiveness using criteria that are based on his own actual abilities and capacities, rather than on criteria based on abilities and capacities that he would like to have or that his agency would like him to have.

Further, the community worker's satisfactions can rely heavily on whether he knows the criteria by which his agency and his community are making judgments about him and his work. Where the criteria are widely separated from each other or from his own, his initial decision in development has to be to initiate a process by which all three can arrive at criteria that they can use together to judge the effectiveness of development work. The question of accountability will then have been worked out to the satisfaction of all concerned. The community worker can walk the tight-rope between his agency and his community: to be an individual in his own right and not a cog in the machinery of either.

W. B. WHALE is Associate Professor of Continuing Education, College of Education, and Head of the Program Development Department, Extension Division, at the University of Saskatchewan, Saskatoon. His field of study is extension education, with special emphasis on the educational component of community development. Areas of particular interest include: role-performance problems of community-development workers and extension workers; structure and functioning of the community; and strategies for increasing learning potential within educational programs. He undertook advanced study in extension education to the Master's-degree level at the University of Toronto and to the Ph.D. level at the University of Wisconsin, Madison.

Section Four

Sharing Experiences

The lack of documentation of field experiences could perhaps be explained by the infancy, innocence, and undisciplined nature of community development. Nonetheless, the dearth of documentation is still somewhat surprising. No one would question the fact that learning does take place without recording and analysis. But it is also known that considerably more learning occurs when the components of documentation and evaluation are added. This would be particularly true in community work, where much emphasis is put on the process of action. In addition to encouraging the field worker to record his experiences, there is also much to be gained from the detached observer-researcher-evaluator, but this component has yet to be introduced widely in the practice of community development.

A good example of analysis and documentation by the community worker is presented by Norman and Fay McLeod. Their article describes situations of hostility and conflict within a community and points out ways in which conflict can be used constructively in community development. Feelings of hostility within a community may be viewed as displaced energy, signifying social impotence. One of the important roles of the community worker is to help community members articulate their needs and help them to identify the alternatives to problem-solving. This article also describes the use of community councils as a way of helping people to organize themselves. Such a topic is also the focus of the last article in this section, written by Willmott.

Florence O'Neill describes with tremendous warmth, humanity and dedication a deep and rewarding experience of working with a community. Other field workers should be encouraged to share their experiences of human interaction.

Many lessons are to be learned from the article written by Jean Lagassé, in which he discusses the first years of community development in Manitoba. One of the main contributions of community development is that of giving people a sense of personal worth and the realization of their collective strength. Government can help to facilitate this, but only if elected representatives and civil servants understand and believe in the underlying philosophy. Special structures are also necessary to deal with the special administrative and supportive problems relating to community development. Lagassé also discusses research methodology and the reconciliation of theory and practice. This article is closely related to Section VI on Indian

Participation. The articles by Deveaux and Compton also deal with the Manitoba experience.

One of the noticeable trends in Canada within the last few years is the attempt being made by numerous organizations to relate more closely to their respective communities. Arthur Stinson's article points out that many of the traditional methods of extension are inadequate. In relating to its community, an organization must have a philosophy for doing so and must understand the methods of accomplishing this. Stinson provides a good example of how an urban organization can function adequately and give adequate support to community self-analysis and action. He discusses such topics as entry into the community, the importance of community representation, supporting services, and information sharing. (These are topics also covered in the articles by McLeod, Willmott, Whale, and McEwen.) Stinson also deals with the concept of the resource centre and points out the mistaken identification of education with schooling, and the tendency to confine education to the classroom. The environments within which learning takes place must be seen in a wider context.

The way in which a community organizes itself for communication, co-ordination, and power is vitally important to its success. Donald E. Willmott discusses the community-development council as a community-development "technique". He distinguishes between community development and community improvement. He talks of the sources of opposition to councils and draws some conclusions that could be helpful to the community-development practitioner and planner.

Experiences with Conflict and Hostility in Two Rural Newfoundland Communities

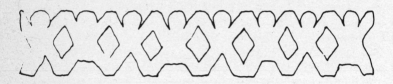

Fay and Norman McLeod

We might as well be frank from the start: this is not a technical article based on objective research. We haven't done much reading, let alone sociological research, on the subject of social conflict and hostility in small communities. Rather, we have worked on two community-development projects in two very different communities over a period of two years; and we wish to describe in simple terms some of our experiences, and try to draw some implications about conflict and hostility in community development. As this is written while we are still very much involved in the second of these projects, we can hardly take the stance of the 'detached observer': hence our goal in this article is realism, and not scientific objectivity.

Our experience in community education and development has been brief, but in many ways unique. We were hired by Frontier College in the fall of 1968 as a husband-wife team, under the relatively new Frontier College service of providing full-time workers under contract to government and other agencies. The two contracts under which we have worked have been with the Newfoundland Department of Community and Social Development. Our first contract placed us in Cox's Cove, on the north shore of Bay of Islands, the last community on the twenty-six-mile road out of Corner Brook.

During and shortly after World War II, Cox's Cove was a boom-town, a major centre for the inshore herring fishery. Since that time, the boom has gone bust; and the community we moved into was a deprived and depressed settlement of about 700 people, with a reputation in the civil service and in neighbouring communities as a 'backward' community. To a large extent, that reputation was a case of self-fulfilling prophecy, but there is no doubt that the community was deprived of public services, lacking in civic organization, and socially, psychologically, and economically depressed.

From what we can gather, Cox's Cove was chosen as the trial site of a Frontier College program by the provincial government, simply because, out of any number of similar communities, it had happened to come to the attention of government employees: a letter from a resident of Cox's Cove to 'Joey' (Premier Joseph R. Smallwood), requesting gravel fill to protect his home from the ravages of the neighbour's garbage and the bog in the back yard, was passed on to officials of the Department of Community and Social Development. It was evidently hypothesized that a better solution to the problem than gravel would be a social-education program; and the services of the Frontier College were employed. In the meantime, the Department provided the gravel as well, under its Community Amenities program.

Our program in Cox's Cove was a hodge-podge of structured and unstructured activities, adult education and community development, informal counselling and group work. Much of it grew out of simply moving unheralded into the community, getting to know it on our own, and listening. We offered basic literacy classes, organized children's sewing and knitting classes, taught sewing to the women, disseminated birth-control information, set up a children's library, held meetings with young people, helped set up a recreation committee, and held study groups on community problems. Out of the study groups grew a development committee that is still in operation; and towards the end of the project, we helped organize a local government. Today, both the Cox's Cove–McIvers Improvement Committee and the Cox's Cove Community Council are going strong; the face of Cox's Cove is changing rapidly, and the Frontier College project has been identified as a visible success.

On the face of it, the prospects for success in Hawkes Bay, where we are now, should be greater than in Cox's Cove. In the first place, the community is reputed to have great development potential and already boasts a brand-new industry. In the second place, we were quite thoroughly introduced to the leadership of the community well before we moved in, and a lot of discussion took place with local leadership around our role here. Of course, there are several versions of just what our job here is, but that was true,in Cox's Cove as well. Yet as it has turned out, the Hawkes Bay project has been more frustrating, and less visibly successful, than the Cox's Cove project.

The three communities of Hawkes Bay, Port Saunders, and Port-au-Choix have been designated growth centres under the resettlement program, and fall within one of the 'special areas' of the Department of Regional Economic Expansion (DREE). There is a new saw-mill at Hawkes Bay and a new fish plant at Port-au-Choix. Of the three communities, Hawkes Bay is the smallest, with only 500 people. It is also the youngest, and the only non-fishing community in the area: Hawkes Bay is little more than a dormitory town for loggers, very much a company town.

There was already a great deal of activity related to community development in the area when we moved in. The Northern Regional Development Association, which was formed a couple of years ago, covers this area, and its president, Martin Lowe, lives in Port Saunders. The Memorial University Extension worker, who was very much involved in the formation of N.R.D.A., is stationed at Port-au-Choix; the parish priest at Port Saunders was a strong supporter of N.R.D.A. and has been instrumental in the formation of the Northern Fisherman's Union; and the Rural Development Officer for the Department of Community and Social Development is stationed in Hawkes Bay. The Department of Community and Social Development was interested in seeing what we would make of the situation, and N.R.D.A. expressed interest in having someone in the area to work intensively on grass-roots involvement within the local area. The Department advocated that we should have an identified role, and it was agreed with regional community leaders that this role should be as teachers in a voluntary adult-education program. It was further agreed that we should live in Hawkes Bay and start work there, as demand was high for adult classes in Hawkes Bay.

Hence our first commitment of time was to adult classes. We set up classes in typing, sewing, and academic upgrading from grades one to ten; and we even held a brief course in the 'new mathematics' for parents. We encouraged discussion and written assignments on community issues, and we helped one of our classes organize a series of 'hot seat' meetings, at which local V.I.P.s were subjected to public cross-examination. At first, we worked closely with the regional leadership around the means of developing better grass-roots involvement; and when it became evident that that direct approach to educating leadership was getting nowhere, we embarked on a visiting campaign to attempt to activate the public around local issues. We helped organize a public meeting to deal with the issue of hiring local labour at the mill. We held a series of small study-group meetings with the mill employees to discuss legal and other aspects of their employment, including the means to assist efforts to establish a union in the mill. We assisted a group of women in staging a three-act play, and then putting on a 'walkathon' to raise money for a children's playground.

After nine months of frustrated efforts at community education and social animation in Hawkes Bay, we were invited by the community council in Port Saunders to assist them in organizing their efforts to get in on more of the developments in the area; and we have spent the last three months of our project concentrating primarily on community development in Port Saunders.

There are undoubtedly a lot of reasons for our successes and failures in Cox's Cove and Hawkes Bay, and we'll go into some of them later. But we suspect that a major factor in the social changes that have taken place in Cox's Cove was the handling of conflict and hostility. Conversely, in Hawkes Bay, we must assume the major responsibility for our own mishandling of conflict and hostility.

We won't bother defining 'conflict' and 'hostility', except to note that conflict is an action or event, while hostility is an emotion. Logically, it would seem, conflict should be a direct expression of hostility. Our experience indicates that in practice, it ain't that simple.

A. Cox's Cove: Constructive Conflict

When we moved into Cox's Cove, there was no visible or structural leadership at all, for, aside from church and school, there was no organization. That is one reason why we were never properly introduced to the community: to whom could we be introduced? We had to stumble on our own into the community, introduce ourselves gradually, and smell out and encourage the natural leaders. Fortunately, there was a latent natural leadership in the community, two or three people in whom at least some citizens were prepared to place their trust.

One of the first things we found in Cox's Cove was hostility. In fact, we were quite impressed with the strong divisions apparent in the community – perhaps unduly impressed. As there was no 'Establishment' in Cox's Cove, the hostility we detected might be called purely horizontal: there was very little social stratification. Instead, hostility was either personal, religious, or based on resentment between working-men and welfare recipients.

We encountered the religious divisions first: one of the first questions we were asked by the children, who were our first contacts in the community, was 'What religion are you?' To a large extent, religious animosity was fed by the denominational school system; and we were very early asked by Pentecostal parents to intervene on behalf of their children, who suspected discrimination by the Anglican high school, when they applied for admission from the Pentecostal grade school.

As we went about visiting our new neighbours, we soon became aware that feelings were even higher between working-men and welfare recipients. There were men in Cox's Cove working for Lundrigans for $1.30 an hour on the road over a period of two or three months, catching a few lobster in the spring, and drawing low benefits from the Unemployment Insurance Commission for the rest of the year. Many of these men were supporting families of six or more children. In the same community, there were men who were classed as physically unfit for work. They had families of similar size, and drew a secure income equivalent to about $300 a month from the welfare department. There are tales (probably exaggerated) of welfare recipients finishing their drinking parties at 5:00 a.m., then going out on the road to jeer their neighbours on the way to work. The working-men deeply resented the long-term welfare recipients, whose life, to them, seemed an easy one.

Then there were the personal hostilities and divisions, all the petty animosities and jealousies that are probably characteristic of any small community, but were magnified in Cox's Cove – in our eyes, at least – to the point of absurdity. We knew of two ladies who had not spoken to each other for over a year, since they clashed over a fist-fight between their children. The kids, incidentally, made up the next day.

We could not, of course, avoid these lines of hostility and division. We were subtly urged to align ourselves in every little feud. At one point we were almost run out of the community, ostensibly because we supported a couple with whom we had been particularly friendly in their complaint against the school principal. The real issue, it turned out later, was that several other couples were jealous of our friendship with the couple in question.

But although we could not immunize ourselves from the hostilities within the community, we could, and did, choose to ignore them and downplay them in the focus of our work. When we heard people asking themselves, 'Whom do I hate?', we sought to refocus their attention to the question, 'What do I want?'. We diagnosed these feelings of hostility within the community as displaced energy, a focus for frustrated aggressions, signifying social impotence. In all our discussions and meetings with people in Cox's Cove, we tried to steer conversation to the articulation of needs and desires common to the whole community. While we did not stop people from talking about their personal resentments and grievances, we never encouraged them to vent them in action. Our hope was that if the community could discover the power to change and to make dents in some of its community-wide problems, then this discovery of social power might take the edge of desperation out of the internal hostilities in the community. Subsequent events in Cox's Cove seem to be bearing out this hope.

The main vehicle we sought to encourage for attacking community problems was the Improvement Committee, which was originally elected to represent fishermen seeking a bait-holding unit for the lobster fishery. This committee turned very quickly to other concerns – primarily community services, which were requested of government agencies. In its first six months of existence, the committee mainly wrote letters, requesting telephone service, a breakwater, road pavement, and other services. The replies they received, from various agencies and from their politicians, were curt, non-committal, and often non-existent. By mid summer, the committee was thoroughly discouraged.

In August, it was learned that the road-paving program would cease at Gillams, halfway from Corner Brook to Cox's Cove. The Improvement Committee had written a lot of letters about that pavement, which had been a political promise in the last election, and they were mad. So were the people of Cox's Cove. The committee managed to bully its way into a meeting with the Premier, who is member for their district, and an angry exchange produced a promise of definite word within a week. When no word was forthcoming after two weeks, the people were madder than ever.

It seemed as though all the frustrations of the people of Cox's Cove were coming to a head in that one issue. Cox's Cove felt generally discriminated against, hard done by, overlooked, and now it was boiling over. They took it out on Joey Smallwood. At a political rally in Gillams in early September, the people of Cox's Cove turned out to boo. They booed so hard that the Premier left the meeting. According to press reports, other people at the meeting begged him to come back, but that's not why he came back: we know the guy who blocked the driveway so he couldn't get out.

Anyway, he did come back, and he met with the Improvement Committee. The meeting was again stormy; and, in fact, the paving didn't go on that year. But a few brick walls began to budge, and they did get a breakwater out of it. And they kept on fighting: today, Cox's Cove is paved.

From that day, when they entered into open conflict and took their battle into the political arena, the Improvement Committee and the newly elected community council have not looked back. We've visited Cox's Cove several times in the last year, and we find the people increasingly proud of their progress, increasingly aggressive in dealing with business and government, and increasingly self-confident. The people of Cox's Cove are discovering their power to effect change: and they learned it, first and foremost, through *conflict* with external forces.

Maybe we're imagining things, but we think the working-men sound a lot less hostile towards welfare recipients nowadays: instead of venting their hostility towards their neighbours, when they talk about welfare now, they talk in terms of criticisms of the welfare system, its failings and abuses.

We know that the religious hostility has died down: the schools are amalgamated today, and there's no static about it. As for personal animosities, they're still there. But they're largely subordinated to local issues, local politics: are you in favour of a law against animals at large, do you think you're getting a fair deal from council when the seasonal jobs roll around, etc. These issues, and many hotter ones, are openly dealt with by the people and their leaders, openly discussed and resolved. Compared to the hidden, unspoken hostilities we used to know, it's like windows and curtains opening in a dark and dank room.

When conflict took place, it was directed outwards; and it was soon channelled into controlled negotiations, and resulted in the discovery of new means to achieve community goals. After the phase of external conflict, community leaders found they had the confidence and the courage to tackle internal problems and divisions. The other day, while we were visiting the Cove, Alex Park, Chairman of the Improvement Committee, was going on about all the rows he'd had with various people in the community. He said, 'They always come to me when they want to row, because they know I can take it.'

'Hell, Alex,' I said, 'you enjoy it, and you know it.'

Alex grinned: 'I love it.'

B. Hawkes Bay: Frustrated Hostility

When we moved into Hawkes Bay, we didn't have any trouble finding leaders. We were invited into the area by members of a regional leadership – the local businessmen, teachers, and clergy who formed the core of the executive and their advisers in the much-publicized Northern Regional Development Association.

The Northern Regional Development Association is a story in community development in itself, a story best told by the Extension Department at Memorial University, which was instrumental in organizing the Association. When we moved into Hawkes Bay, it was an established force; several of its leading lights were also councillors on the Hawkes Bay community council. What was significant for our work was that there was already in Hawkes Bay an established leadership, which had already learned its own style of operating.

We knew, before we even started working in Hawkes Bay, that the regional leadership was very much a social stratum, a loosely knit group of relatively well-educated people from several communities, who formed their own social circle. We knew the leaders were largely out of touch with the people: they told us so. In fact, initially, they asked us to help them develop better grass-roots involvement in community affairs.

This leadership, in itself, was one of our problems in working in Hawkes Bay: re-educating an existing leadership, with well-established habits and practices, is in many ways much more difficult than the education of new leadership. There were other problems too.

To begin with, we were introduced to the community of Hawkes Bay as teachers in a structured program of adult education. We were even given the authority to choose and direct day-school teachers who assisted us in teaching the night-school classes. This meant that the community at large viewed us as night-school teachers, and members of an *élite* of highly educated people with virtually mystical attributes. Whereas in Cox's Cove nobody knew what we were there for, and that made people uncomfortable and forced them to think about how to use us, in Hawkes Bay people were very much at ease in their minds about what we were here for: we were night-school teachers, and if you thought you had something to learn from us, you should go to classes.

That shouldn't have been impossible to overcome, except that whenever we tried to step out of purely formal education, into community education and development, we found we were treading on toes. Community leaders, and some of our colleagues as well, having accepted us as formal instructors in a basic education program, reacted in a defensive manner when we made a bid to put into practice our broader role.

Nevertheless, we tried. We took the leaders at their word when they said they wanted us to help them develop more grass-roots involvement, and set out initially to work with the leaders themselves. We met with them, held informal coffee-klatch meetings, visited them, and tried to focus them on their own approaches to the people. When the council was put on the 'hot seat', and the people yelled at the councillors for agreeing to change to a government-appointed 'local-improvement board' without getting public approval, we followed up with discussions with the leaders, and the councillors said they'd take the lesson to heart and hold more public meetings. The public meetings did not take place.

We talked with them about listening, and they said they'd listen carefully for the concerns of the people. In practice, it didn't work. When the Zone Three Committee of N.R.D.A. held meetings in Hawkes Bay around plans for regional medi-

cal and educational facilities, the leaders were largely unrespon-
sive to the few suggestions offered from the floor.

So we decided to go to the people ourselves. We began a
door-to-door visiting campaign in Hawkes Bay. We found, not
surprisingly, a lot of hostility. In Hawkes Bay, the hostility was
of a different order from Cox's Cove, almost a class phenomenon. There was a religious split between Pentecostals and Ang-
licans, but that was no longer a very emotionally charged issue.
Similarly, the talk of working-men about welfare recipients
held little bitterness. Nor were personal animosities all that
dominant: unlike Cox's Cove, for instance, in Hawkes Bay, we
found that we could make friends with anyone, go out to dinner, and invite people in for dinner quite freely, and there
would be no jealousies aroused.

No, hostility in Hawkes Bay was directed primarily towards
the leadership, towards what people call 'our leading citizens'.
A 'leading citizen', in this sense, is a person better off than
most, probably a businessman, with a high-school education or
better. A 'leading citizen' is regularly elected to committees and
local government, because, it is assumed, he's the only person
who can do it.

In the course of our visiting, aside from the general hostility,
we uncovered one issue very early, that seemed to be a fairly
common one. During the previous summer and fall, while construction was under way on the saw-mill, most of the construction jobs went to people not native to Hawkes Bay: the people
of Hawkes Bay watched while outsiders took the jobs. In the
winter, when the first logs were cut for the mill, a lot of outsiders were hired in the woods, too. Men from Hawkes Bay
who applied for jobs often found the jobs already taken by
someone from outside the community.

This issue had been raised at previous meetings between the
loggers and the N.R.D.A. executive. Now the mill was about to
open in a very few weeks, and hiring was to take place soon.
The great fear of the men was that they would not get jobs
when the permanent positions opened in an industry located in
their own community. As the issue was a pressing one, we cut
short our visiting when we were about halfway through, and
brought the matter to the attention of the local representative
to N.R.D.A. He called a meeting with the men.

At this meeting, it was agreed that it would not do to rely on
the regional executive of N.R.D.A., who had to speak for the

entire region they represented: this was a local issue, and it required an independent local committee to deal with it. The men therefore agreed to organize a public meeting for men and women, to elect such a committee, which might also represent the people of Hawkes Bay to the Local Improvement board and to the N.R.D.A. executive on other issues. We helped the men set up the meeting, and we made a point of consulting with the established community leaders, who told us they thought it was a great idea.

The meeting was a fiasco. Having encouraged people to speak out about their contentions and concerns, and having welcomed people's statements to the effect that 'It's time we took matters into our own hands' – we found that the people were not really prepared to take matters into their own hands. What happened instead was that the people took out their frustrations on the established leaders, blamed them for not having done enough, and generally vented their hostility. The leaders, for their part, became extremely defensive. Two of them resigned from several of their positions. And all of them yelled back at the people, accused them of ingratitude, and then began playing upon their internal divisions, dredging up old feuds and grievances between and among the men, digging into community dirt, and saying, in essence, 'You guys can't stick together anyway.' The people believed them, and the meeting just petered out as one by one they made their exit.

All the hostility and frustration, and the internal divisions of the community, were exposed like raw sores at that meeting. It was a shock to the leaders, a shock to a lot of the people, and a shock to us too. We made several attempts to go back to the leaders and discuss the implications of what had happened, but we were met with distrust. We also made a half-hearted attempt to get out and meet with the people, but the resignation and defeat we found left us feeling defeated ourselves.

Under other circumstances, we might have been able to go back to the people and start over again from the ground up. But in the middle of a brief, one-year project, when we had been identified as school teachers at the outset, this was our one major chance to break into community education and development, and we blew it. From that time on, we found that people and leaders alike preferred to refer to us, sometimes quite pointedly, as 'the night-school teachers', as if to say, 'Keep to your place.'

We have, of course, kept in contact with many of the women in Hawkes Bay, through sewing and typing classes, through the group that is trying to establish a playground, and through social visiting. We have also kept in touch with many of the men, through classes, through social contacts, and through a series of informal meetings around wages and working-conditions in the mill. What we have found has been a continuing sense of frustration and lack of social influence, and continuing subterranean hostility. The men are unhappy with wages and working-conditions in the mill, and frustrated by the slow progress of negotiations by the union; the women are equally frustrated by their inability to get land from the company for the playground, dissatisfied with the efforts of their local government to get land for them, but too discouraged to take matters into their own hands. Hostility in Hawkes Bay is as strong as ever.

Implications

Obviously, we can't draw any final or definite conclusions from two community-development projects, one of which isn't even formally concluded yet. However, there are tentative implications which we'd like to discuss.

Our experiences have led us to believe that internal hostility in a community, which often goes unspoken and is felt as an undercurrent of emotion, is indeed a displaced, frustrated aggression in a situation of social impotence: it is a signification of powerlessness. The petty, often quite irrational, feuds, the social divisions and resentments, are often simply a sign of pent-up frustrations, and not an indication of genuine issues, real wants on which people will act constructively.

In Cox's Cove, we sought to rechannel these energies into activities and issues of common interest in the community. When social frustrations and anger did come to the surface, they came out as a unified demand for action, directed outwards to a politician. Later, in the perspective of success as a unified, organized group, the community was able to deal openly with disagreement and aggression among its own members. Conflict (in this sense) takes place around a specific issue about which people care enough to do something: it is a meaningful confrontation over matters of genuine concern, arising from real wants. Such open confrontation is probably healthy and constructive, both within the community and on issues of contention with outside interests.

Our mistake in Hawkes Bay was to allow, and even encourage, a confusion between conflict over a meaningful issue (the men wanted jobs in the mill), with resentment and displaced hostility directed at community leaders. The issue was real enough, and was basically a quarrel with the company; but the leadership was also implicated, as the men felt they were not doing their jobs, and the result was merely an exacerbation of divisions and hostility within the community. The people did have very real quarrels with their leaders, and there was a need for better communications with the leadership, and possibly new forms of leadership; but these real internal issues were not what came out in the confrontation that took place. What took place was not a conflict, but a mere airing of hostility. The people left that meeting with their hostilities foremost in their minds, more frustrated than ever because their own neighbours had been telling them they couldn't do anything for themselves.

The implication, for us, of these experiences is that conflict as a constructive element in community development–a confrontation over a meaningful issue, in which people take a stand based on their felt needs and wants – is seldom the direct outcome of hostility. On the contrary: whereas hostility and divisions within a community signify a psychological sense of powerlessness, open conflict signifies a growing sense of influence and power. Moreover, once the community as a whole has discovered its collective power through conflict with outside forces, it can deal more readily with openly aggressive conflict within the community, and hostility and resentment will tend to decrease.

To illustrate the difference between conflict over an issue in a community, and divisions of hostility in a community, consider the relationship between the people and their local governments, in Cox's Cove and Hawkes Bay. Shortly after the community council was formally certified in Cox's Cove, and a few months after we left that community, one of the councillors got wind of a rumour that some men were going to circulate a petition to decertify the council. He tracked down the rumour and found the three originators of the petition, who had just started making their rounds. They were evidently motivated partly by personal grudges, partly by personal unwillingness to pay taxes, and partly by sheer devilment. The councillor talked them out of their petition by the simple expedient of threatening to go with them from door to door and argue the other side of the case.

Here was open confrontation over an issue, a conflict within the community, resolved face to face. The story was all over the community within twelve hours, and the council won a lot of respect for its victory.

In Hawkes Bay the council decided, apparently with little prior consultation with the public, to apply to the provincial government for the appointment of a (non-elected) 'Local Improvement' board, which would have increased powers of taxation and borrowing, and could finance a water-and-sewage system. There has been a great deal of grumbling among the people, but the closest anyone came to open confrontation was the 'hot seat' meeting, at which a few of the people present took the councillors to task on the issue of taxation without representation. Instead, the people grumble in their kitchens, complain about the threat of higher taxes, and express distrust of the councillors and plain scepticism that any improvements in services will result. Mixed in with all this grumbling is a growing sense of personal resentment and hostility, and dissatisfaction is expressed largely as a personal grudge, or simple dislike of individual councillors.

Once community divisions have reached this stage, where real issues become submerged, through the sheer sense of impotence, to personal grudges and resentments, it becomes dangerous, and probably destructive, to try and bring the issue into open conflict: things are just too personal and emotionally loaded, and the chances are good that the real issues will never be openly discussed. What is needed is an issue in which the community as a whole can be involved in conflict with outside forces, before internal conflicts can be constructively raised and resolved.

NORMAN MCLEOD was born in Ottawa in 1944, and was raised in the family of a much-travelled economist, moving from Ottawa to Cambridge, Massachusetts; Arlington, Virginia; Jedda, Saudi Arabia; and Toronto. He took his undergraduate studies in political science and philosophy at Queen's University, Kingston, except for his third year, which he spent at the American University, Beirut, Lebanon. In 1965

Mr. McLeod worked for Frontier College as a labourer-teacher on a
C.P.R. extra gang in Alberta; and again in 1967 in a large construc-
tion camp in northern Ontario. He received his Honours B.A. from
Queen's in 1967, and went on to the University of Toronto to take his
M.A. in political economy.

FAY MCLEOD, née Martin, was born in Rocky Mountain House,
Alberta, in 1943, and was raised on a farm near Camrose, Alberta.
She took her undergraduate studies at the University of Alberta, Edmonton, and graduated in 1964 with a B.A. in psychology and sociology. She went to work for the Alberta Department of Public Welfare,
and served for two years as a caseworker in the Child Protection
division. In 1966 she entered the School of Social Work at the University of Toronto to study for an M.S.W. She did her field work for the
School at the Jewish Home for the Aged and the Family Service
Association.

FAY and NORMAN MCLEOD were married in April 1968. By that
time they had committed themselves to working for Frontier College
as a team. They were sent to Newfoundland in October by the College, and they both received their Master's degrees by mail in Cox's
Cove, Newfoundland.

'Thou Beside Me in the Wilderness' [1]

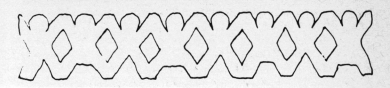

Florence O'Neill

For four years I had secretly desired to work in Land's End, for to me this settlement connoted all that was hopeless and rotten.

'Miss, if you want to see poverty, dirt, misery, and sickness, go to Land's End.'

When I argued, 'But what's wrong with Land's End?' I was told, 'Oh, the people there are no good. They are dishonest, lazy, dirty, ignorant and lawless. You can't do anything with them. If they *have* a few cents they make moonshine, get drunk, and fight. They'd rather buy a plug of tobacco than get a pair of boots for the kids.'

I had never had time to visit Land's End, though it was but six miles away from where I was teaching. Two paths lead to Land's End – one by the seashore, which is dangerous. 'A man fell over the cliff and was killed a long time ago. They say it's haunted, Miss. You'd better not try it.' The other path, cut through the woods and swamps, is difficult to follow, as I learned later from bitter experience. So I had never reached Land's End.

But I made contacts there. Once a week I lay in wait for the little man who carried the weekly mail from Land's End to Toulon and back. We had long chats, and the more I learned about Land's End, the more I wanted to go there. Finally, I decided that I *was* going, and going within a month, and that I would stay and teach there three months instead of the customary two.

But first, many obstacles had to be overcome if my term there was to be fruitful. Most important, it seemed absolutely imperative that the people of Land's End prove that they really wanted my services. Again, living accommodations of some kind must be found; and, finally, the consent of the Department of Education must be obtained. The latter I knew would be forthcoming if my request was presented in logical fashion. But how on earth could I solve all those problems with a full-time program on my hands?

R.S.V.P.

Luck was on my side for once. Shortly after I made my decision, my fairy godfather and godmother – the mailman and his wife – came up my pathway. Not divining the purpose of the visit, I thought quickly, 'Here is my chance to get an invitation to Land's End!' But I soon found that none of my wiles were needed, for, with much blushing and hesitancy, the mailman produced a sealed envelope from his pocket. It contained a petition from forty-nine people, asking me to come to Land's End. With tears in her eyes, the mailman's wife told me of the little children there growing up in ignorance, of the men and women who could not read or write or figure; of the isolation, the poverty, sickness, and privations of the entire population.

I asked her immediately to tell the people of Land's End how happy I should be to come to them as soon as my present work was finished. I would teach both day school and night school, I said, hold meetings, form clubs – do anything I could to help them, if only living quarters could be provided for me. After a long discussion of ways and means, the mailman decided to return to Land's End, hold a meeting at his house that night, and form a committee to build me a place to live. They would cut trees, get the use of a mill now lying idle and saw lumber. They would build a little room on to the school for my use. They would cut enough firewood to heat house and school.

After he left, I was so happy that I could not keep the good news to myself. I told several students and friends. All of them shook their heads. Said one, 'It sounds fine, Miss, and we hate to see you disappointed, but they'll never do it. It is only talk.' Others told me, 'You don't realize what you are up against. You'll need a stove, pipes, a bed, and you can't live in that bleak old schoolhouse alone. Take our advice and forget it. It's bad enough right here, but it's a hundred per cent worse at Land's End.'

With a shock, I realized that I had completely forgotten the stove and bed! Perhaps, after all, my advisers were right. Perhaps I had better wait awhile before I asked the Department for permission to teach at Land's End.

However, after about a week of suspense, the joyful tidings reached me that the people of Land's End evidently meant business. They had turned out in a body, cut trees and firewood, and were now sawing lumber. Adult education had actually begun! A rusty stove was borrowed, pipes ordered from the nearest store. Former students from Coveville sent piles of paper from the mills, and cardboard, cut conveniently for scribblers. (This we later made into books for day and night school use.)

Toward the last of March, the mailman, representing Land's End, proudly asked me to draw a plan for my little house. And could I tell him where and how to get nails and felt and glass! They figured that they would need fifty pounds of nails of varying sizes. That amount seemed to me enough to build a palace, but they should know. They had absolutely no money, but sixteen dollars would provide everything, even sheathing paper with a color scheme included! Things were shaping.

'And what are you going to do for a bed, Miss, and do you want shelves for your books and dishes and pans?' We decided on two benches that would look like day beds and take up little room. I knew where I could borrow one chair, and the young men had promised to make a table.

I was by this time so eager to meet the inhabitants of Land's End (there must be a few more like the mailman up there) that I could neither eat nor sleep. No obstacle seemed insurmountable now. The planning they had done showed that adult education had begun and, to my mind, in the right way.

Some good friends at Terry Brook, twelve miles away, supplied me with a frying pan, dishes, blankets, curtains, cutlery, and a kettle, and, with my first month's groceries bought and paid for, my sole remaining need was a congenial helper and companion. I knew the kind of person I needed. It would help if she knew French. She must be kind, considerate, and cooperative. Either Dorothy or Mary, I thought, might be willing to go with me. Fortunately for her, Dorothy, as a result of studying bookkeeping and typewriting at night school, had just taken a position as assistant bookkeeper and secretary to the manager of the co-operative store at Toulon. But Mary, age seventeen, accepted with delight.

At last all was ready. A message from the Department in answer to my urgent appeal brought the good news, 'Proceed to Land's End.' Early on an April afternoon, seated confidently by the side of our trusted drivers, Mary and I set out. Our teams were heavily laden and the going was rough. Truly we felt like pioneers. Now our wheels were revolving in the snow bank and we made no progress, or we were axle-deep in mud, our way impeded by unforeseen tree stumps or by rocks forced to the surface by the frost.

We Reach Land's End

We were undaunted and joyful and sooner than we expected we were at Land's End. It was all I had anticipated and much more. Drab, weather-beaten buildings stretched sparsely along a bleak, open coast. Broken fences, gates off hinges, pieces of cloth stuffed in broken window panes, roofs of houses sagging in the middle, dirty back yards, a muddy road, and here and there a mossy bank.

But where were the inhabitants, and where was the school building? Little barefoot children ran indoors, and pale faces pressed the window panes as we passed.

'We have to go a good piece yet, Miss. The school is about in the centre. Ah! there it is. Can you see that building with a little shed attached, white-like?' I strained my eyes and soon discerned, standing alone almost on the edge of the cliff, defying storms, unused for years except for very brief periods, what seemed to me a skyscraper – the little school chapel built many years ago by a French priest. As we drew near, a young girl came running up. 'Here's the key, Miss. You'll find kindlings and everything inside.'

As we entered that bare, empty shack, the chilly dampness of new-sawn lumber greeted us. I could not speak. Suddenly I felt terribly inadequate, lost, lonely, helpless, frightened. If I had had the shelter of a home awaiting me, I think I should have been tempted to return to it. One of the drivers, sensing my feelings, said, 'Miss, if you find you can't stand it, you have just to call me, and I'll come up and get you any hour of the day or night.' I smiled and said 'Thank you, George.' Inwardly, I told myself that this would never do and I thanked Heaven that there was no one to greet us.

We all set to work. Soon a fire was crackling in the rusty stove, and smoke issuing from sides and covers gave me the opportunity to have a much-needed cry. Mary was unpacking food. That's what I needed! Ham and eggs, coffee and bread. What a sumptuous meal! Suddenly my spirits soared. The crude legs of the homemade table, the shelves, the wood box – everything was beautiful! After supper, the drivers started on the return journey. Then two women came to clean the stove and help us get settled, and four men came to welcome us. The rest of the evening we spent putting our house in order.

We had no difficulty in arising early the next morning, because neither of us had had a wink of sleep. Just as we had been about to go to bed, the rain came in torrents and pattered incessantly on the sloping roof. In a short while we heard it pouring down either side of the stove pipe. With our newly blackened stove in mind, we sat up for an hour or more emptying containers every few minutes. Finally we gave up, put out the lights, and turned and twisted on our hard damp benches until dawn.

Exploring

The sun shone brightly, the air was invigorating, as I set out at eight in the morning to walk to the farthest end of the settlement to begin what was to me the most important phase of my work. Before seven-thirty that night, I must know my community. I must have visited every one of the twenty-four families and talked with most of the 150 inhabitants. Every contact, every conversation, with man, woman, and child should be an educative experience for both of us. If I could only convince them of my sincerity, could only awaken in them half the enthusiasm I now felt! Somehow, they must be made to know not only their immediate obvious needs, but also hidden desires and interests. Little goals attained must bear fruit and other goals must be made to seem attainable, other interests awakened. They must be made aware of their potentialities for leadership (already evinced); they must be made to feel that they are worthwhile citizens of Newfoundland. They themselves must desire a richer and fuller life. All this could not happen overnight, but if I could succeed in sowing little seeds here and there which would ultimately bear fruit my three months would not be spent in vain.

Three months! Unconsciously I quickened my pace. There was no time to lose. Every minute of the day and night must be utilized if we were to get anywhere. To begin, I must try to think in terms of how I should react, if I were illiterate, living in extreme isolation for years and years, subsisting at the lowest possible standard of living, and so used to hardships that I took them for granted.

I must remember that what I saw represented a gradual decay over a long period of years, that extreme isolation and resultant ignorance accounted for the greater part of the present state of affairs. My soliloquy ended as I approached the first house.

In all the families I visited that day, there were evidences of great poverty, malnutrition, and unhygienic living; in many, there was a history of tuberculosis. On the whole, I found the people very shy. Young men lying idly on a bank would cover their faces as I drew near. I used every imaginable method of approach. One time it would be 'Would you like to help me across that shaky bridge?' Again, 'Are you walking my way? Would you like to come along and tell me about Land's End? It would be a great help.'

Those tactics usually worked, but sometimes it was not quite so easy. On one occasion, as I knocked on the door, I was greeted with what seemed to be a violent outburst of abuse. From the broken English, I gathered that I would be like 'the rest of them' and would not stay longer than a few days. Luckily for me I had already visited a score of families, or I should have been frightened by the ferocious appearance of the unshaven man who finally opened the door. I waited until he had finished his tirade, and then shook his hand. Soon I was invited to sit on the only chair in the shack, and we had a real chat. I sensed that I could win him through his children, and so we conspired to make the day school a success.

Land's End Wakens

It is difficult to paint a realistic picture of just how and why this little sleepy village came to life. Under ordinary circumstances there was an almost perpetual blackout. The majority of the older people went to bed at dusk or sat in the dark (kerosene oil is an expensive commodity when food and clothing are at a premium), while the younger people wandered aimlessly from house to house – nothing to do – nowhere to go.

Suddenly the school building was ablaze with light. People from far and near had come to our first general meeting! The little building was crowded, and I breathed a sigh of relief. My faith was justified – the people wanted to learn. Forty-seven students between the ages of sixteen and sixty registered, and we decided to begin classes for adults the following night and to hold them regularly on Monday, Wednesday, and Friday nights. Thursday night was reserved for the women's club. Regular day school for the children would begin on Monday at nine o'clock.

Volunteer committees were formed to make immediate preparations for classes. Four men promised to come in the morning and use the lumber remaining from the building of my house to make tables and benches for the school. Two others decided to go to Toulon and bring up the portable organ, which the parish priest was lending to us for the term. The younger boys promised to look after the heating for the term. The women would take care of the cleaning of the schoolroom.

Our greatest accomplishment that night was deciding to build a bridge which would ensure a regular day school attendance. Heretofore, little children could not attend school when the river was too high for them to wade. All this and much more was accomplished at the first meeting. Not once were the people found lacking – and these were the people who had been called 'lazy, dishonest, and lawless'.

Classes Begin

After the first week, clubs and classes were in full swing. Rapid progress was made by our thirty-seven absolute beginners. From the start, teaching these men and women was a happy, interesting, and educative experience. Grasping the essentials of the three R's was to me but a minor part of what they learned, but for them it opened the door to an unknown world. I watched them wake up and take an interest in themselves and in their children. Things happened to them. They began to take pride in their appearance; the spirit of good fellowship blossomed; they felt that the success of the school was their responsibility as a group. Before and after classes they discussed their problems, they entered wholeheartedly into the spirit of the sing song and folk dancing. I took every opportunity to teach them good manners, health habits, the care and needs of the body. I tried to awaken a desire for a higher standard of living, which would be strong enough to bring forth action, to broaden their general outlook.

Our women's club might well have been a branch of the Parent-Teacher Association. We had the children in common, and that was the most valuable bond of contact. Together we discussed the care of the child from before birth to adolescence. Mothers talked about their own particular problems.

I was very often in desperation, though I tried hard not to show it. The children were undernourished, half naked, and dirty. I would have given anything for some warm, substantial material, some clothing to make over, shoes – anything to start with. But we had nothing of the kind at hand. We had to do the best we could with what we had. The mothers were anxious to learn cutting and sewing, so we began by each making an apron from a flour bag. Then we ordered a little material from the Co-op store and made a pair of pants, or a dress, for each child. Shirts with half-sleeves and fitted collars were made from flour bags. The women's club also wanted to learn about the planning and cooking of meals. We discussed nutrition, basing our talk on the use of the few foods available, and sometimes we gave demonstrations of cookery in our little room. Our meetings were cheerful, informal, friendly, and invariably ended about midnight or later with folk dancing and a light lunch.

My happiest memories are centred around the day school, perhaps because it was an experiment from the start. I had no idea what to do with forty children ranging from five to fifteen years, nearly all of whom were in grade one, and few of whom had any idea of what 'school' meant. A message to St. John's brought readers and other books. Coveville sent paper and pencils, and soon each child was the proud owner of a scribbler, a pencil, and reader. Many of the children made rapid progress. Almost naked, sometimes sick, and very often hungry, they defied wind, rain, and even parents' advice to come to school. Their average weekly attendance was roughly 95 per cent.

Little incidents stand out vividly – the eagerness with which they waited after school to have their new clothes fitted, their joy when they found real pockets in their pants. I remember especially eight-year-old Lee, who lived with his mother and brother in a shack unfit for a dog house. He wanted a box to put his shirt and pants in – and would I put it away for him? He was afraid to take his clothing home. There was no place to put it, and it might get wet.

Learning to study, work, and play together wrought miracles in these uncared-for children. They could now be trusted. Recess no longer meant bleeding noses, muddy faces, and cuts. They were learning to co-operate and liked it.

Fathers and mothers were proud of their little boys and girls and were beginning to feel responsibility for their development. They provided three motor boats (ordinarily used as fishing boats) for a gala all-day outing to Rocky Cove, a treat that the children will never forget. For most of them, the trip was their first away from Land's End.

Another activity requested by the people was community prayer. On Sunday mornings we met at nine o'clock and recited the Rosary, after which sometimes the children, and very often the whole group, joined in the singing of our favourite hymns. Surely, this was evidence of a unity far greater than I had dreamed of.

School Closes

All too soon, preparations for our official closing were underway. One o'clock in the morning found us busy practising our songs, solos, recitations, and little play. We must try to make our program good, for we expected visitors. Busy men and youths devoted a whole afternoon and morning to the building of the stage for the play – doors on hinges, imitation fireplace, nothing was missing. This again was an educational, as well as a co-operative, experience.

At the exercises, we had a full house, with not even standing room available. Former students of mine came from far and near, from towns a day's run by boat. Our program was a success, and the children's contribution was its most outstanding feature.

Day school and club continued the following week. I did not

mention closing, but I was troubled. I hated to leave. Increasingly, I realized that I had only scratched the surface. Would these people continue to study and work co-operatively, or would they quickly slip back into their former rut?

I was thinking along these lines one evening when I was alone. I must have fallen asleep, for I was awakened by a knock. Willy, one of my most active students, had come to talk with me. He, too, was troubled by the same thoughts. 'Miss, I hate to see you go. You have given us new courage. This is the first time we have had a worker who wanted to stay with us and help us. What *can* we do to get off the rocks? We've been talking about that agricultural society you told us of. Some of the men want to organize. We could start Co-op study clubs, though God knows how we'd get enough money to buy a share. Perhaps Mr. Murphy from the Co-op would come up some time and talk things over with us.' This request was what I had been waiting patiently for. Mary, who had been out for the evening, arrived, we replenished the fire, had lunch, and the three of us talked 'Co-op' well into the night.

At my request, Mr. Murphy came the next day for the first meeting of what we hoped would be an active agricultural society. We discussed the natural facilities of Land's End and listed its assets on the blackboard. There were possibilities for a cod and lobster fishery within immediate reach. There was any amount of good timber, a mill lying idle, and good farm and pasture land. Mr. Murphy led the group into a discussion of clearing of land and co-operative marketing of fish, lumber, and potatoes. The meeting gave a mere overview, he said, of what could be done in the long run. The group was ripe for action, and so an agricultural society was formed and officers elected. Plans were made to meet weekly, with Mr. Murphy as leader as long as he remained on the peninsula. We had reached another milestone!

Would that my story could have a more encouraging ending and that I could say I left Land's End economically secure. Not so! The people still suffer many privations. They lack medical care; they live in uninhabitable houses; they are undernourished. But they now have an understanding day school teacher, who is keeping alive a community spirit. On the survival of that spirit depends the progress of the people of Land's End.

FOOTNOTE

1. This article tells of Florence O'Neill's personal experiences while working in Land's End, Newfoundland, in 1942. The article was first published in *Learning and Society*, edited by Dr. J. R. Kidd and published by the Canadian Association for Adult Education, 1963.

DR. FLORENCE O'NEILL recently retired as Head, Adult Education Section, Indian Affairs Branch, Department of Indian Affairs and Northern Development. One of her main interests throughout her working career was the literacy and basic education of the adult. She frequently emphasized the importance of continuous integrated evaluation and the importance of service-research studies as an integral part of program development.

The First Years of Community Development In Manitoba

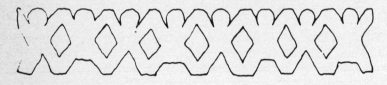

Jean. H. Lagassé

The first thing a social scientist must do when he becomes an administrator is to try to reconcile theory with practice and vice versa. In its search for logic a theory tends to follow a single line of reasoning. Like a laser beam, it penetrates deeply to focus on but a tiny surface at a time. Practice, like the candle, reaches in all directions at once, losing in penetration what it gains in coverage.

The administrator must remain a scientist, however. Only science will enable him to predict the behaviour of people and events. The public administrator in a community-development program must be able to draw explanations from a number of social sciences, especially anthropology, sociology, mass communications, adult education, social psychology and economics. It is his responsibility to structure those particular insights into an institutionalized whole, capable of becoming a government program.

As can be inferred from the title, the purpose of this paper is to relate the attempt that was made to reconcile theory and practice in the launching of a community-development program in Manitoba from 1959 to 1963. The paper is divided into three parts: the background, the launching, and the operation. Each, in turn, will be divided into a number of subdivisions as an attempt is made to give the reader some insight into those administrative problems that may be particular to a community-development activity.

In 'The Talladegha Story' Solom Kimball formulated a principle about new organizations that those involved in the first years of community development in Manitoba kept constantly in their minds as a warning. That principle was: 'New organizations tend to assume the same characteristics possessed by other organizations of the milieu in which they are formed; and, this is true even of those organizations launched to reform or change the existing organizations or the milieu.' It was always feared that it might not be possible to escape the other principles of human behaviour. Many of the things that were done in these first few years must be interpreted as an attempt to create something that would remain different from the standardized bureaucratic units of government administrations.

1. The Background

In the fall of 1959, the government of Manitoba announced that it approved in principle of the main recommendations of a five-hundred-page report (Lagassé, 1959) commissioned three years earlier to investigate the conditions under which the people of Indian ancestry were living.

The report had deliberately kept its recommendations to a minimum. In the belief that there is a tendency to implement only the easy or less compromising recommendations of a study, the report had eliminated all those that were not considered essential. A new approach was being recommended. If that new approach was implemented, the other desirable changes would follow. If it was not implemented, there would be little value, stated the report, in the government's investing more money to expand the existing programs.

That new approach, community development, was introduced in the report as something that the United Nations had utilized in the newly independent less-developed nations and that should be adapted by the province of Manitoba to deal with the Indian and Métis question. By requesting that the director of the study accept the responsibility for helping the province implement the recommendations of the report, the provincial government was indicating its willingness to provide funds for community development.

So much for the chronology of events preceding the launching of the program. There are a number of factors in the political and social make-up of the Manitoba of the 1950s that, more than a chronology of events, can help the reader understand

why a community-development program became a reality in
Manitoba at the time it did.

A. *Public opinion*

From the early fifties on, the Greater Winnipeg Welfare Council, the Manitoba Branch of the Canadian Association of Social
Workers, the Manitoba Council of Women, the Greater Winnipeg Ministerial Association, and many other groups, too numerous to name here, had been conducting studies into the
plight of people of Indian ancestry and making recommendations to the provincial government. It is important to note that
these recommendations were presented to the provincial and
not to the federal government. In addition to 25,000 Treaty
Indians there was in Manitoba an equal number of unintegrat-
ed Métis. There were another 50,000 Manitobans (Lagassé,
1959, Vol. 1, p. 54), descendants of those intrepid *voyageurs*
and fur-traders in the service of the Hudson's Bay Company
and the Northwest Company, who could have claimed some
Indian ancestry, but who were, for all intents and purposes,
known only for their European ancestry. Together these groups
accounted for more than 10 per cent of the population of the
province. Such a heavy concentration, the highest in Canada,
was giving a sense of urgency to every discussion about the
native question.

A province-wide Indian and Métis conference, sponsored by
the Greater Winnipeg Welfare Council, provided those interested in the Indian and Métis question with an annual opportunity to meet, focus upon the most pressing problems, pass resolutions, and, through an appointed delegation, discuss their
points of view in person with members of the provincial cabinet.

By contrast, the provincial government at that time possessed very little information about its native population. Neither the location nor the size of the main settlements was
known. The Cabinet was acutely aware of its shortage of information, as it found little to reply to the delegations that were
presenting resolutions.

It was then that the Member for St. Boniface, Roger Teillet,
himself of Métis ancestry, suggested to his colleagues that the
only way to remedy the situation was to initiate a comprehensive study. His motion before the Manitoba Legislative Assembly stated:

Whereas attention has been drawn to the fact that certain citizens of Manitoba, notably Métis and Indians, are living in difficult circumstances, THEREFORE BE IT RE-SOLVED that this House request the government to consider the advisability of having the Department of Agriculture make a study of this matter, and that the government take such steps as may appear advisable to remedy the situation. (The Orders of the Day, 1956).

The fact that the study was to be placed under the aegis of the Department of Agriculture need not lead one to conclude that the government thought it was faced primarily with an agricultural problem. It often happens in such matters that the personal qualities and interests of individual Cabinet ministers are determining factors in deciding where new programs ought to be lodged.

B. Governmental support

The change that took place in the attitude of the government, under the stimulus of well-informed public opinion, was such that it can be listed here, without hesitation, as one of the factors helping to explain why community development was first launched in Manitoba.

Unless there is political awareness of a problem, suggestions regarding solutions from civil servants are in vain. Prior to 1956, when the study was launched, the government had received many excellent internal reports from its civil servants. Notwithstanding the Cabinet's apparent lack of awareness of Indians and Métis when it received the delegations from the annual Indian and Métis conferences, there were several departments that had close contacts with that part of the population. Included in this group were the Natural Resources branch of the Department of Mines and Natural Resources, the Special Schools Division of the Department of Education, and the Social Welfare and Public Health branch of the Department of Health and Welfare. In each administrative unit, there were several individuals dedicating their best energies to a labour of love, trying to ease the problems they had observed. But their work had not received a sufficiently high priority rating to permeate the upper echelons of government administration.

A similar situation was found to exist in the other provinces. We may have become so accustomed to seeing the Indians and

Métis capture the headlines of our major newspapers that we have forgotten what it was like in Canada for the native population some two decades ago. When, at the Minaki Conference on Citizenship in 1957, the federal Deputy Minister of Citizenship and Immigration, who had responsibility for Indian Affairs, stated as a sign of achievement that, while at the end of the war there were 10,000 Indian children for whom no school was available, that number now had been reduced to 2,000, the participants appeared satisfied. No one, including newspaper editorialists, questioned why so basic a service had been withheld from so large a population for so long.

A labour contract signed between a major international labour union and a large international industrial firm in Manitoba in the mid fifties contained an article declaring that wards of the federal government are excluded from the terms of this contract. That wording had been lifted from a contract that the same union had signed with an industrial concern in British Columbia. These contracts were public documents, available to the mass media, scrutinized by the labour officials of the provinces concerned, and yet no one seems to have found anything strange or out of place in that article. Indeed, prior to the sixties, Indians in Canada were seen very much as public wards and the sole responsibility of the federal government.

Why then would a provincial government accept a new problem? When the Indians from Nelson House were marching in Thompson requesting a greater opportunity for permanent employment from International Nickel, the question was raised in senior government circles. Instead of becoming involved in the situation, the provincial government could have said that since these people were Indians, they were the responsibility of the federal government. But the Premier himself intervened with the reminder that he had been elected by all the residents of the province and could not agree that any segment of the population escaped his jurisdiction.

Mention was made earlier of the futility of a civil servant's devotion to a cause in which the elected officials have but a passing interest. Let the situation be reversed, as it was in Manitoba from the early sixties on, and the civil servants have a real challenge. They find that it is no longer money and support that are lacking, but ideas, clues, solutions, and program outlines.

This is not to say that community development did not meet with some resistance at times. Speaking to the first staff conference, Premier Roblin cautioned that individuals involved in social change could expect conflicts. As Premier he could support community development as a new approach only so far; the rest was up to the staff. Through the quality of their work they had to convince the members of the Legislative Assembly, and the civil servants, of the validity of their approach.

Notwithstanding the above, at some point in the genesis of government policies decisions become quite personalized. Government support for community development was made tangible through three persons: the Deputy Minister of Welfare, the Minister of Welfare, and the Premier. The decisive character of their contribution cannot be overestimated.

C. *The native population*

A third background factor favourable to an early start of a community-development program in Manitoba was the readiness of the native people for change. This is not to say that the people of Indian ancestry in Manitoba were in a better social and economic situation than their brothers in the other provinces. On the contrary, though the author does not have the official statistics available for consultation at this time, it is his recollection that the native population of Manitoba in 1959 rated more poorly than that of the other provinces on most of the items that contribute to the achievement of a high standard of living, i.e. number of rooms per person, electrification, employment ratio, infant mortality, educational achievement, annual income, and so on.

About half of Manitoba's Indian and Métis population lived in the Precambrian Shield and the forest belt adjoining it and depended on fishing and trapping for a livelihood. Their isolation prevented joint action and mutual awareness. Annual meetings of the Manitoba Indian Brotherhood were poorly attended. The main goals of the one Métis association, the Union Nationale Métisse, representing the French-speaking Métis, were cultural and historical rather than social and economic.

In 1959 in Manitoba, the terms 'Indian' and 'Halfbreed', as the Métis were then called, had a very pejorative meaning. As part of the study mentioned earlier, some twenty white officials in positions of authority in or near native communities were asked to define what they meant by these terms. The following is a sample of the type of answer received:

"Halfbreeds are persons of Indian ancestry living in poor houses similar to those of the reserve."

"Any full-blooded or half-blooded Indian who is not living as a white person. In this connection, the attitude of the white neighbours may force certain families to remain halfbreeds longer than they would otherwise."

"A halfbreed is a person who has some degree of Indian blood plus an upbringing which combines factors of primitive living usually in connection with a hunting economy. This applies even when these people have almost embraced the white way of life. A person with a similar degree of Indian blood is accepted into the Canadian way of life only when he conforms to all general requirements of this society; the degree of Indian blood is not too important."

"A halfbreed is a person who when he has money lives like a Whiteman and when he is broke lives like an Indian (Lagassé, 1959, Vol, 1, pp. 56-57).

A number of inferences can be drawn from these definitions. If 'living under poor conditions' was an important element in determining who was a Métis, it follows that the more sordid the conditions, the more 'Indian blood' those individuals living under them were supposed to have. It must be concluded that Manitobans considered the degree of Indian blood to be related to material possessions and the behaviour of individuals. It will be observed that, in this social stratification, Indians were rated lower than the Métis.

Given that people's images of themselves are largely derived from what others are saying about them, one must also conclude that it must have been nearly impossible for native parents, under those conditions, to teach their children self-esteem and pride in their cultural heritage.

Under these conditions native communities were losing much of their potential leadership. One would frequently meet individuals who did not wish to have their native ancestry known. Young students were deprived of models with whom to identify. There was no positive role an adult could play and still remain an Indian or a Métis.

Why then are the above conditions considered to constitute a readiness on the part of people of Indian ancestry for a community-development program? Should they not, on the contrary, have provided a very poor basis for a start?

There are some human aspirations and natural qualities that an environment, no matter how hostile, never quite succeeds in destroying. The report had stressed that the native people had more motivation for self-betterment than existing government programs were providing for. The small lad holding a slingshot knows that the farther away from the fork he pulls the weight, the greater will be the acceleration it achieves when it is released. Community development has precisely that quality when it comes to releasing human potential. The first changes that would take place after the launching of a community-development program could not help but be dramatic and easily visible to outsiders.

The main contribution of community-development is indeed that of giving people a sense of their personal worth and a realization of their collective strength. The opportunity to form autonomous committees and local organizations; the opportunity to appear before authorities with the added strength of vocal community backing; the knowledge that the court of public opinion is favourably inclined to one's cause; the availability of technical advice if and when required: all of these factors were easily recognized by the people of Indian ancestry as desirable assets for them to tap in the facilities offered by a community-development program.

II. The Launching

The study was completed in February 1959, and released in printed form in April. The director of the study was reappointed as consultant to the provincial government in mid November. One of his first assignments was to present a plan for the implementation of what had been described as the main recommendation of the report: the creation of a community-development authority.

A. *The concept*

The first submission he made followed the report's recommendations as closely as possible. The report had said:

It (the Centre for Community-Development) could operate under the joint sponsorship of the Government of Manitoba and the University of Manitoba. It could be administered by a Board of Directors, composed of representatives of the University of Manitoba, the Provincial Government, the In-

dian Affairs Branch, and prominent persons of Indian ancestry. This arrangement would have the advantages of guaranteeing the highest quality of leadership possible for a community development program. It would facilitate consultation with university personnel and still retain the technical
and administrative experience of government departments.
The training of qualified personnel for a Community Development Program would be facilitated as well by this type of
administration as University Departments would, no doubt,
welcome the opportunity to place their students in direct
contact with concrete life experience (Lagassé, 1959, p. 112).

There were many reasons for recommending this formula.
Perhaps, however, the report sought to achieve too many goals
with a single recommendation. There was a need to provide for
an independent operation, which a semi-private body could
provide. There was a need to prevent overlapping of jurisdictions and foster co-operation between the new agency and the
federal Indian Affairs branch. There was the hope that, given a
chance, the university would become less subject-oriented and
more community-oriented. The new agency needed to be in an
influential position in order to conduct a public information
program and change the attitude of the public towards people
of Indian ancestry. There was a need to provide for direct
participation in, and control of, the new agency by the native
population. The latter could be achieved only by providing for
the appointment of native people to a majority of the positions
on the governing board of the agency. A government branch,
of necessity, would have to be responsible to a Minister, and
through him to the Legislative Assembly, and thus be subject
to the priority of interests of the provincial politics of the day.

It is difficult to venture an opinion as to whether the above
structure would have achieved the goals sought more effectively
than the one that was tried. At any rate, the reaction of the
provincial government to the proposal was that it represented
too ambitious a start. It was argued that a new idea, such as
community development was at that time, ought to go through
experimental stages first. The consultant was asked to prepare
a second submission providing for an operation that would
take place totally within the framework of the Department of
Health and Welfare, i.e., that would be a regular branch thereof.

Ironically, this was the only department that the report had
identified as inappropriate for a community-development operation, saying:

Should it prove impractical to create a Centre for Community Development as suggested above, the Provincial Government should consider allocating the responsibility of this program to a department that offers similar services to the rest of the population. It should not be placed in a department that has already established a network of communications with the population under study which would make community development difficult to implement. For example, the majority of the people of Indian ancestry included in this study look upon the Department of Welfare as a relief-granting agency. Such an attitude on the part of the people would conflict with Community Development which suggests that people undertake improvements by themselves (Lagassé, 1959, p. 111).

Industry and Commerce was mentioned by the report as the department that would best serve the interests of community development, on the assumption that those assets that Industry and Commerce represented were exactly those that until then had been least accessible to Indians and Métis. The department had a broad range of contacts with the business world and regulated its activities. It had a Regional Development branch inspired by a philosophy quite akin to that which presently motivates the new federal Department of Regional and Economic Expansion. A location in that department might better enable the community-development officers to open the doors of industry and employment to Indians and Métis. Therein, it was felt, lay the future of the native population. In retrospect, the support that community development did receive from the officials of the Department of Welfare was such that it would be difficult to suggest that this location proved to be a handicap.

B. Program interpretation

By the time the report was completed, there was good readiness for its recommendations. For each of the main subjects studied, advisory committees had been formed. Invited to sit on those committees were officials of public and private agencies most concerned with each topic. Each committee met at least four times: once to help draft the questions that the study should ask on each subject; once to receive a mid-term progress report; and at least twice to discuss and help interpret the main findings of the study team.

The provincial government had requested an action study. It

was felt that maximum impact would be achieved by associat-
ing with the study those persons and agencies who were most
likely to be involved in the implementation of the recommendations. The research team was aware that it would have to recommend new activities that might be seen as threatening. Involvement of the authorities would give them a chance to adjust their programs gradually ahead of the final report and thus
would eliminate the need for many recommendations and negative comments. The discussions that took place in those committees helped the researchers better understand the problems
and anticipate the reaction of the public to their final text, thus
enabling them to tailor their arguments to the requirements of
each particular situation.

The native population had also been prepared for the recommendations of the report. Quite unintentionally, the field work
for the study had been conducted so as to pave the way for
community development. It was decided that, in order to arrive
at an accurate estimation of the size and location of the native
population in Manitoba, the entire province would be
crisscrossed by the field-workers. The province was then divided into three sections: north of the fifty-third parallel, south of
that line, and the Greater Winnipeg area.

In each community where people of Indian ancestry were
found, a questionnaire was to be completed with the help of
respondents selected at random and representative of the major
family names. As some questions pertained to family units and
the siblings of the spouses, this type of selection was felt to be
most profitable. The questions asked had to do with how the
native people saw their problems; what they thought the researchers should recommend to the provincial government;
what they had done until then to try to cope with their problems; what obstacles they had met in trying to better their
situation; and so on.

In order to avoid a certain kind of bias influencing their
findings and to guarantee that the report presented the Indian
and Métis problems as the natives saw them, the field workers
were requested to avoid meeting the local non-Indian notables
as much as possible. This proved to be quite a departure from
'normal' white – non-white relations for those communities. The
native people were somewhat surprised that so much weight
was given to their opinions. The whites were upset because they
were not being consulted. This direct approach, plus the long
discussions they provoked on the rights of all Manitobans to

achieve a decent standard of living, engendered some eagerness
among Manitobans to become involved in the new program.

While Cabinet approval for community development was
quickly given, there was reason to believe that some Ministers
might not have grasped the full impact of the new approach.
There was some fear in the Department of Welfare that when
the first community development officers became effective in
helping local communities achieve their goals, they would meet
with some resistance from those departments responsible for
the things that the local people wanted to change.

This fear was discussed with the Premier, who offered to
invite eight of the Ministers most directly concerned to form a
study group with which the Department of Welfare would discuss the program it was hoping to launch. The group came
together approximately ten times for supper or evening meetings in a downtown hotel, with the Premier himself present at
most of the gatherings. The Manitoba Department of Welfare
(Community Development Services, 1962) put into writing for
the occasion a set of guidelines that were to be reproduced later
as a description of the government's policy towards community
development. A quotation from a section of that paper will
help the reader understand how community development was
conceived in Manitoba:

Every effort is being made to provide maximum flexibility
and autonomy for the implementation of this community
development program. In order to operate effectively a
Community Development program must not be too closely
linked with the administrative policies of other government
departments. . . .
. . . A Community Development Officer must not be allowed
to become a choreman for all government departments.
However, he must be provided with full opportunities (meetings, written materials, etc.) to be acquainted with government policy as administered by departments of government.
He must have channels of communications to acquaint other
government departments as to pressures he sees looming,
and problems as (a) the local community is seeing them, and
(b) how he sees them. The Community Development Officer
must be in a position where he can advise the local community, insofar as he is capable, as to what is government policy
and what the government resources are. On the other hand,
it is readily acknowledged that the Community Development
Officer's function is not primarily, nor necessarily, to pro-

mote to the local community, or defend there, the policy of other government departments.

It is his job, insofar as he can, to be able to say, this is government policy ... here's how you can use it ... you say you don't like it or it works counter to your interests, ambitions or welfare ... you have every right to work as you see fit to get government to recognize your legitimate goals and problems; and I will do my best to interpret your situation to government.

The Community Development Officer will be unable to help the local people work towards or achieve their locally defined goals if they feel he is an apologist or defender of government policies which, they believe, stand in their way. They must feel that when they question a government policy or express the wish to have one changed, the Community Development Officer is not himself playing a role which prevents that policy from being reconsidered by government.

Thus 'helping people achieve their goals' became a prominent feature of community development in Manitoba. When the activities of a particular officer were questioned, the norm that would be used to appraise his behaviour was: 'Was he helping the people achieve their goals or was he promoting one of his own pet peeves ... or getting rid of his frustrations with bureaucracy ... or what have you?'

III The Operation

The problems that arise in the course of the administration of any program are numerous. In a discussion of this type it is difficult to justify the choice of a few or the elimination of most. Problems are subjective things. What constitutes a problem to one individual may not be a problem at all to another with more insights or skills. The few problems discussed below were chosen in the belief that they might help the reader understand those problems that may be peculiar to a community-development program operating within a government setting.

A. Recruitment and training

The advertisements placed in the major national dailies yielded over three hundred applications. It was felt that the candidates appointed should possess at least two qualities, namely, above-average skills in group dynamics, and the willingness to place their skills at the service of native communities for a minimum of two years. Later on, as officers were hired not as consultants but as regular civil servants, the wording used in the official posters had to be more carefully chosen, in order to avoid eliminating the most qualified candidates.

The posters stated that university studies in anthropology or another human science were a prerequisite. In the setting of salary rates the university requirement was a definite advantage. In order still to have access to the large pool of qualified native individuals without a university degree, the posters declared that for the purpose of this competition, a lifetime of close association with people of Indian ancestry would be regarded as equivalent to a university degree in anthropology. The Public Service Commission could accept this exception because the reason anthropology was required was to guarantee that the applicant would understand the native cultures.

The inability to arrive at this compromise elsewhere has led to the establishment of a Community Development Assistant category, to which native persons are systematically assigned and given a lower salary rate, which works against one of the first aims of community development: namely, allowing the native people to regain their self-esteem. Someone who is aware that his employer thinks him worth only one-half to one-third the salary of another group of individuals doing approximately the same job is bound to develop a complex.

Throughout the period under review the staff of Community Development Services was kept small. Saul Alinsky's first remarks to the 1965 Prairie Provinces Banff Training Institute were: 'I see there are 150 persons in this room. You can't all be good community-development officers because ten or fifteen is all that would be needed to completely change the West and I have not yet seen that change.'

In 1954 Nehru had said something in a similar vein to a graduating class of Village Level Workers: 'When community development started in India we had twenty-five Village Level Workers and we were all impressed with the changes that were taking place. There are now more than 25,000 Village Level Workers. There just are not 25,000 Indians who can be trained into becoming good community-development officers.'

It is realized that several concepts of community development can be valid, each applicable to different situations. The Manitoba experience wanted, for a start at least, to focus heavily on giving the native people the opportunity to become a social and political force, to achieve coherence and awareness of their goals, to make their presence felt, to learn the skills of group interaction, to start believing that there were many worth-while goals that they could achieve on their own.

The presence of too many community-development officers could have delayed the achievement of that goal. By making the presence and activities of community-development officers obvious, it would have been difficult for the Indians and Métis to feel that they were themselves responsible for the progress that was being made, let alone convince the white population that it was the native population and not the community-development staff that was expressing itself when demands were being made.

The goal of Community Development Services was to start a movement. No matter how desirable a goal, if the native population was not able to achieve it through their own negotiations with the authorities, no attempt was made to act officially on their behalf. In the absence of prior models, emphasis was put on developing a model that portrayed the picture of dynamic community leaders, giving generously and skilfully of their free time to improve the conditions under which their fellow men were living. The extent to which the people of Indian ancestry in Manitoba have been giving leadership in the last few years to all kinds of activities at the provincial and national level is an indication that this goal was amply realized.

The officers were urged to dedicate much time to studying the economic factors that influenced or controlled the income realizable in each of the occupations in which the native population was engaged. While at first most of these factors might have been foreign to them, it is amazing how familiar they actually became with the economics of such things as bush-clearing, lumbering, fishing, trapping, sub-contracting and construction. They would involve in their learning experience those members of the community most involved or most likely to become interested in each particular topic. Funds were available to call upon outside resource persons for additional information once the more traditional sources (books, government personnel) had contributed what they could.

At quarterly staff-meetings, specific operational problems were discussed with experts in pertinent subjects. Once a year, a week-long residential seminar was planned to which the wives were invited at headquarters' expense. When a person settles in an isolated community, it is the entire family that needs to adjust. The wife may come to regret her husband's decision to leave the material comforts of an urban environment. Under such conditions a wife may come to reject the working conditions and the people who absorb so much of her husband's time. In the early 1960s, the Indian-white relations in many northern communities reminded one of a caste system. The community-development family, on the other hand, was expected to associate itself with the native community, not the white colony. This required maturity and stability of character, plus the willingness to go through a certain acculturation process.

Very few agencies placing families in the North have yet attempted to cope with this problem. Employee efficiency and marital happiness are seriously affected. In an attempt not only to avoid destroying both, but to help the individuals involved achieve a higher level of human experience than would have been possible for them had they remained in an urban setting, a great deal of attention was paid to the needs of the family as a unit.

At the annual staff seminar, the wives would be invited to attend the regular sessions, thereby learning to understand the problems their husbands were trying to meet. In addition, from the second year on, they formed their own study group in human relations and cultural differences, in which their personal experiences could be shared. In this way, the families with more experience could help those who had just joined the staff.

B. Public opinion

The important role of public opinion in helping the program get started has already been discussed. Public understanding and support were even more vital once the program got under way. The mass media were in a better position than Community Development Services to help give Indians and Métis a new image of themselves and make the public aware of the changes that were taking place.

The staff was kept informed of the relative merits of individual reporters and producers and saw it as their duty to help the Indians and Métis obtain the most favourable coverage possible for any of their activities. The staff was asked, however, never to allow itself to be quoted by the media, and to keep referring any inquiries to competent local authorities. Aspiring native leaders were thus given opportunities to strengthen their role and project their image on the entire province. Actually the media quickly grasped what community development was trying to do and frequently made unsolicited contributions of great value.

C. *Freedom of action*

The Mexican Indian Affairs program (Instituto Nacional Indegenist, 1964) is aimed at 'native communities' rather than the 'native population'. Its services are offered to all communities where the presence of some people of Indian background is a factor. By contrast, in the United States and Canada it is the native population, i.e., those Indians whose names are on a government list, that is the object of the service. One of the unintended consequences of this practice is that it tends to segregate the Indians and the administration more than is good for either party. The federal authority is prohibited from spending money or giving its services to non-Indians. Indians have trouble receiving those services that are available to 'all citizens'.

Community Development Services preferred to adopt the Mexican practice. Its staff was asked to make their technical advisory services available to all residents of the communities to which they were assigned. This was made known to the native people as well. An effort had to be made to remain impartial. The example of the lawyer and the doctor was utilized to illustrate how a person can give the best of himself to persons or groups who may at times represent opposing interests.

When an officer was first assigned to a community, he was requested to avoid becoming involved for at least three months. This was difficult to achieve, partly because most appointees were live-wires, and partly because it is natural for a person to want to show the community what he can do from the start. The reason for the request was to avoid having officers acting as technical advisers before they themselves knew what was involved. It was also hoped that as a result the community rather than the officer would set the pace and determine what the officer's concerns should be.

Officers would find this difficult to do. The communities would attempt to involve them from the start. They had to

refuse to give reasonable services at the very time they themselves were trying to be accepted. They were asked to keep in
mind what sociology teaches about 'roles', both 'assigned' and
'achieved'. A community will accept almost any role, providing
it is constant and predictable. Communities can integrate
equally well with the village fool and the village elder, the
preacher and the bootlegger. But let the preacher become bootlegger or vice versa and there is an uproar. The officers' responsibility, especially in the early years when community development itself had to get its message across, was to establish
carefully a new role in native communities: that of technical
adviser. It was realized in principle that role would be whatever
the staff as a group decided to make it. It was important,
however, that once this had been decided, the role would be
played in all communities and by all officers.

Within these limits the officers could experience freedom of
action. Each was in the best position to know what the wisest
advice to give was. The director could not be familiar enough
with a local situation to state what should be said or done. His
role was that of a technical adviser to his staff. If community
development is so good, it must be applied to the administration of a community-development program as well. It would
not have been possible to be directive on the inside and permis-
sive on the outside. This placed a heavy responsibility on the
staff. Only the most mature individuals could function well
with a minimum of direction.

D. Support services

Very few of those who have written about community development have emphasized the degree of outside support a Village
Level Worker (or in the Manitoba experience, a community-
development officer) needs. Attention has been almost entirely
focussed upon the process of change and the skills required to
set it in motion.

At least one half of the energies of Community Development
Services were directed towards what could be called the 'outside world', i.e. factors that were external to the communities
with which the office was ostensibly working. Indeed, most of
the factors that Indian and Métis communities wanted to
change were controlled or influenced by forces outside their
communities. Assuming that there was no situation of permanent conflict present, the outside world had adjusted to the

relative inactivity of those communities and had regulated their services on the basis that nothing was going to change. A closely knit pattern of differential treatment resulted, which could have been called discrimination if that word did not, once used, prevent all involved from co-operative action. On the contrary, the techniques of community development needed to be applied to the outside world at the same time, if not before, they were applied to the native community. Indeed, let the native community evolve and become aware of its potential and let the outside authorities continue in their traditional habits, and in no time a situation of open conflict emerges that serves neither the long-term cause of progress nor of community development.

The author strongly challenges Saul Alinsky's concept of the Establishment as 'the enemy'. Alinsky illustrates his point by asking how effective a labour organizer would be if he were palsy-walsy with management. He adds that people will do the right things for the wrong reasons. The less commendable the things people want to do, the higher the motives they invoke.

In the Manitoba experience, how effective would Community Development Services have been with the outside authorities with this battle cry? To Alinsky's point of view was opposed that of Gandhi, who advised his co-nationals to hate the imperialist system and do all they could to destroy it but at the same time to have sympathy for the individual through whom it was enforced, for these individuals were the victims of the imperialist system as much as the Indians themselves.

The Manitoba officers felt it would have been a lack of faith in community development if they had agreed it could not be made to work effectively in co-operation with the outside authorities. This implied that the head office would make sure the outsiders had access to as much information as possible about the local communities, especially to that information that showed the changes that were taking place. Considerable time was spent interpreting community development and helping outside agencies cope with the problems that were caused by the progress being made in native communities.

Another aspect of support services for community development is the research that must continually be going on in the head office for data and materials that can be of help to the field staff, i.e. technical data to help them give technical advice to their communities, and operational data about government programs and policies so that the communities would be aware of existing government resources. It would be difficult to over-estimate the potential represented by the combined resources of federal and provincial departments. Let the stage be set right and there is little that cannot be done. Let, on the other hand, the problems be approached in a traditional bureaucratic way and the first thing that will be said is likely to be: 'Prove to me that this comes within my jurisdiction.' The community-development officer can witness such a scene and return home hating the Establishment or he can start asking himself 'What would have constituted a better approach?'

The staff of Community Development Services was aware of the different approaches that could be used, from a timid letter of inquiry to an appeal to the Premier or to public opinion. In its discussions with community leaders, the merits of these various approaches were discussed and an effort made to use the most effective one in each case. Above all the case itself needed to be well presented, in a way that met the criteria of those for whom it was intended. The head office, by keeping informed of the climate that prevailed in each government office, could be of real assistance in helping the Indians and Métis understand the system to which they wanted to relate and so establish contact in a way that could lead to the satisfaction of all concerned.

Much more needs to be learned about the dynamics of community development. How can the conflict that accompanies change be kept to a happy level? Winning an individual battle at the cost of augmenting the rejection and hate that frequently results from bitter conflicts is winning nothing at all. The evidence is that there is already far too much conflict in the world. 'Make love not war' is a reminder that 'social-changers' could well heed. In the Manitoba context, the fact that community development was supported by the top echelons of government gave it the opportunity to establish simultaneously two networks of communication, one with the Establishment and one with the native people. It was a difficult navigational course to follow at times, but from the lessons learned others should be able to do much better.

JEAN H. LAGASSÉ is on educational leave from the federal Department of the Secretary of State and is studying at the University of Grenoble, France. His doctoral thesis is expected to deal with the problems of domination in international aid programs.

Mr. Lagassé obtained his B.A. from the University of Manitoba in 1947 and his M.A. from Columbia University in 1956. Between 1947 and 1950 he was a student in theology at Saint Boniface Seminary, an affiliate of the University of Montreal.

Although he has taught briefly at both the collegiate and university levels, Mr. Lagassé's main experience lies in the fields of research and administration. As Director of the Social and Economic Research Office of the Manitoba Department of Agriculture between 1956 and 1959, he headed the study to which he refers in this paper. As Director of Community Services from 1959 to 1963, he helped launch one of the first official community-development programs in Canada. From 1963 to 1970 he served as Director of Canadian Citizenship, a multi-purpose civic-education agency responsible for inter-group relations, educational travel, and human rights in Canada.

As a federal civil servant he was appointed to a number of international delegations: he attended the fifth (1964) and sixth (1968) congresses of the Inter-American Indian Institute in Quito, Ecuador, and Patzcuaro, Mexico; he headed the Canadian delegations to the United Nations Human Rights seminar held in Kingston, Jamaica, in 1967, when the theme topic was 'The Effective Realization of Human Rights through National Legislation,' and the seminar on 'The Problems of Multi-national States' held in 1965 in Ljubljana, Yugoslavia. He has also travelled extensively in the U.S. on a Fund for Adult Education Fellowship (1959), studying American Indian Affairs, and spent some time in Mexico visiting Indian communities in 1966 and 1968.

An Educational Approach to Community Development: Case and Comment[1]

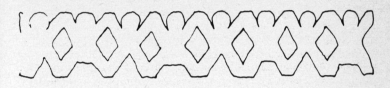

Arthur Stinson

Beginning

It was a simple enough beginning. The very last paragraph in an Extension Division brochure stated:

> The Extension Division is willing to work with organizations and agencies in any region of the five counties of the Ottawa Valley in devising a program or course in community analysis. The purpose of such a course would be to assist people in a region to assess the problems, needs and resources of that area and, in particular, to determine how educational resources may be utilized to assist in the solution of problems or the meeting of needs. Inquiries should be sent to the Director of Extension.

Behind the statement was the knowledge that the traditional extension of adult-education courses outside of Metropolitan Ottawa into the five counties for which Algonquin College had responsibility was inadequate. The Board of Governors had decided not to hire a consultant firm, but instead directed the Extension Division to search for new methods to serve the educational needs of the area.

The Director of Extension and Alan Clarke[2], who then was on contract with the School of Applied Arts, discussed various possible approaches and decided to see if any group would be interested in the idea of a Self Study. Both had an interest and some experience in community work and had studied recent experiments, such as 'Town Talk' in Thunder Bay and the work of the social animators in Quebec. With no specific staff or budget for community development, the Community Self Study idea seemed most adaptable to the style and resources of a College Extension Division.

A basic principle, agreed upon from the beginning, was that the community should approach the College. The need would have to be sufficiently evident, and enough community interest and organization present, to generate such a request. The College would not attempt to impose the idea of a Self Study.

For a few months, this prerequisite appeared to mean nothing would happen. But then, this type of program was unknown in the area and it had received no publicity other than the one announcement.

Then, in the spring of 1969, two inquiries were received almost simultaneously: one from a small town thirty miles outside Ottawa, and one, surprisingly, from a surburban area within the city. The latter came as a surprise, because the city had not been our target and we had not thought of 'community' in these terms.

Entry into a Community

The process began with the first telephone call from an interested individual. This led to a meeting with one or more individuals. The discussion was exploratory.

The process could end there. In one community, for example, we found through discussion that the group had already done considerable analysis and was well advanced into action programs with some professional help at its disposal. We could not see that our approach would help much. In another case, the community had already had several agencies attempting to help it, and the situation was very confused. Although we did not exactly refuse, we required that the various factions in the community would have to make a united approach to us before we could begin to work with them. This did not happen.

In the four cases[3] where the Self Study eventually took place, the interested individuals went back to what was to be the sponsoring organization and persuaded them to take the next step: to call a meeting to consider the idea and invite us to be present.

The meeting stage varied according to circumstances. The

group had to size us up, decide if it could entrust itself to our hands, and determine if the Self Study idea was a project that might meet its needs. From our point of view, we wanted to make sure that what we were proposing suited local circumstances, and we needed to know what the group had tried to do, what they hoped to achieve, and what some of the problems were. Sometimes this took several meetings.

In the meeting stage we used a simple questionnaire, which initiated the process of collective thinking. What are the community assets and liabilities? Where is the community going, and what forces are driving it? What is the power structure, and where are the dissenting views? That kind of thing. Most important, the questionnaire was used to establish where the community was geographically located.

The main questions used to identify the community were as follows: "Community is a place where decisions can be made and action implemented to provide resources". What are the boundaries of the community? What kind of decisions are made within this community? What other kind of decisions would be possible within this community?

The questionnaire, with its emphasis on dynamics and citizen participation, stirred considerable interest, and a follow-up meeting was usually requested to learn the results. The feedback was strictly factual with no interpretation and this led to discussion during which people began to develop their own hypotheses about community attitudes, structures, and action. At this point the decision was usually taken to proceed with the project.

During the discussion process, a number of operative questions were also sorted out. Although precise definitions were not established, 'understandings' were reached on such points as the following:

1. the 'sponsoring organization' was to play a supportive role during the Self Study and to take some responsibility for implementation of results;
2. the College personnel (co-ordinator, faculty, and field-work students) would guide the process, act as catalyst, and provide help and support to the participants;
3. the participants would make decisions on what was important to study and would actually do the research on these problems;
4. some kind of reporting to the general community would be agreed upon;

5. the extent to which the co-operation of the media would be sought would be clarified;
6. some guidelines on the confidentiality of information would be agreed upon;
7. evaluation methods and the potential of action arising out of the Study would be accepted;
8. elected officials would be informed of the proposed Study and their support in principle requested.

During the first two Self Studies we found we had not taken enough time to work these points through with the people in the communities. The result was that later the Self Study process was disrupted while one or another of these points, usually having to do with the clarification of roles, was sorted out. This is not to suggest that everything could be cut and dried in advance; it never worked that way! The people involved in the preparatory discussions wanted to know what they were getting into, but they also didn't want to talk forever. We learned to take our cues from them.

Recruiting and Interpretation

This was an intermediate stage. In one sense it was still part of the 'entry' phase. In another, the Self Study had already begun.

It was regarded as the final phase of entry because it was still possible that the project, and therefore the role of the College, would be rejected. People might have refused to participate.

The Self Study really began, however, as soon as the question came up as to who would be sought as recruits. The sponsoring group had already agreed, on our advice, that between forty and sixty people, as representative of the total community as possible, form the Study group. The recruiting committee, therefore, had to begin by finding out what needs were to be represented: ethnic groups, age groups, language groups, social groups, power groups, underprivileged groups. Our role was to raise all the appropriate questions. In the long run, if the group recruited was not a good cross-section it was the responsibility of the local group. But the process was a lesson in community demography.

Usually, a recruiting committee wanted a piece of paper, a prop, to help explain what the project was all about. After the discussions in the meetings, it was possible for a couple of volunteers to put together an inexpensive brochure, which the

College printed with a map of the community on the front. Experience showed that a recruiting committee, working individually, gave a wide variety of interpretations to what was involved, which caused problems later. The brochure brought some standardization of the interpretations.

The recruiting committee itself might institute a public meeting, a series of recruiting or interpreting meetings, or use the local media extensively. Again, the committee became involved in the analysis process, as it attempted to decide what were the social patterns in the community and how best to reach those interested.

Somewhere along this line deadlines had to be established, dates fixed, a convenient meeting-place found, and a decision made about fees. Again, the characteristics of the community became deciding factors. The College did not insist on fees, but neither did it agree to pay for local expenses. If a suitable hall was provided by the community free of charge, if coffee and refreshments and janitorial service and advertising (i.e. all local costs) were donated, then a fee might not be necessary. The College, normally, paid transportation, meals, and other costs of the personnel it sent to the project.

The recruitment stage was crucial, then, not only for the obvious purposes of getting enough people of the right kinds and interpreting the project reasonably; the committee was already engaged in analysis, was establishing the difference between the community and College roles, and was setting a pattern of organization that might be copied later in social action.

The Structural Model for Self Study

The model we developed was geared to the minimum time and effort needed to achieve something and the maximum time and effort to which volunteer citizens could be expected to commit themselves.

The Self Study project was spread over a twelve-week period, which made it possible to start and complete during a fall or winter semester. It consisted of six evening sessions of about three hours each. In the intervening two-week periods individuals or small teams had task assignments to carry out. These assignments were such that those who were very interested and had the time could do a great deal of work. Sometimes, groups interested in one topic decided to hold extra work-meetings during the intervals. The College staff was also on call for help on task assignments, either by telephone or personal consultation.

We found that the regular sessions were inadequate for many of the more personal services required. Sometimes this was as simple as reinforcement of confidence or as difficult as training someone in a new skill (interviewing, using a library, interpreting statistics). More often than not it was a combination: a vagueness about what to do, a feeling of inadequacy to do it, a lack of confidence, or even fear, regarding community attitudes to inquiry. We discovered that many of the participants needed all the support of the group, and the status associated with the College, in order to get going at all.

The regular sessions were always a mixture of plenaries and small-group sessions. The small groups were the effective, working-bodies. The plenaries were used for general instructions, for presentation of concepts, for feedback from groups, integration of efforts, and some general interpretation of developments. Some skill development took place in both plenary and small groups. As well, individuals and task groups filled out questionnaires or periodic reports of a descriptive or progressive nature.

College personnel operated the plenary sessions; the small groups, however, tended to run themselves. No chairmen or discussion leaders were ever appointed, unless the group itself designated someone to the role. Undoubtedly this was less efficient in the short haul. Our rationale was that it was much more analogous to real community conditions and left the door open for the emergence of a variety of leadership potentials. Students worked with the groups in strictly defined helping-roles. Faculty were sometimes used as group consultants.

The operative principle running through the structure of this model was to make it possible for citizens to become researchers of their own community around issues that were important to them. The College did not do the research; it supported the citizens in every way possible in order to maximize their effectiveness.

The Process of the Model

The main thrust of the sessions and the assignments was based on the statement of a community problem and a subsequent process of redefinition in terms of relevant information, social attitudes and values, and individual commitment to a solution for that problem. The first step was discussion in plenary session of 'problem areas' – family-life, drugs, the aged, community relationships, etc. – which were recorded and shared. The first session also provided the participants with a framework for situating a community problem. This framework emphasized the importance of seeing the problem in relation to the basic structures of society – social, political, economic – to give a clearer picture of the factors involved, the scope of the problem, and the possible entry points for action. The first assignment asked the participants to apply this framework to an interest area chosen from those previously discussed and listed.

The second session concentrated on methods of obtaining information necessary for a further analysis of the selected problem – where to get it, how to get it. It was at this point that the problem areas were identified, and participants were grouped around these according to their interest.

The information collected as part of the second assignment formed the basis of discussion for the third session where the problem was re-examined, clarified, and further informational inputs were identified. In the fourth session groups exchanged information about their problems with a view to problem-solving. The fifth session focussed on plans for action that each group would recommend or undertake. These were then presented to the group as a whole in the sixth and final session.

Concepts Used in the Model

In each of the regular sessions, a basic concept of analysis was used, around which the specific program was built. A listing of these will further illuminate the description of process.

Session 1 – The interrelatedness of problems in dynamic setting. By systematic analysis, aspects of problems may be observed and relations established. Information may be gathered on different aspects of a problem. Then analysis is possible – which may indicate entry points for action.

Session 2 – A problem is stated in terms of information already known. For analysis, resources are then identified. From resources further information is discovered. This information is evaluated in terms of the original statement of the problem, often leading to a restatement of the problem.

Session 3 – As information modifies the definition of a problem, the definition may become more narrow and precise, but, in exploring further resources, the problem may also re-emerge in a broader context.

Session 4 – As specific problems are seen in relationship to each other, certain common themes may emerge which would indicate (a) possible lines for social action, or (b) underlying or causal factors, which must be taken into consideration in devising an action program.

Session 5 – Developing a plan for action is not separate and apart from analysis. This is the point at which a value system (what you think is right) is imposed on the factual information collected. Testing the plan for action with those who must be involved if the plan is to be implemented shows (a) the relevance of the information on which the plan is based, and (b) the validity of your value judgment.

Winding Up the Study

Primarily, in the final session, the participants reported to each other, sharing what they learned. They also included ideas for follow-up action. These reports were, because of pressure of time, sometimes incomplete and often lacked the kind of conclusiveness the participants felt later. This reporting formed the basis for a report to the sponsoring body, except that the emphasis was changed from analysis to social action. The sponsoring body was expected to be the normal agency which would follow up on the suggestions for action, although this was not always the case.

Among the plans for action was usually one for reporting or sharing with the wider community. This plan might be for a special open meeting, a community workshop, or special reports through the media.

Evaluation was of the total process and also of individual learning. Each participant was invited to analyse his own learning in terms of insights, feelings, new understandings, questions, and methods. One or two 'observers' took part in the regular sessions and fed back information that they thought would enhance the process.

The end of the sixth session was the formal close of the College's responsibility. From there on the community could request help from the College for any continuing project. Each request was evaluated for its feasibility on two levels: first, was it a project which would help the community? and second, had the College the resources to be of help?

General Evaluation

What was the effectiveness of the Self Studies? Was there any discernible difference in community life?

To try to find out, we circulated a questionnaire (to 243 persons who had participated) after the conclusion of the fourth Self Study. We were fortunate enough to receive about a 50 per cent reply from participants in each Study, 117 in all. The main questions we asked were what each learned individually, how did the community benefit, were there any specific results, how could the Self Study be made more effective, and what advice they would give to someone in another community contemplating entering into a Self Study.[4]

Several themes emerged from the answers, which were categorized as follows:
1. citizen awareness, involvement, participation, and attitudes;
2. complexity of problems and relationships with local government;
3. community needs, action, and problems of adequate information;
4. identification of contacts and resources;
5. problem solving methods.

Many of these responses were subjective, as for example, 'our community regained some of its lost pride and gained a new sense of direction. People started to communicate.' The *feeling* that citizens could do something about their community was a strong, positive result.

Independent Community Action

We were told that the best measure of effectiveness would be the extent to which citizens would carry on social action independently.

Participants identified twenty-six specific actions that had been accomplished, the initiation of which they attributed to the Self Studies. A sampling of these indicates the range:

1. an executive was formed to develop a neighbourhood park, rink provided and maintained for two winters;
2. initiation of community preparation for marriage course;
3. *l'organisation de pré-maternelles pour les enfants des logis subventionnés;*
4. association of parents of children with learning disabilities has been formed;
5. a new Industrial Commission;
6. a tree planting, gardening campaign, and clean-up of the waterfront;
7. information booklet on existing services prepared;
8. a Planning Board set up, official plan developed, and consultant hired;
9. full-time Recreation Director hired.

In some of the actions reported it was evident that new relationships had been established between citizens and local authorities.[5] A number of other plans and proposals were mentioned which had not yet resulted in action, but continued to involve citizens with local governments, planning boards, and agencies.

Follow-Up Action Involving the College

For the sake of understanding the kinds of program patterns of a community-development nature in which a College may play a constructive role, we have attempted to classify our follow-up experience under the following headings:

Developing Community Leadership Skills;
Linking Developmental Forces in the Community;
Enabling Development Through Consultation;
Mobilizing Resources for Development.

Some of these activities can become as complex as the Self Study itself. The difference is the relationship with the College.

Two good examples of this are activities where the College played a consultative role.

From one Self Study the immediate derivative was a Community Workshop four months later. The College was asked to be consultant to the planning-committee. One result of this was a request to the College to conduct a community-wide survey for the committee using College students. The committee decided what questions they wished to poll the community about.

The College faculty devised the questionnaire. The students organized a door-to-door canvas of the whole town and tabulated the results. The results were fed back to the committee in time for use in the Workshop. This is a useful example of College resources contributing to a developmental process, in contrast to other surveys in which the communities have been used by professors and students for practice field-work, a process which is of no benefit to the community.

The Community Workshop turned out to be a major affair in the life of the town, triggering continuing action in six different areas of concern. The two consultants played fairly conspicuous platform roles as enablers.

From the Self Study in suburban Ottawa, the most visible result was the creation of a new co-ordinating organization to link the French-speaking inhabitants of that area. Participants from the Self Study assumed the leadership roles and requested consultation assistance from the College. This organization became involved in a highly controversial school question, and the College consultants were called upon for advice on a variety of questions, some of which concerned political tactics. This was getting close to dangerous territory, as the issues were highly emotional. The consultants were careful that the decisions regarding social action were entirely those of the organization. The consulting role turned out to be a more sophisticated extension of what was done in the Self Study, i.e. help in analysis, planning, evaluating, and skill-training for more effective participation.

Developing community-leadership skills occurs to some extent in most development work. We reserve that particular title to any projects that have leadership development as the *stated* common goal rather than an individual goal.

One example may provide a useful model for use in other communities. Throughout the Self Study references to adult-education needs kept coming up. Night courses at the High School, however, received indifferent response. Nor did the idea of a Community Adult Education Committee get anywhere. At a meeting called to discuss this situation, the College representative offered to run a course in Education Leadership Development, if the group would find enough people to take it. Besides paying the registration fee and attending, there was one other condition: each participant or team of participants would be obliged, as part of the course, to organize one adult-education activity! The idea was so simple – yet we know of no previous course like it.

The participants in this course received some skill-training, mostly in communication, but the unique feature was that six adult-education activities in the community resulted from it. Each team identified a need and the specific group of people who had that need. Then, in consultation with the people with the needs, a program idea was built. Resources were then explored and related to the proposed program. Resources were found within the College (a trainer for volunteer librarians); they were found with the help of the College (an art teacher, an expert on consumer buying); and the others were found independently.

Linking developmental forces within a community and mobilizing resources for development are two roles which flow rather naturally after the others. The more the College gets to know the area and the more people who come to understand this new role the College plays, the more natural it is to request the College to play the linking-role. We have had not only private but provincial and federal government representatives search us out, and we have been able to link them with community people to their mutual advantage.

The College and its Role in Community Development

This was our experience of community development working from a base in a 'Community' College. It has raised a number of issues and stimulated thoughts about the future potential of an educational institution playing this role. Some of these follow.

The most impressive fact is the great potential of the resources existing in Community Colleges. The Resource Centre concept, for example, is widely accepted and can become strategic in the community-development approach. Histories, reports, statistics, and research about the College area can be collected there. With a little extra effort, the Centre can also become a repository for inventories of program resources, government services, grants, agencies, and human resources. Maps, films, cassette interviews, and newspaper files are examples of media hard to find in ordinary community libraries. When a Resource Centre is linked with a community-development program, it becomes more than a dispenser of information – useful and relevant information becomes mobilized around plans of citizens for social and economic development.

Human resources within a College are rich and varied. There are teachers with practical experience in the trades, technologies, and business. There are teachers drawn from the practical fields of social work, welfare, recreation, and government services. There are professionals in the arts, human relations, group dynamics, administration. And there are students eager to participate in relevant educational experiences outside classroom walls.

They are there, but like many other resources, they are not always easily available. Pressures of heavy workloads may mean the best talents are already fully occupied. Those with specialized skills may be lacking in the ability to work with community groups. Some professionals may demand payment for community work for which there is no budget. Students have a schedule to follow and can't be pulled out of classes for community capers. Or requests come at the wrong time of the year – the students aren't ready yet.

One of the characteristics of community-development activities is that they can't be planned like a curriculum. When the opportunity is ripe, one must be prepared to grasp it. This means the need for a flexibility Colleges have difficulty meeting.

Colleges have not yet developed policies, procedures, or budgets geared to this kind of community service. One approach is to set about establishing these so that a community-development program is possible. The other, which has been followed in this Demonstration Project, is to start doing the job and to try to find the money, change the procedures, and develop new policies when what is needed is evident.

Values to the College

Making College resources available to the community enriches the community but the opposite is also true; involvement in the community enriches the College.

One of the objectives of the Demonstration Project was to make otherwise unavailable educational experiences available to College faculty and students. Through the variety of projects, a number of the faculty have had a unique opportunity to utilize their skills in a community problem-solving setting. This experience, so different from the typical classroom situation, is usually refreshing, challenging, and possibly humbling. The students who are able to get involved find this type of field-work more relevant than most other assignments. Some of them receive a practical training in community-development methods and philosophy, a course which cannot be given successfully in a classroom. The learning situation is genuine 'case study' with the added excitement of uncertainty as to how the 'case' will develop from week to week.

The College also learns about its community: its problems, its dynamics, its leadership, its resources. An educational institution, concerned with meeting needs, may use various research methods, surveys, or studies, but these all have a stale sense of academia about them when compared to true involvement *with* the community.

Often it has been said that such a project must be good public relations for the College, and in the minds of some people this appears to be a valid purpose. This is, of course, an unacceptable goal; to undertake community development with good public relations in mind may well skew the whole approach. Involvement in a community may mean involvement in conflict situations. A public-relations approach could mean attempting to smooth things over in order to leave a 'good image' of the College with everybody.

Good public relations, in the best sense of the word, may, of course, be a serendipital result. The work of the College will be appreciated, not only for what it has done for people and for a community, but for the attitude which it has demonstrated. People come to see the institution in a new light: an institution which really cares about how people live. They see education in a new light too, a process which can help people to cope with real life situations.

The Educational Approach

There are many schools of thought about community development. Our contention is that a legitimate approach is educational and that educational institutions can play a community-development role.

'Learning by objective' has become popular as an education-al methodology, and books are written to show how this may be used in the classroom. Inevitably, there is a sense of strain in adapting this natural process to the artificialities of the class-room community. In the real community, the method is in its natural habitat. This is the method of the Self Study and its many variants in community development.

Problems are specific situations which block the achievement of objectives. Identification of problems and learning how to attack them are fundamental educational techniques. This pro-cess is the basic training-pattern in community development.

The reason why these points must be made at all is the mistaken identification of education with schooling, the confin-ing of education to classrooms. In this process we have collect-ed individuals together in our artificial communities and schools, and have tried to slot them into homogeneous classes. The result of this unnatural process has been to concentrate on individual learning, because the group, the group process, and the community have been so unreal. This has led us to see educa-tional goals in individualistic terms: personal self-awareness, the individual learning-process, the individual ability to analyse and reason, the development of personal maturity. We hope the indi-vidual will become master of himself.

Meanwhile our society has been developing symptoms of serious sickness. Alienation, generation gaps, breakdown of communications, tensions between ethnic and linguistic groups, urban decay, loss of sense of community – the list grows long and depressing – seem relatively impervious to our educational efforts.

These problems are collective or communal in nature. They may be talked about in the classroom, but they can only be tackled in the community.

Can we envisage educational goals in collective terms – com-munity self awareness, the group learning process, ability to analyse community problems, development of a maturity in community relations? Can we see education contributing to a community sense of controlling its environment and institu-tions?

We have seen the educational process at work in a multitude of situations when a group:
1. states and then redefines a problem;
2. systematically searches for the information it needs;

3. devises tactics to approach government or institutions;
4. determines the resources necessary for help;
5. confronts differing opinions and prejudices;
6. attempts to explain and interpret through media;
7. sets priorities and plans for action;
8. evaluates experience.

Individuals learn, yes, but in a situation within which people can realistically come to grips with collective problems.

Working Definition

In professional journals one frequently finds these plaintive questions: 'How can we (the experts) aid the planning process effectively without wresting control from the users?' 'How can the real aspirations of a community be sounded out and realized without imposition?' 'How can we plan *with* people rather than *for* them?'

Educators don't ask the questions often enough. But if and when they do, the answers will lie in the community-development process. The definition evolved at a seminar during which educators did confront these questions went this way, '*Community development is the process of facilitation in solving problems as identified by the community itself.*'[6]

And Where it Stops Nobody Knows

When we embarked on this process at Algonquin, we could not know where it would lead.

What has happened is roughly this. The first two Self Study projects led to several follow-up activities. These in turn resulted in other opportunities.

By word of mouth, the information spread. Each of the first Self Studies has resulted in an invitation from a new community. More and more opportunities arise, and different sections of the College become involved.

Three quite different examples will illustrate the variety and richness of experiences which grew out of community-development activities:

1. members of rural communes visited the College and participated in a teach-in for students on 'Alternative Life Styles';

2. all the students of a Journalism class went to a remote community, lived there for a month with their teacher, and produced four editions of a community newspaper, *The Madawaska Valley*;
3. the College co-sponsored a public forum with the C.B.C., which was broadcast live to the area for one-and-a-half hours on the topic of French-language schools.

An important aspect of this development has been a growing sense on the part of community people that the College is their institution, that they have a modest right to approach it with requests for services.

On our part, we have recognized that equally important is continuity, a continuing and (hopefully) steadily improving ability to respond in a professionally competent manner to community requests.

Conclusion

The Demonstration Project has shown us that an educational institution can play a limited but articulate role in community development.

It has helped us formulate the beginning of an educational philosophy for community development.

It has stimulated our imagination as to where the philosophy could lead us in the future.

FOOTNOTES

1. This article is based on a Demonstration Project in Community Development, for which the author is Research Director, conducted at the Algonquin College of Applied Arts and Technology, Ottawa.
2. In May 1970, the College was given a grant by the Canadian Council on Urban and Regional Research for a one-year project. Alan Clarke became Project Director.
3. The four communities were quite different. Almonte is a town of 3,600 about thirty miles outside Ottawa. Pembroke is a city of 16,000 located one hundred miles up the valley from Ottawa. The other two were residential suburban. 'South East Ottawa' consisted of several mature, fully built-up residential neighbourhoods within the city limits. 'Gloucester North' was a group of new and still-growing developments just outside the city limits and part of a large, predominantly rural township.

4. 'Tabulation of Data from Questionnaires Regarding Community Self Study Projects', compiled by Mrs. Clare Gwyn, Algonquin College, May 1971.

5. 'For years, Council meetings were held monthly, and year upon year passed with no more than the most fleeting glimpse of a citizen in attendance. . . . Today, we not only have individuals regularly at Council meetings: we have groups, and groups of groups. Communication has become the watch-word. Issues are known in advance, discussed in depth, and thoughts made known to Council members. The deliberations of Council are then observed carefully and fully as members wrestle with issues that collectively redound to the public good.' (From a letter to the author dated April 26, 1971, from an elected Council member in Almonte.)

6. 'Ontario Seminar on Community Development', Humber College; Editor – Dorene Jacobs, November 1970.

ARTHUR STINSON is Director of Continuing Education at Algonquin College of Applied Arts and Technology, Ottawa. Although he is a gold-medalist graduate in modern history from the University of Toronto, his work has inevitably combined an interest in adult education and social development, beginning in a one-room school in a rural community. He was one of the pioneers of the community 'Y'. In the fifties he was program organizer for such citizen-involvement programs of the C.B.C. as 'Citizens' Forum' and 'Couchiching Conferences', and later developed the experimental 'Learning Stage' on C.B.C. Radio. Two particular assignments provided unique opportunities to study the Canadian scene – as Liaison Officer of the Second Duke of Edinburgh's Study Conference and as Program Director for the Royal Commission on Bilingualism and Biculturalism. He was Executive Director of the Canadian Citizenship Council and Secretary of the Canadian Commission, International Year for Human Rights. His writings include a paper on 'Canadian Participation in Social Development' and a variety of articles and reports on community development, adult education, broadcasting, and travel and exchange programs.

Case Study of a Community-Development Council

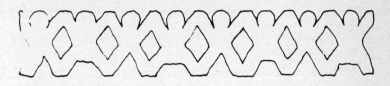

Donald E. Willmott

There is no lack of case studies of successful community-development programs. The case to be analysed here is an example of the successful use of community-development techniques. Yet the problems that were encountered are equally instructive. They will be emphasized here in the belief that the critical analysis of shortcomings in community work may well be as useful as the examination of successes.

The information presented here is based upon informal interviews, direct observation, documentary and periodical research, a sample survey, and 'participant-observation' techniques. These latter materials were gathered by a graduate student who lived in the community for a year, and by other researchers and consultants (from a provincial Community Research Institute), who spent an average of about five days a month in the community over a period of three-and-one-half years.

The Community Development Council of Uptown

For decades, Uptown[1] was what outsiders would call a 'sleepy' rural town. Its existence depended upon supplying farmers with their needs and shipping their products to far-away markets. Farm families within a radius of six or eight miles did all of their regular business and shopping there. In addition, they were served by its post office, its telephone system, its high school, its churches, and its recreational facilities. People from an area two or three times as large also came to Uptown for various specialized commercial and professional services.

In 1957, the American Refining Company (hereafter to be called ARC) began construction of a large industrial plant near Uptown. With encouragement from the company, local leaders began to push forward a program of community improvement. Due to their efforts, the villagers of Uptown voted overwhelmingly in favour of incorporation as a town. The community seemed committed to development in many fields. The new Town Council and the Board of Trade, however, did not move fast enough for some of the younger men. ARC management also favoured a more rapid pace, and clashed with the Town Council. Several businessmen, two or three members of the Company's staff, the high-school principal, and the editor of the local newspaper organized a new Chamber of Commerce. They drew up and began to campaign for an ambitious program for Uptown, including the encouragement of further new industries and the establishment of a water-and-sewerage system, street and sidewalk improvement, a parks and playgrounds development, a dental service, a bakery, and an optometrist.

Other citizens of Uptown began to show concern about the social and economic costs of rapid development. Greatly increased property taxes were a cause of resentment, especially among low-income and retired people. Some of this resentment was directed against the 'upstart' Chamber of Commerce. Its membership, which had never included many of the most influential businessmen of the community, dropped off drastically. After open conflict with the Mayor and the Town Council, it further alienated public support and lapsed into inactivity.

An additional factor in the opposition to rapid development was the feeling that it involved too great a risk. At a public meeting in 1959, an official of ARC urged 'aggressive' town development on the basis of the possibility that, by 1970, several large refineries might be operating in the vicinity. Some Uptown citizens, however, had serious doubts about investing heavily in long-range improvements, since the future of the local industry was as yet uncertain. The example of uranium 'boom towns' turned into 'ghost towns' was recent news at the time.

Thus, there was a sharp division of public opinion as to the proper pace for development in Uptown. Opposition to 'improvements' was especially evident among low-income, retired, and non-English-speaking groups. It appears that at least part of this opposition was based upon misunderstanding, lack of information, and the influence of a few individuals, with vested interests. But for many people, higher taxes involved real hardships. Socially and economically, they were outside the mainstream of community processes and changes. It was primarily votes from these groups that, in early 1959, defeated a by-law intended to authorize further expenditures on the new Uptown school.

Meanwhile, progress-minded citizens were not inactive. Chastened by the failure of the Chamber of Commerce, they sought more effective means for community development, this time by gaining the co-operation of more of the influential people in town. On the one hand, they brought about the election of a more progressive mayor. On the other hand, they established a Community Development Council (C.D.C.) with the co-operation of the Centre for Community Studies from the University of Saskatchewan.

The most important and expensive of proposed community improvements was a water-and-sewerage system. The new Town Council brought this matter to a vote of Uptown ratepayers at the end of 1959. It was clear that there was considerable opposition to the system, mostly among the low-income groups mentioned above. Well before the vote, the issue was discussed in the C.D.C. Although the problems of low-income home-owners were recognized, there was no spokesman for their interests, which might have been served by modifications in the installation layout or in tax regulations. The main problem, as C.D.C. delegates saw it, was to remove misconceptions about the proposed system and to mobilize a sufficiently large vote to defeat the opposition.

At the suggestion of the Mayor, the Council established a committee to promote these purposes. It was decided to use the same techniques that a Citizens' Committee had employed two years earlier in a successful campaign to win votes for town incorporation: that is, in addition to systematic newspaper publicity and several public meetings, every ratepayer was to be canvassed by a personal acquaintance. The twenty-five members of the C.D.C. committee did a thorough job of canvassing in most sections of the community. But because of social and linguistic barriers, there was none among them who could communicate effectively with the people from whom most opposition was expected. In the final balloting, the proportion of voters in favour of the water-and-sewerage debentures fell short of the required two thirds, but by so narrow a margin that the authorities could proclaim the vote sufficient. Before the system was installed in the summer of 1960, a majority of residents of two different streets petitioned against water-and-sewer lines along their properties.

Most projects suggested for action by the C.D.C. were of potential benefit to the whole community and did not clash with group vested interests. In its three-and-one-half years of existence, the Council carried out, or stimulated other organizations to carry out, a considerable number of these. For example, it originated an annual town beautification and clean-up campaign. It assisted in the establishment of a local library. It carried on the initial study and discussions that resulted in a Senior Citizens Home project, which was carried out by the new Elks Lodge, and in plans to build a new hospital and to convert the old one into a nursing-home. Through C.D.C. initiative, organized baseball was provided for school children, and a community recreation program was established.

On the other hand, there were certain kinds of community problems which the C.D.C. did not take up. In the first place, it did not deal with issues that might have created serious controversy in the Council itself, such as the frictions and frustrations that arose in the initial relationships between townspeople and new residents (mostly Americans) employed by ARC. When the community was bitterly divided by a strike at the ARC plant, the Mayor gave a report on the situation to the Council, but it was assumed that no action would be taken.

Rural problems were also avoided by the Council. Originally, it was hoped that the C.D.C. would represent the wider community of Uptown's primary trade area, and that farmers would play an active part in it. But as we have seen, the participation of farmer delegates declined steadily. One explained: 'I've stopped attending C.D.C. meetings because the problems they discuss are of no interest to farmers.' Actually, the Reeve of the Rural Municipality (a regular member of the Council, but not a regular attender) brought rural problems to the attention of several meetings, but little discussion and no action resulted.

Council delegates also showed little interest in projects that would require district or regional co-operation. Before ARC support was obtained, the Senior Citizens Home project appeared to be blocked by the fact that provincial financial assistance was contingent upon the co-operation of near-by towns, which were traditional competitors of Uptown. Throughout the career of the C.D.C., one of the active delegates continually pressed for the establishment of a regional library. The Council promoted a local library instead, and repeatedly deferred consideration of a regional one. In 1962, on the invitation of the C.D.C., two government officials came from Regina to discuss the possibility of provincial aid for a recreational park in Uptown. Again, however, it became clear that such assistance would require regional co-operation, and the matter was dropped.

It was in 1962 that the C.D.C.'s importance in the community began to decline sharply. The Chamber of Commerce had been revived and several new service clubs were now active. On the initiative of ARC, a Community Recreation Association was established. Its constitution provided for executive-level ties with the Town Council, the School Board, and the Company. It quickly built up a large and enthusiastic membership. With ARC donating land and materials and the Town Council providing some financial support, the association undertook to build a swimming-pool, tennis courts, and other recreational facilities for young and old. At the suggestion of the Company, all work was accomplished by volunteer labour.

By 1962, more community-improvement projects had been completed or were in process than had been dreamed of in 1959. The Company was offering major benefits to the community. In contrast to the situation before 1959, it was working closely with the Town Council and had high-level employees in official positions in numerous important community organizations, including the Chamber of Commerce, the School Board, the Library Board, the Town Council, the Recreation Association, the Kinsmen, and the Canadian Legion. There was a general atmosphere of optimism and satisfaction in the community.

Under these circumstances, it was perhaps not surprising that there was little feeling of need for a Community Development Council. In the fall of 1962, the C.D.C.'s president neglected to call a meeting for the election of new officers, and the Council never met again. In reply to an inquiry, he stated that the Chamber of Commerce and the new Recreational Association could handle any new issues or projects that might arise.

When the Rink Committeé faced some difficult problems it called a meeting of 'all organizations'. Because representatives of only six groups attended, a second meeting was scheduled. This time only seven groups were represented, so someone suggested that a meeting of the C.D.C. should be called. The proposal was dropped, however, when past members of the C.D.C. admitted that they did not know the whereabouts of the Council's records of member organizations and delegates. The incident suggested at least an occasional need for a coordinating body, such as the C.D.C. had once been, but the interests and energies of community leaders were now invested in other organizations.

Social Status of C.D.C. Members and Officers

Beginning soon after the C.D.C. was founded, a graduate student in sociology undertook a year of participant observation and research in Upown. In order to investigate the social-prestige system of the community, he used an elaborate procedure not unlike that developed by Hollingshead in studying Elmtown (Hollingshead, 1949, pp. 25-41). After ascertaining that Uptown residents do recognize, however vaguely, 'upper' and 'lower' groups in the community, he asked ten knowledgeable and fairly representative citizens to rate the community standing or 'social bracket' of every Uptown adult into one of the following categories: top, middle, lower, or unknown. He found substantial agreement on the ranking of 206 of the 676 names.

Although only 10 per cent of the adult population were placed by raters in the 'top' group, this category was found to include 42 per cent of the members of the C.D.C. and 58 per cent of its officers. Indeed, to view it in another way, 37 per cent of all people that raters put in the 'top' status group were members of the Council at one time or another between 1959 and 1962 This was true of only 2 per cent of the 'middle' group of citizens.

In an assessment of the occupational status of C.D.C. members as compared to all Uptown adults, women who did not hold jobs were classified according to the occupational category of their husbands.

The figures showed that professional people were very much over-represented in the council. Farmers and manual workers were notably under-represented. Other calculations indicated that two thirds of Uptown professionals participated in C.D.C., as compared to about one sixth of businessmen and white-collar workers, and much lower proportions of other occupational groups.

With regard to educational achievement, a sample survey conducted in 1961 indicated that about one tenth of Uptown adults had completed a college or university course of training. The proportion among council members was found to be over one third. Information concerning all Uptown adults showed that 78 per cent were of non-Anglo-Saxon origin. The corresponding proportion in the C.D.C. was about 58 per cent.

If representation in the C.D.C. is considered from the point of view of attendance and participation in meetings, the taking of responsibility, and the making of decisions, it is clear that farmers and townspeople of lower socio-economic levels played an even smaller part than the figures indicated. The proportion of farmer members declined over the three-year period; so did the attendance and participation of those who remained. The Council had a farmer on its executive only in its first year. The C.D.C. members of lowest socio-economic status attended irregularly, and very rarely spoke in meetings. Nor did they join the informal groups of members who met in restaurants or private homes after each C.D.C. meeting, presumably either because they were never invited to do so or because they would have felt uncomfortable.

C.D.C. and the Organizational Structure of the Community

The C.D.C. obtained its members by inviting the various organizations of the community to name two delegates each year. It was expected that this would provide a fairly articulate and community-minded membership, which would be representative of all significant community organizations. In the three years of its existence, the Council had delegates from thirty-nine clubs and associations (although the number represented

in any single year was considerably smaller). During this period, the total number of groups in Uptown increased from fifty-
odd to sixty-seven. Those not represented either did not receive
invitations or failed to elect delegates. In some cases, organizations declined to name delegates because one or more of their
members were already appointed to the C.D.C. from other
groups. Thus the members of the Council could be considered
to represent considerably more than the official number of del-
egating organizations.

Among the groups not officially represented on the C.D.C.
were the managing-boards of the churches, their choirs and
Sunday School organizations, and seven out of twelve recreational and sports clubs. Several other important 'managing-
bodies' were also not officially represented: the Community
Hall Committee, the Hospital Advisory Board, and the executive of the local telephone company. Perhaps more significant
was the absence of representation from the labour union that
organized the new industry, and from the Polish Club, whose
members were mostly of low socio-economic status. In addition, there were no delegates from the local Fish and Game
League, which included a high proportion of farmers, nor from
organizations that met in near-by hamlets, villages, or farm
homes within Uptown's 'trade area'.

It was hoped that the C.D.C. would be in continual communication with the clubs and associations of the community
through its members. Delegates were expected to report C.D.C.
activities to their own groups, and to bring the concerns of
their groups to the C.D.C. Furthermore, it was expected that
the Council would refer certain suggested projects to appropriate groups for possible action.

In the summer of 1959, after the Council had been functioning a half-year, interviews were conducted with forty-five of its
members. It was found that 67 per cent claimed to have reported C.D.C. activities to their organizations; 16 per cent said they
had consulted their organizations on the position they should
take on Council matters; 22 per cent stated that their organizations had referred certain problems to the Council; and another
22 per cent said that their organizations had been asked by the
Council to undertake certain projects. In the 1960 annual report, the secretary listed as one of the problems of the Council:
'Delegates never bring back problems from their organizations.' A year earlier, however, delegates had been asked to

obtain the opinions of their groups as to the priorities to be attached to a list of fourteen community problems or proposed projects. Many of them had done this.

In summary, we may say that the formal relations between the C.D.C. and other community organizations were significant but not substantial in volume. To a great extent, the Council behaved like an independent organization rather than like a representative or consultative body. Council discussions indicated that delegates usually spoke with community or personal interests in mind; they rarely became spokesmen of their respective organizations.

In order to assess the socio-political position of the C.D.C. in the community, and of its member organizations in comparison with those not represented, a technique, which may be called 'interlock analysis', was applied (Skinner, 1958). This provided two kinds of data: statistical indexes of the relative importance of groups in the organizational structure of the community, and sociometric material on their 'interlocks' (officers in common) with one another.

With regard to organizational importance, it is assumed that a group that can recruit officers who are also officers of many other associations has high socio-political importance. An organization whose officers serve in few other associations may be considered to be relatively less important in the community structure. These assumptions are based upon three further considerations: (a) that acceptance of offers of leadership positions depends at least partly upon the relative prestige and influence of available positions; (b) that associations whose officers hold positions in many other organizations thereby possess wider potential influence on community activities outside their normal jurisdiction; and (c) that influence in the community is exercised primarily by the officers of formal organizations. Although a number of studies have shown the latter proposition not to be true in large cities and towns, it was found to hold in this case. In a reputational study of Uptown leadership, supplemented by interviewing and participant observation, only one 'influential' was discovered who did not hold office in local organizations – the top manager of the new industry. In a Saskatchewan town with a population of about 2,700, Laskin and Phillett (1963) found the same situation.

The index of associational importance used in this study gave an organization credit both for the calibre of its leaders (in terms of the average number of offices they held in other groups) and for the absolute number of their combined officerships in other groups. It was expressed as an 'interlock score'. In 1961, the C.D.C.'s interlock score was about twenty – an indication of very high socio-political importance in the community. Only four out of the remaining forty-nine organizations surpassed this figure: the School Board, the Hospital Board, the Library Board, and the Uptown Telephone Company. In the following year, 1962, the standing of the C.D.C. fell from fifth to eleventh place. The Town Council, the Community Hall Association, the Golf and Country Club, the Knights of Columbus, and the newly organized Figure Skating Club, the Masonic Lodge, and the Chamber of Commerce joined those organizations that surpassed C.D.C.'s interlock score in 1961.

The interlock analysis showed that the Council was generally most closely connected (by overlapping leadership) with organizations offering community services and with those found to be most important socio-politically. In either 1961 or 1962, it had double interlocks (two officers in common) with the Library Board, the Golf and Country Club, the Ladies Hospital Auxiliary, the Red Cross, or the Chamber of Commerce. Least connected with the Council were a number of church groups and women's clubs.

The C.D.C. and the Community Power Structure

In a study of Uptown leaders, 'influence scores' were assigned on the basis of ratings by a panel of ten knowledgeable citizens. Among the thirty top scorers, nineteen were members of C.D.C. at one time or another. The top ten, who may be considered the most influential people in town, included six Council members. Similarly, eleven of the top thirty were among the founders of the C.D.C., and eight served as officers of the Council between 1960 and 1962.

Although C.D.C. members included a fairly representative cross-section of community leaders, there were notable exceptions. None of the three leaders of the local labour union ever served on the Council. They did not have high prestige in the community, and, as will be explained below, they were not interested in the Council. The case was similar with regard to four men who were generally considered to be the spokesmen of low-income, retired, or non-English-speaking segments of the community. Unlike the union leaders, these men were active in community affairs and organizational leadership. Two of these men were members of the C.D.C. during its first few months, but none remained on the Council.

The two organizations with the most influence over the destiny of the community – the Town Council and the new industry – were well represented in the C.D.C. from the first. The Mayor and a Town Councillor were among the founders of the C.D.C. The next Mayor and several other Councillors served as C.D.C. delegates. Through their influence, the Town Council and the C.D.C. co-operated closely and continuously.

Relationships between the C.D.C. and the new Company were almost equally close, except that ARC's top manager took no direct part in the organization. A high-level Company employee was among the founders of the C.D.C., and there were two official ARC delegates from that time on. For three years, the treasurer of the Council was a Company representative, and an ARC delegate served as president for one year. Through its delegates, Company management took a direct interest in community affairs. In view of this situation, a minority in the community – including the inner circle of the labour union – considered the Council a 'tool of ARC'. It was true that the company, like the Town Council, exercised influence on the community through the C.D.C. But in both cases, this influence was generally welcomed. The Company's interests usually coincided with those of the C.D.C. membership: maximum development of community services and facilities.

Summary and Evaluation

The organizers of the Uptown Community Development Council were highly successful in gaining the participation of influential individuals and groups. At a time when town leadership was divided and the new industry's staff was as yet exercising little influence in community organizations, the C.D.C. performed the function of mobilizing and unifying the existing power structure. It brought into one organization leading members of the Town Council, of the upper- and middle-community status groups, and of the Company. For several years, it was the major organizational means through which their common interests in improvement projects were implemented.

The Council died when new organizations, even closer to the upper sectors of the power structure, successfully took over the function of carrying out improvement projects.

In some ways, the Uptown C.D.C. can be regarded as a notable success. Its published accomplishments include: 'good community teamwork'; appropriate use of external resources, such as government and university 'experts'; and completion of nine out of the eleven community projects originally initiated.

In the light of community-development goals, however, our detailed analysis suggests that there were a number of short-comings of the Council, even in areas considered successful. Three shortcomings only will be dealt with here.

Firstly, a distinction between community improvement and community development may be made. The C.D.C. 'improved' the community in many ways, through its beautification campaigns, recreation programs, and so on. In the process, something was added to the human resources of the community. Yet there was little evidence of 'development' in a number of fields. Leadership developed primarily by integrating new leaders from the outside industry into the community power structure. Leaders and spokesmen for disadvantaged groups usually outside this power structure remained outside it. The C.D.C. leaders generally did not develop a wider view of problems and possible solutions – for example, with regard to a park, a Senior Citizens Home, a library, and recreation for rural youth, they failed to co-operate with the relevant communities outside their own. In this respect, they did not listen to the advice of the 'experts'. On the other hand, with regard to the water-and-sewerage system, they unquestioningly accepted the advice of provincial engineers and financial experts, without demanding adjustment of their plans to take local interest groups into account. The C.D.C. did not even attempt to resolve other divisive community issues.

Secondly, the very structure of the C.D.C. prevented it from attaining its goal of serving the entire community. The Council was intended to represent the whole community and to serve the needs of all. It was assumed that this would be achieved by selecting delegates from all local organizations. Such an assumption overlooks some very important facts: (a) Every community has a structure of power and prestige that this kind of council will strengthen if it is 'successful'. Disadvantaged groups will rarely be represented by organizational delegates.

(b) Different social classes have different values in many respects, and the special goals and needs of the underprivileged are therefore rarely understood or taken into account by existing leaders. (c) Because privileges are unequally distributed, the interests of different groups will sometimes conflict. (d) To strengthen the local 'Establishment' usually assures that the interests of the underprivileged will be overlooked, at least when they conflict with the goals of the upper groups – as in the case of the water-and-sewerage issue in Uptown.

Thirdly, the C.D.C. was short-lived. In itself, it did not develop. Membership and attendance at meetings declined in each succeeding year of its brief life of three-and-one-half years. Apparently the educational, consultative, and co-ordinative functions of the Council (which interviews showed were never foremost in the minds of its members) were not sufficiently important to serve as a basis for continued existence. Other organizations began effectively to serve the 'community-improvement' function for the local Establishment. And because the C.D.C. did not become a significant channel of influence for people not ordinarily influential in other town organizations, it did not develop any group of persons especially committed to its continued existence.

There is no desire here to blame or condemn people in Uptown for the shortcomings of the Council. They behaved just as would be expected in any town under similar circumstances.

The consultants from the Community Research Institute who worked with the C.D.C. did not intervene more actively for several reasons. For one thing, because of its emphasis on research, the Institute had a policy of minimum intervention. A second reason was that the consultants tended to see the community through the eyes of its own leaders. This was a natural consequence of the fact that their contacts in the community were almost wholly confined to existing community leaders and members of upper social groups. A third reason was that the ideology of the consultants predisposed them to assume community harmony and common interests, and to overlook conflict and class interests.

With the advantage of considerable research and hindsight, several conclusions for practitioners of community development may be ventured:
1. Intervention strategy can be decided only after choosing between the limited goal of accomplishing specific projects of benefit to certain community groups (community improve-

ment) and the wider goals of developing local human resources (community development). The latter requires a greater degree of intervention because of widespread apathy, and the traditional orientations, élitist tendencies, and geographically limited horizons of existing leaders.'

2. Intervention tactics can be decided only after gaining a clear understanding of community social structure, including class interests and conflict.

3. Organizational techniques can be selected only after deciding whether to mobilize existing influential groups or to activate hitherto uninfluential groups. In the latter case, a council based on delegates from organizations will not be as appropriate as a council based on delegates from block or neighbourhood meetings, or on separate organizations of interest groups.

4. Fruitful evaluation of future community-development projects will require better methods for ascertaining the organizational and social-class structure of the community, for locating the persons who are significant in setting community goals and making decisions, and for assessing the degree of 'development' of human resources, such as leadership skills and participatory involvement. In order to make use of improved research, however, evaluation must be in terms of specifically defined goals.

FOOTNOTE

1. In order to preserve anonymity, all proper names in this report are fictitious.

DONALD E. WILLMOTT was born in China. He received his B.A. in sociology from Oberlin College (1950), his M.A. from the University of Michigan (1953), and his Ph.D. in sociology and far-eastern studies from Cornell University (1958). His doctoral dissertation was on a Chinese community in Indonesia.

During the summers of 1956-9 he worked as a research officer with the Department of Public Welfare, Newfoundland; from 1959 to 1962 he worked as a research officer for the Centre for Community Studies in Saskatoon. Since that time he has worked with many voluntary associations in Metropolitan Toronto.

Dr. Willmott's teaching experience includes Memorial University in Newfoundland (1956-9) and the University of Toronto (1962-6). He is presently on the teaching staff of Glendon College, York University, Toronto.

Relating
to Communities

The principles of community development can be implemented in a great variety of ways. Apart from the involvement of more established organizations in community action, the number of citizen-based organizations has increased considerably within the last few years. Such commitments are prefaced by changing concepts about the term 'community' itself. What communities do we have? What kind of communities do we want? What values do our communities reflect?

As an introduction to this section, and leading directly from the previous section, Barry Wellman raises questions relating to the need for the kinds of neighbourhoods that urban dwellers want. The media and urban communications have had an effect upon the associations one develops and retains. Wellman suggests that we think in terms of 'personal communities' and that we focus on despatialized selective communities rather than on the spatial, geographical community. This takes us beyond the United Nations concept of neighbourhood as the geographic and social unit within which urban community development can be undertaken.

The article by Dorene Jacobs presents an example of a specific group of citizens, linked by a geographical community as well as a 'community of ideas', attempting to control and influence their environment. The case study, as she presents it, shows how citizens exercise choice in the nature of the city or neighbourhood in which they live. The historical development of this citizens' group is important in understanding its present structure, especially the way in which conflict is used constructively (a point also discussed in the articles by Willmott and the McLeods). Jacobs emphasizes the importance of planning and of citizens' groups working with planners. She also discusses ways in which municipalities can encourage and support citizens' groups. Finally, she points out that what is needed is an attitude that urban growth is a process; if its direction is to be influenced by human decisions, there must be opportunity for citizens to participate.

A traditional institution that is attempting to relate to the surrounding community is the public school. The trend is toward the school becoming a resource centre, where the student and adult citizenry increasingly become involved in planning and decision making in matters affecting learning and education. Such is the topic of the third article in this section, written by Dale E. Shuttleworth. If the school views the community as a resource for the enrichment of learning, then the neighbourhood and the larger city become a vast classroom of learning experiences. Some organizations have become fossilized and are in fact barriers to change, a point also made in the article by McEwen. This, Shuttleworth says, must change. The democratization of society cannot be accomplished simply by legislation. Rather, the community and its citizenry must regain control of its institutions.

Whereas the articles by Jacobs and Shuttleworth deal essentially with linkages and action within geographical communities, the article by A. F. Laidlaw emphasizes a community of common interests, beyond geographical boundaries. He talks about the role of co-operatives as a social movement with people working together towards socially desirable goals. One point emphasized by Laidlaw is that the co-operative is an ongoing reality to which people can relate and in which they can test educational theory.

Who Needs Neighbourhoods?[1]

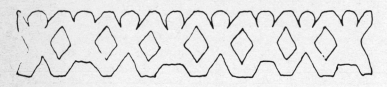

Barry Wellman

Who needs neighbourhoods?

The current battle cry around Toronto – from the bungalows of East York to the salons of the Annex and even to the unchic apartments of St. James Town – is 'save the neighbourhoods'. In the name of Neighbourhood we seek to stop the Spadina Expressway, demolish the developers, and oust the old guard from City Hall. Only in the neighbourhood, it is asserted, can the kind of warm, intimate, and holistic relationships we seek flourish. The rise of the neighbourhood is coming to be seen as the antidote to the alleged impersonality, specialization of interaction, and loss of comprehensible scale of the modern metropolis.

What is not in question is whether the neighbourhood movement seeks worthy goals. What is very much in question is whether we are being wise to hang so many of our hopes for urban salvation on the creation of strong, semi-autonomous urban villages. It is the argument of this paper that the social relationships we so desperately seek are being increasingly provided in non-spatial, non-neighbourhood terms. This makes an extreme emphasis on neighbourhoodness anachronistic, and an over-concentration on the development of neighbourhood autonomy has profoundly conservative implications.

Our concern for the neighbourhood has been in large part traceable to a reaction against previous generations' denunciation of the city as a humane environment. The city, we were told, was cold, it was dehumanizing, it created masses and not persons, it fostered manipulative rationality at the expense of affectivity, and it provided an unsatisfactory matrix for the development of meaningful social relationships (White & White, 1962; Marx, 1964; Schmitt, 1969).

While all these charges were true to a certain extent – as they are no doubt true to a certain extent almost anywhere, in any milieu – they did not stand up to empirical research. For much of the post-war period, hordes of social scientists have brought forth abundant empirical evidence of plentiful, vital, warm, affective, primary ties in the urban metropolis. Such relationships were not left behind in the move from country to city (or suburb) after all. People were found to have close relationships in the city, they rarely felt themselves to be lost amid the masses, and they have been able to use their ties with others as sources of important assistance in times of everyday and emergency stress, as well as in maintaining well-developed networks of sociable relationships (Wellman, Hewson, & Coates, 1971; Jacobs, 1961; Greer, 1962; Lauman, 1968; Adams, 1968; Bott, 1957; Bell & Boat, 1957; Clark, 1966; Keller, 1968).

Much of the intellectual revolution in viewing urban social relationships has focussed on the neighbourhood. In good part, this has been because social scientists have to start somewhere, and spatially delimiting the area of inquiry has been an easy thing to do. The city was seen as a congeries of neighbourhoods: relatively small urban areas with intense interaction within their boundaries. This was a natural reaction to the older view of mass urban chaos. The predilection of many urban social scientists for hanging around street corners to gather data (more elegantly known as 'participant observation') and the ready availability of spatially-mapped census tract statistics and the like also helped form a neighbourhood conception of urban primary relationships (Whyte, 1955; Gans, 1962; Suttles, 1968; Liebow, 1967).

The trouble was, though, that it was a risky business to assume that these special types of 'urban villages' were typical of urban locales, even if one did want to start with the neighbourhood as the point of reference. Indeed, many of the areas studied were chosen for their distinctiveness (and often 'quaintness'): be it ethnic, racial, social class, or life-style.

Our own research, on the other hand, indicates the city has become 'despatialized' (Wellman, Hewson & Coates, 1969; Wellman, 1971). If you start your inquiry by asking where a city-dweller's intimates (close friends and neighbours, and rela-

tives) live and not by asking what is the pattern of social relationships in a given neighbourhood, then you find that the
intimates are spread all over the map. Few people to whom one
feels closest live in one's neighbourhood; most are accessible
only by a vehicular or rapid-transit trip, or by telephone and
mail contacts. For example, in a study of the social relationships of East Yorkers with which I have been associated, only
13 per cent of the respondents' intimates lived in the same
neighbourhood; the great majority, 63 per cent, lived in other
parts of Metropolitan Toronto, while fully 24 per cent lived
outside of Metro (Wellman, *et al*, 1969, p. 9).

Clearly, the neighbourhood is not the basis of close social
relationships for most of these urbanites. Whatever impact the
neighbourhood had previously has been vitiated by easy-to-use
transportation and media. The car, rapid transit, and telephone
have facilitated the maintenance of close ties between intimates
at substantial distances.

Rather than concentrate on spatially bounded neighbourhoods, it seems more fruitful to me to think in terms of the
'personal communities' of city-dwellers. That is, each urbanite
is a participant in a community created by the strong ties that
exist between himself and his intimates and among his intimates. Whether these ties are neighbourhood-based is an empirical question and should not be assumed; our research,
though, indicates that spatial propinquity plays only a small
role in such ties.

Urbanites are forming 'selective communities' consisting of
ties to others with shared interests found in the despatialized
social arena of the metropolis. The size and variety of the city
increases the likelihood that others with similar interests are
available and will be found (Wirth, 1938; Simmel, 1950); communication and transportation media enable one to go afar for
such links. It is in this sense that the despatialized community
is a liberating experience, enabling one to transcend the confines of traditional neighbourhood-based ties.

Some policy implications of this analysis are clear. It is fruitful to build up the neighbourhood as the primary locale of
social interaction. Too many people want to move beyond its
confines for their relationships, no matter how attractive neighbourly interaction is made. Furthermore, concentrating on
neighbourhood interaction works against the liberating effects
of being able to select one's intimates from a metropolis-wide
pool of candidates.

To further such a policy one must enhance transportation and communication channels. Some options that come to mind are the development of more usable public-transportation systems (especially between residential areas), the lowering of long-distance telephone rates, the extension of local telephone boundaries, and the provision of more channels of communication, e.g. picturephone, conference calls, two-way cable systems at a reasonable price (Asimov, 1957). Furthermore, the ability to select one's community effectively from the vast urban pool of potential intimates could well be enhanced by the development of computer matching-systems beyond the present limited service of providing potential bed-partners.

Are neighbourhoods of no use, then? Can we look with urbane disinterest at the slashing of expressways through neighbourhoods and the execution of urban areas under the euphemism of 'urban renewal'? I think not.

There are a number of important functions that vibrant, integrated neighbourhoods can fulfil. One is the maintenance of a diffuse sort of intimacy which strong ties across the metropolis cannot replace. This can range from the venerable cup of sugar to the (Jane) Jacobean notion of neighbourly social control and protection. Walking through local streets, recognizing individuals and their residences, provides an antidote to urban alienation that is an important factor in one's successful social and psychological functioning. In the city, such a sense of control may be not only a product of having a number of strong primary – albeit geographically dispersed – ties; it may be a product as well of being able to relate to the diffuse, often weakly bound, public community of the neighbourhoods.

In some areas, it is often the case that an individual's 'selective community' exists solely within a neighbourhood's boundaries. Neighbourhoods have played an important role as way-stations in the assimilation of newcomers to urban life. An in-migrant or an immigrant is likely to move into an area in which his countrymen live. There he is more apt to find people who think and act more or less as he does and is more apt to have specialized services close at hand which have been attracted by the concentration of his countrymen. It is in such enclaves of immigrants that the closest approximation to true 'urban villages' are likely to occur (Gans, 1962: Breton, 1964).

The neighbourhood may be the locale of communities of shared interests. Homeowners may easily band together to fight high-rise developments or expressways in order to preserve a common way of life. Apartment-dwellers may find a community of interest in seeking to make their landlords more responsive and their environment more humane.

The social importance of neighbourhoods lies in both their heterogeneity and homogeneity. Because of the presence of a wider range of people than is found in one's selective community, urbanites are exposed to a greater variety of experiences, relationships, and points of view. On the other hand, the sorting functions of most neighbourhoods mean one is more likely to come into contact there with people with whom he has the most in common. While not providing all, or even the major part, of one's intimate social relationships, the neighbourhood may well provide the basis for a significant portion of them.

Thus, in a variety of cases, the neighbourhood is an effective unit of collective action to maintain or improve some life-style. The cost of this, though, is the potential subordination of public interests to local interests. No one wants an incinerator in his backyard, yet it can be argued that the placing of an incinerator somewhere is essential to the public good. On the other hand, the neighbourhood is a social unit with which its members can easily identify and over which they feel they have some control. Such a unit, well organized, can do much to make municipal government responsive to local needs, as well as serving the important function of giving urbanites a sense of control over their own individual and group destinies (Kotler, 1969).

However, not all issues are neighbourhood issues, and it would be folly to try to force all conflicts into a spatially determined mode. The political potency of interest groups organized on non-neighbourhood lines is eminently worthy of development as well. It would be unfortunate if we glossed over the fact that the fight for individual self-determination is not always synonymous with the fight for neighbourhood self-determination.

The question we opened with is 'Who needs neighbourhoods?' It is clear that we do, because of the vital functions successful neighbourhoods can fulfil. But it is the central thrust of this paper that a concentration on neighbourhoods as being the chief locale of strong primary social relationships is becoming increasingly anachronistic and doomed to failure in most cases. Only by creating more opportunities for the formation of despatialized selective communities and only by increasing the ease of use of channels of contact between people can the profoundly liberating effect of the modern city be fully exploited.

FOOTNOTE

1. This article has also been published, with minor revisions, in *The Future City*, edited by Eilert Frerichs and Alan Powell, published by the University League for Social Reform, Toronto 1971. Many of the ideas in this paper were developed in discussion with: Donald Coates, Paul Craven, Leslie Howard, Margaret Hewson, William Michelson, Abraham Rotstein, Norman Shulman, Charles Tilly, Jack Wayne, and Beverly Wellman (unbeknownst to them). Editorial advice was provided by Marilyn Whitaker and the (Toronto) *Globe and Mail* (in which a preliminary version of this paper first appeared).

BARRY WELLMAN is an Assistant Professor of Sociology at the University of Toronto, specializing in urban sociology, social perception, and race and ethnic relations.

His principal research-project at the present time is the study of 'Community Ties and Support Systems', and it is from this project that the concerns expressed in his paper in this book have developed. The data for this research are derived from a survey, conducted in 1968, of 845 adults from the East York section of Toronto.

Mr. Wellman is also conducting research into the nature of 'The Future Community'. In it he is trying not only to assess current trends, but to speculate on how technological and social changes will be interrelated with respect to community.

He is also conducting research into the 'Social Identities, Cosmopolitanism, and Networks of Black and White Adolescents'.

Papers by Mr. Wellman include: 'Primary Relationships in the City: Some Preliminary Observations' (with D. B. Coates and Margaret Hewson), 'The Uses of Community', 'Community Ties and Mental Health', 'The Yorklea Study of Mental Health' (with D. B. Coates and Sharon Moyer), 'Social Identities in Black and White', 'Crossing Social Boundaries', 'I am a Student', and 'Success and Self-Conceptions' (with Ellen Murray).

Mr. Wellman received his Ph.D. from Harvard University in 1970. Born in the heart of New York City, he came to Canada in 1967. He now lives in downtown Toronto and bicycles to work every day.

The Annex Ratepayers' Association: Citizens' Efforts to Exercise Social Choice in Their Urban Environment

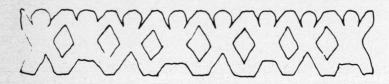

Dorene E. Jacobs

> Probably no other issue is as vital to the success of solving America's urban crisis than the viable participation of urban residents in planning the neighborhoods and cities in which they live and the social programs which directly affect them. City dwellers are demanding to be heard. They want in – they want to help control – not only indirectly through their elected representatives in the councils of central government but also on the block and neighborhood level (Spiegel, 1968, p. 1).

Spiegel's comment is directed towards the acute urban problems of many cities in the United States: it has application to the Canadian urban scene as well.

Can citizens control or influence their environment? Can they exercise choice as to the nature of the city or neighbourhood in which they live? Should they? How?

These questions have become of vital importance in the face of an increasingly complex society, characterized by the accelerated rate of technological change, the growth of knowledge, the expansion of bureaucracy, and the development of larger governing-units, which remove government ever further from the people. What role does the citizen have in such a society? The matter is crucial. According to Franklin (1966), 'In a world of large institutional and corporate control, it becomes increasingly vital for the individual to know he has some influence on his own future' (p. 103).

The emergence of citizens' groups in many centres across

Canada indicates one way in which the desire of citizens to be involved in decisions affecting their lives has found expression. The citizen-group movement, as Carota (1970) calls it, takes various forms – it includes citizens' action-groups, neighbourhood-improvement groups, ratepayers' associations, and tenants' organizations, among others. They are organized around issues affecting a broad geographical area, such as pollution; around regional or city issues such as expressways; around problems of local neighbourhoods – attempting to improve or maintain these neighbourhoods, to promote or prevent urban renewal; around conflicts between landlords and tenants in single apartment buildings or perhaps in large apartment complexes. Generally, they are considered a relatively new phenomenon in Canada, at least in terms of the degree of visibility that they possess today. In some centres, notably Toronto, the emergence of citizens' groups has resulted in sharp conflict between the groups and municipal politicians.

Not all citizens' groups, however, are new, and not all have experienced intense conflict with municipal politicians and officials. One category of citizens' groups has a history going back in some instances as far as fifty years – the local ratepayers' associations. And at least one of these has not experienced the same kind of conflict and opposition that many of the newer citizens' groups have encountered. This is the Annex Ratepayers' Association in Toronto, one of the oldest, and generally considered one of the most successful, of the ratepayers' associations in Canada.

The history of the Annex Ratepayers' Association is intimately linked with the history of the City of Toronto itself, and provides an example of how residents of a local neighbourhood, caught within the process of urban growth in this century, were able to exercise social choice with regard to the nature of their neighbourhood.

Urban Growth and Urban Neighbourhood

Urban growth, of course, is one of the outstanding phenomena of the twentieth century. Its concomitant social problems are becoming of ever-increasing concern.

Sociologists, and others, have not reached agreement in attempting to define the city or to describe and explain the process of urban growth[1] (Davis, 1959; Jones, 1966; Editors of the

Scientific American, 1969). Considerable impetus, however, for the study of the city as an *environment* came from the University of Chicago's Department of Sociology, under the leadership of Robert Park, generally considered to be the father of human ecology (defined as 'a branch of sociology that studies the relationship between a human community and its environment'[2]). Many of the concepts utilized or developed by the Chicago school have influenced subsequent attitudes towards urban growth and are, therefore, worthy of review here.

Using the city of Chicago, burgeoning in the years following World War II, as their laboratory, Park and his colleagues interpreted urban growth as a process primarily of economic determinism, based upon the fluctuations of land values. The Chicago school borrowed from the biological sciences such concepts as dominance, invasion, and succession, and applied them to the growth of the city. For example, Park (1961) writes:

> ... the principle of dominance operates in the human as well as in the plant and animal communities. The so-called natural or functional areas of a metropolitan community – for example, the slum, the rooming house area, the central shopping section and the banking center – each and all owe their existence directly to the factor of dominance and indirectly to competition. The struggle of industries and commercial institutions for a strategic location determines in the long run the main outlines of the urban community. The distribution of population, as well as the location and limits of the residential areas which they occupy, are determined by another similar but subordinate system of forces. The area of domination in any community is usually the area of highest land values. ... It is these land values that determine the location of social institutions and business enterprises (pp. 25-6).

According to the Chicago group, the residential areas surrounding the commercial and business centre of the city deteriorated into rooming-house and slum areas as expanding business and commercial interests invaded these areas and pushed the residential districts farther from the city core. The different sections of the city were considered 'natural areas' brought about by 'natural processes' and were, therefore, immune to influence or direction by human hands.

For many years, the view of the Chicago school was held in

high reverence. According to Bell (1968):

> There is certainly no question of its importance in determin-
> ing belief systems about the nature of urban life among sev-
> eral generations of sociologists and other intellectuals, and
> through them, to a lesser degree, the belief systems of many
> people throughout the society. And although it has been
> revised as a result of the work of many people, in its unre-
> constructed formulation it is not a dead horse even today
> (pp. 135-6).

In fact, Michelson (1970) points out that the concept of 'intervention' has only recently been accepted:

> ... rational intervention in the urban environment is com-
> paratively recent.... When human ecology was formulated,
> Americans were not consciously remaking large sections of
> cities, nor were they building cities of over 100,000 residents
> from scratch on farmland or woods as they are now (p. 21).

In contrast to the determinism of the Chicago ecologists,
Bell posits a 'theory of social choice', which emphasizes that
man makes choices that do indeed affect both where he lives
and the nature of the urban environment (Bell, 1968).

The Chicago school also placed great emphasis upon the city
as a place of social disorganization, of fleeting, secondary relationships which were, in the words of Louis Wirth (1957), 'impersonal, superficial, transitory and segmental' (p. 50). This
view also has been challenged, as a result of studies of urban
neighbourhoods which have revealed the existence of cultures
and subcultures where relationships exist that are primary and
close, where family life is rich and cohesive, where 'ethnic villages' thrive, where a sense of community may exist and be of
real significance to residents (Bell, 1968; Mann, 1961; Gans,
1962; Michelson, 1960; Pfeil, 1968; Young & Willmott, 1957).

As size and complexity become ever more significant factors
in the conduct of urban affairs, the urban neighbourhood becomes more important as a focus for urban life and community
living. This has been recognized by the United Nations (1961),
which has emphasized the concept of neighbourhood as the
geographic and social unit within which urban community development can be undertaken.

In the light, then, of both of these concepts – social choice
whereby citizens may influence the nature of their environment,

and the urban neighbourhood as the setting in which the exercise of social choice may be meaningful in creating a sense of community – it is appropriate to examine an organization such as the Annex Ratepayers' Association, which to a large extent has been successful both in exercising choice and in creating and maintaining a sense of community within its neighbourhood.

The Annex – Citizens and their Neighbourhood

How did the 'natural process' of the Chicago ecologists operate in relation to the Annex?[3]

In the second half of the nineteenth century, Toronto experienced a period of phenomenal growth inspired by the bringing of the railways to the city immediately prior to Confederation (Spiesman, 1967, p. 1). This growth manifested itself in the burgeoning of a variety of commercial activities – manufacturing, warehousing, wholesaling – together with a great expansion in the population. Not surprisingly, and in accord with the Chicago model, the spearhead of growth focussed at, or 'invaded', the city's centre; factories, warehouses, working-class homes, areas of crime and prostitution developed around the lakefront – in what was originally Toronto's fashionable residential district – and served to drive the wealthy out to uninhabited areas where they could acquire space and privacy. A prime example of invasion and succession!

At first the wealthy fled to Church, Jarvis and Sherbourne streets (between the 1860s and 1880s) but, again, the city followed, and by the late 1880s, these streets were also accommodating shops and rooming-houses. Again, invasion and succession. The wealthy were once more on the move, this time to relatively unsettled areas north of Bloor Street – Rosedale and the Annex. Alan Suddon[4] writes:

> From the beginning, the Annex was favoured as a choice residential area. Here is what John Ross Robertson has to say in his *Landmarks of Toronto*: 'The locality has been much built up during the decade ending in 1895 with for the most part a high class style of residences and is evidently destined to be one of the principal residential districts of the city'.

All was not wealth in the Annex, however. The wealthy tended to be concentrated in the southern part of the area, particularly on Lowther and Prince Arthur avenues between Walmer and Avenue roads. Farther north, on the streets running west from Avenue Road – on Tranby and Boswell avenues – could be found the homes of artisans, labourers, and other blue-collar workers, many of them employed in what had been the village of Yorkville, to the east of the Annex. And in the west end of the Annex, a mixed neighbourhood developed, ranging from small entrepreneurs, store-owners, professional people (doctors and lawyers), to white-collar workers whose numbers were growing, and blue-collar workers such as labourers, carpenters, bricklayers, and so on. The diversity of occupation was reflected in the variation in housing types, which included even old farmhouses.

Several trends which were to characterize the Annex until the present time emerged in the early days, prior to World War I. One was that mentioned above – the development of a population mix which was to become extended in several directions in later years. Another was an apparent division between the West Annex and the East Annex, with the area east of Walmer Road representing wealthier, upper-income residents, and the area west of there comprising a mixture of less prosperous low- and middle-income groups. Although today the division is not thought of so much in terms of differentiation on the basis of income and social status, there is still a geographical distinction between the two areas, which was intensified by the widening of Spadina Road after World War II.

Correspondingly, a sense of neighbourhood seemed to develop separately in the East and West Annex (Russel, 1963, p. 21). And along with this sense of neighbourhood grew the concern to maintain the area as it was. Thus, from 1905 on, a series of city by-laws were passed, prohibiting the establishment of various kinds of commercial and industrial enterprises (including apartments) on certain streets of the Annex.

This perhaps marks the beginning of what can be considered the dominant theme of the Annex throughout most of its history – the determination of its residents to maintain it as a residential area, despite the obvious 'natural' processes of urban growth, population shifts, and changes in land use which inevitably occurred to some extent, but whose onslaught was softened, and in some cases turned back, by the determination of the residents.

Changes, however, did occur. They could not be avoided. By

the 1920s and even more in the Depression years of the 1930s, the rich were again on the move, with Forest Hill a favourite destination for many. They left behind their huge, gracious, and spacious homes and, during this time, another trend began – the conversion of many of the larger Annex homes into multiple residences which accommodated, in rooms and flats, the growing numbers of university faculty and students, government employees, and others, who found the Annex both convenient in terms of location and attractive in terms of environment. A 1929 by-law represented an effort to stem the tide by restricting most Annex streets to private residences or, at most, to duplexes (Russel, 1963, p. 21).

It was the Depression, however, that spelled the end of the Annex as an exclusively single-family area. More and more well-to-do families moved out as they found themselves unable to maintain the large homes, and the conversion of houses continued despite the 1929 by-law. During the 1930s, also, many of the larger homes were converted to institutional use by various cultural, educational, religious, or service organizations. Many of the houses were also converted into offices. By the end of the 1930s, the Annex had been engulfed by the expanding city to the point where it was a central district, very convenient to the university, the parliament buildings, and the heart of the city (Suddon, 1964, Vol. 1[2], p. 3).

Next came World War II; the concomitant housing-shortage resulted in wartime orders cancelling restrictions against rooming-houses. This caused a flood of roomers to the Annex, with consequent overcrowding: 'The Annex came to take on a definite dormitory character' (Russel, 1963, pp. 33-4). The result, by 1944, was that the City Planning Board classified the district as vulnerable to blight and decay.

Post-war trends included an increase in the number of rooming-houses, a reduction in the proportion of family units, and, particularly in the East Annex, a preponderance of married couples without children, and of single people, along with an increase in the number of transient tenants, many of them university students (Spiesman, 1967, p. 42).

The Annex Ratepayers' Association

It was during this period of change, dating from the mid 1920s, that the Annex Ratepayers' Association emerged as a significant force in the Annex.

Actually, the Association was formed in 1923, making it the oldest such association in Toronto and possibly in Canada. Its stated purpose was as follows:

> The aims and objectives of the Association are to preserve the residential characteristics of the district, to promote measures to stimulate interest in improving still further the appearance of the area and to assist in preparing and, where necessary, enforcing ordinances and laws for the comfort, safety and good appearance of the Annex (Russel, 1963, p. 29).

Wording it in another way some forty years later, the Association stated that it was

> ... prepared to guide and represent the community in the major battles to protect the Annex from undue exploitation and it is prepared to work with architects, planners, politicians and developers to achieve sound development in our area.[5]

The Association came into being in 1923 because of an application received by the City of Toronto for permission to establish a hospital on the north side of Prince Arthur Avenue, between Avenue Road and Bedford Road, the granting of which would have involved an amendment of the by-laws to permit such an establishment in a residential zone.

> While everyone was sympathetic to the work of the hospital, it was felt that this was a most unsuitable location for an institution of that kind and that the establishment of the hospital would mean the end of the area as a residential district.[6]

A number of prominent citizens in the immediate neighbourhood rallied together and fought the application through the city's Property Committee, Board of Control, and City Council and, losing at that level, to the Ontario Railway and Municipal Board (forerunner of the present Ontario Municipal Board) where they won, and the hospital's application was rejected.

Following this victory, the Association established itself as a watchdog on attempts to violate or change zoning by-laws in the Annex, and during the next ten to fifteen years developed its very considerable expertise in arranging for deputations before the different boards and committees of the City Council and in pursuing the fundamental goal of the Association – to preserve the residential nature of the Annex.

The Association suspended its operations during World War II, when wartime orders cancelled the restrictions against rooming-houses. It resurrected itself in 1948 and was successful in 'preventing the construction of an apartment on a site which is now the only playground in the district and, in one year, it defeated fifteen applications for change of the residential restrictions'.[7]

The Association's major concern in those immediate postwar years was the mushrooming of boarding- and rooming-houses which had occurred during and after the war. The Toronto Planning Board had surveyed residential areas throughout the city and, in 1944, as reported above, had reported the Annex to be 'a sound residential area but vulnerable to decline if steps were not taken to protect it' (Russel, 1963, p. 37). Between 1948 and 1954 the Annex Ratepayers' Association struggled with by-laws and proposed by-laws affecting multiple-dwelling houses, rooming- and boarding-houses. After a series of public meetings, a by-law was passed in 1954 that required that guest-home owners abide by 'Class A' rooming-house regulations, leaving the whole of the Annex zoned for residential use, with high density and certain kinds of institutions permitted on Spadina Road and St. George Street (Johnson, 1962, p. 2). However, the 'Class A' restrictions regarding rooming-houses proved impossible of enforcement and 'an unexpected loop-hole in the by-law resulted in a rash of high-density and high-rise apartments on the larger lots' (Johnson, 1962, p. 2).

Annex Neighbourhood Associations

'Something more than legal protection is required to maintain old values and stimulate new development' was the conclusion reached by the West Annex Neighbourhood Association as the situation described above unfolded (Johnson, 1962, p.2).

Thus, concern in the 1950s for the development of a positive sense of community among Annex residents led to the formation of the West Annex Neighbourhood Association in May, 1952, and the East Annex Neighbourhood Association in November, 1952. The two new organizations saw themselves complementing, rather than competing with, the Ratepayers' Association, in that, while the latter was trying to *maintain* the area, the former were concerned to *improve* the quality of life within it. Thus, they were concerned with improving the condition and appearance of the area and its houses, and with promoting good neighbourly relations. They saw themselves as vehicles for greater citizen participation in achieving these objectives.[8]

The West Annex Association took as its major concern the rehabilitation and restoration of the older homes, neglect of which could pave the way towards blight. It saw 'neighbourhood conservation as slum prevention' (1954, p. 18). In 1954 it published a comprehensive survey of the Annex entitled *Renaissance of the Annex* and was successful in persuading many residents to modernize and restore their homes; the result was an improvement in the soundness of much of the housing stock in the area. The West Annex organization also made representation to the appropriate official bodies of the City of Toronto regarding enforcement of existing by-laws concerned with fire, safety, and health, in the interests of preventing deterioration of the housing.

The East Annex Association concentrated on such projects as neglected parks, garbage and litter conditions, and parking and traffic problems, with its efforts frequently rewarded by co-operative action on the part of civic officials to bring about improvement (Johnson, 1962, p. 2). Taking as its motto, 'It's smart to live in the Annex,' the Association sought to make residents aware of the advantages of the Annex as an urban residential neighbourhood close to the heart of the city. For example, it published a directory of near-by recreational activities, 'Summer in the Annex', and undertook such activities as an interpreter service for New Canadians in the area, a photography contest, picnics, excursions, and other social events designed to further a spirit of community.

During the 1950s, both neighbourhood associations were active and, together with the Ratepayers' Association, sent countless delegations to City Hall. By 1960 the three organizations realized that not only had the appearance of the three separate groups at City Hall become very confusing to city officials, but that the three could also better serve their mutual and frequently overlapping purposes by uniting into one organization to represent the entire geographic area and all of its residents. The Ratepayers' Association agreed to extend its membership to tenants as well as homeowners and the two neighbourhood groups merged themselves into a thereby expanded Ratepayers' Association.

Since that time, in addition to continuing its traditional function of attempting to preserve the residential character of the area, the Ratepayers' Association has also attempted to promote community relations in the district. The latter has been accomplished through public meetings on matters of direct interest and concern to residents, social events of various kinds, art exhibits, walking tours of significant Annex homes, and the publication at different times of a newsletter. The current newsletter is entitled *Voice of the Annex*[9], and attempts to keep members informed of the activities of the Association, particularly of the current issues and 'battles' that are being faced, as aell as to provide general information about the Annex itself and about services and facilities that are available or that the Association thinks should be provided by the city.

A Co-operative Planning Venture

In the late 1950s, the Toronto Planning Board enlisted the co-operation of the Annex Ratepayers' Association in updating the city's Official Plan and Zoning By-law, thereby providing an instance of co-operative planning that could perhaps serve as an example of how the city and other citizens' groups might relate to each other.

The Planning Board divided the city into twenty-five districts for the purpose of studying them in order to 'improve the zoning standards and revise the official plan in the light of anticipated changes in land use, major public works, traffic routes and park requirements' (Johnson, 1962, p. 3). Because of the existence of the Annex Ratepayers' Association as an active, sophisticated, knowledgeable citizens' organization, the Annex was selected as the first district to be surveyed. At the request of the Planning Board, the Association helped to gather and provide information about the character of the Annex in terms of land use, physical characteristics, size and nature of households, location of churches, schools, and other institutions. (Annex residents, who had at an earlier date opposed any land use except single family residences, had by this time accepted the principle of a balance of land uses within the primary concept of the Annex as a residential neighbourhood.)

The appraisal report[10] officially known as 'The Annex District Planning Appraisal', reflected this approach:

The Annex will continue to be mainly a place where people live, but there are many changes to come because of the district's central location, the growth and change of Toronto as a whole and the various subway and expressway proposals. Some of the more important changes expected in the next 20 years are: More conversions (of houses to apartments and flats) ... fewer families ... fewer children ... more apartment buildings ... more student residences ... parks ... institutions ... traffic ... parking ... shopping ... offices ... industries (p. 4).

Following the publishing of the appraisal with its recommendations, the Annex Ratepayers' Association embarked on a gigantic community-education project to enable the residents of the Annex to receive, discuss, and react to the recommendations. The Association of Women Electors co-operated in this effort, and the two organizations distributed 6,000 summaries of the appraisal, arranged small meetings of Annex residents, church representatives, and other interested groups, compiled records of meetings and written submissions, and climaxed the whole endeavour with two public meetings (one in the East and the other in the West Annex) at which the plans were presented, discussed, and deliberated upon (Johnson, 1962, p. 3).

Some revisions were made to the proposals, and the new zoning by-law was passed by City Council in 1959. It permitted more institutional, office, and commercial development on certain specified streets and blocks and – the big change – allowed apartment houses, including high-rise buildings, to be built in almost any residential area in the Annex. The protection regarding the latter was contained in the density regulations incorporated into the zoning category.

It is this last-mentioned feature of the by-law, that permitting high-rise apartments, that has created the biggest headache for Annex residents and the Ratepayers' Association. If the battle of the 1950s was against blight and deterioration of the area, with the enemy recognized as the rooming-house or guest-home operator, that of the 1960s, and the beginning 1970s, has been against spot rezoning, and this time the enemy was bigger, more obvious, and more powerful – the developer. With the completion of the Bloor Street subway, developers saw the Annex as an even more desirable location for profitable high-rise apartments. Many of the old homes on large lots were pulled down to make way for high-rise apartment buildings, and remaining homeowners have been under constant pressure to sell their properties for the same purpose (Russel, 1963, p. 103).

The bigger battle, however, has been with those developers who buy up land and then apply to the city for zoning changes to permit greater density. The Ratepayers' Association sees itself locked in a ceaseless, on-going struggle to maintain adherence to the zoning regulations as set forth in the official plan. It obtains agendas of city and Metro committee-meetings in advance, such as those of the Planning Board's Committee of Adjustment, which receives applications for zoning changes, and it sends representation to meetings when there appears to be a danger of zoning change. Often, these issues are carried to the Ontario Municipal Board. One of the biggest expenses of the Association is the hiring of legal counsel to carry on these battles. So far, it has usually been successful, but it feels the process requires continual vigilance, and there has been widespread apprehension in the area regarding the future. The Association describes the nature of the struggle:

> It is the nature of developers to develop, of planners to plan, of politicians to politick and of homeowners to be steamrollered in the process . . . *unless* they happen to choose to fight back. This fighting back, this attempt to redress the balance of organizational power, is what ratepayers' and residents' associations are all about – including ours. We choose not to be pawns in a multi-million dollar game being played with our properties (which often mean our life savings) [*Voice of the Annex*, Feb. 1970, p. 1].

One method used by the Association has been to provide its members with a description of block-busting tactics, so that they will recognize when it may be about to occur, and, as well, with advice for preventing block-busting: 'Paint up and spruce up, inside and out – show the would-be developer or speculator that the homeowner has no intention of selling out' (*Voice of the Annex*, April 1969, p. 2).

The Association is aware of other threats to the Annex. In an article entitled, 'Battles raging on many fronts,' the Association included the Spadina Expressway, the problem of creeping boundaries (leading to rezoning), the possibility of University of Toronto expansion ('they say they have no plans for the Annex, but we are watching their every move') and possible rezoning of various parcels of land within the district (*Voice of the Annex*, Feb. 1970, p. 2).

The most recent effort of the Association to draw attention to the value of the Annex as a residential area is a housing inventory of all houses built before 1910, to determine their historical value. The project is part of a nation-wide effort being undertaken by the National Sites and Monuments branch of the federal Department of Indian Affairs and Northern Development. However, the Annex Ratepayers' Association is one of only two volunteer groups in the country participating in the survey; the rest will be done by paid help. This again indicates recognition of the capabilities of the Association to handle affairs in its district. Some 2,000 houses will be photographed and analysed with reference to the date each house was built, the architect or builder, the previous owners, residents, and occupants, and all of its interesting architectural and decorative features, both interior and exterior. The Association hopes that the results of the inventory will provide a new basis for arguing for the retention not only of single houses, but of blocks of houses or entire streets, on the basis of their historic value.

The irony of the whole situation in the Annex is that even when the city officials and the neighbourhood residents have co-operated and been able to work out a mutually satisfactory plan, the residents have had to maintain constant vigilance and carry on a ceaseless struggle to maintain the nature of the Annex as agreed upon by both the Planning Board and the residents and, supposedly, as protected by the zoning by-law of 1959.

Citizens' Participation in Neighbourhood Planning

Reference was made earlier to Bell's comment about the influence of the Chicago school's approach of economic determinism regarding urban growth. Certainly, a predominant attitude towards urban growth has been that it is inevitable, that economic values prevail, that progress is to be measured in terms of the physical growth of the city, the increase in population, the size and number of buildings, and the increase in the assessment value of urban land. The significance of the citizens' movement, it would seem, is that many citizens are now saying that these developments are neither inevitable nor desirable, and that greater attention needs to be turned towards the quality of life within the urban environment.

This, essentially, is what the Annex Ratepayers' Association has attempted to achieve. Residents of the Annex developed a concept of the kind of urban neighbourhood in which they wished to live; they managed' to stop or at least control the 'inevitable' or 'natural' invasion of the area by other forms of land use; and, to a considerable degree, they have been able, so far at least, to preserve their neighbourhood. And, as has been shown, they have done this without the opposition and hostility from municipal politicians and officials that a number of other groups have encountered. They therefore can serve as an example for other citizens' groups and other situations.

Granted,. there are some unique features about the Annex Ratepayers' Association. This is not an economically deprived or disadvantaged group. Because the Association represents a basically middle-class neighbourhood, with a range of educational and occupational levels among its citizens, it has had more access than is usual to information about what was happening in the city; it has had more resources available, such as funds for legal counsel; it has, over the years, amassed considerable knowledge and expertise regarding city by-laws, the process of lobbying, and so on. As a result, the Association has always been treated with a certain amount of respect in official quarters, as a body that cannot be ignored.[11]

Perhaps all of these factors are significant in any effort to understand the nature of the present conflict between many citizens' groups and the city.

In 1970 the Bureau of Municipal Research conducted a study entitled 'Neighborhood Participation in Local Government – A Study of the City of Toronto.' In its report (Bureau . . . , 1970), the Bureau points out that:

> The City and the neighbourhood have very different priorities – the City emphasizes the more general problems within the City and the need for professional planning, while the neighbourhood strives to protect and develop the quality of the area (p. 6).

Consequently, the report states, 'the neighbourhood and the City will always tend to be in conflict because of the different perspectives on neighbourhood problems' (p. 9).

According to the Bureau, the city politicians often dislike the neighbourhood groups, an attitude of which the latter are well aware.

... the politicians often do not see the groups as legitimate representatives of the neighborhood, resulting in a widespread lack of trust between the groups and the politicians (p. 11).

On the other hand, the report states:

Among neighbourhood groups there has been frustration and a lack of faith in how the City makes and implements policies (p. 11).

The report reaches the conclusion:

The situation as it exists now has produced neither a desirable nor workable set of relationships between the City and the various neighbourhoods (p. 11).

The Bureau takes the position that 'neighbourhood groups should continue to function as organizations indigenous to their particular area' (p. 15), and proposes a new set of ground rules to help neighbourhood groups to be more effective and to create a better atmosphere between their representatives and the politicians in which to solve problems of mutual concern. Specific proposals include:
1. public funds for the support of community organization;
2. access to information and expertise at both the municipal and provincial levels for neighbourhood groups researching and/or presenting proposals;
3. appointment of group representatives to Committees of Council when issues affecting that neighbourhood are considered;
4. the provision of meeting facilities, such as school or community centres, where the citizen may meet regularly with the aldermen (p. 13).

Implementation of these proposals would do much to remove the inequality in access to resources and information that places citizens in low-income neighbourhoods at a disadvantage in contrast to residents of the Annex.

The Bureau outlines a number of other suggestions for both local government and the neighbourhood groups, all with a view towards creating a situation whereby 'the groups become plugged into the decision-making process in an advisory capacity without usurping any of the final decision-making authority from the elected representatives' (p. 14).

An interesting idea in the direction of shared decision-making was proposed in a letter to the editor of the Toronto *Star*, which had carried an editorial suggesting that neighbourhood groups should offer positive programs for change and improvement rather than simply acting as an organized veto, exercising negative power. The letter suggests,

> The main reason why community groups exercise only a negative power is because of our whole approach to planning and change. When plans are designed without local involvement, this places citizens' groups in an advocate-adversary relationship, with the planning bureaucrats and politicians as advocates and citizens' groups as adversaries.

The letter continues,

> Is it reasonable to assume that planners and politicians can always think of one alternative and that the responsibility for challenging that alternative and creating new ones lies with the citizens – the citizens who frequently do not have the time, energy, information and resources to do what responsible civil servants and politicians should?
> Negative power can be turned into positive power by sharing information and decision-making.[12]

That this proposal has merit has been shown by the example, described above, of the co-operation between the city and the Annex Ratepayers' Association with regard to the Official Appraisal. The city did not bring a ready-made plan to the Annex but, rather, enlisted the help of the Annex Ratepayers' Association in compiling the data necessary for formulating a plan and then developing the plan with all the information available to the residents involved. Together they were able to evolve a plan that was mutually acceptable.

An approach such as this would go a long way towards providing citizens' groups and neighbourhood associations with the opportunity for choice, through the consideration of alternatives for the future of their urban environment. Should such an approach be adopted, the mechanisms of citizen involvement in planning could be developed, perhaps along the lines recommended by the Bureau of Municipal Research.

What is needed, therefore, is an attitude on the part of officials and politicians in local government and among the public at large, that urban growth is a process whose direction can be influenced by human decisions and in which those to be affected by change must have the opportunity to participate in the planning of change.

This is not just a romantic ideal. Recently, considerable attention has turned to the negative aspects of unchecked urban growth. The issues of pollution and traffic congestion in particular have raised serious doubts about the kind of environment man has created in the city. Neighbourhood organizations such as the Annex Ratepayers' Association have consistently placed 'quality of life' values ahead of the 'this is the price of progress' approach, which paid little heed to the positive values of living within an urban neighbourhood. Perhaps now that 'progress' is being seen more and more as a process of destroying much of the quality of life and, indeed, possibly life itself within the urban environment, greater heed will be paid to the concerns of urban residents if urban living is to be viable and satisfying for the future. This presents itself as an urgent issue in the 1970s.

FOOTNOTES

1. *Census of Canada.* 1961, Vol. 1, Pt. 1, Bulletin 1-6.
2. Gove, P.B. (Ed.) *Webster's third new international dictionary.* Springfield, Mass.: Merriam Co., 1966.
3. Although the boundaries of the Annex have changed at different times during its history, they are now generally considered to be Bloor Street on the south, the C.P.R. tracks north of Dupont on the north, Avenue Road on the east, and Bathurst Street on the west. The Annex received its name following annexation by the City of Toronto in 1887. The obvious physical characteristic of the Annex is that it is an area of tree-lined streets containing a preponderance of large Victorian-style homes.
4. Suddon, A. "History of the Annex." In *The Annex*, 1964, Vol. 1 (1) - Vol. 1 (2).
5. *Annex.* Newsletter of the Annex Ratepayers' Association, 1964, Vol. 1 (7), p. 4.
6. *Annex*, 1964, Vol. 1 (1).
7. Johnson, N. "It's smart to live in the Annex." *Habitat*, 1962, January - February.
8. West Annex Neighborhood Association. *Renaissance of the Annex.* Toronto. Author, 1954.
9. *Voice of the Annex.* Newsletter of the Annex Ratepayers' Association, 1969, 1970.

10.City of Toronto Planning Board, *Plan for the Annex*, 1959.
11.*Annex*, 1964, Vol. 1 (3), p. 3.
12.*Toronto Star*, February 24, 1970.

DORENE E. JACOBS is a Project Officer in the Department of Adult Education, Ontario Institute for Studies in Education, where she directs a study of educational needs and interests among the adult population, a project supported by the Ontario Educational Communication Authority. She is also a member of the Steering Committee of the Professional Education Project of the Adult Education Department.

Prior to graduate studies in 1969-70, she served for almost seven years as Education Officer for the Ontario Human Rights Commission and for two years before that as editor of *Ontario Housing* for the Ontario government. She has also held positions with the Canadian National Commission for UNESCO, the United Kingdom Information Services, and the Canadian Association for Adult Education. She was conference co-ordinator for the 1967 International Conference of Commissions for Human Rights held in Toronto and hosted by the Ontario Commission. Part-time activities include tutoring for the Writing Workshop, Atkinson College, York University, and organizing a non-credit course on 'Citizens' Action and Citizens' Issues' for the University of Toronto's Division of Extension.

Miss Jacobs holds an M.Ed. in Adult Education from the Ontario Institute for Studies in Education, a B.S. in Recreation and Community Organization from the Faculty of Education, University of Wisconsin, a B.A. in General Arts from the University of Western Ontario, and is currently enrolled as a part-time Honours Year student in sociology at Atkinson College, York University.

Flemington Road Community School: A Process in Community Development

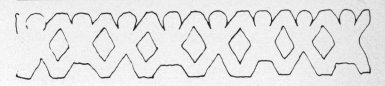

Dale E. Shuttleworth

One of the most influential voices in modern education has been that of John Dewey. As an advocate of education as an instrument of social change, he made the following statement:

> We plead for an improved and enlarged social order that there may be brought into existence all of whose operations shall be more genuinely educative, conducive to the development of desire, judgement, and character. The desired education cannot occur within the four walls of a school shut off from life. Education must itself assume an increasing responsibility for participation in projecting ideas of social change and taking part in their execution in order to be educative. The great problem of American education is the discovery of methods and techniques by which this more direct and vital participation may be brought about (Dewey, 1933, p. 146).

Nowhere have the challenges of twentieth-century education been more apparent, nor the problems more acute, than in our cities. Urban living has become an inescapable fact for the great majority of our families. The heterogeneous nature of urban life, the density of population, the problems of adjustment to a new life-style, and the inability of some individuals to compete economically or cope emotionally: all have led to a major dilemma. Suddenly, traditional methods no longer apply. Our ability to distinguish between the needs of various segments of the population and to provide equality of opportunity is in question.

In many parts of North America, the term 'inner city' has become synonymous with poverty, deprivation, despair, and violence. As Canadian urban-dwellers, we cannot afford an air of smugness about what is happening in the American cities. We are in a position to learn from their experience, to plan for our own future. The late Senator Robert F. Kennedy, when questioned as to the role of urban education, replied:

> We must find new means of increasing the relevancy of school curricula to the challenges students must face in their daily lives, at home, and on the job. As a corollary to this, involve the communities with the schools to a greater degree so that the schools are more accountable to the community and its needs (Kennedy, 1968, p. 58).

Educators have borne the brunt of problems associated with social disorganization, but we are just one of the 'helping professions' shouldering this burden. Many other groups are also frustrated by the problems of the poor and disadvantaged. Municipal government, social welfare, public health, recreation, education authorities, and, most important, the people themselves, must become common partners, if this urban crisis is to be resolved at the community level.

An illustration of the urban problem and what can be done about it is the Lawrence Heights Low Income Housing Development, created in 1957 as a public-housing enclave in Metropolitan Toronto. This community, constructed at the crossroads of Lawrence Avenue and the Spadina Expressway, should be considered as a segregated geographic unit. Patterns of access to the surrounding neighbourhood are limited by physical barriers: to the north, a major thoroughfare, to the south, the institutional buildings along the north of Lawrence Avenue, to the west and east, a fence separating the project population from the neighbouring middle-class, single-family-dwelling community. There are only four routes of access into the community: two from the north, and two from the south. The Spadina Expressway divides the project into two fairly equal areas.

All housing is rented and administered by the Ontario Housing Corporation. Rent is set at approximately one-third of a family's monthly income. Admission is restricted to low-income families, and priority goes to those with the greatest need. There are 1,081 units consisting of walk-up apartments with one to three bedrooms each and row or semi-detached housing with three to five bedrooms per unit.

Total population of the development is about 5,000 persons, 3,000 of whom are school-age children and pre-schoolers. Many families have been relocated from the substandard housing of the core of the city, often on an emergency basis. Almost 30 per cent of the families are one-parent, mother-led. The number of families receiving social-welfare financial assistance ranges from 20 to 40 per cent.

> The family problems found here are no different than can be found throughout the city but are more highly concentrated due to geographic segregation and population density. For some families, their major struggle is that of survival because of their low income and the resulting burdens of debt and other accumulative family problems. A large number of families come from the inner-city slum areas. Although their housing problems were solved, new problems were created, resulting from the loss of such things as familiar neighbourhoods, second-hand stores, easy access to hospital clinics and the corner pubs. Some complaints which came from within the community itself were, and still are: 'children are allowed to run wild', 'parents do not care about their children', or 'families on welfare spend their money on drink' (Oliver, 1968, p. 3).

> Residents of the neighbouring area and trades people visiting the community often see a negative image of the project. Such terms as 'the jungle', 'poverty village' and 'the camp' are commonly used. This stigma hurts personal pride, makes residents feel inferior, and produces the depressing, hopeless feelings that are common attributes of alienation. (Delegran, 1967).

In the midst of this 'problem area' is Flemington Road Public School of the North York Board of Education. This school has grown with Lawrence Heights; it occupies a central location and serves the project exclusively. As probably the first suburban school in Canada to serve a low-income, public-housing area, Flemington has undergone a process of growth and adjustment that transformed it from a traditional, *status quo* institution into a thriving experiment in education, designed to break down the barriers between school and community. During this crucial developmental period, the school was fortunate to have a most outstanding principal in the person of Whittier K. Morris. His enlightened flexibility and democratic style of leadership, coupled with an energetic use of human-relation skills, provided an inspiration to his teachers, and warmth and understanding to his students and their parents. Succeeding principals, A. E. Boddy and J. S. Montgomerie have maintained and expanded this concept.

My own area of the Flemington Road School, the Social Services Project, during the past five years has pioneered the community-school philosophy, based on the belief that the school and the resources that it represents cannot be separated from the community that it serves. As I outlined in a publication (Shuttleworth, 1967), we have extended Flemington Road School as a partner in community development, with these objectives:

1. to improve the quality of living;
2. to use the community as a laboratory for learning;
3. to make the school plant a centre of community living;
4. to organize the curriculum around the fundamental processes and problems of living;
5. to include the community in school policy and program planning;
6. to provide leadership in the co-ordination of community services;
7. to practise and promote democracy in all human relationships.

The community-school concept is interpreted to include three main integrated functions, which I will discuss in the following pages.

The Community-Centred Curriculum

As an extension of the community that it serves, the school views the community as a resource for the enrichment of the program of the school. Other community resources help determine the kind of learning experiences children have. Thus, the neighbourhood and the larger city become a vast class-room of learning experience in developing a more relevant curriculum.

Teachers are exposed to the community's style of living through home visits and through a variety of resource persons and community workers. Through participation in the extended day program, teachers meet parents on an informal basis, leading to greater mutual understanding. Teachers begin to understand the environment and value systems of their pupils and to gear the learning process to develop strengths and compensate for deficiencies.

A curriculum committee was formed on a volunteer basis, representing all educational levels. This group is directing its efforts to writing a curriculum that reflects the particular needs of the community. A further objective is to develop a systematic progression of learning experience through the school. Language programs are studied to evaluate their appropriate use in the setting of Flemington Road School. Field trips are organized and rated according to their learning objectives. Real-life experience becomes a key to unlock the mysteries of reading, mathematics, science, and social studies. An effort is made to meet the child at his level, and to develop a relationship that enriches patterns of educational growth.

Through these experiences, teachers may develop a greater sensitivity to the social, emotional, and physical needs of their students. Certainly a teacher learns that he must meet these basic needs before the academic realm has any meaning for the child. An empathetic rather than a sympathetic relationship must evolve while the teacher continues to enrich the educational environment. Under these circumstances, teachers become need-oriented rather than program-oriented.

A Centre of Community Living

Emphasis is placed upon developing fullest use of the school's physical facilities by both individuals and community groups. Through the community-school framework, space is provided for autonomous programming while the school retains direct responsibility for the use of the building through the principal and community-school director. The school benefits through the supervision of facilities and co-ordination of their use. Participating groups benefit through the use of equipment and facilities under the favourable image that the school enjoys in the community.

The program began in October 1966, with activities for boys and girls on Monday, Wednesday, and Thursday evenings from four o'clock to seven o'clock. These activities included gymnasium, crafts, quiet games, choirs, ballet, story-telling, science, judo, and social-adjustment groups. Leadership was provided by both community volunteers and staff from participating organizations, including the school, the Department of Parks and Recreation, the North York Public Library, and the Lawrence Heights Family and Child Service. Two gymnasiums, kindergarten rooms, and regular class-rooms were used. Programming was developed through student surveys and was highly flexible. Seventy per cent of the students took part in the program during the first year of operation.

The adult program took root much more slowly. School staff first met different groups of community residents to discuss the concept and develop ideas for programming. Booths were set up at School Open House to disseminate information and gather further ideas. School administrators met representatives from community agencies to discuss the program and later to gain their active support. From these meetings, interviews, and conferences, a blueprint of co-operative effort was drawn.

Finally, in February 1967, the program got underway on Monday and Wednesday evenings from seven to ten o'clock. Informal adult get-acquainted centres were developed by Lawrence Heights Social Services. The Department of Parks and Recreation began fitness programs for men and women. Gradually, interest groups were spawned. A Rod and Gun Club and Neighbourhood Association met regularly. The National Council of Jewish Women provided leadership for crafts and dramatic groups. Early in 1968, Thursday evening was established as a Family Night with babysitting provided. Activities included a family-life film series, a homemakers' group, a men's club, a weight-losing group, and an English-improvement class. Coffee parties were also organized in private homes where parents and teachers enjoyed a social evening.

It became apparent, however, that one important segment of the community had been overlooked. The teen-agers soon made their presence felt, and, as a result the facilities were opened on Tuesday evenings for a drop-in centre, tutoring and study centre, and gymnasium program. Table tennis, a TV lounge, dancing, snooker, and discussion groups were later added. An elected board of teen-age monitors helps in development of policy and activities, and in supervision of facilities.

Small interest groups have also begun meeting on Wednesday evenings for activities such as a girls' fitness class, a snooker club, a charm club, a film series, and special projects that include Volunteers Unlimited, in which senior secondary-school students have become community-service workers, and the

Job Improvement Corps where drop-outs are assisted in getting jobs while taking part in educational upgrading and employment training.

The Community-Service Function

As the best-established and most socially accepted resource in the community, the school is prepared to assume an active role in community and social planning and to provide leadership. Administrators try to co-ordinate the activities of many agencies with the school's program.

The school houses a number of services that benefit the whole community. The social-services staff represents the supportive services within the school and provides a liaison with the home and social agencies within the community. The public-health nurse interprets the health of the pupil and his family, and investigates and gives support in combatting problems due to physical or emotional disability. Remedial-reading specialists, a library-resource teacher, and a speech therapist are available to provide assistance in the language area. A full-time dentist and dental nurse provide the dental services for children of the community. A psychologist and psychometrician visit the school to provide an assessment and consultative service in regard to educational and behavioural problems.

The interdisciplinary team constitutes a unified approach to child and family problems. This team represents a collaboration of services among the school, represented by the principal, social-services staff, and public-health nurse, and the Lawrence Heights Family and Child Service, which is a combination of both the Children's Aid Society and the Family Service Association in the area. In addition, representatives of other agencies may be invited to particular conferences. Meetings are held formally on a monthly basis, but interdependence is maintained through informal daily contact. Decisions are made on the basis of all available information and the consensus of disciplines represented. A co-ordinated plan often grows out of a segmented, inefficient plan through such discussions.

Supervision and training are provided for the many volunteers who assist with activities. Seneca College and York University use the Flemington Road community school as a field placement. Workshops and seminars are provided for citizens' groups, teachers, and students of both social work and public-health nursing. In addition, large numbers of community-service personnel and educators from other schools make casual visits and fact-finding tours.

The Community School Advisory Council was organized to guide and evaluate activities and to provide a forum for the discussion of matters of concern to both school and community. Membership includes residents and representatives from agencies or groups either actively involved in the concept or providing organizational support: the Board of Education, North York Council, the Social Planning Council, the Department of Parks and Recreation, the Lawrence Heights Family and Child Service, the North York Public Library, the National Council of Jewish Women, the Neighbourhood Association, the Lawrence Heights Sports Committee, St. Philip's Church, the Ontario Housing Corporation, Seneca College, the Lawrence Heights Judo Club, the Information Centre, the Garden Club, the Metropolitan Police Department, and the Mennonite Brethren Church. Thus, many resources have been brought together under the umbrella of the community school in a co-ordinated effort to improve community living.

The Advisory Council has become the focus for community development in Lawrence Heights. Over the past five years, it has never become structured into a traditional executive hierarchy. The chairmanship rotates from meeting to meeting among community residents. Decisions are reached by consensus. *Ad hoc* work-groups are formed spontaneously to respond to an issue and later report their progress back to the Council. Meetings are open for all to attend and participate, whatever their interests or political views might be. A sense of trust has grown up among people sharing a common philosophy of community action.

This process has resulted in a higher level of skill and involvement throughout the community. Besides the community school, other successful efforts have been a day-care centre, a hot-lunch program, an information centre, a community newspaper, a grocery co-operative, a clothing store, a medical centre, and a hockey arena. Not only have citizens been involved in working for their community, but agencies have been made increasingly accountable to the people.

A Plan for the Future

In reflecting upon the Flemington experience, I cannot help but be appalled by the state of underdevelopment of our resources, both human and physical. Too often, this condition is being reinforced by the very agencies and institutions that society depends upon for leadership. The fact that many of these organizations have become focalized around a hierarchy that excludes the people from the decision-making process has contributed to the problem, rather than alleviating it. It has been my experience, however, that the democratization of society cannot be accomplished simply by legislation. We can only learn by doing. The community must regain control of its institutions and make them accountable to the needs of the people.

Much has been written about the role of the school in low-income areas. The term 'compensatory education' has been coined to refer to programs and techniques designed to improve the success of the school in educating children from low-income families. It seems that too often such efforts are either a reaction to crisis or a type of 'faducation'. By simply modifying the traditional model or by adding a few specialists to the school staff, are we really only perpetuating a system that too often has not worked?

Flemington has attempted to break away from this traditional model of educational behaviour by providing a resource centre for human development. Rather than maintaining a closed institution that only a select group may relate to, we have opened it up to community living. In the process, we have discovered that what people desire are not just services, but access to skills that will give them more control over their resources and a greater sense of fulfilment.

The school of the future must be a democracy that includes parents, teachers, students, and administrators as active partners in decision-making, and curriculum development and implementation. Rather than attempting to extinguish the community life-style, the school should build on it as a basis of communication and learning. Teachers should feel as much at home in the community as in their own class-rooms. In fact, the community should become the class-room, with the human resources actively participating in shaping the learning environment.

The neighbourhood school should encourage human development by reaching out to become part of the life-space of the community. Development activities should begin to happen in small interest groups, possibly meeting in private homes. Activities should most often be action-oriented, leading to the acquisition of skills, directed to the realization of goals. Resource

316 Section 5: Relating to Communities

people might, in the early stages, be drawn from the ranks of professionals or outside volunteers, but as skills are developed, these people must be phased out in favour of indigenous leadership that is self-perpetuating.

These small groups or 'skill teams' should relate to each other through a type of federated 'human-development council'. The council itself would undertake a number of community-betterment projects drawing strength from the skill teams. Many community services traditionally provided by outside agencies would be gradually taken over by the human-development council. Professionals and outside volunteers would become accountable to the human-development council on a kind of contract basis. The human-development council would function as a sort of broker to co-ordinate the effective utilization of community resources.

It is my belief that education can have little relevance to the lives of people unless it has some effect on patterns of community living. By living education as a continuing developmental process, people in fact become emancipated, self-fulfilling individuals who are strong instruments of social change. We must begin at the grass roots, with people of all ages, to practise democracy if democracy is to survive. I hope that the school will have a part in this social reconstruction.

DALE E. SHUTTLEWORTH was born in Windsor, Ontario, and received his early education there. He graduated from the London Teachers' College in 1960 and assumed a position as class-room teacher with the Riverside Board of Education. From 1960 to 1965, he taught in junior and senior public schools and did a lot of coaching, particularly in track and field. In 1964, he graduated from the University of Windsor with a B.A. in sociology. In 1965 he went to North York as a teacher-counsellor at Flemington Road Public School. In 1966 he was named Chairman of Social Services, and in 1967 became Social Services Consultant for North York. In that same year Mr. Shuttleworth received a Master of Education degree from the University of Toronto. During this period he developed the community-school concept at Flemington, the first such program in Ontario. He was also very active in youth work and teacher education. In 1969 and 1970, he served on a curriculum committee on compensatory education for the Province of Ontario. In 1970 and 1971 he was Principal of the compensatory-education summer course for the Ontario Department of Education. Currently he is a doctoral student at the Ontario Institute for Studies in Education, majoring in school-community relations. He is also serving as a member of the Special Task Force on School-Community Involvement of the Toronto Board of Education. Mr. Shuttleworth has written a number of articles in the area of community schools and education in the inner city.

Co-Operatives as Agents of Community Education and Development

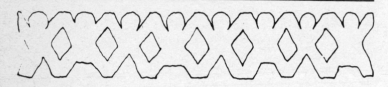

A. F. Laidlaw

In the fluid society of today every institution and organization must be at pains to identify itself and tell its purpose; for not only is society becoming vastly more complex and its various parts thereby in danger of becoming strangers to one another, but the various components of society are constantly changing and therefore view themselves differently from one decade or generation to the next. So it is with co-operatives.

Let us first be clear about the nature of co-operatives, since both friends and foes sometimes have hazy notions about them. They are basically and essentially business enterprises – and usually incorporated businesses, at that. Nor do they make any apology for being businesses, since their prime purpose is to carry out an economic function for members, and they must do this as efficiently as possible. They are, therefore, in essence economic, as much as T. Eaton's or the Royal Bank of Canada – but with a difference. And, as has been said of women, *vive la différence*!

Dr. Georges Fauquet (1951), distinguished writer and formerly International Labor Organization spokesman on co-operatives, expressed it this way:

> The primary aim of the co-operative institution is to improve the economic position of its members, but, because of the methods it employs and the qualities which it requires of its members and which it develops in them, it aims at and achieves a higher goal: to make men with a sense of both

individual and joint responsibility, so that they may rise individually to a full personal life and collectively to a full social life.

Thus, co-operatives serve two functions, those of business enterprise and social movement. Or, briefly stated, they are business plus something else, and it is the something else that concerns us here.

This dual role of co-operatives is not an easy one to play; it often gives rise to conflict within co-operative ranks and is the reason why the co-operative movement sometimes gives the impression of suffering from a split personality. It is simply that economic considerations and the social purpose are often at tug-of-war – a familiar enough game in society itself.

The social purpose in co-operatives is continually asserting itself in various ways. In the rural development program in Ireland led by Horace Plunkett over a half century ago, co-operatives were part of a total movement with the slogan 'Better Farming, Better Business, Better Living'. G.D.H. Cole (1953) viewed the consumers' co-operative movement as having 'two principal functions: to provide consumers with what they want, and to induce them to be sensible about their wants ... and the second involves an active and continuous process of consumer education.' And in the developing countries today, the social values of co-operatives are often stressed equally with the business functions, as reported by one African writer:

> With regard to the co-operative movement, its development since World War II has been one of the encouraging aspects of agricultural policy. ... The official viewpoint is that co-operation provides two politico-economic functions. First, they give the people some degree of independent control of their economic activity; and second, they provide valuable training in business administration which it would be difficult to find elsewhere. The government is not prepared to exchange those for the uncertain economic gains of competition (Oloya, 1968).

So even in times and under conditions when economic considerations tend to be uppermost and business urgencies press hard, co-operatives manage to keep social goals somewhere in the picture, sometimes prominently but, unfortunately, sometimes rather dimly. One of these social goals is to serve members and the community generally in the field of education and development.

The Movement Today

The idea of people working together towards socially desirable goals is very old in the story of mankind, and some historians and scholars have argued that it is mutual aid rather than social conflict that has carried humanity along the road of progress (Kropotkin, 1939). In the making of Canada, especially in the rural communities of bygone days, the spirit of working together in groups was an accepted part of everyday living and, indeed, made survival possible under the difficulties and privations of pioneer life.

But the present co-operative movement, with a network of various kinds of business organizations, now growing quite rapidly in most countries of the world, is of recent development. The idea of co-operation as business enterprise is not old fashioned, but comparatively new. Practically all co-operatives in Canada date from a year after 1900 and most of them from about 1925 onwards. So the adjustments that we see in the movement today are growing-pains rather than the arthritic symptoms of old age.

Here we can sketch the modern development of co-operatives only in broad outline. Starting from Britain in the early part of the last century, consumers' co-operatives have made most rapid progress in Europe, especially in the Scandinavian countries – in Finland they carry on about 40 per cent of the total retail trade. In the U.S.A., the farmers' co-operatives have shown the greatest vigour and growth, even to the point of supplying most of the rural electrification in the country; but as an indication of urban interest too, it should be noted that the largest single housing-project in New York City today is a co-operative, which, when completed soon, will provide apartment homes for about 55,000 people – equal to half the population of P.E.I. In Canada the co-operative idea is taking firm root and is growing well in a number of ways. Perhaps the most dynamic and significant facet of Canada's co-operatives today is the Desjardins movement in Quebec, with over one third of Quebec's population in membership. But that is only one side of the total Canadian movement, which is very far from being one of the largest in the world but which is often regarded as one of the most interesting because of its variety and resourcefulness. Co-operatives appear in many forms in Canada, sometimes without identifying themselves as such. For example, the Wheat Pools are co-operatives, so also is United Grain Growers, and Canadian Press is essentially co-operative though not in name.

In other parts of the world, and in all types of economies, co-operatives are enjoying remarkable growth. They may even be said to be somewhat in vogue in some countries. The constitution of the Republic of Indonesia says, hopefully: 'The economy shall be organized co-operatively'; and Guyana has named itself a 'Co-operative Republic'. In Japan virtually every farmer is a member of a co-operative, and the movement is making an important contribution to the economic miracle of modern Japan.

The coming of age of the co-operative movement is now well recognized in international circles. The world organization of co-operatives, the International Co-operative Alliance, is a consultative partner in councils of the United Nations, and various U.N. agencies, especially F.A.O. and I.L.O., are actively engaged in international-development work with co-operatives.

So much for the broad outlines. What about co-operatives at the community level, in education and social development?

Co-operation and Adult Education

The link between co-operative action and adult education has always been strong. In the last century the co-operative movement and popular education were not merely close friends but twin sisters in the same household. Co-operative societies in nineteenth-century Britain were often the initiators and pacesetters of adult education. Cole (1954) tells us that:

> The Rochdale Society became the owner of the best library in the town, complete with branch libraries and reference libraries scattered all over its area. In 1877 it had fourteen libraries and a total of 13,389 volumes, apart from periodicals ... a wide range of monthly and quarterly magazines. It had a laboratory and a large number of scientific and mathematical instruments, and it lent out for a charge microscopes complete with series of slides.... It was dispensing knowl-

edge pretty much as it sold tea or bread – guaranteeing that its quality was unadulterated and trying to give its members what they appeared to want. . . .

So, also, in other European countries organization for co-operatives started with organizing for knowledge and the two always went hand in hand as the co-operative movement went forward. The attention given to general community education in Denmark, for example, was one of the main features of the Danish co-operatives that visitors from other countries admired most. Lindeman (1961) mentions it several times in his writings. In Sweden the consumers' co-operatives are in the forefront of adult education and have a long tradition of channelling a good portion of their resources into educational activities.

In Canada the story is generally the same, though sometimes, we must confess, pretty spotty. It is interesting to note that four of the sixteen names in *Pioneers in Adult Education in Canada*[1] were men whose names were household words in community education as well as co-operatives. Alphonse Desjardins (1914), father of a co-operative system that now has one third the total population of Quebec in membership, was always conscious of the social significance of the edifice whose foundation he laid. Writing in 1914 he said:

> However important it may be to prevent the farmer and the working man from falling into the clutches of the usurers, it is of even higher importance to educate and to enlighten these same farmers and workingmen so that they may be in a position to protect themselves; to teach them to manage their own business so that they may become thrifty and more valuable members of the community.

The pioneers of co-operative development in western Canada were often the spark-plugs of adult education too, and very often the co-op fieldman was the chief co-ordinator of the educational activities that helped in such a vital way to build 'the West'.

This tradition continues as the co-operative idea is transplanted to the developing nations. Malcolm Darling, who planted much of the seed of co-operative organization that is now beginning to return a great harvest in the Punjab of India, described co-operatives thus in terms of the village: 'Every good co-operative society is an oasis in the desert of inertia.'

Specific Values and Functions

But what, you may ask, is the special value of co-operatives in community education and development? Wherein lies their strength and unique educational role?

Perhaps the first and most obvious answer is that a co-operative is an on-going reality to which people can relate and in which they can test educational theory. There is nothing more frustrating to the learner and futile for the community than educational activity forever divorced from actual life situations. 'Beware how you isolate thinking from doing,' says Lindeman (1961).

This separation of education from effective participation in meaningful social processes has been shown to be the reason why certain programs of community development have ended in disappointment. One writer from Latin America reports:

> Luis Reissig, using UNESCO data, pointed out not long ago that some literacy campaigns have failed so completely that the people who, a few years back, were taught to read and write are now once again illiterate. He argued from this that it was pointless to launch literacy campaigns unless they were combined with structural changes calculated to give the masses a genuine share in the process of development (Co-operación, 1966).

Men of action and social reform know the necessity of tying abstract ideals to something permanent and in the flesh. For example, a man like Cesar Chavez, seeking structural change in society, cannot fool around long with discussion and rhetoric – he must move to embody his beliefs and convictions in an agency for action. In his book, Matthiessen (1970) quoted Chavez:

> There has to be a real organization, a living organization, there have to be people in motion, and they have to be disciplined. . . . I mean a trained instinct so that when the moment comes, we just turn around and hit it. That's real organization. If you organize for demonstration, all you have is demonstration. You must demonstrate, and then return right away to the real work. . . . People come along that have a great love of human beings and have never found a way to channel it.

There is a certain amount of irresponsibility in community

education that does not issue in action, leaving it open to the accusation of being mere propaganda. People in a co-operative at least assume responsibility and test their education against facts and performance. The members of a credit union, for example, are prepared to take on the risk of being their own money-lenders; the members of a housing co-operative light a candle instead of interminably cursing the darkness of the slum landlord.

So, if asked to identify the main educational value in co-operatives, my answer would be: realism. They don't live by words alone.

Secondly, by their very nature co-operatives must follow the old educational principle that says: 'Start at the level of the learner.' In order to succeed they must match need and pro-gram as nearly as possible. The co-operative idea has the flexi-bility for application to the wishes of sophisticated Swedish consumers or the simplest needs of an Eskimo community, or equally to the credit needs of a farmer in India or the housing-needs of a middle-income family in New York City. Wherever there is social need, there is the possibility of co-operative ac-tion of some kind, and the educational program must follow the need. Therefore, theoretically at least, co-operative educa-tion can be a universal vehicle, capable of travelling over the most difficult terrain, a sort of educational jeep that may be found anywhere.

Thirdly, what may be called the 'transformer idea' has great appeal in discussions about community education and develop-ment. The analogy runs like this: Just as a high-voltage current of 10,000 volts must be stepped down to 220 or 110 volts at the community level, so also great national plans and complex ideas must be reduced to an intelligible and usable level re-quired by the community. Obviously, the co-operative organi-zation is such a transformer, ready-made, so to speak. A U.N. publication (United Nations, 1954) explains it this way:

> It is also evident that voluntary co-operation, with its pro-motion of full knowledge, discussion, confidence, equality in control and the greatest possible degree of self-reliance, has no complete substitute. Its results can be cumulative and permanent. For this reason many supervised credit depart-ments, agricultural credit corporations, land settlement au-thorities, administrations for the affairs of indigenous inhab-itants and for community projects, agricultural development boards and other official and semi-official bodies have come

to recognize the need to promote the formation and development of true co-operatives.

Furthermore, in modern times and in all types of society, as the State takes over more and more functions that either regulate or impinge upon the lives of all citizens, it is of paramount importance to maintain voluntary bodies of all kinds to balance the power of omnipotent government. A century ago co-operatives often moved in to occupy a vacuum in the community; today they must be maintained as a countervailing force, and sometimes as a complementary agency, to government authority and action. Of course, voluntary action is of the essence of education, and no educational experience can ever be so lasting and effective as that which ordinary people undertake for themselves. It becomes part of the social metabolism of the community. Lindeman (1961) says: 'Our personalities can be redeemed if we insist upon a proper share in the solution of problems which specifically concern us.' And what could possibly concern the average person more than the everyday matters that are the end and ingredients of co-operatives?

Finally, a Scot must inevitably bring up the question of who is to pay the piper. Community education cannot be kept on air alone – it must be paid for, and co-operators have been paying for it in a somewhat painless way these many years. The co-operative society that does not pay one way or another for community education of some kind is an exception, and a few pay consistently and rather generously.

At the risk of singling out one co-operative in Canada, which is done mainly because its size gives substance to this particular point, it can be mentioned that the Saskatchewan Wheat Pool has spent, aside from business operations, an estimated $100,000 annually in community education since its formation just over forty-five years ago. Where did this money come from? Obviously from the farmer's wheat – and it was his contribution to the variety of community and educational services supported by the 'Sask. Pool'. Community education must be paid for by those who want to keep it alive.

Some Examples

Among the best examples of co-operative organizations engaging in community education and development in the fullest sense are those to be found today in Japan, where agricultural co-operatives have become a vital part of post-war reconstruction and nation-building. My notes of visits to a number of such co-operatives in 1969 contain such jottings as these: '... education built around economic functions ... 400 special-interest groups ... 488 group leaders trained ... co-operative maintains staff of 23 technical advisors + 13 extension workers on home economy ... bookkeeping for women ... wife holds purse and is family bookkeeper ... monthly newsletter to all members ... this co-op has main cultural and community centre in the district ... wedding ceremonies here ... radio-telephone system provides communications service for the community ... quorum of 50% membership for annual meeting ... farmers saving 20% net income in co-op society ...'

Those who wish to examine the factors contributing to Japanese recovery from the devastation of World War II should not miss the record of the remarkable agricultural co-operatives of that country.

But 'community' in the modern world is becoming increasingly urban in character, and in Canada we are often painfully aware of the fact that the community environment that was essentially rural a generation ago has either passed away or is rapidly disappearing. This raises the question of the relevance of the co-operative as a community agent to the modern urban and metropolitan scene. So, for a second exhibit, let us take the work being done in the housing co-operatives of New York City – the largest, called Co-op City, has been mentioned.

One report[2] summarizes their record in this way:

In an ordinary community, neighbors are bound by common ties – schools, government, civic clubs, community affairs. In a housing co-op, neighbors have these ties plus a common interest in their homes.

Democracy, friendliness, common purposes, ways to air and settle disputes, tighter community ties – these explain why the incidence of crime among housing co-op members is very low. One large co-op in New York City has not had a member charged with a felony in more than thirty years. Another large co-op has never had a serious case of juvenile delinquency.

Housing co-ops have succeeded in bringing back the spirit of neighborliness and community that had all but disappeared from many low and middle-income areas of our big cities. They create feelings of permanence and sociability....

Thus we see how the co-operative idea, widely used by farm people to build better communities in North America in past generations, is helping to re-create community in the complexity of modern city life.

These examples are taken from outside Canada simply to make selection easier for the writer, and also because they illustrate a universality about co-operative organization which should have a special appeal for the adult educator. Suffice it to say that rural co-operatives in Canada have long been demonstrating their educational and community-building role, and now urban co-operatives in a few places are beginning to serve in like manner.

Difficulties and Weaknesses

Of course we would be less than honest not to include mention of difficulties in the way of co-operatives playing their educational role. The constant tug-of-war between the economic and social factors has already been mentioned. A business enterprise must first survive and succeed as a business, else it will not be in the community at all, educationally or otherwise.

But this is not the only difficulty. There is also the danger of co-operatives losing their bounce and responsiveness. Organizations, like individuals, tend to become old and too relaxed – they must regularly be given a transfusion of youth and new thinking in order to ward off senility. In earlier times the concept of co-operation was fluid and flexible, and co-operatives were filled with the spirit of a cause and motivated by reform. Now they are more likely to be tamed, set like mortar in the framework of a secure institution, and thereby unable to provide a springboard for imaginative educational action in the community.

This is not a criticism of co-operatives, but rather a warning to them of the process of hardening of the arteries, which can overtake any organization or institution. A good motto for them and for all engaged in community education is contained in the lines of Walt Whitman:

Now understand me well – it is provided in the essence of things that from any fruition of success, no matter what, shall come something to make a greater struggle necessary.

If we are to accept the poet's message, it means this: For co-operatives, as for all organizations involved in community education and development, the task is unending. Having once begun it, we can never be done with it.

FOOTNOTES

1. Edited by Harriet Rouillard (Thomas Nelson and Sons, 1952). The names are Desjardins, Tompkins, Coady and MacDonald.
2. See *Co-operative Housing*, 1967, 4 (2).

A. F. LAIDLAW is a Nova Scotian with long experience in adult education and the co-operative movement.

A graduate of St. Francis Xavier University, Antigonish, he served in Nova Scotia as a school principal, inspector of schools, and Secretary of the Department of Education before joining the staff of the Extension Department of St. Francis Xavier, in which he worked as Associate Director for fourteen years.

In 1958 he became General Secretary of the Co-operative Union of Canada, Ottawa, and while in that position was active as well in several other national organizations. He was also Director of the Central Mortgage and Housing Corporation during 1959-68.

He has had considerable experience in international development, serving as consultant on co-operative training in India during 1956-8, and as Chairman of the Royal Commission on the Co-operative Movement in Ceylon during 1968-9. In connection with the International Co-operative Alliance, London, in which he has served on the executive committee, he has studied co-operatives at first hand in a number of countries.

He took postgraduate studies in education at the University of Toronto, where he obtained the degree of Doctor of Education.

At present Dr. Laidlaw is at St. Francis Xavier University as Professor of Adult Education and Co-operative Studies in the Coady International Institute and the new Department of Adult Education established in 1970.

Section Six

Indian
Participation

This brief section on Canadian Indians provides an example of a specific group of people who are not only trying to define the kind of communities they want, but also are attempting to retain greater control over matters that concern them. Numerous community-development programs have been introduced into Indian communities, notably those by provincial and federal agencies. The degree to which the self-determination of the Indian and Métis people has grown is directly related to the degree to which the basic philosophies of community development were understood and practised by implementing organizations. Accepting self-directed change is one of these basic philosophies.

Edward Rogers focusses on the historical and present-day Indian interaction and non-interaction with Euro-Canadian society. He points out that the Indian is not becoming just another Euro-Canadian, but is reshaping and redefining his own sense of identity. What is necessary, Rogers says, is a new approach to human relationships.

Mrs. Marlene Castellano calls for a partnership relationship between the Indian and the Euro-Canadian. She points out some of the fallacious assumptions made about the delivery of social services: 'The giver is strong and the receiver is weak and should be grateful.' Our assumptions about others are based on our cultural backgrounds, but what is needed is a greater understanding of and respect for the cultures of others. One of the strengths of Castellano's article is that it is not limited to the Indian people of Canada. Her point is that a greater rationalization of social-service programs is required, not only for particular minority groups in Canada but for all groups.

Following in the same spirit, Mrs. Jean Goodwill discusses some of the new horizons for Native women in Canada. She expresses the pride of being Indian and the importance of increasing self-confidence and respect. Strong organizations are necessary to minimize the differences between peoples and build on the strength of commonalities.

Charles A. S. Hynam speaks of the interdependency of men and points out that an essential element in the development of people is good leadership, a theme that runs throughout this section.

The Indian and Euro-Canadian Society [1]

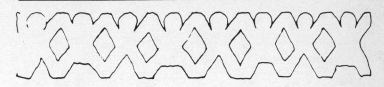

Edward Rogers

Today, an ever-increasing awareness of the Indians[2] of Canada exists, as witnessed, for example, by the frequent mention of them in the public media. Not too many years ago, little public concern was expressed. This greater recognition of Canada's 'first citizens' might suggest that the Indians are becoming more active in affairs outside their home communities and therefore more conspicuous. In other words, they are perhaps becoming an integral part of Euro-Canadian society. On the other hand, the increased attention accorded the Indians may merely reflect a growing concern by Euro-Canadians with social problems such as those experienced by Indian people. Both conditions, it can be suggested, are at work. The present paper, with primary emphasis on the situation in Ontario and the past decade, sketches Indian interaction and non-interaction with Euro-Canadian society.

Since first contact the Indians have, of course, interacted with Euro-Canadian society, but usually the interaction has gone unnoticed except in special instances. Yet economic interaction between the Indians and Euro-Canadian society has been of considerable importance. A classic example is the fur trade. To a certain extent, the Indians living in northern Ontario are still a part of this economic interaction with Euro-Canadians, although they are undergoing rapid change[3] (Dunning, 1958, 1959; Rogers, 1963; Van-Stone, 1963). Such interaction on the part of the Indians might be considered 'voluntary', but often arose out of necessity. Other examples of economic interaction have been guiding for tourists, wage employment, and the production of crafts. These economic activities have been a part of the Indian and Euro-Canadian interaction for many years and several still are. In other areas, such as politics, there was, in the past, much less or no interaction. As an aside, the deep commitment of the Indians to service with Euro-Canadians in times of war should be noted (Scott, 1918-21, pp. 285-328).

During the past ten to fifteen years, Indian activities directed towards interaction with Euro-Canadian society have increased, perhaps not in frequency, but certainly in variety. This started, it can be suggested, with the experiences many Indians had while serving in the armed forces during World War II. Acceptance as equals at a time of national crisis made them fully aware on their return of acts of discrimination against them in civilian life, such as being denied the vote or the right to purchase liquor. Since World War II, the Indians have become increasingly 'noticeable', both through their own endeavours (Cardinal, 1969; Waubageshig, 1970; Deloria, 1969, 1970; Indian Chiefs of Alberta, 1970) and through those of non-Indians (Bodsworth, 1959, 1967; Canada, 1966-7; Fry, 1970; Hendry, 1969; Robertson, 1970; Steiner, 1968). The Hay Lake Indian protest in Edmonton, Alberta, in 1965 (Robertson, 1970, pp. 11-26) and the Kenora march in 1965 (Rogers, 1968, p. 16) all dramatized for non-Indians the Indian's position or his view of that position. The 'plight' of those living at Moosonee and Red Lake, Ontario, as portrayed in the public media, further focussed attention on the Indians and their particular relationship to Euro-Canadian society.

Several factors may have contributed to this increase in activity. The Indian population has increased dramatically, and many individuals have left home and moved to urban areas where they have had a greater opportunity to interact with Euro-Canadians. Furthermore, there has been a lessening of social distance between groups since World War II, with greater opportunity to state one's case. And, in addition, educational opportunities have increased somewhat for Indians, making it possible for them to express their views in terms Euro-Canadians can more readily understand.

Perhaps a critical stage in the interaction between Euro-Canadian society and the Indians of Canada was reached in 1969 when the White Paper prepared by the Minister of Indian Affairs and Northern Development was released (Canada, 1969). This evoked a perhaps unexpected reaction from the Indians, as exemplified by the 'Red Paper' presented to the Prime Minister of Canada by the Indian leaders of Alberta (Indian Chiefs of Alberta, 1970). Indian leaders in other provinces have, or are preparing, similar papers to counter the White Paper (Waubageshig, 1970, p. 46).[4]

The activities that have been occurring in recent years suggest that Indian interaction with Euro-Canadian society has become greater, and that the Indians are slipping into the mainstream of the dominant culture. Yet a close examination of various events in the last ten years, combined with discussions with Indians, strongly suggests that this is all too simple an evaluation. The situation is much more complex, and the Indian is not becoming just another Euro-Canadian. He is slowly and painfully developing a new identity in the eyes of Euro-Canadians. At the same time, he is reshaping and redefining his own sense of identity in the modern world (Deloria, 1969, 1970).

Several ways exist in which Indians, either individually or in groups, interact with Euro-Canadian society. In this paper, attention is focussed on group interaction. Basically, two types of interaction can be defined. There is Indian interaction with Euro-Canadian society that is initiated through the actions of Euro-Canadians. These actions in turn stimulate Indian reactions. The latter can be either 'involuntary' or 'voluntary'. Conversely, there can be interaction instituted by the Indians without direct prior stimulation of an active nature on the part of Euro-Canadians. A response, of course, would not take place without the Euro-Canadian presence, but the actions of the Indians are, nevertheless, an indigenous growth, and Euro-Canadian society responds to them, often negatively. Theoretically, the Indian responses are not guided, to any great extent, by the direct intervention of Euro-Canadians.

In contrast to interaction, there is non-interaction. Attempts have been and are being made by some Indians to withdraw, at least to a certain extent, from Euro-Canadian society. These also are indigenous Indian developments generated in a manner similar to the second type of interaction noted above.

There have been, and are increasingly today, a number of Euro-Canadian actions that have brought forth responses on the part of Indians. The actions or programs implemented by

Euro-Canadians that impinge upon the Indians can be viewed as being of three types: programs legally binding on all citizens including Indians, those for Indians as specified in the Indian Act, and programs for Indians that are not legally binding.

The first type of program or action includes, among other things, welfare services, health and medical treatment, educational programs, and laws regarding criminal and other offences. These programs are automatic, applying to all citizens, and the reaction on the part of the Indians can be considered 'involuntary'. There are cases, however, where the Indians have tried not to comply in the ways designated under the law. Medicare is a case in point. Treaty Number Six specifies that a 'medicine chest' is to be kept at the house of each Indian agent in case of sickness among the Indians (Anon, 1961, part 2, 18; Morris, 1880, p. 218). This, in the eyes of the Indians, means the right to free medical services (Waubageshig, 1970, pp. 35-6). In addition, the Migratory Birds Convention Act has several times been opposed by the Indians as a violation of their treaty rights (Canada, 1966-7, vol. 1, p. 216). Similarly, the Indians are contesting the imposition of customs duties thought to be inapplicable under the provisions of the Jay Treaty. Nevertheless, because of the existence of such legislation, Indians are being forced in many ways to conform to Euro-Canadian cultural patterns.

The second type of action involves those programs enumerated in the Indian Act that require the Indians to follow certain Euro-Canadian edicts or customs that the Indians might not otherwise be accustomed to following. Several examples may suffice. For instance, when an Indian woman marries a person who is not of Indian status:

> ... the Governor in Council may by order declare that the woman is enfranchised as of the date of her marriage and, on the recommendation of the Minister may by order declare that all or any of her children are enfranchised as of the date of her marriage and, on the recommendation of the Minister may by order declare that all or any of her children are enfranchised as of the date of the marriage or such other date as the order may specify (Canada, 1963, p. 35).

In the educational field, the Minister of Indian Affairs may:

> require an Indian who has become 16 years of age to attend

school for such further period as the Minister considers advisable, but no Indian shall be required to attend school after he becomes 18 years of age (Canada, 1963, p. 38).

Furthermore, the Indian Act specifies the form of government the Indians will have:

Whenever he deems it advisable for the good government of a band, the Minister may declare by order that after a day to be named therein the council of the band, consisting of the chief and councillors, shall be selected by elections to be held in accordance with this Act (Canada, 1963, p. 24).

This is in violation of the customs of many Indians, both in the past and by sentiment today.

Finally, arrangements are made by the government regarding inheritance. It is decreed that the property of the husband shall go to his wife and children (Canada, 1963, p. 15). Many Indian societies have operated under other principles and even recently some have attempted to maintain the traditional customs (Rogers, 1962).

The third type of action mentioned, of greatest concern in this paper, involves those programs instituted by Euro-Canadians that are not legally binding on Indians. The federal and provincial governments and citizens' groups have, over the years, developed a number of programs. These programs are not designed to meet the needs of all the citizens of Canada; rather, they have been established to 'benefit' the Indians, whether in the whole of Canada, within a particular province, or in a special group. It must be pointed out, however, that some of these programs are only part of larger schemes that also involve non-Indians. In all programs of this type, the Indians are under absolutely no obligation to interact. Nevertheless, Indian interaction has occurred with most, if not all, such programs. The stated aim of some of these programs is that eventually the Indians will be completely in charge.

Federal programs have emanated primarily from the Indian Affairs Branch of the government in Ottawa. These programs have been manifold: political, educational, economic, social, and cultural.

With regard to political programs, the federal government during the early 1960s began to alter its view of local Indian government. In 1965 the Indian Affairs Branch granted self-government to certain Indian bands who had been advocating such a step. Through this program, the Indians gained more independence from federal control, but certainly not complete autonomy.

Indian education, following the Euro-Canadian system, has for a number of years been the responsibility of the federal government. Formal education is, of course, mandatory (Canada, 1963, p. 37). Other programs, such as Manpower retraining, which are not mandatory, have been made available to Indians, often under arrangements with the provincial governments.

Economic programs were intensified by the Indian Affairs Branch in the 1960s. For example, a program to develop parks on Indian reserves was started. In 1965 a camping-area was developed at the Kettle Point Reserve and by 1967, at least one park, the Cape Croker Indian Park, was opened (Penhale, 1968, p. 8). There were many other similar programs, such as the development of tourist camps and marinas, as, for example, at Moose Deer Point (Penhale, 1968, p. 10). Other economic endeavours exist, such as the charcoal factory and pheasant hatchery and game preserve at Christian Island (Penhale, 1968, p. 10).

In the socio-political field, the bands were given the option of voting in 1965 on whether or not to have liquor on the reserves. In 1966 a cultural section of Indian Affairs was established, and the first major endeavour was the Indian Pavilion at Expo. Other programs for Indians have been financed during the years since.

As far as provincial programs are concerned, only a few of those initiated by the Ontario government will be mentioned. During the past ten years, this government has started on its own, or in co-operation with the federal government, a number of programs that impinge upon Indians. Perhaps initially most active in this field was the Ontario Department of Lands and Forests. The Department placed Indians in the Junior Rangers School, employed Indians for fire-fighting and tree-planting, established goose-hunting camps and wild-rice projects, and worked with the Indians in game management. Also, at one time, the Department had an Indian advisory committee reporting directly to the Minister.

The Ontario Department of Education has been conscious of the need for work among Indians, and several years ago appointed an Indian to act on their behalf in promoting, in co-operation with the Indian Affairs Branch, a five-week credit course for teachers of Indian children held at Trent University.

The Provincial Secretary's office has under its wing the Indian Community Branch, officially created in 1966 when a federal-provincial agreement was signed. It has been active in hiring community-development officers to work in Indian communities and has been promoting, through financial assistance, various Indian projects within the province.

In 1964, the federal Indian Affairs Branch, in co-operation with the Department of Agriculture, began a pilot project in which, each fall, Indians were brought to southern Ontario to aid in the harvest of crops. Some of these individuals came from as far away as James Bay.

Other programs and actions relating to Indians have been the concern of the Churches, universities, and other citizens' organizations. Although these organizations are not government structures, they often gain considerable financial support from various levels of government in order to carry out their aims.

The Churches have for a great many years spent considerable time and effort in attempting to convert the Indians. Officially, all Indians have been converted and are members of one Church or another, and a number have become clergymen. But not all Indians are active members in any Church. In fact, in recent years there has arisen a reaction to Christianity and an attempt on the part of the Indians to re-establish their own rituals and beliefs.

But the Churches have done more than attempt the conversion of the Indians and the eradication of native religious beliefs and practices. They have been active in educational, social, and economic programs. Indian children for years have been educated in mission schools under the authority of the Minister of Indian Affairs (Canada, 1963, p. 37). But today such mission schools are rapidly disappearing – Shingwap, Horden, and the Mohawk Institute have been closed, and few are left.

Other enterprises in which the Churches have been active should be mentioned. The Presbyterian Church in Kenora and the Methodist Church in Parry Sound have both promoted Friendship Centres, and the Catholic Church organized the Widjiitwan Corporation, an attempt to establish an Indian community based on the cutting of pulpwood. In these endeavours, Indians have interacted with Euro-Canadians, and in the case of the Parry Sound Friendship Centre, they have eventually gained a degree of control.

Universities have had limited interaction with Indians, although a few have carried out research among them. A notable exception is Trent University with its program of Indian studies, whereby Indians are directly concerned at both the professional and student level. The limited interaction of universities with Indians is reflected in the miniscule number of Indian students enrolled. The reasons for this are complex and no one factor can be isolated to explain why so few Indians attend college.

Although attempts by citizens' organizations to intercede on behalf of Indians began as early as the first part of the 1800s, (Aborigines' Protection Society, 1839, p. 22), probably the greatest amount of activity has occurred in the past decade or two. The Indian-Eskimo Association of Canada, started in 1960, has been most noticeable. On occasion it has established a provincial chapter, such as that for the Province of Ontario, organized in 1965, but now disbanded. The Association has operated as a 'political pressure group', supposedly on behalf of the Indian peoples of Canada, and at the same time has elicited the support of some Indians to this cause.

Through a series of conferences and workshops, the Association has endeavoured to develop Indian leadership along Euro-Canadian lines, and a political awareness of the intricacies of parliamentary procedures so that Indians could themselves advance their cause. As time has passed, Indians have become more and more interested in the Association, if not, perhaps, in terms of numbers, at least in terms of a greater commitment on the part of those who had become associated in the first place. At present, an Indian is president of the Association, and the Board is composed in large measure of Indians. It may be that the Association has now moved as far as possible in the realm of political action and is beginning to move in the direction of educational programs. This will become clear only in the years ahead. The Indian-Eskimo Association, as a body of interested citizens, is not alone in its work among Indians. There are many local groups constituted for a variety of reasons and purposes, although the chief aim is to 'benefit' the Indians.

Although the Churches have been involved in the establishment of friendship centres, so have citizens' groups in such locations as Toronto and London. In the case of Toronto, however, the North American Indian Club has played a significant role. Such centres provide a place where Indians may come voluntarily to seek aid, if needed, and to relax and meet others. The centres' personnel give guidance and counselling, having individuals on staff for that purpose, and act as mediators between the Indians and various urban organizations. An example of the latter is the services rendered to Indians involved in court cases. The centres also organize and initiate programs, such as summer seminars for youth and handicraft training.

Indians have joined the friendship centres and act in various official capacities. They sit on the governing-boards, act as directors, social workers, and program organizers. Some of these centres are becoming, more and more, organizations run solely by the Indians, although the trend is a slow one.

Although other programs initiated by Euro-Canadians might be mentioned, those already outlined should suffice to indicate what has been taking place. Indians, on the other hand, have initiated actions and programs without initial sponsoring by Euro-Canadians. Although such actions have occurred in the past, it is only in the last few years that they have become numerous. Many of these have been directed to interaction with Euro-Canadian society. Others have been conceived of as ways of reducing interaction and are here referred to as 'non-interaction' programs.

The Indians, in forging their own programs, are following a number of different approaches: political, educational, economic, cultural, and religious, and both group and individual endeavours. These courses of action are not always clear cut, but are often, if not always, interwoven one with another. Those programs aimed at interaction with Euro-Canadians, once they have been conceived, rely on securing financial assistance from Euro-Canadian institutions and individuals. The economic resources of the Indians are too limited to do otherwise. However, those programs directed towards non-interaction attempt to be totally self-sufficient.

Perhaps the most important avenue of interaction that the Indians have evolved in the past few years is in the realm of politics. An attempt is being made on the part of the Indians to organize and unify so that they may have an effective voice at both the federal and provincial levels of government. Probably for the first time in their history of contact with Euro-Canadians, the Indians are to a certain extent being listened to, although their requests are not always followed. There have been Indian organizations in the past, but they do not appear to have been very effective on major issues. Perhaps, however, the Indians have never been so severely threatened in the past as they presently are by the implications of the federal White Paper.

The first attempt on the part of Indians to organize across Canada resulted in the National Indian Council, which dissolved in the mid sixties after several years of existence. This has now been replaced by the National Indian Brotherhood, with offices in Ottawa. Because of its lack of funds, this organization, like all others established by Indians with possibly a few exceptions, is dependent upon securing financial support from Euro-Canadian agencies, both governmental and private. To a certain extent at least, this tends to curtail its freedom of operation.

The Union of Ontario Indians came into existence not too many years ago. Its aims are political, although it is concerned with other endeavours of a socio-economic nature such as a study of the Indians of Toronto, started this year. In name the Union is a relatively new organization, although its roots extend back in time to the last century, when the Grand Council represented some of the Indians of Ontario. Another political force within the province is the Association of Iroquois and Allied Indians, which has existed for centuries in one form or another.

Thus political interaction with Euro-Canadian society initiated by Indians, although of limited extent, is finally beginning to emerge. This can be seen as a forced reaction to the federal White Paper. The Indians must first try by every constitutional means to preserve their rights, culture, and identity. They will need vast public support, since they have little or no political power of their own.

Economic developments on the part of the Indians are somewhat more difficult to isolate than political movements, since the former tend to be smaller in scope and often individual in nature. But whatever the case, they are subject to approval and control by the Indian Affairs Department. It is not possible here to review the individual economic enterprises that have been undertaken by Indians. Rather, an attempt will be made to mention a few that have involved more than one person, although these, no doubt, were initially conceived by one individual.

An early undertaking of this nature was the Cape Croker furniture factory. Some of the Indians of that reserve desired to manufacture furniture for commercial sale, and in 1962, four members of the reserve formed a private company for that purpose. In November 1964, vocational training under Program Five was authorized by the provincial government, the first time that such training had been made available to Indians in Ontario. Approximately a year later, however, a review was made by the Ontario government as to the economic feasibility of the factory. The conclusion was that it was not a sound business proposition. Nevertheless, the Indian Affairs Branch made available at about this time a business-manager whose services were terminated not long afterwards. Since then progress appears to have been made. The operation has been under the control and management of an Indian entrepreneur and in summer employs five to six men.

Another venture, which by all reports has been economically successful, is the production of handicrafts at Curve Lake. Production is now sufficient to supply a national market. On the Six Nations Reserve, a thriving pottery industry has been developed which cannot keep up with the demand both in Canada and in the United States; and at the St. Regis Reserve a lacrosse factory has done well.[5] In 1970, the Wikwedoong Native Development Association was established in Thunder Bay to promote economic development among Indians in northwestern Ontario in such areas as handicrafts.

Co-operatives (the term is used very loosely) are another form of economic development that Indians are engaged in. A store at Weagamow Lake in northern Ontario is one example. The Indians of Webique established their own tourist industry a few years go, albeit under the stimulus of a guide-training program sponsored by the provincial and federal governments. At Sutton-Hawly Lake, the Indians have been involved for some years in a tourist operation.

Most economic endeavours, however, from the point of view of the Indians, have met with limited success for a variety of reasons. The principal one, no doubt, is the lack of sufficient capital to compete with comparable Euro-Canadian enterprises. The trend is towards more economic endeavours being started by the Indians on their own initiative; but the paternalistic laws and Euro-Canadian attitudes governing the Indian have stunted his initiative and prevented him from developing efficiency and responsibility. They have had a consistently deadening effect. The Indians have not been given the freedom to do the things they have wanted to do because it is often thought they are not 'ready' or 'competent'.

Social interaction of Indians with Euro-Canadians, of course, occurs every day at an individual level. Visiting with Euro-Canadians, giving talks to various Euro-Canadian groups, and intermarriage with Euro-Canadians are all part of this process. It would appear that this form of interaction is primarily of an individual nature rather than a group enterprise. However, local fairs and pow-wows sponsored by Indians are a form of group social interaction when Euro-Canadians are invited to attend.

Cultural activities by Indians appear to be a relatively new development, if, for the moment, one disregards dance groups and the production of handicrafts. Recently within the Province of Ontario, several developments in the cultural field have taken place. One is the Indian Travelling College through which, it is hoped, the conditions and cultures of the Indians can be made known to Indian youth and other interested persons. A second is the Manitou Art Corporation, established in 1970 to promote painting, music, drama, and other forms of artistic talent among Indian peoples. (Of course, there have been individual artists, singers, and writers [Morrisseau, 1965; Johnston, 1970; Clutesi, 1967, 1969] of national and international fame, and more are emerging yearly.) A third group is the Nishnawbe Institute with headquarters in Toronto, which is involved with religious and cultural affairs and which organized the first Indian religious conference, held in Montana in 1970 and attended by delegates from all over North America.

Pow-wows, such as those held at Wekwemikong on Manitoulin Island, are another expression of the interest the Indians are taking in their own cultural heritage and their desire to revive and retain it. Furthermore, the concern that Indians have expressed regarding the portrayal of their life and history by television, the movies, and other forms of the mass media indicate a willingness to interact with Euro-Canadian society in an attempt to rectify the erroneous image that for so long has been presented of the Indians. Other examples of cultural programs established and undertaken by Indians are radio programs, such as 'Our Native Land', on the C.B.C., and newspapers, such as the *Kenomadiwin News*, Thunder Bay, written and edited by and for Indians.

Programs of non-interaction by Indians with Euro-Canadian society do occur. No doubt they have always existed to a certain extent in one form or another since the arrival of Europeans. They are often religious in nature and frequently based on past conditions thought to be typically Indian. What perhaps distinguishes them to a large extent from the other activities already mentioned is the desire on the part of the group to do what the individuals feel they should do, without particular concern for attitudes held by Euro-Canadians. The survival of these movements depends in large measure on the group's own initiative. They are largely, if not completely, independent of Euro-Canadian society, except for the fact that the latter has influenced their emergence. In a sense, some of these movements might be considered as a withdrawal from Euro-Canadian society, reacting to the Euro-Canadians' attempted assimilation or integration of the Indians into Western society.

Within Ontario there are at least two religious movements that reject Euro-Canadian society as expressed in terms of Christianity. They represent a sincere desire on the part of Indians not to be 'consumed' by Euro-Canadian society and to prevent the extinction of Indian culture. One, the Iroquois Longhouse religion, has, of course, a long history. At present, it seems to be gaining adherents and strength. There are also indications that the Midewiwin may be having a revival.[6]

Aside from the religious movements, a strong desire on the part of the Indian people to retain their language is developing. This is seen as fundamental to cultural preservation. In many communities the Indians have commenced programs of instruction in the local dialect for their youths. Occasionally Euro-Canadians become involved, and accordingly the programs cannot be considered as cases of non-interaction.

As yet, within the Province of Ontario, there is no real attempt by any Indian group to sever its relations with Euro-Canadian society as has happened in Alberta. There a group of Stoney Indians and the Smallboy Cree have moved away from intimate contact with Euro-Canadians and established their own communities. The nearest approach to this type of movement in Ontario might be at Angling Lake, several hundred miles north of Sioux Lookout. Indians from the settlement of Big Trout Lake became dissatisfied with conditions in the village and moved away and established the settlement of Angling Lake. Here they were away from the interference of non-Indians.

The above sketch indicates something of the degree and type of interaction or non-interaction that the Indians have with Euro-Canadian society, and some of the reasons involved. Certain salient features of the relationship between the two groups are clear.

First, Euro-Canadians have been the ones most active in promoting programs for Indians. Accordingly, the programs are generally, if not always, designed to conform to the conception that Euro-Canadians have of Indians, who must attempt to operate in a fashion suitable only to Euro-Canadians, and not as they, the Indians, might wish to operate. This is perhaps beginning to change somewhat. Today the Indians desire to help themselves in their own way, although they want the support and co-operation, though not the paternalistic domination, of the Euro-Canadians.

Second, Indian reaction to these programs has been primarily (outwardly at least) passive, although today it is becoming more active, vocal, and aggressive. The Indians have interacted, in some cases perhaps out of a genuine desire to do so, at other times because there is no other alternative open to them. In other words the Indians have really had no choice, or at best a very limited choice, but to do as the Euro-Canadians dictated.

Third, programs of interaction initiated by the Indians have begun, but are as yet still minimal. But these are perhaps of crucial importance. Most programs of this nature are dependent upon the goodwill and financial assistance of Euro-Canadians. The lack of a financial resource base has, at times and perhaps frequently, inhibited Indian interaction with Euro-Canadian society on the former's own terms. Accordingly, through the bureaucratic structure with its paternalistic philosophy, the Euro-Canadian remains the dominant force, imposing his will upon the Indians. This is something that can and must be changed if the Indians are ever to stand on their own feet. Yet the Indians are grappling with the problem and slowly developing a political consciousness and acumen; they are attaining a degree of political influence and of participation in the decision-making process. This has meant a considerable expenditure of energy on their part, leaving little time as yet for activities in other fields.

Fourth, some Indians have chosen a course of non-interaction in so far as they are capable of doing so. This is not a new approach, but one often taken at those times when the pressures of contact with an alien culture become unbearable. The present appears to be such a time. Indigenous religious movements are increasing and, it is predicted, will continue to do so. It is in this area of activity that Indians can find freedom from Euro-Canadians. Such movements act as an escape-valve for the frustrations generated by Euro-Canadian programs and attitudes.

Fifth, the attempts to interact with Euro-Canadian society have left deep scars on Indians which only time can heal, and then only with the appropriate understanding on the part of Euro-Canadians (Rogers, 1968, pp. 15-21).

All the evidence clearly indicates that, with few exceptions, Euro-Canadians have dominated the lives of Indians either through force, legislation, or a pervasive benevolence based on an attitude that the 'great white father' knows best. Euro-Canadian attitudes have, in many ways, deeply affected the form and type of interaction taken by Indians in relation to Euro-Canadian society and vice versa. Although attitudes are one of the most difficult features of a culture to isolate, it is perhaps safe to say that those held regarding Indians range from dislike and distrust to condescension. Rarely does one find that Indians are considered as equals, unless they mirror the image that the Euro-Canadian has of himself. Benevolent tolerance seems to be the most the Indian can expect.

In the early days of white settlement, Indians were looked upon at best as children who must be civilized, and at worst as heathen savages who should be eliminated. The former attitude is still reflected in the Indian Act, whereby farming is stressed as a way of life for the Indian. Formerly it was explicitly stated that through agriculture the Indians would become civilized and could then be converted (Thwaites, 1959, Vol. 8-(57), p. 59). At the same time, there was a theological problem as to whether or not Indians were even human (Josephy, 1968, p. 5; Hallowell, 1967, p. 320; Slotkin, 1965, p. 42).

Although the Indians are now becoming of more concern to the general public, it must be realized that, because of their past experiences in dealing with Euro-Canadians and their differing cultural values, Indians do not always respond as expected. Their past history of contact explains the wariness with which they approach Euro-Canadian society and those who profess to be helping them.

The Indians, in formulating their own actions and programs, are attempting to devise ways and means whereby they will not be hurt again. They are also trying to break out of a stifling paternalistic, bureaucratic structure to do things for themselves, by themselves, and in their own way. Accordingly, while recognizing the need to interact with Euro-Canadian society, the Indians are attempting to do so without becoming assimilated.

As Dr. Gilbert Monture has said:

> I am glad you used the word integration rather than assimilation, because I think there is a great deal of difference. To me, integration means still retaining pride of your own racial characteristics, pride in your tradition and the achievements of your race, but blending if you like with the other people. Whereas assimilation, and this is the thing that I would hate to see take place, is where the Indians as a racial or ethnic group would be completely merged and lost in the Canadian economy or citizenry (Canadian Broadcasting Corporation, 1966).

The history of contact between Indians and Europeans in southern Ontario is clear[7](Surtees, 1968, pp. 87-98). The former have been 'legally' dispossessed of their land, no matter how their former title might be defined, and their culture has been shattered. Indians were not given the vote until 1958, and no provisions have been made for proportional representation in the government. Furthermore, all registered Indians are in a special category of citizenship defined by the Indian Act. Because of the circumstances in which they find themselves, the Indians feel their losses deeply and resent them bitterly. Today they have no intention of proceeding any further with the process of assimilation if they can help it. Instead, they are attempting to reverse the process, so far by peaceful means but this may not last for long. There is the possible danger that violence may emerge, and, if so, most likely in the North where expectations have been raised high but means to achieve them have not been created.

There is no doubt that the Indian's existence is recognized –

administrative structures grow and programs proliferate. And yet nothing changes to any great extent, nor has it for the last several hundred years. A basic reason for this can be discovered in a review of events of the past ten years. Euro-Canadians have refused to relinquish their positions of authority and responsibility in matters pertaining to Indians.

Only if Euro-Canadians accept Indians as equals who have much to contribute to Western society can there be optimism for the future. But equality is not to be measured by programs calculated in dollars and cents. Programs initiated to date are far too often limited to housing, health, and education. Although such programs are necessary, they are thought sufficient in themselves to make for equality. No more need be done; one's conscience has been cleansed; heaven is in sight. Why should Indians continue to make a fuss? The Euro-Canadian is hurt by their ingratitude.

Is it possible to improve the situation when Euro-Canadians hold attitudes and values that inhibit them, consciously or unconsciously, from dealing with Indians as equals? Perhaps, but a new approach to human relationships is needed. To start with, any approach taken should be completely divorced from the political system, so that programs, once established, can be given sufficient time to have a fair chance of success. The programs themselves should represent the wishes of Indians and not always be those deemed 'good' by Euro-Canadians. For this, more detailed knowledge in depth is needed regarding both the Indians' desires and aspirations and the potential for them that exists within the Euro-Canadian system as it is presently constituted. Often, if not always, programs are initiated without this background information. Furthermore, constructive change is often inhibited because the programs are not unified. Too often there is duplication of effort and lack of coordination. Finally, Indians should be given sufficient financial support without paternalistic strings attached, in order to accomplish what they themselves have set out to do.

It is time serious thought be given to what has been and is being done *to* the Indian, not for him, in order to understand why so much planning has resulted in failure, and why so much money has gone not to Indians, but to maintaining Euro-Canadian structures devoted to 'aiding' Indians. The Indian never has been and is not today a child. The Indian needs concern, understanding, acceptance, and support. He is a person who can take his place in Euro-Canadian society, if only given the same consideration that others are.

FOOTNOTES

1. The observations and views expressed in this paper are the result of the author's work among the Indians of Ontario, Quebec, and elsewhere, during the past twenty years, and his involvement during the past decade with the provincial and federal governments in matters regarding Indians. To all those individuals – Cree, Ojibwa, Ottawa, Potawatomi, Delaware, Iroquois, and Euro-Canadian – who made this work possible, I am most grateful. Dr. Garth Taylor closely read the manuscript and expressed his opinions, which were most helpful and for which I am thankful. Special thanks are due Miss Delia Opekokew and Messrs. Walter Currie, Bob Davis, Harvey McCue, and Basil Johnston, who critically read several drafts of the paper and candidly expressed their opinions, which resulted in my drastically rethinking views I had originally held. They also clarified many points of fact. Where the paper does not conform to the views expressed by those consulted, it is due solely to my inability to comprehend fully the true meaning of 'Indianism'. In this connection, it must be pointed out that there are those who feel I have been 'soft' on the Euro-Canadians.

2. The term 'Indian', aside from the problem of whether or not it should be employed at all, presents a problem of definition. What really is meant by the term 'Indian'? The term can be defined in one of several ways depending upon one's frame of reference. Because of varied meanings, the term 'Indian' is frequently used wrongly. This can sometimes be a serious mistake.

   Four ways, at least, exist in which the term can be defined: legally, biologically, culturally, or from an individual point of view.

   A legal definition of 'Indian' is given in the Indian Act: 'Indian means a person who pursuant to this Act is registered as an Indian or is entitled to be registered as an Indian ' (Canada, 1963:1). Accordingly, an individual of European ancestry under certain circumstances can be registered as an Indian. The opposite is also true.

   A second definition of 'Indian' is biological. Use of the biological definition is possible only in so far as the geneological background of any particular individual is known and diagnostic physical traits are present. In other words, is the particular individual, at least to some degree, of prehistoric Asiatic origin? Of course, the problem is to establish to what degree one must be of prehistoric origin to qualify biologically as an Indian.

   Thirdly, there could be a cultural definition of 'Indian'. At the time of European contact, the cultures exhibited by the Indians of the New World were quite distinct from the cultures of the arriving Europeans. Over time, however, both cultures altered tremendously. Overt Indian culture in many particulars has disappeared completely or become incorporated into Euro-Canadian culture (Hallowell, 1967, pp. 317-45). Little remains, therefore, to identify readily Indian culture or cultures from the point of view of observable traits. The Indians have adopted and often reinterpreted concepts and other cultural items derived from the Europeans. Today, a lack of a clear-cut cultural distinction seems to exist between the two groups. However, although this may appear to be the case at first glance, it is in many ways a superficial view. To this day there has been maintained among many peoples an 'Indianism', a quality that is difficult to define. Since it is rooted in values and attitudes, and generally little more, it is difficult to describe in standard ethnological terms. Yet this difficulty seems in large measure to reside in the observer. Investigators have yet to devise and define a meaningful way in which to present this aspect of 'Indian' culture.

A fourth definition of 'Indian' is based merely on who claims to be an Indian, regardless of any legal, biological or cultural definition. It seems most convenient in this paper to employ this definition of 'Indian'. If this were not done, complications would continually arise. For example, if the legal definition were employed, it would exclude as many individuals who are biologically Indian as it includes.

Besides the problem of the definition of the term 'Indian', there is the problem as to the legitimacy of its use. To be sure, it has become a part of the English vocabulary, but there are those 'Indians' who do not wish to be referred to by the term. Yet no suitable substitute has been found to refer to all the original inhabitants of the New World. In the United States 'Native American' is coming into use. Some Canadian Indians have suggested that 'native people' is a more appropriate designation. 'The People' might be suggested, since many if not all groups referred to themselves in this way. Perhaps those directly concerned will solve this problem.

3. Liebow, E. & Trudeau, J. 'A preliminary study of acculturation among the Cree Indians of Winisk, Ontario.' *Arctic*, 1962, Vol. 15, (3), pp. 190-204.

4. The White Paper, the Indians felt, would strip them of their lands and their rights under the Indian Act and subject them to undue pressures from the non-Indian. Some years ago the United States Government had followed a similar course of action which because of the consequences has been abandoned. This knowledge added to the Indians' concern.

5. Lingard, W. 'Lacrosse – the fastest game on two feet.' *Beaver*, 1969, outfit 300, autumn, 12-16.

6. The Midewiwin was an Ojibwa society composed of both men and women who were medical practitioners caring for the needs of the community.
7. Rogers, E.S. *Indian farmers – rural victorians, 1820-1930.* Ottawa: National Museum of Man. In press.

EDWARD S. ROGERS was born in Lee, Massachusetts. He served in the United States Infantry in the European theatre of operations during World War II. In 1958 he received his Ph.D. in anthropology from the University of New Mexico. He carried out archaeological field-work in Quebec and Maine between 1947 and 1950 and ethnological field-work among the Mistassini Cree in 1953-4, the Miscalero Apache in 1957, the Round Lake Ojibwa in 1958-9, and also worked in South India in 1965, and among the Parry Island Ojibwa, the Pawtowatomi and the Ottawa during the summers of 1963-7. He is a consultant to the Ontario Department of Lands and Forests, a member of the Archaeological and Historic Sites Board of Ontario and the Board of Indian Crafts of Ontario, and a Fellow of the American Anthropological Association. At present he is Curator of the Department of Ethnology, Royal Ontario Museum, part-time Professor of Anthropology at McMaster University, and Adjunct Professor in the Department of Anthropology, State University of New York at Buffalo. His publications include 'The Round Lake Ojibwa' (1962), 'The Hunting Group – Hunting Territory Complex among the Mistassini Indians' (1963), 'The Material Culture of the Mistassini' (1967), 'Mistassini Albanel' (with Charles Martijn, 1969), 'Forgotten Peoples' (1969), 'New Guinea: Big Man Island' (1970), and articles on various topics dealing with the Canadian Indian.

Out of Paternalism and into Partnership: An Exploration of Alternatives in Social Service to Native People

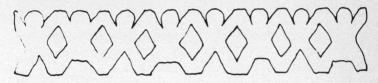

Marlene Castellano

Most Indians who participate in non-Indian society with a modicum of success are asked repeatedly to take part in dialogues to encourage a better understanding of Indian people and their aspirations. Many of the talented young Indians, currently visible on the horizon, decline to engage in this activity, because they have become convinced that the search for 'understanding' between two cultures must always end in frustration. Inevitably in such a study, one starts with his own definition of what is and what is not good, his own institutional methods of dealing with his environment, his own expectations in relationships with others, and, most especially, his own systems of thought embodied in his native language. It is impossible, even by the greatest act of discipline, to set all this aside because, without familiar means of structuring and interpreting experience, a person is incapable of absorbing and making sense of new stimuli to which he is exposed.

In seeking to acquire 'understanding' of Indian culture the non-Indian starts with the framework of his own culture and then, by reading papers and talking with people who profess to know how it is with Indians, he puts Indians into the picture in relation to his own world view. The pursuit of better intercultural relations by this means is not only fruitless; it is probably even destructive because, to a people trying to develop autonomy, the persons who represent the greatest threat are those white liberals, and Indian liberals, who are convinced that they understand Indians. This does not mean that Indians and whites cannot know each other. But such knowledge demands involvement, person to person, eyeball to eyeball, without the protection of the roles behind which people in white society like to hide.

If you say, by your manner or through your expectations: 'I will be your business friend,' or 'I will be your neighbour friend or your club friend, or your helper friend,' the traditional Indian will not comprehend you. He recognizes only two categories: friend and stranger. If you are friends, there is no need to define the boundaries within which you can trust each other. Conversely, if you are strangers, a boundless lack of trust must be taken for granted.

It seems that this peculiarly Indian trait of being unable to trust within limitations explains why Indians of both sexes are so easily seduced into exploitative relationships.

Distinctions between Indian and white values and life styles are usually drawn with the assumption that the Indian is the laggard who must catch up. Increasing numbers of young Indians who have experience in both societies hold a different view. They observe that people in white society develop techniques like sensitivity training to teach them how to engage in authentic personal relationships, that they queue up at Mental Health Clinics to seek help in putting themselves in touch with people and with their environment, while, on the other hand, Indians who live this authentic, rhythmic kind of life are crucified every time they step off the reserve. It is a cruel irony that many Indians, particularly those now in middle age, subscribe to the idea that their first priority should be to keep pace with white society in its headlong pursuit of production, consumption, and personal fragmentation.

The disparity between the cultural orientation of Indian and white society is nowhere more evident than in the interaction which takes place around the delivery and use of social services.

Social services extended not only to Indians but to all disadvantaged groups in Canadian society are predicated on a destructive kind of contract, which assumes that the giver is strong, wise, and generous, and the receiver is, by definition, weak, ignorant, and grateful. An offer of help on these terms is not help at all, but rather a violence perpetrated against the person allegedly helped. Disadvantaged persons have instinctively recognized this violence for what it is, and they have reacted with a variety of devices to save their sense of integrity.

Therefore, even massive infusions of personnel and money will not improve the condition of the persons and groups who are being dehumanized and repressed by the institutions which purport to serve them.

An illustration of the hostility that is engendered by the traditional helping situation came to light during a recent field-study in which the author was engaged. A woman, well-known in the district for her good works, reported that she went out to deliver a box of used clothing to a poor family in an impoverished native settlement. The clothing was in good condition, the kind of articles an average mother would gladly send her children out in. The family in question were clearly in need, partly because of the intemperate drinking of the father. However, when the donor delivered the gift, the husband and father, who happened to be at home that day, carried the offering to his back yard and burned it in full view of his would-be benefactor. She was incensed at his disregard for the value of the property and his rude rejection of her generosity. She was inclined to attribute the man's action to his being under the influence of alcohol at the time. Nevertheless, she had never returned to that household bearing gifts.

Not everyone whose self-esteem is bruised by the expectation that he should assume a dependent posture is able to respond with such dramatic force. Many others who feel buffeted and frustrated by their circumstances remain inarticulate and unheard.

In an effort to evoke the reality of these others we have set down here a composite case history. The details do not refer to a particular Indian girl, though it would be easy to find in any reserve community individuals who have lived through a similar succession of experiences.

An Indian girl, who occupied a somewhat marginal position in her community to begin with, established a liaison with a non-Indian and, over a period of time, bore a couple of children out of wedlock. These children were duly registered as members of the mother's band. Then, pressured by the church and the respectable elements in the community, and by her own civilized conscience, she married her white lover and took up residence off the reserve. In time she bore three children more. Then the marriage broke down, for any of the numerous reasons that marriages break down, or perhaps because of the special stresses which bear upon Indian-white marriages. Alone with the responsibility for five children, the woman returned to the sanctuary of the reserve and by doing so she unwittingly compounded her problems, for she placed herself in a no-man's land between bureaucracies.

Since there are very few capitalists on Indian reserves, there is scarcely any rental housing available. This prevailing situation may change as more band councils use housing loans, made available to Indians in recent years, to move into the field of public housing. However, given the scarcity of houses not occupied by their owners, the only real choice open to this particular girl was to return to her parents' home, which was already peopled with assorted grandchildren and other relatives.

Now consider her position: By her marriage she has forfeited her formal membership in the reserve community. Although her return is tolerated, it is not really welcomed, because, particularly in southern Ontario, the band administration is anxious, like all other municipal administrations, to keep their rates of dependent persons at a minimum. There are housing loans and grants available, but only to persons with legal Indian status. The woman has little hope of escaping from the deprived and overcrowded conditions in her parental home, unless she chooses to try coping with her responsibilities away from the reserve and away from the supportive network of familiar people and surroundings.

The needs of mothers of dependent children do not go unheeded in our society and, after a waiting period, the girl becomes eligible for Family Benefits, whereby she receives a sustaining allowance from the Province for herself and her children. But in an elastic family unit, it is extremely difficult to withhold whatever resources are available and ensure that they are used exclusively by the individuals whose names appear on the record in Toronto.

In time, one of the girl's children falls seriously ill and is taken into hospital, and it is there discovered that the child is suffering from poor nutrition or one of the infections associated with inadequate sanitation. The Children's Aid Society is called in to apprehend the child for his own protection. The child is placed in a foster home or group home away from the reserve, at a cost to the community of $100 per month. The cost of supporting a child away from his own home might be more than that now, but it certainly would not be less.

A social worker undertakes counselling with the family in an attempt to raise the standard of care available for the child and to ensure that the family can provide adequate parenting on the child's return. The situation that ensues is inherently frustrating for everyone concerned. The family, cut off from one of its members, powerless in face of an institution, not comprehending the legislative machinery which has defined them as neglectful, inarticulate in the language in which they are being evaluated, can formulate only one question: 'When are you bringing back our child?' The social worker, on the other hand, is struggling to communicate that the child is in care because of an occurrence of neglect within the meaning of the Child Welfare Act, and the child can be returned only when the conditions leading to neglect have been alleviated. In face of insufficient income, family disintegration, inadequate housing, and communication problems aggravated by hostility, her words, which are essentially the only resources she has, are useless.

Now the Indian girl, who first was victimized by the bureaucratic regulations which circumscribe her legal status and her options as a reserve resident, is further victimized by the fragmentation of services which dictate that a child welfare worker is empowered to deal with only one aspect of the client's experience, that is, her neglect of a child. The child welfare authority is powerless to deal directly with the multiplicity of problems that may have contributed to that neglect.

After a period of two years, the Children's Aid Society is faced with the decision of whether to return the child to the basically unaltered home situation or to request that the court make the child a permanent ward of the Province. If the latter course is chosen, the child's likely fate is to join the roster of the hundreds of Indian children who are having their souls destroyed in a succession of foster homes, while the provincial adoption clearance service advertises in vain for homes into which these hard-to-place children can be adopted.

Meanwhile, the Indian girl, who still retains some shred of hope that life may be worth clinging to, establishes a continuing relationship with a man on the reserve. The relationship is mutually rewarding, and there seems some possibility that they could make a good life together. But he has limited education and consequently cannot depend on more than seasonal employment. The girl is caught in a dilemma. If she establishes a common-law union she will jeopardize her eligibility for Family Benefits. Without the provincial allowance she would submit the entire family to the uncertainties of irregular income and the indignities involved in repeated applications for welfare. If she opts for the security of maintaining her eligibility for the provincial allowance, she must resign herself to continuing indefinitely with little hope of achieving a more personally rewarding arrangement.

One degrading accommodation to these circumstances, which is worked out when the welfare investigator is more humane than moral, is a tacit agreement with the welfare officer that the common-law husband shall remain invisible.

Again, the recipient of service suffers from the irrationality of a structure of services that militates against individual mental health, self-respect, and mutually supportive social relationships.

We could take this case history further, through involvement with the courts and the confusion of trying to sort out who pays for what when two of the children are Indian, and three are white, and all five are enrolled in consolidated schools, but perhaps enough has been said to illustrate that at critical points of the Indian person's experience the maze of social services operate in such a manner as to constitute disservice to the individuals and families involved.

The Indian client probably believes, because she is told so repeatedly, that she is part of the 'Indian Problem' confronting society. That, of course, is nonsense, for the obstacles which she encounters in trying to survive are the same obstacles encountered by her impoverished single-parent counterpart downtown in the city. The Indian client's situation is distinctive because it is transposed to the milieu of the reserve and complicated by factors of culture and divided governmental jurisdiction.

In selecting material to illustrate this paper, most of the examples that came to mind involved women. This could be attributed to the author's background of working in family and child welfare, but it could equally well be due to the fact that Indian men are not so often harassed by social-service institutions. With Indian men the dichotomy between good Indians and bad Indians is sharper and more easily discerned, since one need only look at whether the man stays sober and holds down a steady job in order to make the judgment. Good Indians do not need to be rescued and bad Indians are subtly encouraged to do away with themselves as quickly and noiselessly as possible.

The thesis of this paper has been that present approaches to social services directed to Indians are grossly inadequate. When such a criticism is levelled, the standard response, from the society which pays to support services and from the persons who deliver services, is a challenge to the critic to offer a better alternative. When no alternative solution is forthcoming, the white initiator is vindicated in continuing to do things his way, and the age-old drama is repeated, with the white man defining the choices and judging the results.

There is a reason why no alternative solutions can be offered in response to the challenge thrown out. The problems under discussion are not primarily Indian problems; they are human problems which plague Canadian society in the nineteen-seventies and which, on a national scale, threaten to break up the nation itself.

In 1970, a Toronto newspaper gave prominent coverage to a reporter's visit to a squatter settlement of Indians near a northern Ontario town. With supporting pictures, the report presented a dramatic picture of the misery which prevailed in the settlement. Because the Indians there were not on a reserve, they were outside of the area of federal responsibility; since they had established their residence on Crown land outside of town limits, they were outside of municipal responsibility; as for provincial services, the conditions on which they might be available were unknown, and therefore they were inaccessible to the people involved. The people spoke an Indian language; they sent their children to school only sporadically; they were unemployable except on a seasonal basis; they were housed in tents and makeshift cabins; and when they roused themselves from their apathy or alcoholic haze sufficiently to speak at all, they talked of life as if it were a living death.

Here was a description, not of an individual, but of a whole group of persons in whose experience the major social problems of our time converge: the problem of how to occupy and subsidize with dignity the growing proportion of the population whose skills are not needed in the employment market; the problem of how to design an educational system that serves more than a small *élite*; the problem of how to house a population with rising expectations of what constitutes necessities; and the problem of how to offset the deterioration of community cohesiveness and individual mental health.

Clearly, if Indians or their leaders had solutions to these problems they would be saviours to more than their own people.

What is unique about the incidence of these common human problems among Indians is the racial overtone which the situation perhaps unavoidably takes on. While the squatter settlement described above embodies all the evil characteristics associated with irredeemable Indians, well-adjusted Indians tend to live inconspicuously among the general population. Often, where Indians are concerned, racial characteristics operate as a convenient means of labelling, isolating, and exerting pressure on those persons who cannot or will not conform to the expectations society has of them.

In the midst of this dismal scene there are promises of better things to come, but Indian people know that there have always been white promises and, consequently, they are not buoyed up with hope. Preliminary press releases from the Senate Committee on Poverty have focussed on the urgent need for rationalizing, if not radicalizing, our present system of social services. In late 1970, at a conference convened by the Indian Association of Alberta, a representative of the federal government admitted that policy initiatives had concentrated on economic development to the neglect of social development, and he gave assurance that in future more attention would be paid to social needs in setting policy priorities. Occasionally, one hears of experimental programs, not often in Ontario, regrettably, such as Newstart, again in Alberta, which has been singularly successful in developing a sense of involvement and hope for the families engaged in a multi-dimensional educational program in preparation for fuller participation in the social and economic life of modern society. The May-June 1970 issue of *Canadian Welfare* described a Saskatchewan experiment in reassigning to a native community the responsibility for child protection.

In the field of child welfare, there is currently a surge of support for the concept of shared parenting, which was part of tribal life before it was undermined by conversion to a cash economy. Briefly, the philosophy behind the shared-parenting concept proposes that every child, as well as being the child of his parents is, *de facto*, a child of the community, for a society will be devastated if it permits significant numbers of its children to be thwarted and warped and tossed on the ash-heap. It has become increasingly evident in the past decade that the traditional approach of child welfare, of sorting out the inadequate from the adequate parents and providing substitute care for neglected children, is no longer sufficient. The method has become obsolete, because our economy cannot support enough institutions and treatment centres for the emotionally disturbed children who are collected in this way, and because this approach constitutes a one-way street. Once a situation has been permitted to deteriorate to the point where the family breaks up, it is extremely difficult to put it back together again and make it stick.

Now that the concept of shared parenting has evolved, it seems very simple to discern that of course it is more economical and more rational and more child protective to add to the resources of the natural parents rather than to try to provide a complete substitute for them.

A document which was published in June 1970, titled 'One Million Children', looks at some of the issues raised in this paper, in relation to the estimated one million children in Canada who have special needs by virtue of their physical health, their learning capacity, their social and economic condition, their anti-social behaviour, or their mental health. If this very thorough and widely supported study comes anywhere near realizing its potential as a blueprint for a new deal for children, all segments of society, including Indians, will benefit from it.

In conclusion, some comments are offered here on the direction we are taking, or should take, in reacting to the issues raised in this paper.

There is an urgent need for Indians and non-Indians alike to recognize the many common features in the social problems experienced by Indians and by other segments of Canadian society. This is not a suggestion that the special problems of Indians can be dismissed. People have sometimes suggested that concern for the distress of impoverished northern Indians is exaggerated, since the whites living in the same region suffer the same hardships. To say that there is white suffering does not reduce the magnitude of Indian suffering. It should, rather, increase the urgency with which we seek remedies.

Because there is undeniably an element of racism, which tends to make the social problems experienced by Indians more difficult of solution, it is absolutely essential that the decision-makers and the front-line personnel in human-service programs should be Indian. This does not mean that the contribution of non-Indian technicians and professionals is unnecessary or unwelcome. At this stage of history, the Indian people do not have sufficient numbers of skilled personnel of native origin to mount the programs that should be initiated immediately. However, white men have established such a discouraging record of taking control of any field into which they are invited and then manipulating things to achieve their own goals, that Indian leaders now are extremely wary of offers of assistance from whites. One method of accommodation, which seems to work fairly well, is that in which Indians control the financing of a project; they then can hire or fire professional advisers.

As well as the rising numbers of young Indians who are acquiring the credentials to assume responsibility within existing institutional structures, a new resource is coming to light. Reserve Indians, who hold few academic qualifications, are becoming increasingly involved in political leadership, destroying the stereotype of the 'dumb Indian', as they engage in tough negotiating and apply their native intelligence to contemporary problems. In the past, the bulk of Indians who were eased out of an uncongenial school system at the lower levels accepted that, in relation to white expectations, they were incompetent. Subservience to a system which downgraded them was distasteful and altering it was inconceivable, so the only choice was non-participation. Partnership to replace paternalism is no longer inconceivable, despite the communication difficulties that persist between Indian communities and political, welfare, educational, and correctional institutions.

Indians are disillusioned with the adequacy of white methods of socializing the young, caring for the dependent, and rehabilitating the delinquent members of Indian society. Their disillusionment can be the first step towards reclaiming these functions, if white society is prepared to recognize that a lifetime of Indian experience represents a unique qualification for human-service roles among Indians. In the past, Indians have shown themselves unwilling to act as agents of white society in imposing controls on their brothers. If a serious effort were made to develop Indian-operated group foster homes, half-way houses, community education, and services supportive of family life, the readiness of Indian personnel to function in a given program could be read as a barometer of the relevance of the service to the perceived needs of the native people it purports to serve.

In suggesting that personnel in human-service programs should be Indian, we do not mean to suggest that Indian problem-solvers necessarily have better solutions than anyone else.

The concept of common Indian identity is not even applicable in this context. The social and psychological distance between the affluent, well-integrated Indian field-worker and the self-destructive, transient alcoholic is as great as the distance which exists between their white counterparts. It would be foolhardy to claim that Indian personnel can provide instant salvation.

What Indians have to offer to their own is an approach which is saddled with fewer prejudices arising from cultural difference. We know, at various levels of our consciousness, that the myths that have evolved around the term 'Indian' are simply not valid. Perhaps starting with this knowledge, we can more easily than anyone else establish the kind of relationships that build roads out of insufferable conditions.

MARLENE CASTELLANO is a Mohawk from the Bay of Quinte, presently living in Peterborough, Ontario. She holds the degrees of Bachelor of Arts from Queen's University and Master of Social Work from the University of Toronto. As well as maintaining close ties with her home reserve she has worked professionally and in voluntary associations with Indians in Winnipeg, Toronto, and smaller centres in southern Ontario.

Her essay 'Vocation or Identity' appeared in the recently published book *The Only Good Indian* (Waubageshig, ed.). Current responsibilities include an assignment from the Union of Ontario Indians to act as a member of the Management Committee, overseeing an action-research project on Indians in Toronto, and part-time work with Sir Sandford Fleming College of Applied Arts and Technology, Peterborough, as a consultant on services to Indians.

A New Horizon for Native Women in Canada

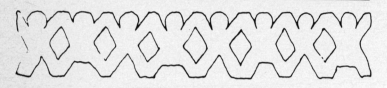

Jean Goodwill

Those of us who have been involved in helping the Indian cause for many years have witnessed a great many changes, particularly in the last decade.

In the early sixties the development of native organizations had been for the most part the concern of long-standing leaders of Indian ancestry, who for many years had carried on without government support.

Generally conferences of native people were sponsored by non-Indian groups such as social agencies, organizations interested in ethnic groups, churches, universities, and colleges. There was much concern about the migration of native people from reserves to near-by towns and cities. Because of overpopulation in Indian communities and lack of job opportunities, the desire of these people was to seek a new and possibly a better way of life. The result of this was the establishment of Indian Centres in most major urban areas across Canada.

Through conferences, seminars, human-relations courses, and other gatherings, a number of capable, articulate, concerned, but determined Indian people emerged. Among this group were Indian women of all ages.

Historically, for social and cultural reasons, Indian women remained in the background with the responsibility of the home and family. Other than the Mohawks in eastern Canada, who followed the matriarchal system, women of other tribes did not sit on council nor did they have any say in the affairs of the tribe. In the ensuing years, living with great courage under dire circumstances and through many hardships, they continued to support their families and tried to maintain their homes.

They lived through an educational system that separated them from their children physically, culturally, and religiously. Although some schools were built on reserves, there were many others that required the children to be away from their homes ten months of the year. Many lost their language, culture, religion, and respect for parents and elders. All this was totally contrary to their way of life and the teachings of their forefathers.

Many of those who went through this form of educational system, having to live with two distinct cultures, began to realize what was happening to their children. They no longer took a back seat in any activities and gatherings sponsored by non-Indian groups.

Although very little publicity was focussed on them as a group, many of these women made their mark in the professional world as graduates from universities, nursing-schools, teachers' and business colleges. Others trained as technicians, held executive positions in government and non-government offices, or became known through their talents in art and writing. Several found permanent residence outside their reserves and community, others, such as teachers and nurses, returned to Indian communities to work in whatever capacity they were trained in. On the community level, they were elected as chiefs and councillors, they sat on school committees, and assisted public-health nurses as capable community health workers.

The National Indian Council, one of the several attempts by Indian leaders to form a national body, included both men and women on their executive. Within three years this particular national group had to disband and to separate into two groups, the status and non-status Indians. At that time, it seemed the only way each group could deal with their particular legislative problems. The status or treaty Indians were a federal responsibility, and the non-status Indians came under provincial jurisdiction.

The National Indian Brotherhood was formed for the status Indians, and in later years non-status and Métis provincial organizations began to develop.

When Centennial celebrations were being planned, there was a negative response from many Indian groups. Looking at the dilemma of their people across Canada for the past hundred years, many felt they had no reason to celebrate.

The Indians of Canada Pavilion at Expo 67 provoked a great number of people, not only Canadians, but also visitors from many parts of the world. For the first time the Indian people of Canada were able to portray their living-conditions as they are. Many Canadians were quite upset – as taxpayers they felt Indian people should be grateful for what had been done for them. Those who had some understanding of the situation were glad to see that at last the truth was being told to the world.

Most of all, religious groups were very annoyed at what they saw and at what the Indian people said about the churches and Christianity. After all, they had spent many years of dedicated work to Christianize these people and take them away from their pagan beliefs.

Through the Centennial Commission some Indian groups took advantage of the grant program to carry on their traditional celebrations, to gather for meetings, and to strengthen their ties provincially and nationally.

The following year, 1968, was declared the International Year of Human Rights. Many meetings were held throughout Canada. Again, without question, 'The Indian' was the main topic. He was becoming a constant festering sore on the Canadian society. By the end of the year, many Indian people, both men and women, sensed that this exercise was not creating any impact on the non-Indian society nor on some individuals. 'Brotherhood Week', sponsored by the Canadian Council of Christians and Jews, was an example of tokenism – giving once-yearly recognition to Indian people, and other ethnic groups for that matter.

For the first time government was finally accepting the idea of giving grants to Indian associations. Meetings were no longer organized, managed, and conducted by government officials. A great number of capable Indian men and women were now taking over the leadership role.

Native-women's groups, started several years ago as home-makers', handicrafts, and sewing clubs in some provinces, were never actively organized on any large scale except within their own communities and districts. Along with many of the new developments among native people during this period, with better communication facilities and a greater awareness of the need for improved conditions, many of these women's groups were beginning to organize provincially.

Most of them had seen progress made in some areas, but were more than aware of the failures of government and non-Indian groups in their attempt to improve conditions for native people. Memories of life under dire circumstances on their reserves and communities were fresh in their minds. There were still examples of ridicule and derogatory remarks by non-Indians. Then there was the general criticism that they could not even work together to help their own people solve their problems. Somewhere along the way, in their fight for a better place in this country as a minority group, their people appeared to have lost stamina and strength, because of their many divisions. They were divisions created by legislation, by many outside forces, and sometimes by forces within their ranks.

Unlike other existing native organizations, right from the beginning, women's groups, through their provincial conferences, involved both status and non-status women in overcoming some of the major problems of Indian unity. They took advantage of provincial and federal funds to hold meetings. They reassured male-dominated organizations that they would not interfere in their fight for land and treaty rights, but, as mothers, wives, and community workers, they could deal with many other critical issues, work on many projects, and offer their support to programs that existing organizations were not able to cope with, for a variety of reasons.

During the studies for the Royal Commission on the Status of Women, the Voice of Alberta Native Women's Society presented a brief, giving views from all native women, status and non-status and Métis, from reserves, communities, and from the city. Throughout the study this particular brief was used as a basic reference by the Commission. Other presentations were made by individuals and groups of native women across the country. The Commission was impressed by their practical understanding of their problems, their willingness to handle many of the problems themselves, and their confidence in their ability to do so.

The Royal Commission contains nine recommendations pertaining specifically to the native and Eskimo women of Canada. While these recommendations are presently under study by the government, a special sub-committee consisting mainly of native women is dealing with the specific issues.

By early 1971, the Voice of Alberta Native Women's Society took on the task of planning, organizing, and conducting the first National Conference of Native Women in Canada. Their initial contacts were made through fairly well-known native women of other provinces, some of whom had attended previous meetings with the women of Alberta. Although some provinces were not as well organized as Alberta, representatives from active groups were invited.

In most areas, because of wide interest and the desire to attend a national meeting of native women, additional delegates were sponsored by their local government, native organizations, or other interested groups. Some came at their own expense. A few young people hitch-hiked from Vancouver just to be there.

For many of these women, it was an entirely new experience. Being isolated in their homes and communities, tied down with their families for most of their lives, they had never travelled outside their immediate surroundings. Hotel living was a new and rather frightening experience. With the help of those who had travelled, and with the enjoyment of meeting so many other native women, they adjusted to the situation in no time. Those who came from the Maritimes were amazed at the size of Canada, as they looked back at the speed of their flight and the length of time it took to get to Edmonton.

Many of the delegates were fascinated to learn that there were many distinct language differences among themselves, while their tribal and cultural differences were not always noticeable.

Most of the women were dressed in modern clothes, from the most up-to-date pant-suits for the young to matronly types of dresses and suits for the elderly ladies. A few from Saskatchewan and Alberta wore their traditional shawls, and their hair hung in beautiful long braids.

Throughout the conference it was quite obvious they had common concerns. They talked of the educational system and what it had done to their homes and families. They were concerned with community improvement, child welfare, the lack of basic facilities that most Canadian women can take for granted. They talked about the perpetual dilemma created by welfare hand-outs, the major unresolved problems of alcohol, and how they were now faced with drugs, which were already affecting their young people. They expressed their concern over the exploitation and imitation of crafts. What was once a truly creative skill was gradually being replaced by mass-produced commercialized copies of traditional designs, lowering quality and standards.

One of the major issues was the question of Indian women losing their Indian status upon marriage to non-status Indians or to a non-Indian person (Indian Act). This was obviously one of the biggest concerns of many Indian women in Canada, and they are fully aware that this will need some form of statutory change before the problem can be solved.

The formal-education background of these women ranged from none to elementary grades received at reserve and residential schools. Others were graduates of universities, colleges, and were working in many fields, with a variety of travel and conference experience. Those who expressed themselves were very articulate speakers, but it must be noted that educational background is certainly no criterion for the type of natural expression that Indian people possess. By gaining greater self-confidence and with their experience in dealing with basic issues of family and community life, these women will no doubt succeed in exerting greater pressure on governments and non-Indian agencies for improved and expanded programs.

By their presentations it was clear they were prepared to step forward and catch up on many of the things that were always the sole responsibility of men. They wanted their ideas to become realistic and most of all they wanted to change the image of the Indian woman in the eyes of their own people and the non-Indian public.

Although the various Indian associations and the National bodies (the National Indian Brotherhood and the National Native Council) have succeeded in gaining greater recognition by government and non-Indian groups, Indian women have always been closer to reserve and community situations. From this vantage point they also recognized that sometimes too many splintered groups were trying to serve their people. Too often barriers created by these groups delayed meaningful progress.

The majority of the delegates agreed that there was a need for a national association of native women. An association, open to all women of Indian ancestry, would help to remove existing barriers among the native people. It would provide a means of communicating inter-provincially, thus creating a stronger united voice for all. It would also give support to other organizations in their struggle for land and treaty rights, and at the same time seek to find ways of gaining for its members their rightful place in society as Indian people and as women. With the support of a national organization they would have a greater part to play in the education of their children by sitting on school boards and curriculum committees and by helping to investigate all other aspects of Indian education. In housing, they would have a say in the kind of homes that were suitable for their families. They would help to promote recreational programs in their communities and to alleviate the problems of alcohol, drugs, and child neglect. A national body would also encourage better health facilities and involve more women in community health programs.

While there are many positive aspects in favour of the formation of a national association, many of the delegates felt they should consult with other women on their reserves and communities before making a decision. As a result, a steering committee was formed, representing the two Territories and most of the provinces. As the elected chairman of this committee I was responsible for the co-ordination of on-going discussions as to the viability of a national organization for native women. My first responsibility was to bring together members of this committee, to study the recommendations, and to work on a proposed constitution. At the time of writing this meeting was being planned.

The whole idea of getting a group of native women together from many parts of Canada was a great experience for all delegates and for any observer. Throughout all sessions and at social functions it was obvious they had common concerns as mentioned earlier. Although these delegates came from different cultural groups and spoke different languages, they all expressed the same concern with the impending loss of culture through the pressure of a rapidly changing society. This unique culture, distinct and different from that of any other race of people on the continent, has always been the strongest common bond of these people in spite of all kinds of pressure.

This was quite evident on the final evening of the conference. Following the custom of the western tribes, a traditional pow-wow was held in honour of all visiting delegates. Dancers and singers from the Blackfoot, Blood, and Cree tribes came with their colourful dancing outfits. One has to be a participant to understand the drumming and singing and to truly understand the feeling of pride of being 'Indian'.

Honour songs were sung for all visiting delegates and they were invited to dance. Those who did not know how tried, while others who did showed them how. Following the honour song each delegate was given a necklace and one dollar attached to a small branch of a tree. The gift of a necklace is a tradition carried on for centuries when visiting tribes were presented with gifts of clothing, blankets, and beaded buckskin outfits; the branch from a tree represents a horse – one of the greatest gifts one could bestow upon an honoured visitor.

It was a moving ceremony, the delegates each in turn expressing their appreciation for what was truly 'western hospitality'. They had learned so much and appreciated the fact that although they had many common concerns with native women from many parts of Canada, they were more than aware of the distinct tribal differences that exist between the Kwakiutl, Blackfoot, Cree, Ojibway, Dakota, Mohawk, Micmac, and Maliseet from the southern parts of Canada and the Loucheaux, Dogrib, Chilcotin, and Inuit of the north.

The culture of these people will always be their strongest common bond.

JEAN GOODWILL is a direct descendant of Chief Poundmaker, a noted chief and leader of the Crees during the 1885 rebellion in Saskatchewan. She speaks Cree fluently. Born on Little Pine Reserve near Paynton, Saskatchewan, she attended the reserve school up to the eighth grade. She graduated from Bedford Road Collegiate, Saskatoon, and later received her Registered Nurse's degree from the Holy Family Hospital, Prince Albert, Saskatchewan.

From 1954 to 1960, she worked with the Indian and Northern Health Services at Fort Qu'Appelle Indian Hospital, the La Ronge Nursing Station, and with Public Health in Prince Albert and northern regions of Saskatchewan.

After a year of nursing in Bermuda, she returned to Canada with different objectives and became the Executive Director of the Indian and Métis Friendship Centre in Winnipeg, a position she held for over two years.

Mrs. Goodwill joined Indian Affairs and Northern Development in the Cultural Development section and later worked as co-editor of *The Indian News* on a contract basis. In 1969 she entered the civil service, and was assigned to the Cultural Development division as editor of *TA WOW* – a new Canadian-Indian cultural magazine.

She has been a member of the following: the Indian-Eskimo Association of Canada, the National Indian Council, the National Indian Princess Pageant Committee, the National Native News Service Committee, and was a consultant on the committee for the Canadian Correction Association report 'Indians and the Law'. She toured with the Canadian Prairie Inter-Tribal Dancers in Holland and France in 1969. Lately she has been involved in the study for the Royal Commission on the Status of Women, with particular reference to recommendations concerning Indian and Eskimo women; has assisted in the planning and co-ordination of the National Indian Cultural Conference 1970-1; has reviewed textbooks for the Ontario Department of Education; and has served as Chairman of the Steering Committee for the formation of a National Native Women's Association.

Mr. and Mrs. Goodwill recently left Ottawa and are now in Saskatchewan. Mr. Goodwill is Director of the Indian Cultural College. Mrs. Goodwill is with the Saskatoon District office in Saskatoon.

Community Development and the White-Indian Problem[1]

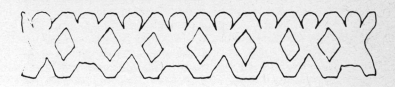

Charles A. S. Hynam

The many letters and articles that from time to time appear in the press and elsewhere make it clear that there are big differences of opinion among sincere, well-meaning people, some of whom are in positions of authority, as to what they consider is 'good' for the Indian. For example, there is unlikely to be consensus on answers to the following questions: To integrate or not to integrate? Is the existing state of affairs on reserves a form of Indian culture or not? Is Canadian culture truly 'white-man's culture'? Unfortunately, the person who is likely to suffer most when there is disagreement among his 'helpers' is the Indian himself. It may be useful, therefore, to pose the question: 'How many of these "differences" are real and how many are due to misunderstandings?'

I think it would be safe to say that hardly anyone who is in any influential position would want to see the Indian integrated[2] into the so-called 'white man's culture' other than *as an Indian*. There is general agreement that the Indian should be proud of his Indianness; but of what aspects of his Indianness should he be proud? Or of what should he be made proud by functional education? There seems to be the point of view in certain quarters that he should be encouraged to be proud of his existing state of affairs, which may not be much, but which 'works'. There are those who disagree strongly with this point of view. They argue that 'what is' is often only a travesty of the old Indian culture and is neither functional for the

Indian nor for the Canadian community of which he is now a part.

Without taking sides, I would like to suggest that the most useful action can be taken in an area where, again, there *is* agreement. For instance, no one I know of would question the desirability of making the Indian aware, for example, of the fact mentioned by Charles Gallenkamp in his book *Maya* (1962) that 'When Caesar was subduing the barbarous tribes in what is now the greater part of continental Europe, a vast complex of ceremonial cities was beginning to rise proudly in colorful splendor in the tropical regions of Middle America' (p. 9). Furthermore, no one I know of would deny the Indian the pride of learning in respect to the magnificent Mayan and Aztec American Indian civilizations that they are among the 'high civilizations' of the world, nor would they be against the Indian learning that:

> about three quarters of the foods which the world eats today were first cultivated by the South American Indians of the Andes. From that region came maize in twenty different varieties, potatoes, yams, squash, many types of beans, manioc, peanuts, cashews, pineapple, chocolate, avocados, peppers, strawberries and blackberries. Some have been domesticated for so long, or have run wild, in other parts of the world that we have forgotten their South American origin (Calder, 1966, p. 13).

There would not be much disagreement as to the functionality of the Indian culture in North America before the advent of the white man. In fact, there are many white men who feel that there is still much in the old Indian cultures that is worthy of emulation, for example,

> Indians believed that hospitality was automatic if there was food and that to contradict was disgracefully bad mannered. ... Of all personal qualities, truthfulness was the one most prized. That this particular virtue was less esteemed by the white intruder was one of the facts which earned him the undying distrust and contempt of the Indian (Symington, 1969, p. 62).

In addition to what has been referred to above, the area of disagreement appears to lie in whether or not the *existing* state of affairs is a form of true Indian culture or just an unfortunate hybrid imposed on the Indian by the white man. Cannot this area of disagreement be by-passed as much as possible? Perhaps not; certainly by-passing it is made more difficult by the implication, if not by the direct statement made in certain quarters, that the Indian is happy or at least satisfied with his existing culture. It may be extremely difficult to get a valid answer to this because of the fact that proud and sensitive people will be loathe to admit, even to themselves, that their way of life is not 'good' for them.

There is also the question as to whether the term 'white-man's culture' is really descriptive of the facts. In any age in recorded history, the fundamental contributions to the peak culture by the bearers of that culture have been minimal. They have been fortunate in that circumstances have put them in the position where they can make the best use of the elements that have been contributed by previous cultures. 'None of the complex societies to be found on earth today ("white" or otherwise) created more than a very few of the total number of cultural elements to be found in it' (Bierstedt, 1970, p. 144). All of them have 'borrowed' elements from other societies. This is admirably documented by Ralph Linton (1936) in the following quotations:

> Our solid (Canadian)[3] citizen awakens in a bed built on a pattern which originated in the Near East but which was modified in Northern Europe before it was transmitted to America. He throws back the covers made from cotton, domesticated in India, or linen, domesticated in the Near East, or wool from sheep, also domesticated in the Near East, or silk, the use of which was discovered in China. All of these materials have been spun and woven by processes invented in the Near East. He slips into his moccasins, invented by the Indians of the Eastern woodlands, and goes to the bathroom, whose fixtures are a mixture of European and American inventions, both of recent date. Before going out for breakfast he glances through the window, made of glass invented in Egypt, and if it is raining, puts on overshoes made of rubber discovered by the Central American Indians and takes an umbrella, invented in southeastern Asia. Upon his head he puts a hat made of felt, a material invented in the Asiatic steppes.
>
> On his way to breakfast he stops to buy a paper, paying for it with coins, an ancient Lydian invention. At the restaurant a whole new series of borrowed elements confronts him. His plate is made of a form of pottery invented in

China. His knife is of steel, an alloy first made in southern India, his fork, a medieval Italian invention, and his spoon a derivative of a Roman original. He begins breakfast with an orange, from the eastern Mediterranean, a cantaloupe from Persia, or perhaps a piece of African watermelon. With this he has coffee, an Abyssinian plant, with cream and sugar. Both the domestication of cows and the idea of milking them originated in the Near East, while sugar was first made in India. After his fruit and first coffee he goes on to waffles, cakes made by a Scandinavian technique from wheat domesticated in Asia Minor. Over these he pours maple syrup invented by the Indians of the Eastern woodlands. As a side dish he may have the eggs of a species of bird domesticated in Indo-China, or thin strips of the flesh of an animal domesticated in Eastern Asia, which have been salted and smoked by a process developed in northern Europe.

When our friend has finished eating, he settles back to smoke, an American Indian habit, consuming a plant domesticated in Brazil in either a pipe, derived from the Indians of Virginia, or a cigarette, derived from Mexico. If he is hardy enough he may even attempt a cigar, transmitted to us from the Antilles by way of Spain (pp. 326-7).

Ralph Linton also estimated 'that in no case does the number of indigenous or native elements exceed 10 per cent of the total culture.' This being so, the Indian has every right to participate fully in a culture to which his ancestors have already contributed a great deal.

Finally, it is suggested that all areas of disagreement will fade into relative insignificance, if there is agreement that what is of prime importance is for those of us who want to be helpful to the Indian to convey to him that we are sincerely interested in *his* welfare, not only in the satisfaction that *we* get from 'doing good'. If, indeed, we are sincere in this, then we must be willing to learn from the school of experience which indicates clearly that we can provide opportunities, timely advice in the right spirit, facilities, etc., but if the Indian is to develop *his* potentialities, he has to be encouraged to decide for himself and to help himself as his ethnic brothers did so magnificently in the past.

In his long, arduous journey forward from savagery to a civilized state, the first five steps by which man has advanced are generally admitted to be the following: control of fire, invention of agriculture, domestication of animals, tools of metal, and discovery of the principle of the wheel. All of the tremendous building program of the ancient Maya was accomplished without the aid of a single carrying animal other than man himself. . . .

The principle of the wheel was unknown to the ancient Maya. They had no wheeled vehicles of any kind . . . and most students of aboriginal American ceramics are agreed that the potter's wheel for turning pottery was also unknown. . . . In short, the Maya were acquainted with and enjoyed the use of only the first two of the foregoing five 'steps towards civilization'.

On this primitive horizon, and on this alone, may the Maya civilization be fairly compared with the prehistoric civilizations of the Old World. And if this comparison be made, it will be found that, starting from the same cultural scratch, no Neolithic people of the Old World ever reached such heights of achievement as did the ancient Maya of Middle America (Gallenkamp, 1962, pp. 176-8).

Today there is a real danger in an affluent society like Canada of being too dependent on assistance and on such assistance being measured too much in terms of money. Ross and Van Den Haag warn that: 'Investment or even donation of capital need no more be the remedy (for underdevelopment) than sugar is the remedy for diabetes. The causes of the lack of capital and the use that would be made of it must be determined first' (Ross & Van Den Haag, 1957, p. 461).

No ethnic group can be fully self-respecting, if it remains *indefinitely* dependent on hand-outs from government. This poses a real problem for Indian leaders. The argument that the money being handed out is only some of the value of what was misappropriated in the past from the Indian people only confuses the issue. Misappropriation was, of course, wrong. But *continual dependence* on hand-outs is also wrong, because of its debilitating effect on a people; and two wrongs never make a right.

Our definition of community development (Hynam, 1968) includes 'process' as 'program'. During recent years in many parts of Canada, the community-development process has thrown up Indian leaders who are animating their people quite effectively, but the next stage is likely to be more difficult, i.e., the formulation of self-help programs that will eventually lead animated people by the wise use of government and other assistance to true independence. Independence, however, may be the wrong word to use. We are really interdependent. It may be that what is often called independence is really equity in the comity of Canada. There can hardly be any disagreement that this is a desirable goal for the Indian people: an achievement that would make them as an ethnic group no longer dependent on special assistance for the underprivileged.

This is a real challenge to Indian leaders. The leader who has the interests of his people at heart cannot always be pandering to popularity. The idea of self-help is often not very popular. D. S. Hatch, rather too pessimistically perhaps, states that 'The self-help leader may be idolized in the next generation, but he is not likely to be in this' (Hatch, 1949, p. 14). Yet there have been some truly great leaders, like Gandhi and Churchill, who have offered their people the equivalent of 'blood, sweat, and tears', and increased their popularity by so doing.

The next decades in Canada are likely to be critical ones for the Indian people. It can only be hoped that, as is so often the case, crises will produce appropriate leaders.

FOOTNOTES

1. In the preparation of this article, the author is particularly grateful to Glen Eyford for his critical and constructive comments.
2. For the writer integration is *not* synonymous with assimilation.
3. The substitution of the word Canadian for American, which is in the original, does not detract from the relevance of the quotation.

CHARLES ARTHUR SYLVESTER HYNAM was born in St. Michael, Barbados, British West Indies. He was educated at Combermere School (Barbados), Harrison College (Barbados), the Imperial College of Tropical Agriculture (Trinidad), and Cornell University. Receiving the Diploma of the Imperial College in July 1930, he spent an additional year as a postgraduate in sugar technology. He received his M.S. from Cornell University in 1958 and a Ph.D. (majoring in rural sociology with a minor in sociology) in 1964.

Appointments in public and other services have been as follows: Headmaster and Farm Manager, Glen Community School, St. Vincent, British West Indies, 1933-5; Government Agriculturist, Netherlands Windward Islands, Netherlands West Indies, 1935-41 (he received a permanent appointment in the Netherlands Service in February 1941, but resigned in July 1941 to serve in the British Overseas Service); agricultural extension officer in such places as Antigua, Trinidad, British Honduras, and Barbados; Assistant Professor of Sociology, Muhlenberg College, Pennsylvania, 1961-2; Assistant Professor of Sociology, University of Alberta, 1962-7; and Associate Professor of Sociology, University of Alberta, 1967 to date. From 1965, there has been a joint appointment with the Department of Agricultural Economics. In October 1967, he was appointed Chairman of the interdisciplinary committee for the M.A. program in community development. From July 1, 1969, to August 31, 1970, a sabbatical leave was spent at the Institute of Commonwealth Studies, London University, doing research work on certain aspects of community development.

Application
and Analysis

.Previous articles, including those by Kidd and Lotz, have pointed out the lack of discipline in community development. Up until now, full advantage has not been taken of the research and theory developed in the social sciences that have relevance to community development, and only limited attempts have been made to develop theory out of community practice. One of the purposes of this section is to point out the practicality of good theory.

The theory and practice of community development are not limited to rural and poor areas. Similarly, 'community' is not limited to just the usual geographic-sociological definition. Such are some of the points made by Freeman H. Compton as he emphasizes the need to be clear about the concepts we use in community-development theory and practice. Community development must be placed in an administrative setting that is not inhibiting. This applies as well to the research and evaluation components of community development. Compton re-emphasizes what it means for government to be committed to community development, and summarizes community development as a process, program, movement, or a method of working with others.

John W. Frei strongly points out the need to apply a scientific approach to the problems of societal development. This implies the formulation of a theory of practice, and an understanding of action research. The article includes a detailed outline of the survey method as a means of collecting and interpreting data, a practice also emphasized in the article by Stinson. According to Frei, since the process of intervention is basically a social-learning process, there is a need for more fact finding and descriptive research, evaluative and predictive studies, and rigorous measurement of results. The field of societal development is so complex that no single profession can hope to master it alone. Thus a theme that frequently occurs throughout this book is that of interprofessional and interdisciplinary co-operation and action.

The third article in this section, written by Coolie Verner, examines the concepts of development and action. Some of the references to earlier writings help to put present-day practices into a historical perspective. Verner sees community development as an adult-education method. He distinguishes between social action and community action, discusses role differentiations in community development, and outlines in detail the steps in community action.

The article by Charles E. Hendry brings together many of the concepts previously discussed by other authors. The article is further strengthened by the example it gives of collecting and interpreting field data. Furthermore, the study is of the BAEQ (*le Bureau d'Aménagement de l'Est du Québec*), which is one of the most ambitious development-planning projects ever undertaken in Canada. This project represents an intensive effort to apply scientific methods to assess total resources and project plans, within the philosophy of social animation. Hendry's article raises some of the basic questions concerning the social aspects of policy, science, and intervention. He also discusses the role of the change agent and the scientist.

Community Development Theory and Practice

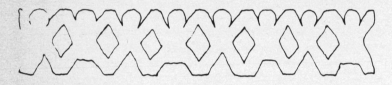

Freeman H. Compton

What Community Development Is

'Community development' has a variety of meanings. The way in which it is defined often depends on the orientation of the sponsoring agency, i.e., whether the agency is economic- or resource-development-oriented; whether it is primarily social-development- or local-government-oriented, etc. A letter in a recent issue of *Maclean's* sets out the ultimate objectives of community development clearly: 'What we should seek is justice and equality for men and women who may be Indian or Quebecois or Doukhobors or even Wasps. We should never allow group politics to obscure the fact that the goal of valid social action is material sufficiency and intellectual freedom for all human beings.'

A genuine community-development sponsoring-agency must be people-oriented. But community development is not a 'welfare' program, nor just an anti-poverty program. However, effective anti-poverty programs do use community development as a significant intervention process, since it involves victims of poverty circumstances in the fight.

Community development is not just for blight areas, not just a poor peoples' movement. In Manitoba, an effective community-development effort is being carried out by one of our universities in a middle-class, suburban, residential area. Community development can be a means of making even good communities better. 'Community', when used in this sense, is not restricted to the usual geographic or sociological definition. The community-development process is equally valid for area and regional development and, in fact, is a vital part of it.

Because community development takes an holistic, ecological approach, care must be taken to place the service in an administrative setting where it will not be inhibited by (a) narrowly defined agency objectives or particular-purpose orientations or models; (b) traditional methods of delivering service to people. The process, when set in motion, will defy any attempt to restrict it to special areas of man in his total environment.

Definitions

The Canadian Welfare Council (1970) defines community development as:

> A process aimed at promoting citizen participation in social affairs, developing people's awareness of problems, enabling them to define their needs in relation to the total environment, making possible their enlightened choice among various options and channelling the results into effective action for social change (p.17).

This is basically the problem-solving process, not unique to community development.

The classical United Nations definition (1955) is that community development is:

> a process of social action in which the people of a community organize themselves for planning and action; define their common and individual needs and solve their problems; execute their plans with a maximum reliance upon community resources; and supplement these resources when necessary with services and materials from governmental and non-governmental agencies outside of the community (p.2).

Finally, the Manitoba Department of Health and Social Development Planned Program Budgeting System (1970) states that the purpose of community development is:

> To assist people to develop economically and socially viable communities which can strengthen and support adequately individual and family growth and enhance the quality of life.

Emphasis in this definition is on competent, viable communities – the only real merit of which is the extent to which such competence and viability improves the quality of life of people, both individuals and families.

Reduced to its essence, community development is not much more than 'people participating in the improvement of their lot.' This has been the primary goal of community development in Manitoba since it was introduced into Indian and Métis communities ten years ago. This was the essence of the justification for a community-development approach to Indian and Métis problems put forward by Jean Lagassé (1959, Ch.6) in 1958, as an alternative to traditional methods of working with Indian people. The experience in Manitoba and in other parts of Canada has proven that encouraging and facilitating meaningful participation is an effective way of breaking through barriers of apathy and hopelessness, and of getting people, in co-operation with government, to seek solutions to those problems that they themselves identify as contributing to their socio-economic plight. Where the desire or ambition to achieve or to change is low, or when those involved are slow or sluggish starters, the animation or motivation dimension of community development is a stimulant. But there can be no half-way measures. Participation has to be genuine both in intent and application. Inconsistencies will quickly be interpreted as tokenism and phoniness, and will not be tolerated.

The Two Phases of Community Development

There are two phases to the community-development process, best articulated by the Hon. John Munro in a speech to the Winnipeg Canadian Welfare Planning Council in February, 1969, when he said:

More recently, we have begun to move in the direction of seeing the development of communities as a two-phase process. The first phase is the process of community animation, motivating the poor to organize and work toward the identification of their own needs, the establishment of their own institutions to meet these needs and the development of a sense of community and capacity for collective strength in place of individual alienation and resignation. Some of these experiments, although modest, have produced rather startling results. Clearly there is within the culture of the poor and the alienated minorities a tremendous latent potential and capacity for self-improvement and self-betterment.

Phase one begins with a group of alienated individuals, resigned to impotence, with no sense of capacity to relate to the larger society or win for themselves a place in it. Grievances are suffered. The belief that by their act they can set in motion events which will lead to the correction of these grievances is absent. Phase one ends with a sense of community, an awareness that the grievances are shared and that in the collectivity there is the capacity to demand that these be corrected.

It is phase two of this process that confronts us with the far greater challenge. If we meet the articulation by this community of its grievances and aspirations with a stone wall of either opposition or apathy, we will either destroy it or transform it into an army determined to destroy us. If community development is to be a reality and not a mere sham, then we must be prepared to mobilize the necessary resources – (including a willingness to share some of our own power) – to meet the legitimate demands of the new community (pp. 5-6).

The animating or stimulating is not easily achieved, and, even when achieved, it must be emphasized that it is only the first phase: a phase of 'turning on' communities, and a phase during which the system (and especially the government system) will prepare in many ways to respond to the inevitable community representation. The second phase, the long-term development phase, will give effect to the first phase. It is during the second phase, especially in a government-sponsored service, where it will be seen whether or not government has the courage of its conviction. It is here, too, that one encounters the problem of reconciling citizen participation with political accountability.

It should be emphasized that community development is no short-cut to changing years of conditioning. It is no panacea, and there is nothing mystical about it. It is important to emphasize and to acknowledge this, lest there be those who, when the process does not produce miracles overnight or when it begins to manifest some growing pains, as it is bound to do, will be all too apt to say 'Ah, ah – I told you so. See! It is producing nothing but disturbance.' Often, the inevitable disturbance caused by the identification and articulation of the problem by the people is attributed to the community-development process, or the community-development worker. Often the issues are lost while attempts are made to blame either the agency or a particular worker.

It is also important that the community-development practitioner recognize this, because his enthusiasm for, commitment to, and identification with, community development and change often will alienate him from colleagues and build up resistance in an Establishment that is already characterized by resistance to change.

Based on the evidence that exists, there is no doubt that the community-development approach is valid. People are gaining power through more access to information, organization, access to financial and technical resources, and leadership development. The process is causing many changes in government attitudes towards Indians; societal attitudes towards the poor; student recognition in universities; as well as in urban renewal and regional socio-economic development in many parts of Canada. Until recently such involvement by the people in forcing social change was literally unheard of, was not to be encouraged or even tolerated. These developments notwithstanding, however, the results of community development and particularly the experience that communities gain through it are not very well documented.

This failure to adequately record and evaluate our experiences has resulted in a poor job of communicating what we have been about to the public and in particular to our politicians. The need for communication represents a very real challenge, which could probably best be met through the combined efforts of the public, academicians, and the community-development program administrators.

Community Development – Program, Method, Process, Movement

To the very practical, uninitiated, hard-nosed administrator, community development is:

A program: A combination of plans and strategies for achieving some very concrete, tangible objectives, e.g., promoting an industry, building a community hall, digging wells, building playgrounds. The program emphasis includes the agency policy, the objective, the various activities and their objectives, the administrative structure, the support services, the financial resources and people, all of which are required to provide a particular type of service. The program also includes provision for evaluation and testing. The program is that collection of things that facilitates the community-development process.

To the practitioner, community development is:

A method: A method of working with people; an approach to delivering service; a means of achieving certain specific objectives.

In Manitoba, community development has been adopted officially by many departments and agencies as a method of working with people. In the part of the province designated as the North, under a Northern Affairs Act, community development is a major emphasis of the Manitoba Department of Northern Affairs. In Agro-Manitoba there is a similar emphasis by the Department of Agriculture. In other parts of the province, and particularly in urban and suburban areas, this function is assumed by the Department of Health and Social Development. This department would prefer to use community development as a process of people problem-solving rather than a program, i.e., they tend to use community development as a *method*, as they would use casework, group work, or community organization as legitimate and appropriate problem-solving or intervention processes. Finally, Mines, Resources and Environmental Management (responsible especially for renewable resource management, i.e., development and conservation) is tending towards a greater involvement of the people primarily affected by resource development, so that natural-resource development takes into account social as well as economic consequences.

An area of northern Manitoba has been designated a 'Department of Regional Economic Expansion Special Area'. In that area community development, or 'Community–Information' as it is being called, is to be used as a means of involving the local people with government, in planning for development. Manitoba Newstart Inc. is also in the same area. A new model for the administration of community development may emerge in this area.

In addition to government inputs, in Manitoba a significant community-development function is carried out by the Manitoba Indian Brotherhood, on Indian reserves and in the cities where Indians tend to congregate as a result of the rural-to-urban population shift; by the Manitoba Métis Federation, in rural and urban areas where there are concentrations of Métis people; by Neighborhood Services centres in the Winnipeg downtown area; and by the University of Winnipeg as a part of its Urban Renewal Studies program.

As more and more agencies get involved in communities, a significant social-development planning function will include the co-ordination of services so as to: (a) avoid duplication; (b) avoid unnecessary competition, with its inevitable confusion, among agencies; (c) bring together expertise in planning for such service; (d) ensure greatest return on this investment in developmental services; (e) make the most efficient use of scarce resources, e.g. for consultation, training, etc.; (f) rationalize the use of scarce field-services practitioners.

To the practitioner in any of these sponsored services, community development is:

A process: A series of stages, from very simple problem-solving to applying the competence gained to more complex situations, through which people and communities progress in achieving objectives and in effecting change.

To the fervent, whose vision of community development is beyond the parochial, community development is:

A movement: A philosophy of life; a cause; a way of relating to people in various kinds of communities – homes, schools, universities, offices, neighbourhoods, etc. In the movement sense, it may be looked at now as a very informal association of communities or groups who are pursuing a new-found road to problem-solving and freedom. Thus, we may refer to the community-development movement in Canada to denote the way in which groups throughout the country are using a similar approach to come to grips with their problems, and the way in which these groups, regions, etc. are identifying with each other. Sometime in the future, people may see purpose in more formally structuring this 'movement'.

A Summary of the Major Characteristics of Community Development

Community development is *people involvement* in decision-making; it is a means of broadening the political power base – it implies meaningful, as opposed to token, citizen participation.

It is a *problem-solving* process, designed to make people aware of their problems and to stimulate them to do something about their problems: to plan and choose between alternative solutions, to take action, including drawing on government and other resources, to evaluate the experience, and to apply any learning to new problem-solving, or additional tasks to be undertaken.

It is a *learning* process, geared not to the acquisition of knowledge, but to a change in behaviour. It is learning by doing, not so much for the doing as for the experiences gained by doing.

It tends towards increasing individual, group, and community competence for managing their own affairs.

It is a social-action program geared to material sufficiency and intellectual freedom for all human beings.

It is not 'extension' in the classical sense – not a method of selling and promoting preconceived plans and programs. It cannot be an 'elitist' approach, dealing only with status leaders or, for example, producers of a certain prowess – e.g. only those farmers or fishermen who have the resources and the latent skills to manage well. Community development is more of a grass-roots approach than that, but it is not only a grass-roots approach. It is necessary also at the intra-agency and the inter-agency level, if the two stages identified by the Hon. Mr. Munro are to be achieved successfully.

Community development gives effect to good planning because it involves people in developing the plans. Research (Lippitt, G., 1969; Bennis, 1968; Likert, 1969; McGregor, 1969) shows that people are more deeply committed to a course of action if they have had a voice in planning it. There is a difference between a set of ideas or concepts and a plan. The plan reflects and incorporates the reaction to the ideas or the tentative plan.

Community development is a process of developing and meeting the needs of people, not agencies. The two are not necessarily incompatible; in fact, with some sensitivity (ear-to-the-ground sort of thing), meaningful dialogue (as opposed to telling) between agency and the people, enlightened modern participative management, and good planning that provides for the meaningful involvement of the people, the needs of the people and of agencies will be one.

In community development there can be no channelling of the process in a particular direction. There can be no sacred cows or forbidden fruits, so that, for example, economic development is pursued to the exclusion of development in the area of education, or development of local government is sought but medical services ignored. The approach is a holistic one; people participation is people participation in whatever areas people are motivated to participate.

Community development is 'not a manipulative process for achieving political and/or agency ends. Once it has become rooted and gained momentum, there can be no turning it off without risk of causing considerable frustration and possible militancy or, to use the reference in Mr. Munro's speech, 'If we meet the articulation by a community of its grievances and aspirations with a stone wall of either opposition or apathy, we will either destroy it or transform it into an army determined to destroy us' (p.6). A radio commentator, referring to the current representations being made by the Indians and Métis of Fort Chipewyan in Alberta, who made use of peaceful demonstrations and the mass media to articulate their concerns, remarked, 'Let's not cause them to turn these tools into weapons.'

Community development implies development and change, so community-development workers are sometimes referred to as change agents (NTL, pp. 57-8).

Change is inevitable, yet people and human systems react to it in various ways, some negative. For instance, they may refuse to acknowledge that it is happening and, in fact, actively resist; or they may be prepared to accept the fact that it is happening in many quarters but not to them, and so display a passive resistance. Some are negative through their indifference and neutrality and allow change to take place without resistance – 'what will be, will be,' while others behave much more positively, and not only recognize the inevitability of change, but help it to evolve and to that extent are change agents or catalysts for change.

Helping change to take place and causing it to happen is much less frustrating and ultimately much more satisfying and productive than resisting it. The former is what 'the system', including government, does in preparing for that second phase of community development referred to earlier in Mr. Munro's speech.

Basic Beliefs

Being developmental, in contrast to being traditional, in one's approach to people is largely a matter of attitude and belief.

Developmentally oriented people subscribe to certain fundamental beliefs about people generally (Sanders, 1958, Nos. 1-4):

1. All people, no matter how unambitious they may appear to be, do want to help themselves and will help themselves if they are given the chance.
2. Backwardness and poverty are not necessarily caused by laziness or lack of ambition, but often come about because the difficulties to be overcome are too great for the human and technical resources available, or known by the community to be available. The remedy lies not so much in stimulating people as in effecting change in the environment.
3. Communities and individuals will try to help themselves when they are motivated to do so and when they are allowed to work out their own terms for doing so.
4. If lasting change is to be achieved, it is necessary to influence many aspects of behaviour at the same time, otherwise we create imbalance and possible social disintegration.
5. People are competent to participate in decision-making now. It's a question of starting where they are; there is no point at which people are more or less ready to be involved, any more than there is a point at which people are more or less ready to be free.
6. People have a right to expect that government technical expertise will be made available to them to achieve developmental goals they set for themselves.
7. All people should have equal opportunity, and that opportunity, to be real, will often require provision for more than identical services to all. A letter to the editor in a recent issue of *Maclean's* referred to the inequity of our 'court fines' system, and referred to inequality in opportunity in this way: 'A $100 fine may be nothing for one man, an annoyance for another man, an impossibility for a third man. The person who can't pay has a jail record while the rich man committing the same offense does not.'

Community Development in a Government Setting

Community development cannot survive in isolation from the rest of the system. It relies on the willingness and the ability of the system to respond to change. Also, it must rely on the impact it can make on the political decision-maker.

Community development must operate out of a total government social-development perspective (a government philosophy). Community development will not survive if its source of motivation and dynamism is the philosophy of a single department. It is a simple fact that a single department lacks the authority to make government policy.

All government departments must be prepared to respond to people-initiative and be prepared also to relate to people in a developmental way. The result of different departments using different approaches to working with people is frustrating, disillusioning, and stifling. A designated community-development branch or division (which is but one administrative model for a community-development service in government) can and should give leadership in how to work effectively with people, and it should be the central source of expert knowledge, know-how, and resource material; but a community-development branch has no monopoly on the approach. This fact has many implications for government services, not the least of which are:

1. The necessity of providing for the reorientation and training of the many categories of government and other agency field-workers and program administrators.
2. The necessity of allocating to the branch the resources that will be necessary, not only for administrative and field staff, but also for back-up resource material and support services so that the branch can function effectively in the agency setting as well as in the field. This includes provision, for example, for well-focussed interdepartmental seminars and other forms of interdepartmental communication.
3. The necessity of recognizing that the costs of instituting a community-development service, therefore, are usually higher initially (as are most new services) than government administration may be used to in providing services in traditional ways. But once the program is launched, the ratio of benefit to cost tends to be greater than one.

Towards a Community-Development Management Style

A community-development service requires a management style that is developmental and that will be consistent with developmental activity in the field. Styles of management range along a continuum from authoritarian and autocratic to consultative to participative.

Since community-development is predicated on people-participation, the appropriate style of management is one that will involve people in decision-making. This means that the director and staff of a community-development branch, for example, constitute a management unit with well-defined shared areas of management responsibility. Field staffs may not be expected to reflect any kind of relationship to people-attitude other than the one that is reflected in their relationship to their superiors. A worker who is told what to do may be similarly authoritarian in his relationship to people. The best practice for a field-worker in involving people in problem-solving is to be involved himself in the problem-solving of his agency. Maslow's theory of Hierarchy of Needs applies to staff needs as well as to client and community needs, and the implications are similar.

Douglas McGregor in his book *The Human Side of Enterprise* (1969) has developed two theories to explain human behaviour:

Essentially, Theory X builds on the lower order of human needs. Theory Y assumes that, once met, these needs no longer motivate. It builds on the higher order of needs. Human behavior is based on theory – we do A because we theorize it will produce B. It is important that the leader examine his assumptions – his theory – about what makes people behave as they do. His assumptions reflect his value system and determine his practices and how he organizes for decision making and action.

It may be useful to check our own assumptions against the following:

Theory X:

1. The average human being has an inherent dislike of work and will avoid it if he can – he is naturally lazy.
2. Because of the human characteristic of dislike of work, most people must be coerced, controlled, directed, threatened with punishment to get them to put forth adequate effort toward the achievement of organizational objectives.
3. The average human being prefers to be directed, wishes to avoid responsibility, has relatively little ambition, wants security above all.

Theory Y: (These are the basic assumptions underlying community development as an approach to working with people couched in modern management concepts).

1. The expenditure of physical and mental effort in work is as natural as play or rest.

394 Section 7: Application & Analysis

2. External control and the threat of punishment are not the only means for bringing about effort toward organizational objectives. Man will exercise self-direction and self-control in the services of objectives to which he is committed.
3. Commitment to objectives is related to the rewards associated with their achievement.
4. The average human being learns, under proper conditions, not only to accept but to seek responsibility.
5. The capacity to exercise a relatively high degree of imagination, ingenuity, and creativity in the solution of organizational objectives is widely, not narrowly, distributed in the population.
6. Under the conditions of modern industrial life, the intellectual potentialities of the average human being are only partially utilized.

The need is not so much to choose up sides as to which theory is 'right' but to make our assumptions about human behavior more explicit and to check how well our own behavior reflects our assumptions. Theory Y is more dynamic than X, more optimistic about the possibility for human growth and development, more concerned with self-direction and self-responsibility, more consistent with available social science knowledge.

Theory X or Theory Y would influence how we organize for decision making and action. If we accept Theory X, then it would make sense to have:

One-way communication – telling
Strategy planning by the top leaders only
Decision making at the top level only
A handing down of decisions to be implemented by middle management
A handing down of instructions to be carried out by the workers (Nothing goes up except reports).

Theory Y would make it worthwhile to have:
Two-way communication
Involvement in goal setting, planning, and decision making at each level (NTL, pp. 36-7).

'In getting the job done, the amount of influence a manager exerts over subordinates, is determined by how much he allows himself to be influenced by them' (Bell, 1971).

It is the management style which recognizes this fact that is most likely to encourage developmental attitudes.

The management style has implications both for how administration (a) manages staff; (b) manages money and materials which constitute their program. The good manager causes things to happen – the traditional administrator manages things that happen. What we do here, close to home, under our noses, will be reflected in what we expect our workers to do 'out there' and vice versa.

Community-Development Strategy

It would be difficult to define a community-development strategy. Effective strategy has many facets, depending on a number of factors related particularly to the point of development at which a community is. There are many strategy models. There is the conflict and/or the conflict-reconciliation model. There is an information-communication model being developed. Some agencies approach community development through adult education. Economic development forms the base for another model. Other models emphasize manpower development. Some regard social animation as a model in itself. There are many types of social-action models identified largely by the strategy or strategies employed.

Regardless of the model or combination of models used in any situation, the one essential feature of a development strategy is people-power. People achieve power through education (enlightenment), organization, resources, and leadership. Governments and other sponsoring and/or supportive agencies can assist in people-development by:
1. keeping people informed and enlightened through providing effective information, adult or community education, and communication systems with provision for feedback as well as information dissemination;
2. recognizing and assisting in the development of organization;
3. giving people access to government technical and financial resources. In a day of mass media, communication, public sympathy for peoples' movements, and access to other than government resources, the most that government jurisdictions can do is to prolong the inevitable. These jurisdictions are no longer in full control of what goes on in their backyards;
4. providing opportunity for leadership development.

It seems essential, therefore, that regardless of what else

community-development effort is about, it must be oriented to the mobilization of people for action.

FREEMAN H. COMPTON is currently Special Adviser in Social Development to the Assistant Deputy Minister of Research, Planning and Development in the Manitoba Department of Mines, Resources and Environmental Management.

He was a student at St. Francis Xavier University in Antigonish, Nova Scotia. For twelve years he was with the Newfoundland Co-operative Movement, six years as a co-operative extension worker and six years as Director of Co-operative Extension Services for the province. Prior to that, he was a teacher in Newfoundland.

In 1961 he joined the Northern Administration branch of the federal Department of Northern Affairs as that department's first Community Assistance Officer. A year later he joined the Manitoba community-development program as a community-development worker in The Pas, and from 1963-8 was Director of Community Development Services for Manitoba.

In 1965 he was awarded a Nuffield Travel Fellowship and used it to study community development and extension methods with Dr. T. R. Batten at the University of London.

From 1968-70 he was Director of Programme Consultation Services with the Manitoba Department of Health and Social Services.

Practice-Research in Social Development

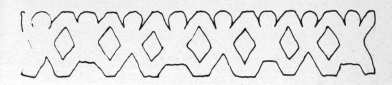

John Frei

1.0 Introduction

This article tries to present a review of some of the most important ideas of several of the more significant contemporary so-
cial-scientists, and to pull together, in a meaningful way, a few
of their very different approaches to the phenomena of change,
with the hope that subsequently we will be able to understand
them better, and to formulate a theory of practice-research
serving societal development. It seems that only this kind of
dynamic attitude and comprehension can provide the insight
necessary to cope effectively with our complex, post-industrial
society and its problems.

For the purpose of this paper, societal development includes
the methods of 'community organization', 'community development', 'community action', 'social action', 'social animation', etc. Because of the complexity of the field and its dynamics, research in these areas is still at the beginning of its
formulation and evolution.

Basically, societal development deals with the present social
meta-problems and their sub-systems at various levels of societal organization. Complex systems of interdependent social
structures and feelings are heterogeneous, volatile, and difficult
to identify and measure. In this setting the classical methods of
well-structured academic or sociological research, which tend
to formulate general laws, seem to be neither suitable nor satisfactory. In fact they are often in conflict with the flexibility

required for successful change-oriented action. This conflict extends from theory into practice.

Freeman and Sherwood (1965), who studied several community-based programs funded either by the federal government or by the Ford Foundation in the U.S., confirm the need for the accumulation of experience and for better understanding of the environment in which researchers have to work, and agree that such work suffers from considerable, almost day-to-day change, and that the classical independent-dependent variable model of research does not fit such a complex situation. In spite of this, however, they maintain that the social-science researcher must insist on the development of an 'impact model' that is based on theory, logically interrelating a 'set of principles and procedures with desired outcomes'. Such a model should be the basis of action for the practitioner, and should enable him to formulate programs and even to make 'practical decisions about day-to-day program situations'. They state that:

> ... unless the social science researcher participates, *indeed leads* (author's emphasis) the dialogue and bargaining required for the development of an impact model – *including the identification of goals* (author's emphasis), the description of input-output variables, and the elaboration of a rationale that specifies the relationship between input variables and goals – these tasks are likely to remain undone. Once the impact model is formulated, the researcher must continue to remain within the environment, like a snarling watch dog, ready to oppose alterations in program and procedures that could render his evaluation efforts useless (p. 16).

Consideration of this model description suggests a serious problem arising for the practitioner: how to reconcile its rigidity with the principle of the participation of people in the community in the development action, participation that leads inevitably to changes, not only in the 'procedures' or process, but possibly even in the goals of action.

For this reason Brooks (1965) opposed the Freeman-Sherwood model and introduced the principle of the necessity of continuous feedback of research findings into the action programs, which, in turn, produce adjustments and improvements in their operation. This, of course, requires flexibility in the methodology of the action process, and is contrary to the Freeman-Sherwood thesis.

Weinberg (1967), who evaluated the Youth Training and Employment Project, East Los Angeles, came to similar conclusions:

> It was impossible to be inventive, flexible and expedient on the one hand and at the same time do careful, scientific, controlled research on the other (p. 198).

Marris and Rein (1967) see the dilemma in the difference between an interest in action and experimental research. Research cannot interpret the present until it knows the answers to its ultimate questions, whereas action cannot foresee what questions to ask until it has interpreted the present. They finally came to the conclusion that experimental research and action aimed at benefitting the community are incompatible. Instead of experiment, they recommend exploration and imaginative serial analysis, the results of which can be rapidly communicated and applied to adjustment of the action. To minimize the lack of precision, they also recommend breaking down the action into a series of steps, making it possible to revise the action program of the next step as the previous step is completed. This conforms with Warren's theory (1963) of episodic community planning and action.

2.0 The Concept of Societal Development

Before exploring the possibilities of practice-research design and function in societal development, let us discuss the function of this development. It is, in reality, a composite of functions characterized by *change*, a movement from an existing state to a new one, which, in turn, includes a social-learning process as well as, in most cases, a change in the attitudes or even the values of the system involved, or of its sub-systems. In nature, systems tend to resist change, and the change process generates stress, which has to be overcome before the change can take place.

Several theories describing and explaining this process can be suggested.

Selye (1956) developed his theory of stress (of change) based on studies of biological systems which tend to maintain equilibrium or homeostasis. When any kind of stressor (any substance strange to the system structure) is forced into the system, it results in either a Local (in a sub-system) or a General (in the whole system) Adaptation Syndrome, which sparks action within the system (or its sub-system) aiming at elimination of the stressor. The symptom of stress can be an increased temperature, a swelling, or any other physical change produced by this action. In this process the system's homeostasis is disrupted until the action succeeds in eliminating the stressor and the system re-establishes its homeostasis or, if the stress is too powerful for even the whole system, death follows. Selye's theory can be applied in principle even to social systems.

The Cooks (1960), however, developed a special theory for social systems of 'emergents'. According to this theory, if such a system (tending also to maintain stability) is subjected to the stress of change, new events or conditions arise (called emergents) that help the system to overcome the stress and regain equilibrium.

Ashby (Ashby & Frank, 1967) conceived another theory which is important for our discussion: that of the step-function of social systems. He considers them to be composed of a number of sub-systems, each of which has its range of fluctuation. When stress is applied, some of the sub-systems can absorb the stress and enable the system to maintain its stability. When, however, one or more of the sub-systems are forced to start operating under stress beyond their normal range of variability, the whole system undergoes a 'step-function' and shifts to a 'new track' of operation.

Finally, we should consider Hardin's theory (1968) of a homeostatic plateau limited by two boundaries within which conditions of the system can change according to a laissez-faire principle and maintain stability. Should the system tend to work beyond the boundary limits either on its positive or negative side, it cannot establish homeostasis and cannot survive.

It is suggested that combining these four theories in a model of societal development can serve as a base for the possible identification of the role and function of research in this development. The assumptions for the construction of this model are that social systems change in repeated steps, alternating with stable periods as they compete or co-operate with each other and as they adjust to the turbulence of the environment in which they operate. Furthermore, the homeostatic plateau of our society of which the systems are a part is a fairly wide one, which enables the progression or regression of development from a lower to a higher state or vice versa.

We can also assume that even this plateau can move within the general ecological field of human societies, and does so continually and progressively in episodic and orderly steps as long as societal reformation takes place, and in abrupt, disordered, and extensive step-functions should revolutionary change occur.

The proposed general model is composed of repeated step models, each of them based on Selye's General Adaptation Model (fig. 1) with the addition of the theories of Cooks and Ashby. From a balanced (homeostatic) state of the step, the system tension curve moves into the rising stage of stress caused by introduced change stimulus followed by a period of adjustment that often modifies the requirements of the original stimulus (compromise), and reaches a new equilibrium (homeostasis) on a higher (or lower) level of well-being. This ends the 'step', or 'episode' in the development, and the equilibrium lasts until the next change stimulus attacks the system, leading to another step process.

A system of such steps (fig. 2) represents the dynamics of societal development, and a curve joining the periods of equilibrium (homeostasis) of the system shows the resulting process movement.

The feasibility of this model seems to be supported by:

2.1 Selye's model of the General Adaptation Syndrome accepted today as a scientific demonstration of the process of change caused by the introduction of a stressor into a biological organism (Selye, 1956);

2.2 Etzioni's theory of Mixed-Scanning in Decision-Making, according to which the contextuating, or fundamental, long-range-planning decisions are made from 'bit' (or item) decisions, made 'incrementally' (piecemeal), but within the context set by the fundamental decisions (Etzioni, 1968);

2.3 Lippit et al's theory that the process of change does not develop continually but in 'spurts' (steps) of learning, separated by longer periods of apparent stability, needed to gain insight, integration of the learning, and reorganization of the system (Lippit, Watson, & Wesley, 1958);

2.4 Lewin's theory of quasi-stationary equilibrium (similar, in broad terms, to Hardin's theory of homeostatic plateau), the levels of which can be changed by social forces (stressors) changing social habits in three steps – unfreezing their present level, moving to the new level, and freezing this new level (Lewin, 1962);

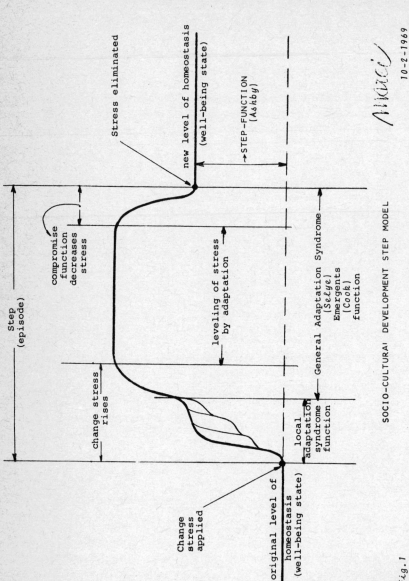

SOCIO-CULTURAL DEVELOPMENT STEP MODEL

Fig. 1

10-2-1969

SOCIO CULTURAL DEVELOPMENT

PROCESS MODEL

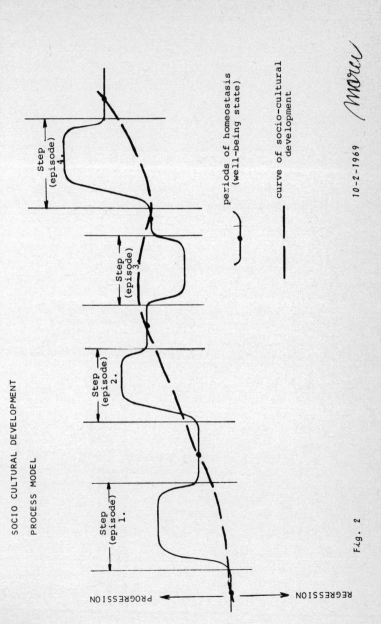

Fig. 2

2.5 Homans's Equilibrium Model in which the relationship of parts and the interplay of dynamic social forces in a system (group) cause the system to be sometimes in balance, sometimes out of balance, and in which the deviance from conformity is seen as an integral part of the system (Homans, 1950).

Within each step of our model, the process of societal development is influenced by the various community sub-systems involved in the process, and by repeated causal trains, or stimuli and responses of the cybernetic feedback, which activate the structure, thus enabling the achievement of the step-function and the acceptance and integration of the results of the social-learning process by the sub-systems. During this process, which is a give-and-take experience, the sub-systems, in accepting adjustment to the change, have also to adjust their structure or structural constraints. The whole process thus becomes a form-changing or morphogenic continuum.

3.0 Overview of Evaluative and Predictive Research Studies in Societal Development

The emphasis here is on the *process*. In such research we still lack experience. Lippit (1965) calls for more effort in its development:

> It has become clear that we have to develop new skills of retrieving and organizing research-based knowledge in such a way that it links to the need of social practitioners or client population – there is a necessary linkage function of helping practitioners work through the implications of new knowledge for specific models of practice and specific operational skills (p. 669).

Chin (1962) recommends organizing research used for decision, policy, or future situations, and utilizing some methods of psychometrics, another theory of games, in studying the effects of decisions based on predictions in social affairs. He also suggests the development of research of action programs aiming at the improvement of specific procedures, techniques, treatments, or interventions.

Kahn (1963) speaks about diagnostic or descriptive studies or exploratory and descriptive studies, with one of the objectives being to get an accurate picture of the dynamics of the process, which also would generate hypotheses for further studies and which could – combined with experiment – lead to predictions.

All these methods have to be considered in the framework of the episodic process development. As mentioned, Marris and Rein (1967) recommend reducing the unknown factors relevant to a decision on further steps in the action process by breaking this action down into a series of proximate steps that can be researched and that will make the rational choice among them much easier.

> The ultimate purpose can then be only vaguely, or even inconsistently stated, since it is no more than an indication of the general direction of the initial efforts, a justification of the appropriateness of the first steps. As it will be continually reinterpreted in the light of experience, a precise and inflexible definition of the ultimate goal would only be an encumbrance.... Action is tentative, non-committal, adaptive. It concentrates upon the next step, breaking the sequence into discrete, manageable decisions ... evolving the future out of present opportunities (pp. 204-6).

This is the philosophy that brings Marris and Rein to the suggestion that instead of rigid experimental research we should use the technique of exploration, an imaginative serial analysis that can be rapidly communicated and that can enable us to project its results into the formulation and planning of the next action steps. This method is valid both in the change process, the goal of which comes from within the community (typically: Ross & Lappin, 1967), and in purposive-change type of process, in which the ultimate goals are brought into the community by an outside change agent (Warren, 1965).

This process always contains, consciously or subconsciously, an evaluation of the process-continuum, of its *past and present, as well as projections into the future*. At the same time, as Mills (1959) stated:

> Three kinds of interludes – on problems, methods, theory – ought to come out of the work ... and lead to it again; they should be shaped by work-in-progress and to some extent guide that work (p. 198).

This leads to new (repeated) diagnoses. According to Lippit (1965),

> The principles which govern the transformation of diagnostic insight into change goals and intentions are a very prominent part of theory of planned change. . . . Perhaps the most common single source of failure in change efforts is the difficulty of converting information about a given problem into strategic and tactical projections of what should be done about it (pp. 258-9).

To this purpose, Chombart de Lauwe (1964) recommends controlled observation, action process, group discussion, and their evaluation, and use of successive hypotheses and syntheses. Observation can be, alternatively, indirect, from documents pertaining to the action process.

Biddle and Biddle (1965) developed, from practical experience, their research model, in which the important role is performed by the citizen group, which sets both the action and research design. Their model combines action and research into a continuous evaluation and adjustment of the process, with action periods followed by evaluation and by new decisions leading to new actions, etc. This model is worth studying and, with adjustments, possibly adopting.

In all the different methods of this process-evaluation type of research, *recording* has an important function, as it can become the basis for the analysis and evaluation of the past and present, as well as for projection into the future or anticipation of the process development. This seems to be more and more accepted as a valid research technique.

Merton (1962) speaks about the post-factum social interpretation of events and states that the

> . . . procedure in which the observations are at hand and the interpretations are subsequently applied to the data has the logical structure of clinical inquiry. The observations may be case-history or statistical in character. The defining characteristic of this procedure is the introduction of the interpretation *after* the observations have been made rather than empirical testing of a pre-designated hypothesis (p. 93).

As a logical consequence of the episodic or step structure of the societal development process, evaluative and predictive studies and research into the individual steps are essential for guidance and evaluation of the results of the process, and should be built into each intervention project design as an indispensable component.

Chin (1962) recommends the development of a systematic body of principles and theory through research for the building and testing of the practitioners' theory of change. In Shyne's terms:

The process of social work intervention has been sorely neglected in social work research because it is the most difficult dimension to study (p. 770).

This statement, of course, is of importance not only to social work, but to all professions that intervene today in societal development.

How, then, should we plan, in this complex process, to use the various research methods that are at present available to us?

4.0 Practice-Research Problems

First, let us explore the roles of the practitioner in the societal development process. Sanders (1964) identified them in his model of professional roles in planned change and intervention as those of: *analyst*, in which the practitioner has to research the problem; *planner*, in which he projects the results of the research analysis into a plan of action; *organizer for change*, when he begins implementing the plan through preparation and then initiation of the action process; *program administrator*, when he directs the operations. These roles are more or less clearly identifiable in all change activities, even though they are not all necessarily performed by the same professional.

Complications arise when we consider the episodic or step nature of the societal development process that aims at the solution of a given problem. In such cases we can assume that the original "analyst" role at the outset of the process has to include first the social study of the systems involved and, second, the analysis of the problems and conditions that can initiate the action in the first episode (step) of the developmental process. Similar distinctions could be assumed for the 'planner' and 'organizer' roles, which deal with the process of development or change, and especially for the role of the 'program administrator', in all of which relevant and well-organized research elements are essential but are largely still missing.

It is necessary to stress that we have in mind operational

research focussing on the process, its development, changes, methods, and techniques. Such research can be done in 're-search bits' following, and/or preceding, individual action epi-sodes or stages, in which the functions proposed by Sanders can, or have to be, repeated.

If we consider Sanders' identification of roles a feasible, and, in practice, a validated model; if we accept the thesis that there is an urgent need to apply a scientific approach to the problems of societal development, and, finally, if we accept as a basic principle that, in the change process, concern for the people involved, and not mere sociological or clinical curiosity should be the basis for any research introduced, the following practice-research methods are indicated.

4.1 For The Analyst's Role

After identification of the developmental problems, the re-search work pertinent to this role should be fact-finding and evaluation, with the possible steps of:

4.1.1 Gathering of demographic data concerning the area of intervention;

4.1.2 Gathering of results of available studies or surveys, or doing the necessary research in general problems pertinent to the developmental situation in the area of intervention. This may be, for example, studies or surveys of the influence of physical planning on the social life of families and individuals; of transportation and its influence on changes in the inner city and suburbs; of development of income and purchasing-power of citizen groups in similar areas; identification of the needs of the population in the intervention area or in other, similar areas; identification of existing citizen groups and of the degree of their participation in decision-making in such areas, etc.,

4.1.3 Gathering information and describing experiences gained in other activities in similar environments aiming at similar goals, even those where no research was involved;

4.1.4 Studies or surveys of specific problems and conditions existing at the outset of the intervention process in the action area and its population, in the frame of reference of the goals proposed by the population and/or the change agent (e.g., gen-eral ecology, social pathology, etc.);

4.1.5 Gathering of information and data about existing services and resources systems at the local, municipal, regional, provin-cial (state), and federal levels available or accessible from the local level for the purposes of the intervention;

4.1.6 Analysing and evaluating the collected data as to their relevance and importance for the purpose of planning the intervention;

4.1.7 Recording of all the gathered facts and information, and organization of their filing in preparation for use at any time in further planning analysis.

4.2 For the Planner's Role

4.2.1 Based on the results of the analyst's research, organizing, if necessary, additional fact-finding or research to fill the gaps in the information pattern that appears in the analysis and evaluation necessary for successful planning of the specific intervention;

4.2.2 Preparing a summary of the data and information, and making it available to the workers and people involved in the development of the intervention plans on the local, neighbourhood, or municipal level (councils, citizen groups, change agents, population in general);

4.2.3 Participating as closely as possible in the development of intervention plans and actions as an observer and, if asked by the change agents, as an expert, to gain understanding of the function of planning in the intervention process;

4.2.4 Establishing close relationships and co-operation with the workers and/or leaders of the planned action, to gain acceptance by them and to work out with them successively the design of practice-research bits that will support the action process and its steps. The objectives should be to enable better and easier decisions concerning the alternatives emerging in this process to be made, and to gather data and experience gained by the change agents (citizens and workers involved), thus building a body of knowledge emerging from this process;

4.2.5 Organizing as soon as possible a small but representative committee, including the citizens and workers, that would advise and possibly direct the process of the research work.

4.3 For the Organizer-of-Change's and the Program Administrator's Roles

The practice-researcher's work, and his help to the change agents responsible for the intervention action in the community, are very delicate functions that must be considered *secondary*, or supplementary, to the intervention action itself, which has to be the *primary* or leading function in the process. The research work should therefore never block or disturb the action, but should be a tool enabling its enhancement.

This principle requires flexibility in design and methodology. No rigid design of a long-lasting research can be accepted. The principle should be to follow the action process; to register its steps and their outcome; to analyse the decisions forming the bases of the individual action steps; to evaluate repeatedly the past steps in the process, and its present situation, and to propose to the change agents, based on this evaluation, the alternatives for the immediate future episodes or steps of the action process.

In this work the practice-researcher often has to undertake partial research actions that rapidly produce facts and information necessary for the timely orientation of the change agents so that they can reach better and safer decisions in the next episodes of the action process.

Both the research design and methods must be carried out in steps following the episodes of the action process, and can, therefore, consist of a number of separate research actions, or bits, forming a research pattern helping the change agents in their intervention actions, and, when summarized, analysed, and evaluated, giving an insight into the total intervention process that could lead to generalization.

Such practice-research has to take into consideration the available theories of action processes; record synoptically the studied process, its episodes and steps; include successively suitable other theories and/or develop its own theories fitting the process episodes and steps; repeatedly analyse, compare, and evaluate the effectiveness of such theories in the light of the results of the individual episodes in the action process and of its final results.

The scope of such practice-research will vary according to the scope of the intervention action, its goals, and its individual episodes and steps. However, even a fairly simple intervention should include at least some of the research functions described above.

Wherever possible, some measurement techniques should be included to evaluate the effectiveness of the intervention action.

5.0 Practice-Research Methods

Various kinds of research techniques can be used in the practice-research and its research bits, depending on the development of the intervention action. In the first stages, there is a need for fact-finding and descriptive research, later for evaluative and predictive studies, and, finally, some measurement of results should be undertaken.

5.1 Descriptive and Exploratory Studies and Surveys

These studies and surveys have to help in the formulation of the problem, in the finding of facts which form the basis of the intervention steps, and for the planning and decision-making regarding action. The emphasis is on helping the dynamic action process. Therefore the practice-research at this stage cannot use long, time-consuming studies and complex surveys requiring elaborate instruments. Short and precise studies with clearly defined objectives and/or simple, short-term surveys with a minimum number of instrument questions are indicated. The time limitations should be fully respected.

The various techniques of this type of research, as described above, may have to be repeated during the following stages (episodes, steps) of the development process, as the need for additional data or revision of the originally gathered data arises. Such research steps can become very important for the development of new theories, as the process of intervention is basically a social-learning process. They can spark formation of new, generally valid action models, methodology, and techniques of the intervention process.

5.2 Measurement and Evaluative Studies and Surveys

The most difficult problem of social work, as well as of other professions in the field of societal development, is the lack of a positive yardstick with which to measure the effects of intervention. Various methods are being used and tested: the survey, the field of experiment studies, occasionally the classic experiment; the case study and records' evaluation; projective techniques applied in the evaluation of case movement, etc. Few of the methods used, whether of the inquiry or observation type, can be accepted as fully satisfactory, and then only in specific cases.

Kogan (1963) defined the problem of measurement as assigning symbols to things or to the properties of things according to specified rules and operations. In societal development, some emerging items or events are of a physical or economic nature and can be measured in generally accepted standard units of different kinds. Others are of a psychological or sociological nature, and their measurement is and can be done basically only through the use of judgment. Theory of scales enables us to select and use scales from the 'all-or-none' type to the ordinal and multi-dimensional type with many ranks and factors. Generally, the use of practitioner judgments, according to MacDonald (1958) are called for when objective data are inadequate.

Ideally, the effect of societal development interventions should be evaluated by field-experiment studies, by comparing the changes occurring in the action population with a control population of similar characteristics during a determined period of time. Such experiments, however, have to be built into the intervention or action programs at its outset, and tend, therefore, to disrupt the process by their rigidity, as was discussed in the introduction to this paper. Exceptions can be observed when the field experiment is used to validate a result of an intervention at the end of its developmental process, through repeating the same action with a similar population.

If it is not possible or desirable to include the experiment in the intervention program, or to repeat the action after the results become apparent, a survey method can be used to find out what has happened, and to whom. In many cases, a survey before and after the action is used even in an experiment. A survey (with an interview schedule) is not an ideal method of measuring the effect or results of a societal-development intervention. It can be used with success and without involvement of judgment in a follow-up of change in measurable facts of a physical or economic nature. As soon as it has to measure feelings of any kind, judgment is immediately involved. The design of the interview schedule or instrument is difficult, and very often its difficulties are underestimated. The questions that are included have to be selected and formulated very carefully, to eliminate those that are not pertinent to or necessary for the clarification and measurement of the issues studied.

Open-ended questions can lead to misunderstanding and biased responses. Responses to questions trying to clarify or verify deep-seated psychological states or problems have to be considered very cautiously, as people tend to reply to such questions readily and truthfully if the cause of such states or problems is external to them and to the group (family) in which they live, but do not respond readily and truthfully if the cause is internal.

Other problems to be considered when survey methods are used are: the influence of the interviewer on the quality of responses; the projection of his biases; the interpretation of the open-ended questions to the interviewee; the lack of relationship needed for sincere responses to difficult or embarrassing questions. Can instrument-testing and training of interviewers eliminate these problems? What is the influence of the analysis in evaluation of the responded instruments, especially in the case of open-ended questions, where personal judgment was involved? These problems are not new. They are common to all empirical-research efforts.

Mills (1959) expressed his experience as follows:

> ... no-one, regardless of skill, can obtain, in a twenty-minute or even a day-long interview, the kinds of depth materials which we know, from the most skilled and prolonged interviews, are to be gotten. Nor is to possible to obtain by the usual sort of sample survey the kind of information – which we know is available from studies properly oriented to history (p. 70).

Woolins (1963) evaluated the use of the survey as follows:

> ...descriptive survey is started which seeks to find out what has happened and to whom. When this information becomes available, the focus shifts to: 'What was done?' or 'Why did it happen?' Then the descriptive survey with its broad sweep and relatively shallow inquiry becomes inadequate; case studies and experimental studies usually follow (p. 252).

The author's experience seems to confirm this criticism of the use of the survey. A suggestion is to use the survey with caution and to limit its scope to only those issues that are directly tied to the evaluated events.

Questionnaires sent by mail can be used with fair results for verification of clearly formulated problems. The number of questions should be as limited as possible, and questions should be put in the simplest and clearest possible language. Questions concerning feelings in this case have even greater limitations than in the interview survey.

Generally, for measuring the effect of social-work intervention, Woolins (1963) recommends the use of a combination of methods (survey, experiment, case study):

> ... each providing information which clearly described the

subject, the stimulus, and the result, and shows their relationship to one another (p. 251).

The problem of measurement, and evaluation of societal intervention can be compared, at present, to an iceberg. We perceive only a very small part of it. Very much will have to be done, especially in the development of measurement methods, before we are able to discover and clarify its as yet unexplored ramifications.

In speaking about the methodological problems of change, and of obtaining reliable data for measuring it, Lippit *et al* (1958) stated:

> Setting aside for a moment the problems of measuring change, we still find many difficulties in the way of obtaining any kind of measurement for these variables. What, for example – is a good measure of mental health? ... Can mental health be measured by verbal instruments, calibrating, so to speak, the words which the individual uses about himself and his world?
>
> ... Similar questions can be asked about groups, organizations, and communities. What do we need to know about them in order to make the relevant social and psychological evaluations, and how can this information be obtained?
>
> The crux of the problem is that many social-psychological variables are internal-process phenomena, without clear external symptoms, causing difficult measurement problems. Attempts to redefine them in terms of public symptoms for measurement may reassure the researcher but they do not alter the nature of the subjective experience (pp. 262-64).

This statement must not discourage us in our future work. We have to accept the present limitations of this kind of research, and, by using the best of our creativity and skill, try successively to eliminate them.

Herzog (1959) can be quoted here to encourage us to do so.

> ... Don't be afraid of unpretentious research. Better be simple, clear and forthright about limitations than to employ techniques more ambitious than the data warrant (p. 83).

This is how we have to begin. However, we have to promote and practise the development of more sophisticated research of this type, because it can become one of the most important instruments in the solution of our present and future complex societal problems.

6.0 Dilemma of Practice-Research

Practice-research as described above will often result, of necessity, in a conflict between the exact, scientific, knowledge-enhancement thinking of a scientist following, identifying, and verifying facts, and the artistic thinking of the practitioner, using with sensitivity, tact, and diplomacy, himself and his personality set-up and feelings to relate to the change actors to help them gain insight, and sometimes to change their motivation, attitudes, habits, and even values.

The combination of both, the scientific knowledge and the artistic traits of the practitioner, develops skill, which is an ability to use both of them in a delicately balanced way to achieve the goals of the societal change. An equation can be proposed:

$$(\text{Knowledge} + \text{Art}) = \text{Skill}$$

in which, if Knowledge $>$ Art, or Art $>$ Knowledge, the result is lopsided skill, causing problems in its application in practice. Either we see cool rigidity of theory prevailing over empathy and making the establishment of human relationships difficult or impossible, or emotional involvement, possibly resulting in our losing sight of facts and conditions important for the successful attainment of action goals.

If we accept this thesis, we can suggest that:

6.1 Special education should be directed towards the development of social-work practitioners, to motivate and sensitize them to understand this problem and learn how to balance knowledge and art in practice, so as to be able to direct both the research and action processes in societal development.

6.2 Special research workers should be trained, who would accept this thesis and design and direct their research efforts towards combining scientific principles with practice-science flexibility to enable the practitioners to perform successfully their change-action role.

Finally, the work in the field of societal development is so complex that no single profession can hope to master it alone. The interdependence of the numerous open systems in the societal matrix forces us to accept and practice interprofessional co-operation, without which we cannot succeed.

7.0 Summary

Research in societal development is still at the beginning of its development. Conflicts arise between the scientifically rigid researcher and the action-flexible practitioner, when long-term research designs are built into action programs. To enable better understanding of the societal-development field, a model of it is proposed, dividing its process into episodes or steps (based on several validated and/or accepted biological and sociological theories), following a curve of general development. This, in turn, can move from one level to another when the whole field is limited by boundaries of a homeostatic plateau which itself can change both its span and direction in the general ecological field. Each step is analysed as to the stresses or forces that arise in it when change stimulus or a stressor is applied. This model can help in partializing the process into sections which, as suggested, could be more easily researched.

The research efforts in societal development have to follow the process and its episodes. Research here should be a secondary function, helping the primary function of intervention in societal development. Analysis of such research has been presented, adjusted to the roles of the change agents and using practice-research bits undertaken to furnish facts and information necessary for decisions on further intervention episodes.

This type of research, emphasizing the process study, is not yet sufficiently developed, but some existing methods could be applied in it; measurement and evaluation of results can utilize many of the existing methods and techniques based on the use of judgment, although they are still in the process of development. It is suggested that the problem of conflict between the research and practice requirements in the action process be seen in the light of a combination of knowledge and art concepts. These must be delicately balanced in order that both may be productive in enhancing sociocultural development. There is a need for the training of specialists, practitioners, and researchers for this field, and for acceptance and use of a multi-professional approach.

JOHN W. FREI is presently the Executive Director of the Social Planning Council of Metropolitan Toronto. He emigrated from Czechoslovakia in 1951 and became a Canadian citizen in 1956. He received a

Doctor of Law degree from Charles University, Prague. In Canada he has studied administration, executive training, psychology and vocational guidance at Sir George Williams University in Montreal. He received his Master of Social Work from McGill University.

Mr. Frei has lectured in the School of Engineering at Charles University. In addition, he has been a lecturer in the McGill University School of Social Work, l'Université de Montréal Ecole de Service Sociale, and the School of Social Work and the Department of Urban and Regional Planning at the University of Toronto.

In Europe Mr. Frei has had wide experience in engineering, commerce, and law. In Canada he has worked in construction and planning engineering. He has been a member of such organizations as the Canadian Association of Social Workers, and the Canadian Council of Social Development as well as the society of Automotive Engineers, New York. He has also been Past-President of the Quebec Welfare Council.

Community Action and Learning: A Concept Analysis

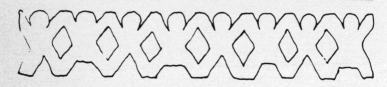

Coolie Verner

Every new field of social practice encounters difficulties in finding terminology to designate the phenomena with which it is concerned. The physical and natural sciences are apt to create a new language, but the social sciences use common words that are associated with the specific phenomena identified. This practice inhibits precise scientific communication in the social sciences because of the many variations in meaning that collect around words in common usage (Wootton, 1950, pp. 12-14). The social phenomena to which words are attached as terms are often imprecisely identified at the time the term is applied so that several discrete phenomena may be identified by a single term. Conversely, a number of different words and phrases may be used to identify a single phenomenon in the initial period of identification. Such is the situation with respect to the idea of community development where two discrete concepts – action and development – are equated and variously identified by the terms 'community development', 'community action', 'community improvement', 'community organization', 'social action', or other similar phrases. It is the purpose of this paper to examine the concepts of development and action to differentiate between a process of community change on the one hand and a process of learning how to instigate such change on the other.[1]

Organization

Every social grouping has some structure that defines the relationship among the members of the group and provides the organization through which group functions are achieved. The form and complexity of this structure will depend upon the size of the social grouping, which may vary from a family to a tribe or from a community to a society. The structure of larger units is traditionally referred to as 'social organization' (e.g. Firth, 1967), while the term 'community organization' originally referred to the analysis of the social structure of the community (Cooley, 1919). Both terms represent static concepts that are descriptive of a situation or structure as it existed at a given moment in time within the social unit described.

Some initial confusion was created when the descriptive term 'community organization' became attached to a process designed to achieve a particular pattern of organization within a community for some special purpose (Steiner, 1925; Fitzgerald, 1948; McMillan, 1945). Further confusion resulted from the inclusion of the concept 'action' as an integral part of community organization defined as a process. Fortunately, this use of 'community organization' is no longer popular and the term is reverting to its original meaning. The notion of 'action' that is currently in favour has created a new sort of confusion, which needs clarification.

Action

Deliberate and planned change may occur at several different levels within the structure of a community, and each level of action represents a different degree of involvement of the members of the community in the action program. In codifying the potential levels of action no attempt is made to ascribe values to the action at this point, since the value assigned to action will relate to the nature of the change as well as to the process through which the change is accomplished. The general value-orientation of a society will determine the specific value attached to the form of the action and to the structural level at which it occurs. Thus, a community imbued with the democratic process will reject changes of an authoritarian nature originating at the individual level, while one not so conditioned will accept such changes as the normal course of events.

The levels of potential action in a community are as follows:

1. Individual Level

Change may be initiated and carried out by a single individual without reference to other members of a community even though they may be affected significantly by it. This may occur in a community with a pyramidal power structure, such as that dominated by a political boss or a corporate manager in a wholly owned single-industry town. Such power for action may derive legitimately from ownership, as in the case of the mine manager in a wholly owned mining-town, or it may result from feelings of powerlessness or apathy on the part of citizens in a situation where the political boss is dominant. In either situation, the individual inducing the change is acting in an authoritarian manner which contributes to the deterioration of democratic values.

2. Small-Group Level

A few individuals working together may initiate change in a community on some matter of particular concern to that group. Small-group action appears to be growing more frequent at the moment in an attempt to counteract the feeling of individual powerlessness that is a product of a mass society. Neighbourhood groups may attempt to prevent some local civic change or an interest group may attempt to block a proposed law, but whatever the motivation, small-group action is rarely successful in accomplishing the desired change unless it is directly meaningful to larger segments of the community.

3. Sub-Organization Level

This level is similar to the preceding except that the proposed change is legitimized by representing (in theory at least) the approbation of an established group in the community. In this case, change is initiated within and for an organization by a sub-unit of that organization, as in the case of a municipal planning department acting for government. The ultimate success of action initiated at this level depends more upon the importance and power of the parent organization than upon the significance of the proposed change to the community.

4. Organization Level

A single unit within a community may initiate some change perceived to be important to the community. The unit may be a voluntary association or local government. In general, this is the level at which most successful community change is initiated. The success of the action depends upon the power of the organization, as in the case of government, or the ability of the organization to move the action to the next level, as in the case of voluntary associations.

5. Multi-Organizational Level

Except in special circumstances, a voluntary association rarely succeeds in bringing about change unless it wins the support of other community associations. It is at this level that much non-governmental action is successfully accomplished, but the problems associated with co-ordination and the development of common interests sometimes inhibit action at this level (Verner, 'The Structure of Community Adult Education', 1962, pp. 23-28). Action is almost never initiated at this level because of the difficulties of reaching agreement among diverse organizations.

6. Community Level

Change is brought about at this level when the community acts as a social unit. Consequently this is the only level at which community action can occur. This is the only level in the community structure at which all segments of the community have an equal opportunity and responsibility to participate in the change program. Not all members of the community may become involved in the action, but all must share the responsibility for the action.

7. Pan-Community Level

Change may be initiated and concluded by forces external to the community. Such changes may affect the local community significantly, but the local level rarely influences the change. National organizations or regional, provincial, or national governments are usually the sources of changes at this level. Neither social action nor community action occurs at this level.

Social and Community Action

There is a variety of different kinds of action to produce change that may be found in a community, but the concern here is with those actions that involve community members in producing change deemed desirable in the community. Action programs leading to changes that affect a community and that are initiated and carried out, by segments of the community constitute 'social action'. Thus, attempts to solve a community problem by a single organization in the community is social action. On the other hand, 'community action' is a process of change conceived and carried out by a community acting as a discrete social unit. While community action can occur only at the community level (level 5), social action may occur at any subordinate level (i.e., levels 2 through 5). Because social action is the most common source of planned change, it is sometimes misconstrued to be community action.

This differentiation between social and community action may imply that one is more valuable than the other when, in fact, it only identifies the position of the action in the structure of the community. Any values attached to action are external to the level at which the action occurs. The specific changes resulting from community action are not necessarily more valuable to a community than those achieved through social action in so far as only the change itself is concerned.

Community Development

Community action is distinguished from community development as the product is differentiated from the skill that produced it. Community development is an adult-education method through which members of a community learn to manage the action process in a setting of reality while dealing with real problems. Action can and does occur in a community without community development, but community development will not occur without some action resulting. Because of the inevitable and continuing association between learning and action inherent in community development, the educational process leading to action is confused with the action itself. Community development can be related either to social action or to community action, but it is not the only educational method that produces the learning essential to deliberate and planned change in a community (Verner & Booth, 1964).

The learning with which community development is involved was first identified by Alexis de Tocqueville (1948) when he described the process of social and community action as he perceived it at that time:

... a citizen may conceive of some need which is not being met. What does he do? He goes across the street and discusses it with his neighbor. Then what happens? A committee comes into existence and then the committee begins functioning on behalf of that need, and you won't believe this but it is true. All of this is done without reference to any bureaucrat. All of this is done by the private citizens on their own initiative. (p. 191)

In 1921, Edouard Lindeman (1921, ch.9) systematized this occurrence that de Tocqueville described into ten steps, which he identified as follows:

STEPS IN COMMUNITY ACTION
It appears that there are certain definite steps which community groups pass through in arriving at points of action. The division of these steps, here attempted, is quite arbitrary, and should not be considered in a strictly scientific manner. Persons who have studied these summaries do not agree on the classification here used. Further study and analysis of a larger number of projects may change the classification materially.

A portion of these steps in community action are sociological, and some are psychological. There is no apparent means by which the sciences of sociology and of social psychology can be separated in this analysis.

STEP NUMBER ONE

Consciousness of need; some person, either within or without the community, expresses the need which is later represented by the definite project.

STEP NUMBER TWO

Spreading the consciousness of need; a leader, within some institution or group within the community, convinces his or her group, or a portion of the group, of the reality of the need.

STEP NUMBER THREE

Projection of consciousness of need; the group interested attempts to project the consciousness of need upon the leadership of the community; the consciousness of need becomes more general.

STEP NUMBER FOUR

Emotional impulse to meet the need quickly; some influential assistance is enlisted, in the attempt to arrive at a quick means of meeting the need.

STEP NUMBER FIVE

Presentation of other solutions; other means of meeting the need are presented.

STEP NUMBER SIX

Conflict of solutions; various groups lend their support to one or the other of the various solutions presented.

STEP NUMBER SEVEN

Investigation; it appears to be increasingly customary to pause at this point, and to investigate the project with expert assistance. (This step, however, is usually omitted and the following one takes its place.)

STEP NUMBER EIGHT

Open discussion of issue; a public mass meeting or gathering of some sort is held, at which the project is presented, and the groups with most influence attempt to secure adoption of their plans.

STEP NUMBER NINE

Integration of solutions; the various solutions presented are tested, with an effort to retain something out of each, in the practicable solution which is now emerging.

STEP NUMBER TEN

Compromise on basis of tentative progress; certain groups relinquish certain elements of their plans in order to save themselves from complete defeat, and the solution which results is a compromise with certain reservations. The means selected for meeting the need are not satisfactory to all groups, but are regarded as tentatively progressive.

The steps outlined by Lindeman indicate the range of specific learning-tasks that must be accomplished if the action program is to be successful. Individuals involved in community action must learn to manage the tasks at each stage in addition to learning how to proceed from one stage to the next. The learning involved in community development differs materially from that encountered in most adult-education activities, for the learning content is derived from and contributes to the community-action process. In this, community development illustrates Dewey's concept of learning by doing, and the learning is immediately useful and meaningful.

In some situations community action may develop independently, and the participants learn to manage the process by trial and error in a kind of community self-education (Ogden and Ogden, 1946). Through community development the element of chance in learning is reduced, because the management of the learning is directed by the adult educator so that the skill and knowledge necessary for community action can be acquired systematically and with greater efficiency.

Since community development is principally concerned with learning, the operation of the educational process is of greater importance than the community action which results from it. In other words, community development focusses attention upon what happens within an individual's consciousness to mould him into an intelligent, participating member of a democratic society (Lippitt, Watson, and Bruce, 1958). The specific change program, therefore, is the vehicle for learning to handle co-operative group study and action. Through such learning, individuals develop the skills that enable them to identify and solve community problems intelligently in ways appropriate to their specific community. In addition to the specific knowledge and skill associated with an action objective, participants are also acquiring values and learning to apply those values to the community-action process.

Action and Values

Community development is concerned with producing the kinds of group-learning experiences that will strengthen democracy and further the operation of the democratic process at the community level. Thus, the basic values of community development are *means*-oriented in that the way action occurs is more important than the specific change that results from the action. This concentration on the means is transmitted to the participants in community development so that the subsequent action-program is also concerned more with the means than with the result of the action. Thus, community development is involved not only with learning the skills of action, but also with establishing the appropriate value base for action (Batten, 1953).

Because it operates on a value system in which process is paramount, it is doubtful that community development can function in other than a democratic society. Even within a society in which the values of democracy are basic, community development cannot function unless it is free to establish such a value base in the community in which it operates. This accounts for the frequent failure of government-established community-development programs in which they are perceived as tools to accomplish a specified objective. Failure is inevitable in such circumstances because community development is process- rather than result-directed.

Social action can be distinguished from community action with respect to the basic value orientation of the action program. Social-action programs are almost always directed towards the achievement of some specific socially desirable objectives identified by the segment of the community conducting the action. In this case the process is of less importance than the results of the action; consequently, social-action programs are not specifically concerned with the education of participants. Community action, on the other hand, is processes-oriented and the education of participants in the management of co-operative action is equally important with the way in which the objective is achieved. Thus, if the education of community members in the ways of democracy is important, then community action may be assumed to have greater value for the community than does social action. When community development is a part of social action, its value to the community is enhanced.

The value base that undergirds community development as an educational process also determines the ultimate value of the objective achieved through community action. Since the objective of community action is set by those participating in it, that objective will be valuable for that community regardless of any other considerations. The ultimate objective is not the only value derived from community action, for the individuals involved also learn the ways of intelligent participation in community affairs. This not only strengthens local democracy, but also builds defences against intermittent or persistent authoritarianism in local government and organizations. Such authoritarianism develops in response to apathy or resistance, which grows out of the alienation of man in modern society. Apathy and resistance are indications that the methods and processes of change are defective, for as Kolb and Brunner (1949) note: 'The naive assumption that any group of persons will fall in with any plan about which they have not been consulted and which has not taken the social situation into account has been proved false so often in history that its survival is one of the world's mysteries' (p. 5).

Application

The precise identification of community development as a method of adult education distinct from the action that results, clarifies the role of the professional leader in community development, and provides a basis for systematic research into the educational process and the action process as two distinct phenomena.

1. Role Differentiation

By separating the learning process, which is community development, from the change program, which is community action, the role of professional leadership in community development is clarified. The community-development leader is concerned only with the design and management of a learning situation to insure that it achieves its objectives. In this role the leader is solely an adult educator. He has no role in the community-action process, as he is not involved directly in the action that results from community development.

The continuing interrelationship and interdependence of community development and community action makes it difficult for the leader of the learning process not to assume also the leadership of the action process. In order to function as an educator in the situation, he must retain objectivity and remain aloof from the action as it occurs. In other words, the leader can identify areas for study or analysis and insist upon the careful appraisal of decisions reached by the group, but he cannot himself propose solutions to problems or initiate action. Community development breaks down when its leader assumes that his values are axiomatic or that his expertise in educational matters automatically insures an equivalent expertise in those areas of knowledge that constitute the action program. The leadership for community development is usually from outside the community or group involved, while the leadership for community action is usually indigenous. Adult education has an important role to play in the training of community-action leadership, but such leaders are not adult educators since their principal concern is the action process itself rather than the educational process that is prerequisite to action (Batten, 1962; Ross, 1965).

In many places the term *animateur social* identifies leadership trained to manage the action process, and it is sometimes confused with the designation 'adult educator'. Both roles are distinctive and both require specific specialized training but each requires a different sort of training with respect to content and skills. By identifying the different roles of the specialist, an

428 Section 7: Application and Analysis

administrator is in a better position to seek the specific kinds of leadership skills required for the task at hand.

2. Research

There is little empirical evidence to explain either community development or community action. The two processes are usually undifferentiated; consequently, research in the area lacks clarity and precision in identifying precisely what happens or in what sequence. In separating the educational process from action, research can identify the kinds of learning tasks required, the instructional processes most appropriate for each task, and the sequential ordering of the learning-experience that will contribute most effectively to the achievement of the objectives. On the other hand, the detailed analysis of the action process should identify the procedures and characteristics of action that contribute to or prevent successful action programs.

FOOTNOTE

1. This paper is a revision of an earlier work. See Verner, C., 'The Community Development Process', *Community Development Review*, 6 March 1961, pp. 49-58.

COOLIE VERNER is a Professor of Adult Education at the University of British Columbia, where he is Head of the Department of Adult Education in the Faculty of Education, and Director of the Adult Education Research Centre. He also holds an appointment in the Department of Agricultural Economics in the Faculty of Agriculture, where he teaches rural sociology and supervises the graduate program in agricultural extension. The graduate program in adult education at the University of British Columbia was the first of its kind in Canada. Professor Verner received his doctorate in rural sociology at Columbia University under Professor Edmund deS. Brunner. Early in his career he worked with Jean and Jesse Ogden on the famous experiment in community development at the University of Virginia, and later was Professor of Adult Education at Florida State University. His principal interests have centred on the introduction of change in communities and particularly on educating people for change. Over the years he has produced an extensive bibliography of research and writing in rural sociology and adult education related to the adoption of innovations, participation, and adult learning and instruction. In recent years, the Research Centre has completed an extensive socio-economic survey of the rural areas of British Columbia for the Canada Land Inventory. Professor Verner has been a consultant to many local and national organizations, to the Canadian government on rural sociology and adult education and to the United States and other foreign governments.

Investigation and Intervention in Social Development

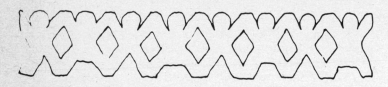

Charles E. Hendry

The value of this document lies principally in its attempt to identify and make explicit the basic assumptions underlying one of the most ambitious development planning projects ever undertaken in Canada, and to raise and discuss certain basic questions concerning the social aspects of policy, science, and intervention. What is covered here relates and is limited to the first phase of a continuing process in the pursuit of planned social change, namely, the assessment of resources and the involvement of the people in such an assessment. A companion piece is now needed to record and review what has occurred in the second phase of the project, the follow-through on implementation in terms both of priorities and strategies.

What follows is an informal recording of the impressions of the writer after a two-day visit to Mont Joli in June 1965 for the purpose of learning at closer range something of the meaning and the method of B.A.E.Q., le Bureau d'Aménagement de l'Est du Québec (known in English as the Eastern Quebec Planning Bureau). Although influenced to some extent by the reactions of his nine colleagues who participated in the exercise, the views here expressed are solely the responsibility of the writer.

For many years it has been the practice of the University of Toronto School of Social Work to make use of field observation as a means of helping keep its teaching staff realistically related to significant changes in society, and sensitive to their implications for the School's three major functions – teaching, research, and consultation. Possibly the most ambitious such undertaking was the School's Round Table on Man and Industry, involving systematic studies and repeat visits to six industrial-impact areas in Ontario. This three-year project has been described and assessed by Sir Geoffrey Vickers, the project's chief consultant, in his *The Undirected Society*, published in 1959 by the University of Toronto Press.

At the outset it must be emphasized that the writer's impressions of B.A.E.Q. are based on limited and inadequate opportunity for observation and study. Less than two days was spent in the Gaspé, and that mainly at B.A.E.Q. headquarters in Mont Joli. One might accurately assert that what follows in this statement, which concerns a project involving a massive attack on poverty, is derived largely from meetings with B.A.E.Q. staff and from examining a few scientific and technical documents, without benefit of direct study or contact in the area with the poor or with poverty as such.

We flew to Rimouski from Quebec City after a day spent with officials of the Provincial Department of Family and Social Welfare, were driven by limousine from Rimouski to Mont Joli, stayed at a delightful modern motel overlooking the St. Lawrence, and had our meals at a hotel capable of satisfying quite sophisticated tastes.

Even though it may be assumed that the reader of these very informal notes is thoroughly familiar with the purpose and program of B.A.E.Q., a brief recapitulation is included at this point simply by way of indicating the writer's own perception of the situation.

B.A.E.Q., it would appear, constitutes a dramatic and determined initiative to assess the economic and human resources of a chronically depressed and economically underdeveloped region in the Province of Quebec, and to formulate a comprehensive, long-range plan to rehabilitate the area and to lay the foundations to insure its maximum productivity and development.

The Gaspé, which is the location of this significant pilot project, comprises 16,000 square miles and a population of 325,000. Over $100,000,000 annually is distributed by way of public assistance and transfer payments to maintain its population. In some sections of the Gaspé between 90 and 100 per cent of the population is maintained by such payments. Unemployment and underemployment are chronic and a sense of hopelessness hangs like a pall over the area.

In every major sector of the economy – fishing, forestry, mining, agriculture and tourism – serious problems exist. Many of the younger and more enterprising are leaving to seek employment and try out life elsewhere. It is estimated that during the last twenty years, 100,000 people have left the Gaspé. Incomes are very low. The average Gaspé fisherman's family income is $2,500 of which 50 per cent comes from social security. In Gaspé-Sud county the per capita income is only $680, less than one half the national average.

It might be useful if, at this point, one were to attempt to portray some appreciation of the Gaspé with respect to its past and especially what it has meant to have been bypassed, as it were, in the sweep of economic growth elsewhere.

Over the years, it would appear that the natural resources of the Gaspé have been exploited with little regard for the well-being of the people. Until recently very little initiative has been taken to cope with the basic economic and social problems of the region. In 1956, however, a regional organization was formed in the Lower St. Lawrence area, outside of government, known as the Lower St. Lawrence Economic Guidance Council, and some modest efforts were begun. Later, a second Regional Economic Expansion Council was created for the Gaspé and the Magdalen Islands. When ARDA was established in 1961, the Quebec government found it both possible and advantageous to use these two existing Councils as a nucleus and to encourage the formation of a private non-profit corporation composed of five members of each of the two Councils. In 1963 Quebec passed parallel legislation and signed an agreement with Ottawa to co-operate with the federal government. A new corporation – B.A.E.Q. – was then formed to develop a master plan for the development of the Gaspé. The project was given three years of life and a $4,000,000 budget. It is the largest single ARDA project in Canada. There is close liaison between the B.A.E.Q. and Quebec's Permanent Interdepartmental Committee on National Resources, presided over by the Deputy Minister of Agriculture.

B.A.E.Q. represents an intensive effort to apply scientific methods, through a broad, interdisciplinary research program, to assess total resources, and to project plans for their fullest possible development in the interests of a viable economy and the well-being of the people of the area. Research is chanelled chiefly along three lines: bio-physical, economic, and social. Upon the basis of systematic inventories in all sectors of the economy and discussions by the people through some 200 local community committees and eight zone committees, a master plan was projected and recommended to the government of Quebec.

Paralleling the research program is a program of 'social animation'. In many ways this is the unique and most imaginative and strategic part of the total effort. Field-workers or 'community-development workers', now over twenty in number, some of them graduate social workers, are deployed throughout the Gaspé to work closely with local committees. Their function is to animate the committees and the people, to spark them into awareness of their situation, to encourage them to examine and discuss the problems they face, to contribute their views to the B.A.E.Q. and, through representation in eight committees at the zone level, to react to proposals presented by the B.A.E.Q. research and planning staff, and to help decide upon which specific, alternative lines of action they would recommend be forwarded to the provincial government for final political action.

What impresses one in visiting Mont Joli, headquarters of the B.A.E.Q., is the youthfulness of the staff (average age twenty-seven years, the oldest member being thirty-six years of age), their sophistication (especially in terms of scientific research and technical competence), and their dedication (and one senses exhilaration on every hand, something approaching religious zeal in their commitment to the necessity and wisdom of rationalizing economic, social, and political arrangements). The type of cars in the parking lot, MG's for example, the informality of the clothes worn, the overtime spent on work at night and over weekends, these and many other indications abound to support this interpretation. A quality of idealism, a sense of urgency, a commitment to social and economic justice, permeates the very atmosphere. One gets the impression that these are intensely concerned young men who have seen a gleam and who have a new faith in the future.

As a matter of fact, this emphasis on social animation, on attempting to harness the deep discontent of the people and on arousing new aspirations and high expectations, goes far beyond a mere exercise in applied social science. Many of the staff are convinced, as are professional social workers and others who work directly with the people, that if the B.A.E.Q. recommendations are not accepted and implemented, there may well be quite serious social consequences. Such is the morale and *esprit de corps* of the B.A.E.Q. staff that they are anxious to continue as a kind of task force, to move to new locations, and to tackle other similar assignments. Some of the staff go so far as to indicate that, if the government should give any sign of failing to support the plan being formulated for the Gaspé, they would not hesitate themselves to enter the arena of political action.

As one stands back to gain perspective on what one has been able to observe in a visit to B.A.E.Q. headquarters in Mont Joli, and on what one has been able to read in the several policy documents made available for study, the writer has found it useful to organize his impressions and to formulate his further questions in terms of three rather broad categories: (1) Socio-Economic Policy; (2) Natural and Social Sciences; and (3) Social Practice or Social Administration.

One overarching comment is both necessary and appropriate before engaging in more specific and detailed discussion. The theoretical formulation as outlined in the writings of Guy Coulcombe and François Poulin (especially in their paper entitled 'Planning and Socio-Economic Structures' [mimeographed February 1965]) is essentially faultless. A companion paper, actually an extract from the second Report, entitled 'Essay on Interpretation and General Hypothesis' (also mimeographed, March 1964) provides further highly useful background interpretation. The conceptual quality of the philosophical and scientific assumptions underlying B.A.E.Q. is characterized by unusual clarity, sophistication, and conviction. Where questions inevitably arise in the mind of the transient observer is in the area of the implementation of the objectives set forth in these excellent policy guides. Under each of the three categories, adopted for convenience of analysis, two divisions will be found, one for use in attempting to identify and, for the most part, to paraphrase *basic assumptions*, the other for use in venturing to indicate *basic questions* – questions that the writer finds himself raising, not so much concerning the underlying philosophy (assumptions) of the undertaking, as the difficulties or dangers encountered, actual or potential, in the administration of the project.

A. Basic Assumptions

I Socio-Economic Planning

1. The purpose of regional-development planning is to achieve

a rational organization of a region's total resources to provide
for its harmonious development and the prosperity of the
population living within it.
2. It is stated explicitly that 'The most fundamental characteristic of our project is beyond doubt its global approach.'
3. There cannot be an infallible and universal method of planning because socio-economic structures differ from country to
country and region to region, and because they have a profound and determining effect on the very texture of any planning at any level and in every aspect of planning – theoretical,
methodological, and administrative.
4. Interrelations must be defined between the four main factors
or elements of regional development: resources, socio-economic
organization, population, and space.
5. Limitations obtain within the Canadian setting, despite the
closest possible co-operation between ARDA (at the federal level) and B.A.E.Q. (through ARDA's provincial counterpart), and
one such limitation may be noted in efforts to redistribute national and provincial wealth among the various regions, districts, and communities in Quebec because 'this distribution is
based on a welfare-state policy rather than a policy of true
planning'.

II Natural and Social Sciences

1. Chief reliance is placed on systematic, scientific studies
aimed at finding the most complete and rational use of the
region's human and material resources.
2. Such regional-development planning calls for the utmost in
interdisciplinary, scientific collaboration.
3. The viewpoints of the various scientific disciplines must be
integrated (not juxtaposed) with those expressed by the various
rural and urban communities, by the associations, pressure
groups, and elected representatives of the population. That is
not a simple democratic preoccupation, but a definite recognition of the fact that the population alone can assume and undertake the required structural transformations.
4. A large and diverse group of professional research workers
is required for such global assessment and planning: *ecologists*
and *forest engineers* to inventory the region's physical resources
(forests, soils, fisheries, mines, tourist sites); *pedologists*, *geo-
morphologists*, *agro-meteorologists* and *agronomists* to determine the bio-physical possibilities of the various agricultural
zones and sub-zones of the territory; a team of *geologists*, *fishery engineers*, *town planners*, and *geographers* to verify the min-

ing potential, the fish stock, the main tourist sites, and the space distribution of socio-economic activities; *economists* to study the present methods of utilization of these resources, in order to determine how they can be effectively put to advantage in terms of income and employment; and *sociologists* and *political scientists* to examine the structure and evolution of the population, the prevailing mentality of the various strata of the regional society, and the system of organization presently adopted by the population.

III Social Practice

1. It is necessary that the population be present and participate to the fullest extent in the establishment of the regional goals.
2. Socio-economic development planning must be based on the population's participation and willingness to accept scientific and technical guidance.
3. Participation itself, however, has to be structured. That is why, besides its staff of some fifty research workers, B.A.E.Q. employs some twenty-five social animators (community-level or community-development workers), journalists, and radio and television specialists, who work at the creation and animation of structural participation and precise information that will also reach the population at large. A National Film Board team has produced fifteen films. Some of these are being used as tools to encourage citizen participation in some two hundred communities. Over three hundred and fifty 'Farm Forum' type radio-discussion groups have been organized. A weekly newspaper is also published by B.A.E.Q.

Basic Questions

I Socio-Economic Policy

Strategy might well be a more appropriate term here than policy although the two terms are inescapably linked in any realistic consideration of either. Rationalization seems to be the central and controlling concept, falling somewhere between the valuelessness of ecology and natural evolution and the value-laden thrust of social revolution. Sir Geoffrey Vickers contributes significantly to our understanding of the dynamics of planned change in two brilliant essays, one entitled 'The Psychology of Policy Making and Social Change' (*British Journal of Psychiatry*, Vol. 110, No. 467, July 1964), and the other 'Ecology, Planning and the American Dream' (*The Urban Condition*, edited by Leonard J. Duhl. New York: Basic Books Inc., 1963). Reference has been made earlier to Sir Geoffrey Vickers and might properly be directed also to his book, *The Art of Judgment* (Chapman and Hall, 1965).

The major question arising in this category of 'Socio-Economic Policy' centres in the attitude or attitudes that seem to be implied in the use of the term 'welfare state'. Does this mean to imply that welfare services are equated with attempts to adjust people to the economic structure rather than the economic structure to the needs of people?

Is welfare seen as an instrumentality of 'Establishment'? In various ways and at various times during discussion with B.A.E.Q. staff members at Mont Joli, one got the impression that the Department of Family and Social Welfare was considered of peripheral importance in the project and that, despite valiant efforts towards realistic reorientation and the appointment of very bright and competent staff members at the provincial level, the Department was critically handicapped by traditional structures at the local level.

On the other hand, there was evidence that B.A.E.Q. was making new and effective use of basic information and statistical data in the Department of Family and Social Welfare, and that senior members of the Department were co-operating actively and constructively with B.A.E.Q., especially in the Magdalen Islands.

One finds oneself wondering if the term 'welfare state' is not as inappropriate and inaccurate in describing socio-economic policies in the Gaspé, as the term 'doctrinaire socialism' would be if it were used to describe the socio-economic policies of B.A.E.Q. Such terms oversimplify and result inevitably in inaccuracy. How, one wonders, would one categorize what is happening in Prince Edward Island under A.D. Margison & Associates, consulting professional engineers? Clearly, in B.A.E.Q., indicative rather than directive planning is intended. One gets the impression that much of the theoretical framework of B.A.E.Q. has been derived from relatively recent developments in the applied social sciences and in social administration, much of this in France and in former French colonial countries of Africa. Canadians and Americans, in the so-called affluent

West, have much indeed to learn from areas of the world that have experienced the chaos of war's aftermath and sudden emergence into the contagion of rising twentieth-century expectations. B.A.E.Q. would seem to, be committed to moving into the midst of massive disadvantage and chronic discontent with a view to encouraging and engineering planned and radical socio-economic change with a minimum of disruption and dislocation.

II Natural and Social Sciences

The two questions uppermost in the writer's mind, under this category, concern the role of the scientist and the research specialist as change agents, and the relationship between the role of the research scientist and the professional practitioner, whether he be an engineer, social worker, public-health official, or educator. The dependence on research scientists in B.A.E.Q. is pronounced. The disciplined search for 'hard facts' and the meticulous care taken in their refinement, display, and documentation, are nothing short of inspiring. This is notably apparent in the sophistication with which so much of the basic data have been transferred to maps. On the other hand, one gets the impression, up to this stage, at least, that considerably less reliance is being placed on professional personnel from certain major, relevant professions in the areas of health, education, and welfare.

The three models discussed by Everett Hughes in his *Men and Their Work* (Free Press, 1958) – science, business, and profession – afford useful commentary. Frankly, one wonders whether or not, and under what circumstances, a scientist skilled at *investigation* can or should engage also in actual *intervention.* Is there not a highly useful differentiation of roles here that needs to be safeguarded? Might not the contributions of each be maximized if there were more complete collaboration?

How objective can a scientist be as a scientist when he becomes committed to radical social-reform objectives? Do some B.A.E.Q. staff members have such faith in science that they believe rational manipulation of economic forces is sufficient to set things right? One is both elated and apprehensive in speculating on an approach that may lead individuals engaged in such an operation to develop a frame of mind that attracts or produces intensely earnest, if not angry and indignant, young men, in a great hurry, who embrace scientific planning (rationalization) as though it were a religion, young men who seem determined to use the necessary political pressure or to create the necessary political power to break through social injustice, economic inequality, and the political apathy that have come to hold the people as in the grip of a vice.

What are the meanings and implications of the fact that the average age of the staff at B.A.E.Q. is twenty-seven years, also evidence, sometimes quite subtle, sometimes quite open, of lack of confidence in scientists, professionals, and scholars who are beyond thirty-five years of age, who have managed to adjust or accommodate over the years to the 'Establishment' under the 'Bossism' of a Duplessis régime? Obviously such a heavy concentration of young research scientists and social animators means a correspondingly heavy emphasis on rationality and an inevitable questioning or rejection of tradition, values, outlook, and methods, both of inquiry and social action.

III Social Practice

In discussing B.A.E.Q., especially the work of the 'social animators', the group that visited Mont Joli deliberately used the term 'social practice' rather than 'social-work practice', the focus of its own specialized competence, because the community-level worker, social animator, or community-development worker, as the case may be, draws upon the knowledge, principles, experience, and techniques derived from agricultural extension, public health, co-operatives, education, including adult education, technical assistance of various kinds, as well as from social work and social welfare.

Needless to say, the question was asked, 'Does the approach taken by the "social animator" conform to or utilize recognized principles of professional social-work practice?' Also, 'In what respects does the approach depart from well-defined principles of social work?' And finally, 'In what respects, if any, does the approach of the "social animator" hold the possibility of enriching social-work practice?'

One finds oneself, inevitably, asking some very fundamental questions here, the kind of questions, for example, that were raised by J. William Fulbright, Pierre Mendes-France, Viscount Hailsham, and others who participated in a vigorous dialogue on the occasion of the tenth anniversary of the Center for the Study of Democratic Institutions in January 1963. Their subject was 'The Elite and the Electorate: Is Government by the People Possible?'

What strikes one most forcibly in the B.A.E.Q. project is the deliberate provision made to involve the people who are most directly concerned, namely the population of the Gaspé itself. The principal device used, as has been noted, is the 'social animator', some twenty in number, deployed to work at the local community level with some two hundred community committees.

A chief function of the 'social animator' is to help insure that the research program of B.A.E.Q. is kept action-oriented. That is to say, paraphrasing Kurt Lewin who did so much to develop the idea of 'action-research', (1) to insure a sharp focus on problems that are relevant, meaningful, and real to the people and to those who carry major responsibility for shaping policy and administering programs; (2) to serve as a bridge of communication between the users and the producers of research; and (3) to emphasize in every appropriate way, and at every step along the way, the translation of research findings into practical results.

What this means, basically – and with all due respect to the impressive inventories of the natural resources of the region – is that, in the last analysis, what is *really* important is not what is on the land or under the waters that lap upon its shores, but what is in the minds of the people, who they think they are, how they perceive their present situation and their future prospects, in a word, what it is they really think or feel they need or want and what they are convinced is possible of realization. This represents bed-rock, and the foundations of planning, in the Gaspé or anywhere else, must be built solidly on the most genuine participation, understanding, and commitment of the people themselves.

In his scholarly and perceptive statement on the occasion of the tenth anniversary of the Center for the Study of Democratic Institutions of the Fund for the Republic on 'The Elite and the Electorate', Senator J. William Fulbright made the following observation:

> The case for government by élites is irrefutable insofar as it rests on the need for expert and specialized knowledge. The average citizen is no more qualified for the detailed administration of government than the average politician is qualified to practice medicine or to split an atom. But in the choice of basic goals, the fundamental moral judgments that shape the life of the society, the judgment of trained élites is no more valid than the judgment of an educated people. The knowl-

edge of the navigator is essential to the conduct of a voyage, but his special skills have no relevance to the choice of whether to take the voyage and where we wish to go. . . . The experience of modern times shows us that when the passengers take over the navigation of the ship it is likely to go on the rocks. This does not mean that their chosen destination is the wrong one or that an expert would have made a better choice, but only that they are unlikely to get there without the navigator's guidance. We must guard against allowing the navigator to determine our destination, but we must allow him to steer the ship without amateur supervision of every turn of the wheel. A political leader is chosen because of his supposed qualifications for his job. If he is qualified, he should be allowed to carry it out according to his own best judgment. If his judgment is found defective by his electors, he can and should be removed. His constituents, however, must recognize that he has a duty to his office as well as to them and that their duty in turn is to fill the office but not to run it. We must distinguish between the functions of *representation* and of *government*, *requiring* our elected leaders to represent us while *allowing* them to govern.

Another way of looking at all of this is to draw a distinction between 'development planning' and 'community development'. Development planning, characteristically, involves very large geographical areas, whole nations, provinces, and regions. Community development, on the other hand, involves much smaller geographical areas, local communities, concession lines, rural hamlets, and urban neighbourhoods. They are interdependent, however, and the knowledge and skills needed at the community-development level are no less sophisticated and demanding than those needed at the development planning level.

Charles Frankel, the philosopher, participating in the same symposium in which Senator Fulbright made the statement quoted above, made these cogent comments:

One of the questions that is often raised is why the people with their passion and their foolishness should be allowed to rule and to get in the way of those who know better. An assumption here is that technical experts agree. This is just not so. Technical experts do not agree.

A second assumption is that the decisions made in the political field by so-called 'experts' or the 'élite' are technical decisions. They are, but within extremely narrow limits. I can think of very few important political decisions that do not involve the weighing and assessing of evidence from a wide variety of different specialties. This means that even those who are experts in one field quickly become laymen the moment they move into another field. The view that expertise is a prerequisite for holding competent opinions on public affairs is one that does not disqualify only *some* of us 'people'. It disqualifies all of us. . . . What is called for in making public decisions, accordingly, is not omniscience or omnicompetent knowledge but something closer to wisdom, and common sense, and an understanding of when and where and for what reasons to rely on the advice of experts.

It is often necessary for democratic government to take the lead in organizing the unorganized, in providing the voiceless with a voice; the problem of the relationship of the electorate to the élite is essentially, I think, a problem of association and organization. The sense of impotence at the local level is the crucial issue.

Here then, in the light of the immense importance one must attach to the crucial role of the social animator, are a few of the questions one must raise:

1. Are the social animators engineers of consent, agents of discontent, salesmen of antibiotics, educators, therapists, catalysts, or simply enablers?
2. Has a clear distinction been made between the role of the social animator in the present research and planning phase and his role in the next phase, namely, the implementation phase, when the master plan, in whatever form it is officially endorsed and proclaimed by the government of the province, is to be implemented?
3. What in essence are the qualifications of the social animators? What in their personalities, education, and performance fit them especially for their present functions?
4. It was remarked by one of the staff of B.A.E.Q. headquarters that the methods used and the approach taken by the social animators have changed as the project has moved along. What changes were made and why?
5. How, actually, do the social animators intervene in a local community? How do they help the community to move from traditional to more rational ways of perceiving the reality of their situation and the relevance of the total B.A.E.Q. effort in terms of their needs? Is there available or emerging a discernible body of knowledge and skill that can be transmitted in a systematic way, through formal professional education and

training, capable of being built into disciplined professional behaviour?

6. What is the meaning, and what are the implications, of the use of such terms by B.A.E.Q. staff members as 'hard and soft facts', the 'hard facts' being those sought by the research scientist, the 'soft facts' being those sought by the social animators?

7. Again, what about the implications of social animators identifying and encouraging the removal of 'straw men' (apathetic, inhospitable to 'hard facts', opposed to change, lacking in foresight, withdrawn from conflict and strain) and their replacement by 'strong men' (more dynamic, ready to face up to 'hard facts', hospitable to change, committed to planned change, capable of confronting discontent and conflict constructively) in local community committees?

8. In the frequent use of the phrase 'mentality of the population' is there some suggestion of derogation, a categorizing of the people as representing a whole 'generation of dependency', a concern chiefly as to whether or not the people are willing to take part in the changes to be proposed? Or is 'mentality' intended to include attitudes, values, beliefs, sentiments, levels of aspiration, and the other components that go to make up one's perception of social reality?

9. One is not entirely clear if and how politicians are related to, or involved in, the project. What policy within B.A.E.Q. determines the extent to which, and how, municipal, provincial, and federal elected representatives are consulted or otherwise engaged in the undertaking?

10. What becomes of the functions of the social animators at the end of the three-year B.A.E.Q. contract period?

These, then, are some of the questions one finds oneself raising after even a brief exposure to B.A.E.Q. On the other hand, a few very firm and positive conclusions stand out in clear relief:

1. B.A.E.Q. represents a first encounter, an initial phase, a beginning of an extended and continuing operation whose purpose is the rehabilitation and redevelopment of a whole region.

2. The $4,000,000 invested in B.A.E.Q., both in development planning and community development, spread over a three-year period, represents a very small fraction of the $300,-000,000 that is likely to flow into the Gaspé region in government financing (public assistance, and transfer payments of

various kinds) during the same period.

3. The integrity of the enterprise is unassailable. Devotion, sincerity, and dedication mark the B.A.E.Q. staff off as a very special group indeed, and their competence matches their character.

4. It is to be hoped that political scientists will now be used by B.A.E.Q. in devising political structures capable of sustaining the momentum generated by this inspired initiative and suited to the highly technical interdisciplinary and interprofessional collaboration that increasingly must underlie and influence major political decisions.

5. One cannot escape relating what is taking place in ARDA and B.A.E.Q. to a paper of the Council of the Tavistock Institute of Human Relations on *Social Research and a National Policy for Science* (August 1964). B.A.E.Q. constitutes an experiment of national and international significance.

6. In addition to the substantial contribution being made by B.A.E.Q. in so many ways, and because of the emphasis it is placing on the role of the social animator, it is to be hoped that provision will be made to document this sector of activity within B.A.E.Q., and to describe and evaluate such activity with a view to identifying basic principles with special reference to their usefulness in the professional education and training of such functionaires.

In Retrospect

During our very first hours at B.A.E.Q. headquarters in Mont Joli, the writer found himself thinking back to a comparable experience in Recife, headquarters of SUDENE (Superintendency for the Development of the North-east) in north-east Brazil, in 1962. He was struck by the marked similarity between the problems of the two regions and the two massive efforts of development planning. Despite extreme differentials in the dimensions involved (SUDENE territory has a population of nearly 22,500,000 as compared with B.A.E.Q's 325,000), the parallels are quite remarkable.

Two documents on SUDENE might be mentioned. One is a pamphlet published by the Canadian Institute of International Affairs entitled *Change in Latin America: Example of North-east Brazil*. It is Vol. XXIV, No. 3 (December 1964 issue) of the Institute's 'Behind the Headlines' series, Baxter Publishing Company, 228 Bloor St. West, Toronto 5. Its author, Barry Lando, is a native of Vancouver and a graduate of Harvard and Columbia Universities. He was then staff correspondent for Time-Life in Rio de Janeiro. The other document is a mimeographed report entitled *The Brazilian Northeast* – SUDENE – *And its First Guiding Plan*. It was prepared and released under the authority of the Presidencia Da Republica Superintendencia Do Desenvolvimento Do Nordeste, Recife, 1962.

In one respect B.A.E.Q. differs fundamentally from SUDENE. B.A.E.Q. has attempted to balance its *reliance upon scientists* and its commitment to rationalization, by the deployment of 'social animators' whose function it is to develop a *reliance upon citizens*, and to induce and enable the people themselves to become involved in confronting their own plight and prospects. This would seem to be the most significant and strategic ingredient in the B.A.E.Q. model. At the same time, it highlights the most difficult, delicate, and demanding forces in the total operation.

One is profoundly impressed with the quite amazing effort going forward in the Gaspé and Magdalen Islands. Incredibly important results, both positive and negative, are in the offing, from which, apart entirely from what actually happens in the immediate territory involved, we can learn a great deal about how best to articulate scientific *investigation* (inventories and assessment of total resources) and professional *intervention* (to enlist and enable the 'client', in this case the community, to become actively and responsibly involved in social discovery and decision-search.

Actually all of this boils down to *Resolving Social Conflict*, the title, incidentally, of a collection of essays by the late Kurt Lewin. The great challenge faced in dealing constructively and creatively with chronic and massive disadvantage and discontent is the challenge of achieving disciplined interdisciplinary, interdepartmental, and intergovernmental collaboration and of perfecting a genuine partnership between citizen and specialist. B.A.E.Q. is a laboratory well suited to this lofty pursuit.

CHARLES E. HENDRY was born in Ottawa, Ontario. After graduation from McMaster University in 1925, he spent two years in Alberta in the field of the youth services. He cut his eye teeth on community work in New York City's Upper East Side while doing graduate work at Columbia University and Union Theological Seminary. For varying periods during his twenty-year stay in the United States, he was Supervisor of Field Studies in the Department of Educational Sociology at New York University; Director of a pioneer experimental youth project in Kenosha, Wisconsin; Professor of Group Work at George Williams College in Chicago; National Director of Program and Personnel with the Boys Clubs of America; Director of Research and Statistics with the National Council of the Boy Scouts of America; and Director and Co-ordinator of Research for the Commission on Community Interrelations of the American Jewish Congress – these last three positions with headquarters in New York City. He held teaching posts at Teachers' College and the School of Social Work of Columbia University, Smith College, and Wellesley College, and was a Research Associate attached to the Department of Industrial Relations at the Massachusetts Institute of Technology, when he accepted an invitation to return to Canada as Professor of Social Work at the University of Toronto in 1946.

In 1951 he succeeded the late Harry Cassidy as Director of this school. As may be noted in his article community development in the *Social Work Encyclopedia*, his interest and activity reflected considerable comparative study.

In 1950 he received the first U.N. Welfare Fellowship awarded to a Canadian, for field studies in Scandinavia. Subsequently, with the Council on World Tensions, as well as under other auspices, he travelled widely throughout the world examining community development or its equivalent in over sixty countries in many different regions of the world. In 1958-9 he visited the People's Republic of China. A major emphasis during his twenty-three years at the University of Toronto was on interprofessional and interdisciplinary collaboration and the involvement of citizens in partnership with professionals. His publications are extensive, the latest being a study of Establishment policy with respect to native Canadians. The book is entitled *Beyond Traplines* (Toronto: Ryerson Press, 1969).

Dr. Hendry retired from the University of Toronto in June 1969. He is Consultant to the Government of Ontario's Department of Social and Family Services, a member of the Advisory Committee to the Attorney General on Legal Aid, Chairman of the Long-Range Planning Committee of the Canadian Red Cross Society, and President of the Canadian Council on Social Development.

Bibliography

BOOKS

Adams, B. *Kinship in urban setting.* Chicago: Markham, 1968.

Adelman, H. & Lee, D. (Eds.) *The university game.* Toronto: Anansi, 1968.

Alinsky, S. D. *Reveille for radicals.* New York: Vintage Books, 1969.

Anonymous. *The treaties between Her Majesty Queen Victoria, and the Indians of British North America.* Reprinted by the Provincial Committee on Minority Groups, in co-operation with the Federation of Saskatchewan Indians, 1961.

Apter, D. E. *Ideology and discontent.* New York: Free Press, 1969.

Arensberg, C. M. & Niehoff, A. H. *Introducing social change.* Chicago: Aldine Pub. Co., 1964.

Asimov, I. *The naked sun.* New York: Doubleday, 1957.

Axline, J. M. *Play therapy.* Boston: Houghton Mifflin, 1947.

Baker, W. *Community development and national development.* New York: United Nations, 1963.

Barnett, N. G. *Innovation: The basis of cultural change.* Toronto: McGraw-Hill Book Co., 1953.

Batten, T. R. *Communities and their development.* London: Oxford University Press, 1965.

Batten, T. R. *Training for community development.* London: Oxford University Press, 1962.

Batten, T. R. & Batten, M. *The human factor in community work.* London: Oxford University Press, 1965.

Bauer, R. (Ed.) *Social indicators.* Cambridge, Mass.: Massachusetts Institute of Technology, 1966.

Bennett, J. W. *Hutterian brethren. The agricultural economy and social organization of a communal people.* Stanford, California: Stanford University Press, 1970.

Bennis, W. G. *Changing organization.* New York: McGraw Hill, 1966.

Bennis, W. G. *The planning of change.* New York: Holt, Rinehart & Winston, 1968.

Berlo, D. K. *The process of communication.* New York: Holt, Rinehart and Winston, 1960.

Biddle, W. W. & Biddle, L. J. *The community development process.* Toronto: Holt, Rinehart and Winston, 1965.

Biddle, W. W. & Biddle, L. J. *Encouraging community development.* New York: Holt, Rinehart & Winston, 1968.

Bierstedt, B. *The social order.* Toronto: McGraw Hill, 1970.

448

Blondin, Michel. *'Animation Sociale'*. Montreal: Conseil des Oeuvres de Montréal, October 1968.

Bodsworth, F. *The sparrow's fall*. Garden City, New York: Doubleday, 1967.

Bodsworth, F. *The strange one*. New York: Dodd, Mead & Co., 1959.

Bott, E. *Family and social network*. London: Tavistock, 1957.

Bruyn, S. T. *Communities in action*. New Haven: College and University Press, 1963.

Canadian Council for International Co-operation. *Community encounter: Programme models for the community*. Ottawa: Canadian Council for International Co-operation, 1971.

Cardinal, H. *The unjust society: The tragedy of Canada's Indians*. Edmonton: M. G. Hurtig, 1969.

Cary, Lee J. (Ed.) *Community development as a process*. Columbia, Missouri: University of Missouri Press, 1971.

Cassirer, Ernest. *An essay on man*. New Haven, Conn.: Yale University Press, 1944.

Chambers, M. (Ed.) *The fall of Rome. Can it be explained?* New York: Holt, Rinehart and Winston, 1966.

Clark, S. D. *The suburban society*. Toronto: University of Toronto Press, 1966.

Clark, T. N. *Community structure and decision-making: Comparative analysis*. San Francisco: Chandler Publishing Co., 1968.

Clutesi, G. C. *Potlatch*. Sidney, B.C.: Gray's Publishing Ltd., 1969.

Clutesi, G. C. *Son of raven, son of deer: Fables of the Tse-Shaht people*. Sidney, B.C.: Gray's Publishing Ltd., 1967.

Coady, M. M. *Masters of their own destiny*. New York: Harper & Brothers, 1939.

Cockburn, A. & Blackburn, R. (Eds.). *Student Power*. H Harmondsworth: Penguin, 1969.

Cole, G. D. H. *A century of cooperation*. London: George Allen & Unwin, 1945.

Compton, F. H. *Social policies for Canada*. Part I. Ottawa: Canadian Welfare Council, 1969.

Connor, D. M. *Diagnosing community problems*. Ottawa: Development Press, 1966.

Connor, D. M. *Strategies for development*. Ottawa: Development Press, 1968.

Connor, D. M. *Understanding your community*. Ottawa: Author, 1969.

Cook, L. A. & Cook, E. F. *A sociological approach to education*. New York: McGraw Hill, 1960.

Cooley, C. H. *Social organization*. New York: Schocken Books, 1962.

Coser, L. *Continuities in the study of social conflict*. New York: Free Press, 1967.

Coser, L. *Men of ideas: A sociologist's view*. New York: Free Press, 1965.

Cox, F. M. & Erlich, J. L. *Strategies of community organization: A book of readings*. Hasca, Illinois: F. E. Peacock Inc., 1970.

Daly, M. *The revolution game.* Toronto: New Press, 1970.

Davis, K. *The world's metropolitan areas.* Berkeley: University of California Press, 1959.

Deloria, V. *Custer died for your sins: An Indian manifesto.* New York: MacMillan, 1969.

Deloria, V. *We talk, you listen: New tribes, new turf.* New York: MacMillan, 1970.

Desjardin, A. *The cooperative people's bank: La caisse populaire.* New York: Russel Sage Foundation, 1914.

Dewey, J. In Kilpatrick, W. H. (Ed.) *The educational frontier.* New York: Appleton Century, 1933.

Dimock, H. G. *Selecting and training group leaders.* Montreal: Centre for Human Relations and Community Studies, Sir George Williams University, 1970.

Dimock, H. G. & McDonald, R. *An external intervention into federal community development programs.* Montreal: Centre for Human Relations and Community Studies, Sir George Williams University, 1967.

Downs, James F. *Cultures in crisis.* Beverly Hills: Glencoe Press, 1971.

DuBois, Rachel Davis, and Li, Mew-Soong. *Reducing social tension and conflict.* New York: Association Press, 1971.

Dunning, R. W. *Social and economic change among the Northern Ojibwa.* Toronto: University of Toronto Press, 1959.

Etzioni, A. *The active society.* New York: Free Press, 1968.

Experimental Projects Branch, Department of Forestry and Rural Development. *Survey of literature on the community with selected annotations, reading lists and periodicals.* Ottawa: Department of Forestry and Rural Development, October, 1968.

Fauquet, G. *The cooperative sector.* Manchester: The Cooperative Union, 1951.

Findlay, Suzanne and Peter. *Community self-analysis: Effectiveness and future implications.* 1970.

Firth, R. *Elements of social organization.* Boston: Beacon Press, 1967.

Fitzgerald, G. B. *Community organization for recreation.* New York: A. S. Barnes, 1948.

Franklin, R. (Ed.) *Patterns of community development.* Washington: Public Affairs Press, 1966.

French, R. M. *The community: A comparative perspective.* Hasca, Ill.: F. E. Peacock Publishers, 1969.

Fry, A. *How a people die: A novel.* Toronto: Doubleday, 1970.

Galbraith, J. K. *The new industrial state.* Toronto: New American Library of Canada (Signet Books), 1967.

Gallenkamp, C. *Maya.* New York: Pyramid Publications, 1962.

Gans, H. *The urban villagers.* New York: Free Press of Glencoe, 1962.

Gluckman, M. *Politics, law and ritual in tribal society.* Chicago: Aldine Co., 1965.

Goodenough, W. H. *Co-operation in change.* New York: Russel Sage Foundation, 1963.

450

Greer, S. *The emerging city.* New York: Free Press, 1962.

Hall, Edward T. *The silent language.* Greenwich, Conn.: Fawcett Publications, Inc., 1965.

Hallenbeck, W. C. (Ed.) *Community and adult education.* Chicago: Adult Education Association, 1962.

Hamilton, I. *The children's crusade.* Toronto: Peter Martin Associates, 1970.

Harvard University Program on Technology and Society. *Social innovation in the city, new enterprises for community development.* Cambridge, Mass.: Harvard University Press, 1969.

Hatch, D. S. *Toward freedom from want.* London: Geoffrey Cumberlege, Oxford University Press, 1949.

Hauser, A. *The social history of art.* London: Routledge and Kegan Paul, 1962.

Hawley, W. D. & Wirt, F. M. *The search for community power.* Englewood Cliffs, N.J.: Prentice Hall, 1968.

Hawthorn, H. B. (Ed.) *A survey of the contemporary Indians of Canada.* Ottawa: Queen's Printer, 1966-67. 2 vols.

Head, W. *Neighborhood participation in local government.* Toronto: Bureau of Municipal Research, 1970.

Head, W. *A relevant war against poverty.* New York: Metropolitan Applied Research Center Inc., 1968.

Hendry, C. E. *Beyond the traplines: Does the church really care?* Toronto: Ryerson Press, 1969.

Herzog, E. *Some guidelines for evaluative research.* Washington, D.C.: U.S. Department of Health and Welfare, 1959.

Hollingshead, A.B. *Elmtown's youth.* New York: John Wiley & Sons, 1949.

Homans, G. C. *The human group.* New York: Harcourt, Brace & World, 1950.

Illich, I. D. *Celebration of awareness: A call for institutional revolution.* Garden City, New York: Doubleday & Co., 1970.

Jackson, J. D. *Community development: Ideology and technology - a comparative study of three community development agencies.* Montreal: Centre for Human Relations and Community Studies, Sir George Williams University, August, 1971.

Jacobs, D. *Community development in urban areas.* New York: United Nations, 1961.

Jacobs, J. *The death and life of great American cities.* New York: Random House, 1961.

Janowitz, M. *Community political systems.* Illinois: The Free Press of Glencoe, 1961.

Johnston, P. *Tale of Nokomis.* Toronto: C. J. Musson Ltd., 1970.

Jones, E. *Towns and cities.* New York: Oxford University Press, 1966.

Josephy, A. M. *The Indian heritage of America.* New York: Knopf, 1968.

Keller, S. *The urban neighborhood.* New York: Random House, 1968.

Kolb, J. H. *Emerging rural communities.* Madison: University of Wisconsin Press, 1959.

Kolb, J. H. & Brunner, E. de S. *A study of rural society.* Toronto: Nelson, 1949.

Kornhauser, W. *The politics of mass society.* Illinois: The Free Press of Glencoe, 1959.

Kotler, M. *Neighborhood government.* Indianapolis: Bobbs-Merrill, 1969.

Kropotkin, P. *Mutual aid: A factor of evolution.* Boston: Extending Horizon Books, 1955.

Laidlaw, A. *Rural progress through cooperatives.* New York: United Nations Department of Economic Affairs, 1954.

Langdon, S. (Canadian Union of Students) *Canadian Dimension,* 1970, Feb.-Mar., 6-8.

Lappin, Ben. *The community workers and the social work tradition.* Toronto: Canadian Association for Education in the Social Services, 1970.

Leighton, A. H. *My name is legion.* New York: Basic Books Inc., 1959.

Liebow, E. *Tally's corner.* Boston: Little & Brown, 1967.

Likert, T. *Human organization.* New York: Merediths Corp., 1969.

Likert, T. *New patterns of management.* New York: McGraw Hill, 1967.

Lindeman, E. *The community.* New York: Association Press, 1921.

Lindeman, V. *The meaning of adult education.* Montreal: Harvest House, 1961.

Linton, R. *The study of man.* New York: Appleton-Century-Crofts Inc., 1936.

Lippit, R. Watson, J., & Westley, B. *The dynamics of planned change.* New York: Harcourt, Brace & World Inc., 1958.

Lippitt, G. L. *Organization renewal.* New York: Merediths Corp., 1969.

Lloyd, Antony John. *Community development in Canada.* Ottawa: Canadian Research Centre for Anthropology, Saint Paul University, 1967.

Loomis, S. *Paris in the terror: June 1793-July 1794.* Philadelphia: Lippincott, 1964.

Lorimer, J. *The real world of city politics.* Toronto: James Lewis & Samuel Publishers, 1970.

Lorimer, J. & Philips, M. *Working people.* Toronto: James Lewis & Samuel Publishers, 1971.

Loring, W.C., Jr., Sweetser, F. L., & Ernst, C.F. *Community organization for citizens participation in urban renewal.* Boston: Housing Association of Metropolitan Boston, 1957.

Lotz, James. *Northern realities.* Toronto: New Press, 1970.

Mann, W. E. (Ed.) *Social and cultural change in Canada.* Vol. One. Toronto: Copp-Clark Publishing Company, 1970.

Mann, W. E. (Ed.) *Social and cultural change in Canada.* Vol. Two. Toronto: Copp-Clark Publishing Company, 1970.

Marsh, Leonard. *Communities in Canada.* Toronto: McClelland and Stewart Limited, 1970.

Marx, L. *The machine in the garden.* New York: Oxford University Press, 1964.

Matthiessen, P. *Sal si Puedes: Cesar Chavez and the new American revolution.* New York: Random House, 1970.

McEwen, E. R. *Community development service for Canadian Indian and Métis communities.* Toronto: Indian-Eskimo Association of Canada, 1968.

McGregor, D. *The human side of enterprise.* Toronto: McGraw Hill, 1969.

McMahon, Ernest E. *Needs – of people and their communities – and the adult educator.* Washington, D.C.: Adult Education Association of the USA, 1970.

McMillen, W. *Community organization for social welfare.* Chicago: University of Chicago Press, 1945.

Merton, R. K. *Social theory and social structure.* Glencoe: The Free Press, 1962.

Michelson, W. H. *Man and his urban environment: A sociological approach.* Don Mills: Addison Wesley Co., 1970.

Miller, P. A. *Community health action.* East Lansing: Michigan State College Press, 1953.

Mills, C. W. *The sociological imagination.* New York: Grove Press, 1959.

Minar, D. W. & Greer, S. *The concept of community.* Chicago: Aldine Publishing Co., 1969.

Morris, A. *The treaties of Canada with the Indians of Manitoba and the Northwest Territories.* Toronto: Belfords, Clarks & Co., 1880.

Morriseau, N. *Legends of my people: The great Ojibwa.* Toronto: Ryerson Press, 1965.

Myrdal, G. *Beyond the welfare state.* New Haven: Yale University Press, 1960.

National Training Laboratories and National Education Association. *Reading book: 19th annual summer laboratory in human relations training.* Washington, D.C.: National Training Laboratories Institute for Applied Behavioral Science, 1969.

Nehru, J. *Five speeches on community development.* New Delhi: Ministry of Community Development, 1954.

Nisbet, R. A. *Community and power.* New York: Oxford University Press, 1962.

Ogden, J. & Ogden, J. *Small communities in action.* New York: Harper, 1946.

Rapoport, A. *Fights, games and debates.* Ann Arbor: The University of Michigan Press, 1970.

Rapoport, R. N. *Community as doctor.* London: Tavistock Publications, 1960.

Robertson, H. *Reservations are for Indians.* Toronto: James Lewis & Samuel Publishers, 1970.

Rogers, C. R. *Client-centered therapy.* Boston: Houghton Mifflin, 1951.

Rogers, E. M. *Diffusion of innovations.* New York: The Free Press of Glencoe, 1962.

Ross, M. G. & Lappin, B. W. *Community organization.* (2nd ed.) New York: Harper & Row, 1967.

Ross, R. & Van Den Haag, E. *The fabric of society.* New York: Harcourt, Brace & Co., 1957.

Rossi, P. H., & Dentler, R. A. *The politics of urban renewal.* New York: Free Press of Glencoe, 1961.

Ruopp, P. (Ed.) *Approaches to community development.* The Hague: W. van Hoeve, 1953.

Sanders, I. T. *The community: An introduction to a social system.* New York: Ronald Press Co., 1966.

Schaller, L. E. *Community organization: Conflict and reconciliation.* New York: Abingdon Press, 1966.

Schmitt, P. *Back to nature.* New York: Oxford University Press, 1969.

Schon, D. A. *Displacement of concepts.* London: Tavistock Publications, 1963.

Scientific American. *Cities.* New York: Alfred A. Knopf, 1969.

Selye, H. M. D. *The stress of life.* New York: McGraw Hill, 1956.

Selznick, P. *TVA and the grass roots.* Berkeley: University of California Press, 1949.

Sennett, R. *The uses of disorder.* New York: Alfred A. Knopf, 1970.

Skinner, G. W. *Leadership and power in the Chinese community in Thailand.* Ithaca, New York: Cornell University Press, 1958.

Slotkin, J. S. (Ed.) *Readings in early anthropology. Chicago: Aldine Publishing Co., 1965.*

Smith, A. H. & Fischer, J. L. (Eds.) *Anthropology.* Englewood Cliffs: Prentice-Hall, 1970.

Spicer, E. H. (Ed.) *Human problems in technological change.* New York: Russel Sage, 1952.

Spiegel, H. B. C. (Ed.) *Citizen participation in urban development.* Vol. I-II. Washington: National Training Laboratory, Institute for Applied Behavioral Science, 1968.

Steiner, J. F. *Community organization.* New York: Century, 1925.

Steiner, S. *The new Indians.* New York: Harper & Row, 1968.

Stinson, Arthur. *Canadian participation in social development.* Ottawa: The Citizenship Branch, Department of the Secretary of State, 1968.

Stinson, Arthur. *Submission to Canadian Council on Urban and Regional Research for shared cost support.* March 1970.

Suttles, G. *The social order of the slum.* Chicago: University of Chicago Press, 1968.

Symington, F. *The Canadian Indian.* Toronto: McClelland & Stewart Ltd., 1969.

454

Thwaites, R. G. *The Jesuit relations and allied documents.* New York: Pagent Books Company, 1959.

Titmus, Richard M. *Essays on the welfare state.* London: Unwin University Books, 1958.

United Nations. *Social progress through community development.* New York: United Nations Press, 1955.

Verner, C. *A conceptual scheme for the identification and classification of processes for adult education.* Washington, D.C.: Adult Education Association of the U.S.A., 1962.

Verner, C. & Booth, A. *Adult education.* Washington, D.C.: Center for Applied Research in Education, Inc., 1964.

Vichers, G. *Value system and social progress.* New York: Basic Books, 1968.

Vickers, E. *Groups advisory to government.* Toronto: Canadian Association for Adult Education, 1968.

Vidich, A. J. & Bensman, J. *Small town in mass society.* Princeton: Princeton University Press, 1958.

Warren, R. L. *The community in America.* Chicago: Rand McNally & Co., 1963.

Warren, R. L. *Studying your community.* New York: Free Press, 1965.

Waterston, A. *Development planning: Lessons of experience.* Baltimore: Johns Hopkins Press, 1965.

Waubageshig (Ed.) *The only good Indian.* Toronto: New Press, 1970.

Wellman, B., Hewson, M. & Coates, D. B. *Community-network-communication.* Toronto: Centre for Urban and Community Studies, University of Toronto, 1971.

Whipple, James B. *Community service and continuing education: A literature review.* Syracuse: Syracuse University Publications in Continuing Education, 1970, No. 20.

Whipple, James B., and Chertow, Doris S. (Eds.) *The university and community service: Perspectives for the seventies.* Syracuse: Syracuse University Publications in Continuing Education, 1970, No. 64.

White, M. & White, L. *The intellectuals versus the city.* Cambridge, Mass.: Harvard University Press, 1962.

Whyte, W. F. *Street corner society.* (2nd ed.) Chicago: University of Chicago Press, 1955.

Wootton, B. *Testament for social science.* London: G. Allen, 1950.

Yee, A. H. (Ed.) *Social interaction in educational settings.* Englewood Cliffs, N.J: Prentice-Hall, 1971.

Young, M. & Willmott, P. *Family and Kinship in East London.* London: Routledge & Kegan Paul, 1957.

REPORTS AND STUDIES

Unpublished Papers, Speeches and Theses

Bell, W.L. *Departmental reorganization.* Manitoba: unpublished paper, 1971.

Bremner, R. H. *The role of government in promoting social change: A historical perspective.* A paper prepared for the Columbia University School of Social Work Arden House Conference, Harriman, New York, November 18-21, 1965.

Calder, R. "B.B.C. world service talk." Quoted in *The Bajan.* 1966, January.

Carota, M. *The citizen group movement among the low income citizens of urban Canada.* Ottawa: Canadian Association of Neighbourhood Services, under the auspices of the Department of National Health and Welfare, 1970.

Clarke, L. *Community development in Canada: A background paper and proposal.* Prepared for the Urban Assistance Study, Policy Planning Central Mortgage and Housing Corporation, December, 1970.

Cohen, N. *Should government take a direct hand in promoting social change?* A paper prepared for the Columbia University School of Social Work Arden House Conference, Harriman, New York, November 18-21, 1965.

Cole, G. D. H. *Democracy and authority in the cooperative movement.* A lecture given at the London School of Economics, London, November, 1953.

Compton, F. *Community development program material.* Winnipeg: Department of Health and Social Development, 1970. (Unpublished).

David, P. T. *Government as agent of social change: Some problems in theory.* A paper prepared for the Columbia University School of Social Work Arden House Conference, Harriman, New York, November 18-21, 1965.

Delegran, W. *Life in the heights: The tenants' viewpoint.* Unpublished research study, 1967.

Frei, J. W. *The potential of planned change – forms of intervention – organizing and planning functions in the council and fund field.* Ottawa: Community Funds and Councils, Canadian Welfare Council, 1968.

Guisinger, S. *Local participation.* Unpublished report of the Abt Associates, Inc., Cambridge, Massachusetts, 1969.

Haggstrom, W. C. *The moral case against social action.* A paper prepared for the Columbia University School of Social Work Arden House Conference, Harriman, New York, November 18-21, 1965.

Head, W. *The Don district study.* Toronto: Social Planning Council of Metropolitan Toronto, 1970.

456

Laskin, R. & Phillett, S. *Formal versus reputational leadership.* A paper delivered at the annual meeting of the Pacific Sociological Foundation, Portland, Oregon, April 1963.

Laumann, E. O."Interlocking and radial friendship." *Detroit Area Study, Working Paper #5.* Ann Arbor: University of Michigan, 1968.

Levy, Charles S. *Power and ethics in personal service occupations.* Unpublished manuscript, pp. 442, School of Social Work, University of Toronto, Toronto.

Lorimer, J. *Expertise versus participation: Who will govern Canada's cities?* Paper prepared for Liberal Conference, Harrison Hot Springs, B.C., November, 1969.

Mackenzie, J. H. *Strategies for change – an historical examination of community development in Manitoba.* Thesis for the University of Southern Illinois.

Mosher, A. T. *Interrelationships between agricultural development, social organization, and personal attitudes and values.* Ithaca: New York State College of Agriculture, 1960.

Munro, the Hon. J. *Citizen participation – community development process.* Ottawa: Dept. of National Health & Welfare, 1969.

Oliver, G. *Adapting agency structure and program to offer co-operative outreach services.* Paper presented at The Canadian Conference on Social Welfare, Ottawa, June 19, 1968.

Oloya, J. J. *Some aspects of economic development with special reference to East Africa.* East African Literature Bureau, 1968.

Russel, C. *Social change in the Annex.* Unpublished thesis, University of Toronto, 1963.

Sim, R. A. *Government grants to voluntary agencies.* Paper based on a study made by the Canadian Association of Adult Education for Canadian Citizenship Branch.

Sim, R. A. Intervention: The ethics of helping others. A paper given at the Boston University Workshop on Community Development. 1969. (Unpublished).

Spiesman, S. *The development of the "Annex" In the mid-1920's.* Unpublished thesis, University of Toronto, 1967.

Steward, J. H. *Limitations of applied anthropology: The case of the Indian new deal.* Ottawa Citizenship Branch, Secretary of State, file No. 3967.

Warren, R. L. *Types of purpose social change at the community level.* Brandeis University Papers in Social Welfare, 1965, II.

Welch, Hon. R. *Citizen participation in community development.* An address to the First Ontario Provincial-Municipal Conference, April 24, 1970.

Wellman, B. *The uses of community.* Paper presented at the annual meeting of the Canadian Sociology and Anthropology Association, St. John's, Newfoundland, June, 1971.

Wellman, B., Hewson, M. & Coates, D. B. *Primary relationships in the city: Some preliminary observations.* Paper presented at the annual meeting of the Canadian Sociology Association, Toronto, June, 1969.

Willmott, D. E. *The role of the community council in a developing community.* An unpublished paper.

Proceedings and Statements

Canada Department of Indian Affairs and Northern Development. *Statement of the Government of Canada on Indian Policy, 1969.* Ottawa: Queen's Printer, 1969.

Canadian Broadcasting Corporation. *The way of the Indian.* Thirteen documentary programs broadcast on C.B.C. Radio, 1966.

Canadian Civil Liberties Association. *Poverty and civil liberties.* Proceedings of the Special Senate Committee on Poverty, Ottawa:1970, #32.

Clague, M. *Proceedings of the Special Senate Committee on Poverty.* Toronto: Just Society Movement, 1970, #28.

Compton, F. *Community development proposal.* Winnipeg: Manitoba Indian Brotherhood, 1969.

Government of Canada. *Office consolidation of the Indian act.* Ottawa: Queen's Printer, 1963.

Hynam, C. A. S. "Community development, an example of conceptual confusion." In Card (ed.) *Perspectives on regions and regionalism.* Western Association of Sociology and Anthropology Proceedings, 1968.

Indian Chiefs of Alberta. *Citizens plus.* (The red paper). A presentation by the Indian Chiefs of Alberta to The Right Honourable P. E. Trudeau, Prime Minister, and the Government of Canada, 1970.

Klein, A. F. *Back to the neighbourhoods to involve citizens.* Ottawa: Citizenship Branch, Secretary of State, Research and documentation file No. 3806.

Lagassé, J. *Community development services: A community development program for Manitoba.* Winnipeg: Department of Welfare, 1962.

Lotz, J. A. *Directory of Canadian non-governmental organizations engaged in international development assistance.* Ottawa: Canadian Council for International Co-operation, 1970.

Mogulof, M. B. *Advocates for themselves: Citizen participation in federally supported community decision/program organizations.* O Ottawa: Citizenship Branch Termatrix No. 4621, 1969.

Proceedings. The Orders of the day, March 23rd, 1956. *Legislative papers.* Winnipeg: Queen's Printer, 1956.

Student's Administrative Council. *Brief to the Commission on University Government.* Toronto: S.A.C., University of Toronto, 1969.

458

Reports

Aborigines Protection Society. *Report on the Indians of Upper Canada.* London: J. Haddon, 1829. (Reprinted: Toronto; Canadiana House, 1968.)

Abramson, J. *Rural to urban adjustment.* Ottawa: ARDA Research Report, No. RE-4, Department of Forestry and Rural Development.

Aged and Long-term Illness Survey Committee. *Report and recommendations.* Regina: Government of Saskatchewan, 1963.

Baker, W. *Key to community series.* Saskatoon: Centre for Community Studies, 1963.

Canada Department of Agriculture. *A review of the rural development program in the United States of America.* Ottawa: Author, 1960.

Canadian Welfare Council. *Housing and people.* Report published by Canadian Welfare Council, June, 1970.

Commission on University Affairs. *Report.* Toronto: University of Toronto, 1969.

Connor, D. & Curtis, J. E. *Sociology and anthropology in Canada: Some characteristics of the discipline and their current university programs.* Montreal: Canadian Sociology and Anthropology Assoc., 1970.

Draper, James A. (Ed.) *National workshop on community development: Teaching and research.* Toronto: The Ontario Institute for Studies in Education (Department of Adult Education), 1968.

Draper, James A. (Ed.) *Second national workshop on community development – 1969.* Toronto: The Ontario Institute for Studies in Education (Department of Adult Education), 1969.

Duff-Berdahl Commission. *Report.* Toronto: Association of University Teachers and the Association of Universities and Colleges of Canada, 1966.

Dyck, H. J. *Social futures of Alberta, 1970-2005.* Edmonton: Human Resources Research Council of Alberta, 1970.

Lagassé, J. H. *The people of Indian ancestry in Manitoba,* Vol. I-III. Report to the Manitoba Government. Winnipeg: Queen's Printer,1959.

Lagassé, J. H. *Realidades y proyectos: 16 anos de trabajo.* Mexico: Instituto Nacional Indegenista, 1964.

McCrorie, J. M. *ARDA: An experiment in development planning.* Report of the Canadian Council on Rural Development, Ottawa: Queen's Printer, 1969.

The Minister of University Affairs of Ontario. *Report.* Toronto: Government of Ontario, 1967.

Morris, P. & Rein, M. *Dilemmas of social reform: Reports of the Institute of Community Studies.* London: Routledge & Kegan Paul, 1967.

Parsons, G. F. *Arctic suburb: A look at the North's newcomers.* Ottawa: Northern Science Research Group, Department of Indian Affairs and Northern Development, 1970.

Presidential Advisory Committee on Undergraduate Instruction in the Faculty of Arts and Science. *Report.* University of Toronto, 1967.

Presidential Committee on Disciplinary Procedures. *Report.* University of Toronto, 1969.

Rogers, E.S. *The Round Lake Ojibwa.* Occasional Paper No. 5, Art and Archaeology Division, Royal Ontario Museum, University of Toronto, 1962.

Rogers, E. *Native rights in Canada.* Toronto: Indian-Eskimo Association of Canada, Legal Committee, 1970.

Royal Commission on Agriculture and Rural Life. *Report.* Vols. 1-14. Regina: Government of Saskatchewan, 1957.

Shuttleworth, D. E. *The community school and social reconstruction, a demonstration project.* Toronto: Ontario Educational Research Council, 1967.

Sim, R. A. *Community development: A case study of a six months action-research project.* Unpublished paper, February, 1966.

Task Force on Government Information. *To know and be known: Report.* Ottawa: Queen's Printer, 1969.

Willmott, D. E. *Industry comes to a prairie town.* Saskatoon: Centre for Community Studies, 1962.

ARTICLES

Audain, M. "Tenant management." *Canadian welfare,* 1970, 46, pp. 3-7.

Bailey, J. "The charrette: New vehicle for citizen participation." *City,* 1970, June-July, pp. 42-45.

Baker, W. B. "Saskatchewan approaches community development." In *Community organization, community planning and community development.* New York: Council of Social Work Education, 1961.

Baker, W. B. & Solomon, D. D. "A survey and asssessment of the role of agricultural extension in resource development. In *Resources for tomorrow.* Ottawa: Government of Canada, 1961.

Batten, T. R. "Social values and community development." In Ruopp, P. (Ed.) *Approaches to community development.* The Hague: W. van Hoeve, 1953.

Beers, H. W. "Social components of community development." *Rural sociology,* 1958, p. 23.

Bell, W. "The city, the suburb and a theory of social choice." In Greer, S. *et al* (Eds.) *The new urbanization.* New York: St. Martin's Press, 1968.

Bell, W. & Boat, M. D. "Urban neighborhoods and informal social relations." *American journal of sociology,* 1957, LXII, January, pp. 391-398.

Bird, C. "The GNP – A beast to be bridled." *Think,* 1970, 36(3), pp. 2-8.

Breton, R. "Institutional completeness of ethnic communities and the personal relations of immigrants." *American journal of sociology,* 1964, LXX, September, pp. 193-205.

Brooks, M. P. "The community action program as a setting for applied research." *Journal of social issues,* 1965, 21(1).

Brox, O. "Maintenance of economic dualism in Newfoundland." *Newfoundland social and economic studies,* 1969, 9.

Bureau of Municipal Research. "Neighborhood participation in local government: A study of the City of Toronto." *Civic affairs,* 1970, January.

Chin, R. "Problems and prospects of applied research." In Bennis, Benne, & Chin (Eds.) *The planning of change.* New York: Holt, Rinehart & Winston, 1962.

Chombart de Lauwe, P. H. "Field and case studies." In Hauser, P. M. (Ed.) *Handbook for social research in urban areas.* Paris: UNESCO 1964.

Connor, D. & Curtis, J. E. "A perspective on rural sociology in Canada and some implications." *Rural sociology,* 1970, 35(2), pp. 267-274.

"Cooperación popular: A new approach to community development in Peru." *International labour review,* 1966, September.

CUSO. "Every day is a confrontation of challenges." *CUSO bulletin,* 1970, Summer, pp.6-7.

Daly, M. "Ottawa debates how best to give money to citizens' groups." *Toronto Daily Star,* 1970, September 26.

Dewitt, R. L. "Public policy and community protest: The Fogo case." *Newfoundland social and economic studies,* 1969, 8.

Dubey, S. N. "Community action programs and citizen participation: Issues and confusions." *Social work,* 1970, January, pp.76-84.

Dunning, R. W. "Some implications of economic change in northern Ojibwa social structure." *Canadian journal of economics and political science,* 1958, Vol. 24, pp. 562-566.

Frank, L. K. "The need for a new political theory." *Daedalus, journal of the A.A.A.S.,* 1967, Summer, pp. 814-815.

Freeman, H. E. & Sherwood, C. C. "Research in large-scale intervention programs." *Journal of social issues,* 1965, 21(1).

Gans, H. J. & Glasgow, R. W. "The Ayn Rand syndrome," *Psychology today* 1970, March, pp. 58-82.

Gilbert, N. & Eaton, J. W. "Who speaks for the poor." *Journal of the American Institute of Planners,* 1970, November, pp. 411-416.

Griffiths, H. "Case studies in community development: The uncompleted bridge." *Community development journal,* 1970, 5, pp. 6-10.

Hallowell, A. I. "The backwash of the frontier: The impact of the Indian on American culture." In Bohannan, P. & Plog, F. (Eds.) *Beyond the frontier.* Garden City, N.Y.: National History Press, 1967.

Hardin, G. "The cybernetics of competition: A biologist's view of society." In Buckley, W. (Ed.) *Modern systems research for behavioral scientists.* Chicago: Aldine Publishing Co., 1968.

Hassiger, E. "Social relations between centralized and local systems." *Rural sociology,* 1961, p. 26.

Horton, J. "The dehumanization of anomie and alienation: A problem in the ideology of sociology." *The British journal of sociology,* 1964, 15, pp. 283-300.

Iverson, N. & Mathews, D. R. "Communities in decline. An examination of household resettlement in Newfoundland." *Newfoundland social and economic studies,* 1968, 6.

Kahn, A. J. "The design of research." In Polansky, N. A. (Ed.) *Social work research.* Chicago: University of Chicago Press, 1963.

Katadotis, P. "FRAP, FLQ and Drapeau: Or how to win an election." *Our generation,* 1970, 7(3), pp. 76-80.

Kelner, M. "Ethnic penetration into Toronto's elite structure." *The Canadian review of sociology and anthropology,* 1970, 7(2), pp. 128-137.

Kennedy, R. F. "Federal education policy." *Phi delta kappa,* 1968, June.

Klein, D. "Sensitivity training and community development." In Schein, E. & Bennis, W. (Eds.) *Personal and organizational change through group methods.* New York: Wiley, 1965.

Kogan, L. S. "Principles of measurement." In Polansky, N. A. (Ed.) *Social work research.* Chicago: University of Chicago Press, 1963.

Krause, E. A. "Functions of a bureaucratic ideology: Citizens participation." *Social problems,* Santa Barbara, Calif.: Department of Sociology, University of California, pp. 129-143.

Kristjanson, L. F. "Who solves what problems." In *Research review.* Saskatoon: Centre for Community Studies, 1962.

Lagassé, J. H. "Community development in Manitoba." *Human organization.* 1961-62, 20, Winter.

Leibow, E. & Liebow, J. T. "A preliminary study of acculturation among the Cree Indians of Winisk, Ontario." *Arctic,* 1962, Vol. 15(3), pp. 190-204.

Lewis, K. "Quasi-stationary social equilibria and the problem of permanent change." In Bennis, Benne, & Chin (Eds.) *The planning of change.* New York: Holt, Rinehart & Winston, 1962.

Lippit, R. "The use of social research to improve social practice." *American journal of orthopsychiatry,* 1965, 35(4).

MacDonald, M. E. "Capability of theory and method." *In Use of judgement as data in social work research.* New York: National Association of Social Workers, 1958.

Mair, L. "Power and politics." *New society,* 1970, 407, pp. 113-114.

Mann, W. E. "The social system of a slum." In Clark, S. D. (Ed.) *Urbanism and the changing Canadian society.* Toronto: University of Toronto Press, 1961.

Marshall, D. "Tenant power." *Maclean's magazine,* 1969, April, pp. 21-26.

Marshall, D. R. "Who participates in what?" *Urban affairs quarterly,* 1968, 1(2), pp. 201-223.

Nicholas, A. "New Brunswick Indians: Conservative militants." In Waubageshig (Ed.) *The only good Indian.* Toronto: New Press, 1970.

Park, R. E. "Human ecology." In Theodorson, G. A. (Ed.) *Studies in human ecology.* Evanston, Ill.: Row, Peterson & Co., 1961.

Peattie, L. R. "Drama and advocacy planning." *Journal of the American Institute of Planners,* 1970, Nov., pp. 405-410.

Pfeil, E. "The pattern of neighboring relations in Dortmund-Nordstadt." In Pahl, R. E. (Ed.) *Readings in urban sociology.* London: Pergamon Press, 1968.

Repo, M. "The fallacy of community control." *Transformation,* 1971, 1(1).

Richardson, N. H. "Participatory democracy and planning – The Canadian experience." *Journal of Town Planning Institute,* 1970, February, pp. 52-55.

Rogers, E. S. "Changing settlement patterns of the Cree-Ojibwa of Northern Ontario." *Southwestern journal of anthropology,* 1963, Vol. 19(1), pp. 64-88.

Rogers, E. S. "Within two worlds." *Rotunda,* Vol. 1(1), pp. 15-21. Toronto: Royal Ontario Museum.

Rostovtzeff, M. I. "The decay of the ancient world and its economic explanations." In Chambers, M. (Ed.) *The fall of Rome. Can it be explained?* New York: Holt, Rinehart and Winston, 1966.

Rowan, H. (Ed.). "The world of Whitetown: Neglected blue-collar communities." *Carnegie quarterly,* 1970, 18(4).

Rowan, M. K. "Poor Peoples Conference delegates represent 250 groups across Canada." *Globe and Mail,* 1971, January 8, p. 23.

Sanders, I. "Professional roles in planned change." In Morris, R. (Ed.) *Centrally planned change.* New York: National Association of Social Workers, 1964.

Sanders, I. "Theories of community development." *Rural sociology,* 1958, 23(1).

Scott, D. C. "The Canadian Indians in the great world war." In *Canada in the great world war.* Vol. 3. Toronto: United Publishers, 1918-21.

Seeley, J. "What is planning?" *Journal of the American Institute of Planners,* 1962, 28(2), pp. 91-97.

Sewell, J. "A new alderman discovers flaws in the power game." *Globe and Mail,* 1971, January 6, p. 7.

Shulman, N. "Mutual aid and neighbouring patterns: The lower town study." *Anthropologica,* 1967, 9 (2), 51-60.

Shyne, A. W. "Social work research." In Laurie, H. L. (Ed.) *Encyclopedia of social work.* New York: National Association of Social Workers, 1965.

Sim, R. A. "The agricultural rehabilitation and development act" (ARDA) *Interim.* Toronto: Canadian Association for Adult Education, 1963.

Sim, R. A. "Community action in a twilight zone." *Royal Institute of British Architects Journal,* 1970, Oct., pp. 445-453.

Simmel, G. "The metropolis and mental life." In Wolff, K. (Ed.) *The sociology of Geog Simmel.* Glencoe, Ill.: Free Press, 1950.

Smith, E. "Planning for people: The Gaspé project." *Canadian dimension,* 1966, 4 (1), pp. 20-23.

Stern, G. G. "Myth and reality in the American College." *AAUP bulletin,* 1966, winter.

Sternlieb, G. "Hawthornism and housing." *Urban affairs quarterly,* 1970, 6(1).

Stutt, R. A. "Opportunities for rural development in Canada." *Canadian journal of agricultural economics,* 1961, 0 (2) pp. 22-23.

Sun, R. A. "Stranger in the community." *Canadian welfare,* 1969, November-December.

Surtees, R. J. "The development of an Indian reserve policy in Canada." *Ontario history,* 1968, Vol. 61(2), 87-98.

Taylor, C. C. "Community development programs and methods." *Community development review,* 1956, December.

Thompson, J. D. & Bates, F. L. "Technology, organization, and administration." *Administrative science quarterly,* 1957, pp. 325-343.

Vanstone, J. W. "Changing patterns of Indian trapping in the Canadian sub-arctic." *Arctic,* 1963, Vol. 16(3), pp. 159-174.

Verba, S. "Democratic participation." *The annals of the American Academy of Political and Social Science,* 1967, 373, pp. 53-78.

Verner, C. "The structure of community adult education." In Hallenbeck, W. C. (Ed.) *Community and adult education.* Chicago: Adult Education Association, 1972.

Wadel, C. "Marginal adaptation and modernization in Newfoundland." *Newfoundland social and economic studies,* 1969, 7.

Weiers, M. "New-style social worker helps fight politicians." *Toronto Daily Star,* 1970, October 16.

Weinberg, J. L. "Evaluation study of youth training and employment project, East Los Angeles." In Morris, P. & Rein, M., *Dilemmas of social reform.* London. Routledge & Kegan Paul, 1967.

Wirth, L. "Urbanism as a way of life." *American journal of sociology,* 1938, XLIV, pp. 8-20.

Wirth, L. "Urbanism as a way of life." In Hatt, P. K. & Reiss, A. J. (Ed.) *Cities and society*. New York: Free Press, 1957.

Woodcock, G. "How can we make democracy work between elections?" *Macleans,* 1971, April.

Woodcock, G. "I'm a WASP. . . .Which minority do you belong to?" Macleans, 1971, February.

Woolins, M. "Measuring the effect of social work intervention." In Polansky, N. A. *Social work research*. Chicago: University of Chicago Press, 1963.